ttled by 12 Car. II. cap. 4. §. 2, 7. [illegible] Geo. I. cap. 7. §. 2. and other ACTS of PARLIA-
ge: With the Total Amount of [illegible] DUTIES to be REPAID
ACT of PARLIAMENT, intitled, AN [illegible] Majesty a Subsidy of Poundage
his Kingdom, Anno Domini 1747, [illegible] such as are not rated, but pay
aid DUTIES to be REPAID, [illegible] Exportation to foreign Parts

S.

begin with Letter B.

		RATES. By 12 Car. II. cap. 4. &c.			RATES. By 11 Geo. I. cap. 7.			[illegible] to be paid on Importation. By British.				[illegible] to be paid on Importation. By Strangers.				REPAID on Exportation in Time by any Persons.			
	☞	l.	s.	d.	l.	s.	d.	l.	s.	d.	20ths	l.	s.	d.	20ths	l.	s.	d.	20ths
— — —	1	0	17	10	—	—	—	0	3	5	$3\frac{9}{10}$	0	3	7	$17\frac{2}{3}$	0	3	0	$2\frac{1}{4}$
— — — —	2	0	13	4	—	—	—	0	2	6	16	0	2	8	16	0	2	3	0
of Rates, for every 20 s. of their — — — }	3	—	—	—	—	—	—	0	5	8	17	0	5	11	17	0	5	1	5
— — —	4	—	—	—	2	0	0	0	11	5	14	0	11	11	14	0	10	2	10
— — — —	5	0	5	0	—	—	—	0	0	11	11	0	1	0	6	0	0	2	10
— — —	6	—	—	—	—	—	—	0	0	3	15	0	0	3	15	0	0	3	15
e — — —	7	1	6	8	—	—	—	2	6	9	12	2	7	1	12	1	19	6	0
ther country — —	8	1	6	8	—	—	—	2	0	1	12	2	0	5	12	1	19	6	0
— — —	9	2	8	0	—	—	—	0	9	2	$17\frac{3}{5}$	0	9	10	$1\frac{3}{5}$	0	8	1	4
12 lb. of iron in the locks —	10	—	—	—	—	—	—	0	4	8	5	0	4	8	5	0	4	8	5
— — —	11	1	12	0	—	—	—	0	6	1	$18\frac{2}{5}$	0	6	6	$14\frac{2}{5}$	0	5	4	16
2 lb. of steel in the rings. —	12	—	—	—	—	—	—	0	5	1	$17\frac{1}{2}$	0	5	1	$17\frac{1}{2}$	0	5	1	$17\frac{1}{2}$
— — —	13	—	—	—	—	—	—	0	0	11	5	0	0	11	5	0	0	11	5
oath — — —	14	—	—	—	—	—	—	0	6	0	0	0	6	0	0	—	—	—	—
— — —	15	—	—	—	0	4	0	0	0	11	$9\frac{4}{5}$	0	1	1	$1\frac{4}{5}$	0	0	10	7
— — —	16	5	6	8	—	—	—	1	0	6	8	1	1	10	8	0	18	0	0
— — —	17	2	13	4	—	—	—	0	10	3	4	0	10	11	4	0	9	0	0
— — —	18	3	11	2	—	—	—	0	13	8	$7\frac{9}{10}$	0	14	7	1	0	12	0	$2\frac{1}{4}$
, containing 112 lb. thereof —	19	—	—	—	—	—	—	0	4	8	5	0	4	8	5	0	4	8	5
e thereof — —	20	—	—	—	—	—	—	0	0	11	5	0	0	11	5	0	0	11	5
— — —	21	12	0	0	—	—	—	2	6	2	8	2	9	2	8	2	0	6	0
— — — —	22	12	0	0	—	—	—	3	8	8	8	3	11	8	8	3	3	0	0
— — — —	23	0	12	6	—	—	—	0	2	4	$17\frac{1}{2}$	0	2	6	15	0	2	1	$6\frac{1}{4}$
— — — —	24	0	12	6	—	—	—	0	3	6	$18\frac{3}{4}$	0	3	8	$16\frac{1}{4}$	0	3	3	$7\frac{1}{2}$
Britain or Ireland, or foreign built	25	0	12	6	—	—	—	0	3	8	$16\frac{1}{4}$	0	3	8	$16\frac{1}{4}$	0	3	3	$7\frac{1}{2}$
— — —	26	5	0	0	—	—	—	0	19	3	0	1	0	6	0	0	16	10	10
— — — —	27	5	0	0	—	—	—	1	8	7	10	1	9	10	10	1	6	3	0
Britain or Ireland, or foreign built	28	5	0	0	—	—	—	1	9	10	10	1	9	10	10	1	6	3	0
— — — —	29	2	0	0	—	—	—	0	7	8	8	0	8	2	8	0	6	9	0

Portsmouth Record Series
Portsmouth
Customs letter books
1748–1750

Fig. 1 REVENUE CUTTER CLOSE–HAULED 1790, an anonymous oil painting

Portsmouth Record Series
Portsmouth Customs letter books 1748–1750

Edited by G. Hampson
with an Introduction by G. Hampson and J.G. Rule

Hampshire County Council: Winchester: 1994

Published by Hampshire County Council, The Castle, Winchester SO23 8UJ
ISBN 1 85975 023 0
Bound in Black Devon Cloth. Text set in Linotype Baskerville No.2 by Inset Phototypesetting and printed on Victory Cream Cartridge 100g/m² by Hobbs the Printers Limited.

General Editor's Preface

Mr Hampson wishes to acknowledge the help he had in the early stages of the work from the late Mr R.C. Jarvis. I am grateful to Mr Hampson and Professor Rule for their patience over delays in publication and for agreeing to substantial rearrangement of the Introduction. This involved some expansion of chapter 4, and I accept full responsibility for its final form. I am alone responsible for the Appendices. I am grateful too to those who have greatly assisted the later stages of preparation of the book with knowledgeable advice and help on particular questions: Mr C.D. Chalmers, Mr H.S. Cobb, Dr A.I. Doyle, Mr D. Francis, Mr M.A. Grist, Mr A. J. Heesom, Professor P.C.G. Isaac, Dr R.J.B. Knight, Dr B. Lavery, Miss S.J. Lewin, Miss L. Macfarlane, Dr N.A.M. Rodger, Ms J. Springall, Dr J. Stedman, Mr N.W. Surry, Professor G.B. Townend, Miss J.M. Wraight and Mr I.F. Wright.

P.D.A. HARVEY
University of Durham

Contents

List of Illustrations

List of abbreviations

Beawes	W. Beawes, *Lex mercatoria rediviva: or, the merchant's directory* (2nd edn, 1761)
Beck	S.W. Beck, *The draper's dictionary. A manual of textile fabrics: their history and applications* [1886]
B.L.	British Library, Reference Division (formerly British Museum)
Carson (1974)	E. Carson, *Smugglers and revenue officers in the Portsmouth area in the eighteenth century* (Portsmouth Papers, no.22; 1974)
Carson (1977)	E.A. Carson, 'The Customs records of Portsmouth', *Journal of the Society of Archivists*, v, no. 7 (April 1977), pp. 429–36
C.J.	*The Journals of the House of Commons*
Crouch	H. Crouch, *A complete guide to the officers of His Majesty's Customs in the out-ports* (1732)
Hoon	E.E. Hoon, *The organization of the English Customs system 1696–1786* (1938)
O.E.D.	*The Oxford English dictionary* (13v., 1933)
Postlethwayt	M. Postlethwayt, *The universal dictionary of trade and commerce* (2nd edn, 2v., 1757)
P.R.O.	Public Record Office. The following classes of records are cited:

CUST 3	Customs, ledgers of imports and exports
CUST 18	Customs, establishments, series I
CUST 21	Customs, miscellaneous books
CUST 28	Customs, Board and secretariat, minute books
CUST 29	Customs, Board and secretariat, minute entry books
CUST 31	Customs, Board and secretariat, out-letter books, intra-departmental
CUST 32	Customs, Board and secretariat, in-letter books
CUST 39	Customs, establishment, staff lists
CUST 41	Customs, copies of counsel's opinions
CUST 42	Customs, headquarters departments
CUST 58	Customs, outport records: Portsmouth
PRO 30/32	documents acquired by gift, deposit or purchase: Leeds papers
T 42	Treasury, registers, Customs establishments, England

Saxby	H. Saxby, *The British Customs: containing an historical and practical account of each branch of that revenue* (1757)
Wilhelmsen	L.J. Wilhelmsen, *English textile nomenclature* (Skrifter fra Norges Handelshøyskole, no.1; 1943)

Introduction

1 Organisation of the Customs service

THE BOARD OF CUSTOMS

The Customs service in England and Wales was under the control of the Board of Customs.[1] This was set up in 1671 when the system of farming the collection of Customs was abolished, and it consisted of between five and nine Commissioners. Its duties were to regulate Customs procedure, in London directly and in other ports – outports – by letters, to prosecute evasions, to supervise the staff, to consider merchants' petitions and to formulate policy. The Secretary to the Board was its most powerful officer and throughout the years covered by this volume this was William Wood, who held the post from 1742 to 1765.[2] The Board Room and other offices were in the Custom House in London; this, rebuilt after a fire in 1718, stood beside the Thames, just above the Tower of London. The Board might meet every weekday except holidays, but in practice it met rarely on Monday or Saturday.[3] The Board was directly answerable to the Lords of the Treasury, and acknowledged no other authority under the Crown except the Privy Council and Parliament, but there was much co-operation at the highest level with the Secretaries of State (especially over action against smuggling) and with the Boards of Trade and of Excise. Justices of the Peace and other local authorities were required to help the Board of Customs and its officers.[4]

The most senior posts were granted by letters patent but few of these patent officers served in person; most appointed deputies to act for them, often choosing them with the advice of the Board.[5] London was by far the most important port, though in the eighteenth century the outports were growing in importance. The officers at the Custom House in London who were concerned with the outports were the Secretary, the three or four Solicitors, the Receiver-General, who was in charge of payments as well as most non-penal receipts, and officers who dealt with other financial matters: the Receiver of Fines and Forfeitures for the Outports, the Accountant of Petty Receipts, the Paymaster of Incidents and the Receiver of the Superannuation Fund.[6] Throughout the Customs service there was almost a parallel structure of controllers and examiners to check the accounts of all officers who handled money. The chief of these was the Controller-General of Customs, but the Receiver of Fines and Forfeitures for the Outports and the Receiver of the Superannuation Fund had each his own Controller and outport accounts were checked by a separate group of officers, much of whose work was really done by clerks: four Examiners of the Outport Books, the Surveyor of Outport Accounts, the Inspector of the Outport Collectors' Accounts and the Inspector

---

1 E.E. Hoon, *The organization of the English Customs system 1696–1786* (1938), is a definitive account of the Customs service in the eighteenth century. Two shorter works give valuable surveys of the Portsmouth Customs records of this period and their contents: E. Carson, *Smugglers and revenue officers in the Portsmouth area in the eighteenth century* (Portsmouth Papers, no. 22; 1974), and E.A. Carson, 'The Customs records of Portsmouth', *Journal of the Society of Archivists*, v, no. 7 (April 1977), pp. 429–36.

2 Hoon, pp. 56, 62–9.

3 Hoon, p. 71; H. Chamberlain, *A new and compleat survey of the Cities of London and Westminster, the Borough of Southwark, and parts adjacent* [1770], p. 552.

4 Hoon, pp. 45–7, 81–3, 85–6, 186.

5 Hoon, pp. 14–17, 20–2, 195–6.

6 Hoon, pp. 92–6, 99–106.

of Exchequer Books. By the mid-eighteenth century the system was extraordinarily elaborate and in many ways was both cumbersome and inefficient. Intermediate between the central Custom House and the outports were the Surveyors-General, of whom there were seven by 1771; each supervised the local officers in one area of the coast.[7]

LOCAL ORGANISATION

The Customs organisation for London, covering the whole of the Thames estuary, was more elaborate than for any other port. It was centred on the Long Room on the first floor of the Custom House, where the chief officers, known as bench officers, sat on a raised platform: the deputies of the Collector Inwards, of the Collector Outwards, of the Controller and of the Surveyor of the Port and, in person, the Surveyor-General of the area. The first three of these each had charge of other officials in this large but overcrowded room, receiving money from the ships' masters and merchants who came there to pay duty and dealing with the relevant paperwork. But the Long Room was only the tip of the organisation for the port. Beyond the Custom House was a vast number of officers and subordinate employees supervising and watching the movement of dutiable goods on and off ships, with attendant administrators and controllers. Tidewaiters (directed by a Tidesurveyor) accompanied every ship in each direction between London and Gravesend or other point downstream to prevent illicit loading or unloading of goods. In London itself, goods loaded for export were controlled by searchers, the landing of imports by landwaiters (directed by a Landsurveyor), backed up by a force of weighers and watchmen. Separate groups dealt with those kinds of coastal traffic that were subject to duties. Many were employed. By the 1780's there were about 550 tidewaiters in the London service and from 400 to 600 men were involved in unloading, weighing and warehousing imports.[8]

This elaborate organisation was simplified in the outports; depending on the size of the port, functions might be combined. Some outports were called head-ports, where there were three patent officers, Customer, Controller and Searcher. Others, called member-ports, were subject to these patent officers at the head-port for the area but were otherwise independent. Although imports and exports were allowed only at the outport itself, the Customs officers' responsibilities extended along the whole coastline as far as the limits of the neighbouring outports' stretches of coast; within this area there might be other ports, called creeks, where foreign business was not allowed but where Customs officers were stationed to deal with coastal traffic. In 1784 there were 71 outports (20 head-ports and 51 member-ports) and 32 creeks. The coastline was taken to extend as far up each river as the first bridge.[9]

The three patent offices at each head-port were of medieval origin. By the mid-eighteenth century they were almost always served by deputies, though the principals took the fees that accrued to each office. A patent officer might appoint more than one deputy, so as to divide the work of the port; he might, for instance, have a different deputy in each member-port. Equally, one man might be the deputy of more than one officer, or might also hold some other Customs office in his own right. This could result in anomalies, where an officer held also the post that was meant to act as a check or control on his own work. With the passage of time and successive changes in organisation, some of the work of the patent officers had been modified. By the mid-eighteenth century it was not a patent officer but the Collector who was primarily responsible for collecting the duty in an outport and for sending to the

---

7 Hoon, pp. 106–13.
8 Hoon, pp. 122–66.
9 Hoon, pp. 167–9.

Custom House in London regular accounts as well as the money, either in cash or in the form of bills of exchange; he also had overall charge of the outport's staff and of warehousing. Nominally the Customer (or his deputy) also returned full accounts, but in practice his responsibility was confined to coastal business and this responsibility was shared with both the Collector and the Controller. The Controller (or his deputy) now served as a check on the Collector as well as on the Customer; he shared general responsibility for the port with the Collector, kept similar accounts and countersigned documents.[10] This had come about through successive measures by the Treasury and Board of Customs to tighten control at the outports. In 1698 the Controller was ordered to keep accounts of the Collector's remittances and to send duplicates to the Receiver-General. In 1706 the Board resolved to send its letters and orders to an outport's Collector and Controller jointly and ordered them similarly to write jointly to the Board. In 1708 the Controller was made jointly responsible with the Collector for the safe custody of cash and in 1739 the Collector was ordered to consult the Controller in everything concerning the outport 'and not to take upon him to give orders or directions relating to the management of the Port without first consulting him and having his consent'.[11] The Board of Customs itself kept close control of the day-to-day business of an outport by its letters and orders; by 1783 it was answering 9000 letters a year from the outports. However, the Surveyor-General for the area might deal with particular problems and would occasionally make a full examination, with detailed report, of the conduct of business in the outport. Sometimes officers were sent from London for some special investigation.[12]

The third patent officer of a head-port, the Searcher, had originally been responsible for surveying the movement of all goods, but now, as in the port of London, dealt only with exports. Imports were dealt with by landwaiters and coastal traffic by coastwaiters, while tidewaiters exercised surveillance afloat; the tidewaiters, with those who assisted them, were also known as tidesmen. In most outports a single Surveyor would be in charge of both landwaiters and tidewaiters, and his post was an important one: the Board of Customs ordered in 1739 that the Surveyor as well as the Controller should be consulted by the Collector on all aspects of the outport's business.[13] To prevent smuggling an outport would maintain both waterguard and landguard. The waterguard of boatmen operated with smacks and sloops which were reinforced in the course of the eighteenth century by an increasing number of armed cutters, but the waterguard often depended on the assistance of naval vessels.[14] The landguard of Riding Officers, under Riding Surveyors or Riding Supervisors, patrolled the coast and might keep watch up to ten miles inland.[15]

Some of the London patent officers were appointed for life, but in the outports patent officers held their posts only at the Crown's pleasure. Other officers – Collectors, Surveyors, landwaiters, tidewaiters, coastwaiters – were appointed by a warrant from the Treasury to the Customs Board, but normally the Customs Commissioners had supplied the name in the first place. These officers were paid their salaries from the Treasury's Customs establishment account, but some came to be given further regular allowances from the incidents account, intended to meet non-regular exigencies of every kind. The incidents account was used to pay men who did occasional work for the Customs on a daily basis, but it was also used, increasingly, to provide retaining fees for these occasional workers and

---

[10] Hoon, pp. 5–13, 16, 173, 174–6.
[11] Hoon, pp. 187–8.
[12] Hoon, pp. 65, 113–14, 189–91.
[13] Hoon, pp. 11, 173, 188; Carson (1974), pp. 3–4.
[14] Hoon, pp. 177–8. Smacks, sloops and cutters were all single-masted vessels; cutters, with a square topsail, were generally the largest.
[15] Hoon, pp. 169, 182–3.

regular salaries for further full-time staff, mostly tidewaiters and other lower-ranking officers, who were appointed by the Board of Customs alone, not by the Treasury. Some staff, such as clerks, might be appointed and paid simply by their principals. Political patronage played a part in appointments, although qualifications and training were required of the appointee. Officers were forbidden to serve in the town where they had lived previously and they had to have no other business or employment outside the service. They had to give security for carrying out their duties and had to swear to take no more than the legal fees and payments. Fees were fixed by statute but special gratuities might be paid by merchants or by the Board of Customs itself for work out of hours or other particular services. The sale of contraband or other goods seized was an important source of profit: the officer making the seizure would normally get one-third or one-half of the proceeds.[16] The Board appears to have treated outport staff reasonably as to leave of absence and sick leave, but the contemporary custom of selling one's office to a successor was forbidden.[17] Dereliction of duty was met by instant dismissal, as happened at Portsmouth in August 1750, when casks were run ashore from the Lion while tidesmen were aboard.[18]

Any description of the local structure of the Customs service in the mid-eighteenth century is bound to make it seem cumbersome and confusing – a result of its long history and successive changes in its organisation. Contemporaries compared it unfavourably with the slicker, more efficient organisation of the quite separate Excise service (the two were not combined until 1909).[19] In practice, however, Customs business at an outport was carried on in a reasonably straightforward, uncomplicated way, as appears in the records of operations at Portsmouth.

CUSTOMS ORGANISATION AT PORTSMOUTH

Long after the re-organisation of 1671, and still in the mid-eighteenth century, Portsmouth was formally a member-port with its head-port at Southampton, to which the three or four patent officers were appointed: Customer (or separate Customer Inwards and Customer Outwards), Controller and Searcher.[20] It was from them that Portsmouth's Deputy Customer and Deputy Controller took their office and much of their remuneration. However, except in 1676–83, Portsmouth is consistently separated from Southampton in the establishment lists,[21] and from the letter books edited here it seems in effect to have operated independently of Southampton.

In 1671 the Customs establishment at Portsmouth was modest: a Collector, a Surveyor, one Waiter and Searcher at Portsmouth and another at Gosport and four employees called tidesmen and boatmen. This staff expanded rapidly in the late seventeenth century and again from the 1720's onwards. By the 1740's nearly 30 men were paid from the establishment account, while from the incidents account salaries were paid to a further 20, as well as small retaining fees to 20 more who were paid by the day when their services were called on. The largest number were tidesmen and boatmen, but others included the commander, mate and crew of the yacht Greenhill and officers – Waiter and Searcher or

[16] Hoon, pp. 195–215, 218–19. The development of regular payments from the incidents account can be traced at Portsmouth in P.R.O. CUST 58/349 (accounts of expenses, 1689–1702); cf. Appendix VI. The amounts produced at Portsmouth by seizures condemned in the Court of the Exchequer in 1748–50 appear in Appendix I.

[17] Nos 11, 40, 242.

[18] nos 719, 728.

[19] J. Brewer, *The sinews of power: war, money and the English state 1688–1783* (1989), pp. 101–14.

[20] Saxby, p. 392; P.R.O. CUST 39/183, 185 (copies of letters patent etc. for Customs appointments, 1671–1716, 1727–34); T42/2, f. 33r (list of established and other Customs officers, Michaelmas 1717).

[21] References for the establishment lists are given in Appendix V. Those of 1676–83 are P.R.O. PRO 30/32/20–27, CUST 39/12, CUST 18/1B–17.

Riding Officer or both – at Cosham, Emsworth, Fareham, Gosport, Stokes Bay and Titchfield.[22]

Portsmouth was not a busy commercial port, like Bristol, rapidly rising Liverpool, or even Hull, where in 1749 there were at one time 33 ships from the American plantations lying in the harbour with only 35 tidesmen to supervise them. However, as the letter books make clear, its relatively large establishment was kept active enough by the special problems of a naval port. In 1748–50 its management was effectively in the hands of the Collector, William Cooley, who was still holding that post 30 years later, and the Deputy Controller, Robert Turvin, and it was they who sent the letters and reports to the Board of Customs. The letters and instructions received from London came mostly from the Board itself, signed by whichever Commissioners were sitting that day, but sometimes from the Secretary to the Board, William Wood. Portsmouth's lower-ranking officers like the Tidesurveyor, William Baskerville, or the captain of the yacht, Charles Coombes, did not communicate directly with the Board, but there are frequent glimpses of their activities and concerns in reports and requests forwarded by Cooley and Turvin.

Many of the letters deal with matters of employment: hiring and firing, pay and allowances. There seems to have been a proper concern with the efficiency of the tidesmen. One was considered unsuitable for being 'almost continually Drunk'. Two others were dismissed for neglect of their duty when contraband was discovered to have been run from the vessel they had been placed on board. Objection was raised to another seeking to combine the post of coal meter with that of a settled tidesman, 'two inconsistant Employment's'.[23] On the positive side several of the letters reveal an anxiety to keep reliable tidesmen, by securing them sick pay and trying to ensure their allowances were paid on time.[24] Tidesmen were paid £30 a year. At a time when, according to Adam Smith, the common wages of unskilled labour in England were around 7s. a week, this clearly implies pay parity with skilled artisans for a job which required watchfulness and reliability rather than special skill. From the fact that he was unable to sign a deposition, one at least of the settled tidesmen at Portsmouth was illiterate.[25] Nevertheless, eighteenth-century Portsmouth with its busy Dockyard was a boom town, and with plenty of employment available it was not easy to recruit and retain reliable tidesmen. This was especially so when special advantages such as superannuation schemes for established workers, although not generally available for the lower orders, were to be had in the Dockyard. The situation was not made any easier by the fact that the Customs paid on a national scale and the cost of living in Portsmouth was high compared with other outports:

> an Officer may live as well at most other Out Ports, with a Sallary of £40 as here with £50, And the settle Tidesmen at £30 Per Annum, we are Persuaded must have been very hard put to it to live during the War.[26]

It is easier to come by information on the quality of the lowly tidesmen than on the higher-ranked Customs officers. However, one letter, the outcome of an inspection of the port, is revealing in this respect. The Collector himself did not escape criticism both for the way he managed his staff and the way in which he kept his books. The Landsurveyor was criticised for inadequate supervision of his staff and the Riding Officer at Titchfield was ordered to live

---

[22] See Appendices IV and VI.
[23] Nos 643, 719, 358.
[24] E.g. nos 200, 701.
[25] A. Smith, *An inquiry into the nature and causes of the wealth of nations*, ed. R.H. Campbell, A.S. Skinner and W.B. Todd (2v., 1976), i, p. 92; no. 552.
[26] No. 200.

nearer to the coast. The coastwaiter was warned to make his own book entries, instead of transcribing those made by the Deputy Customer. Most severely censured was the master of the yacht, Charles Coombes. He claimed wages and allowances for a ship's boy he did not have and spent too much of his time ashore, 'which affords a bad Example to the Mate & Mariners under your Command'. [27]

2 Commercial and fiscal policy

REVENUE AND THE REGULATION OF TRADE

For many people, conditioned by tales of running contests with smugglers, 'revenue man' is a complete enough synonym for 'Customs officer'. The prime purpose of the Customs is commonly seen as the securing and protection of the revenue due to the Treasury from duties imposed on imported or exported goods. This suggests that the function of the Customs service was overwhelmingly fiscal: the maximisation of the public revenue. In fact its role was much wider. It was the leading edge of the comprehensive economic system which afterwards became known as mercantilism. [28] Under this policy the state regulated the economy under the belief that trade was a form of warfare and that only through active intervention and direction could a nation ensure that it secured and maintained a share sufficient to bring national prosperity. There were many facets to mercantilism, but the cornerstone was the control of foreign trade. To this end the Customs were the essential agency that operated an incredibly complex system of import duties, export bounties, re-export 'drawbacks', prohibitions and exclusions. Special interest groups, like the old-incorporated guilds of London, had long been able to use their influence to secure special protection for their products. The Portsmouth Customs officers were reminded in 1750 that foreign-made combs were a prohibited import under an Act secured by the Company of Comb Makers in the reign of Edward IV: 'The Commissioners direct you to give it in strict charge to all the officers at your Port, to prevent the Importation and Entry of Combs, except from Ireland, & incase they meet with any, they are to Seize & prosecute the same agreeable to Law'. [29]

But in the eighteenth century such idiosyncratic measures of protection gave way to a more general intent of encouraging the export of manufactured goods and restricting their import. The realisation had dawned not only that they had a greater value than raw materials and thus assisted the achievement of a positive balance of trade, but also that they increased the employment available for the larger population and thus lessened the perpetual problem of the poor. England was foremost among the economically progressive nations that were beginning to count their strength in terms of the population they were able to support as well as the bullion they were able to accrue. Both of course had implications for their ability to wage war. [30]

Before turning to wider economic functions of the Customs, their importance to the revenue needs to be examined. Gross figures suggest it was increasing. The Treasury was receiving an annual £3.8 million by the 1780's compared with a little over £1 million in 1700, but in relation to other sources of revenue Customs duties did not advance despite the growing importance of overseas trade. Averaged through the eighteenth century they

[27] No. 677.
[28] For a general discussion of mercantilism see the introduction to *Revisions in mercantilism*, ed. D.C. Coleman (1969), pp. 1–17.
[29] No. 699. See Appendix VII for the full titles and citations of Acts of Parliament mentioned in the Introduction.
[30] C. Wilson, *England's apprenticeship 1603–1763* (2nd edn, 1984), pp. 265–7.

fluctuated narrowly around providing a fifth of public revenue. The Land Tax was of equal importance and the two moved inversely. In peace the Land Tax, the only source of direct taxation, was levied at 10 per cent of an admittedly dubious valuation. In war the landed classes, who after all were the lawmakers, suffered a doubling to 20 per cent. Wars disrupt trade and they invariably decreased Customs revenue. Since eighteenth-century England was as often at war as not, the two sources tended to rough equivalence. Significantly more important than either was the Excise. This inland tax was imposed on a range of commodities, although particularly on alcohol, and, administered quite separately from the Customs, delivered usually twice as much as either of the other two revenue sources.[31]

The Excise service, as we have seen, was a by-word for efficiency and was often contrasted with the Customs in this respect. Its career structure was open to talent and rewarded efficiency, while the Customs service was full of placemen who owed their positions to influence and did their duty through proxies to whom they side-slipped a small part of their unearned salaries. At the lower levels working Customs officers supplemented inadequate wages through connivance with duty-evaders – a fact recognised in 1746 by their own chief official, the Secretary to the Board.[32] Just as important in the increasing role given to the Excise was that it was much easier to police an inland levy at the place of production than to control the amount of coastal smuggling. Sir Robert Walpole was appreciating the gain of drawing even more of the revenue from the Excise in 1733 when he attempted to replace its levy on specified commodities with a general Excise from which exemptions would be specified. The freedom-cherishing English people, anticipating the impact of an expanded army of Excise inspectors and snoopers, would have none of it.[33]

Had there been a general Excise, Customs duties might have dwindled rather than stagnated in relative importance. As things turned out, it was largely under Walpole that the Customs were systematically moulded into an instrument of economic regulation. To their critical strategic role in shifting the make-up of exports away from raw materials to manufactured goods and in achieving an inverse effect on imports was added the regulation of the important colonial trade, especially with North America. The presumption that colonial economies should be allowed to develop only in ways which advantaged the metropolitan country was already enshrined in the general principles of the navigation Acts passed between the 1650's and the 1730's. Under these most imports from Europe had to come into England either in an English ship, or in one from the country where they originated. All colonial trade was restricted to English or colonial ships and a key group of so-called enumerated colonial products could be exported only to England; tobacco was the most significant and valuable of these. European goods, with one or two exceptions, could not be exported directly to the colonies but had to be carried by English ships or routed through England. In origin the Acts clearly sought to disadvantage trade rivals like the Dutch and French. In effect when they were added to by Acts aimed at discouraging the development of competing activities by the colonists, such as the bans on their exporting woollen cloth in 1699 and beaver hats in 1732, they also formed part of a wider colonial policy.[34]

---

31 J. Brewer, *The sinews of power: war, money and the English state, 1688–1783* (1989), pp. 95–100.

32 In a report to the House of Commons on 24 Mar. 1746, printed in *C.J.*, xxv , pp. 101–10. For the suggestion of Customs connivance see the evidence of the Secretary, William Wood, pp. 107, 109.

33 The standard account of this critical moment in English fiscal history is P. Langford, *The Excise crisis: society and politics in the age of Walpole* (1975).

34 Only small amounts of enumerated colonial goods passed through Portsmouth, though see the return of tobacco in no. 715. Of other plantation crops rice is mentioned (e.g. no. 22).

Fig. 2 SIR MILES STAPYLTON, BART, COMMISSIONER OF CUSTOMS 1750–2, a mezzotint published by T. Fleming, York

The export of wool had been banned from the early seventeenth century. It was one of the few commodities in respect of which the Customs had to prevent out-smuggling, popularly known as owling.[35] Its intent to encourage the cloth manufacture was reinforced with the removal of export duties on woollen cloth in 1700. The general removal of duty from manufactured exports did not come until Walpole's reforms of 1722. From this date it is clearly inadequate to view the role of Customs legislation only from the perspective of the revenue, for the imposition or increasing of import duties was now motivated as much by simple protectionism as by fiscal considerations. Commodities such as linen or silk of which it was felt Britain could increase its production, lessening or removing its need to import, were especially favoured. Encouragement could go beyond the erection of tariffs and embargoes to the granting of bounties to encourage exports. Linen exports were so encouraged in 1742 and the cost was borne by an additional duty on imported cambrics. British silk manufacturers were able to secure in 1721 a ban on wearing the printed calicoes which they considered threatened their position in the market for printed light fabrics.[36]

So far as export bounties were concerned, much as certain manufacturing interests benefited from them, they did not generally do so to any greater extent than did the landed interest. As T.S. Ashton remarked, 'Like rulers in all ages, the landlords who sat at Westminster, tended to identify the interest of the nation with that of the class to which they belonged'.[37] Under the series of Acts which were not repealed until 1846, not only did the landed interest secure a sliding scale of duties on imported cereals, but under the Corn Bounty Act of 1689 grain sent abroad received a bounty. This could be suspended whenever there was a crisis in food supply following bad harvests. Exports could then be placed under a temporary ban. This happened in 1698, 1709, 1740, 1757 and 1767. The great period of grain exporting was between 1732 and 1766 when more than half of the total for the century took place. The effects of the corn laws were always a matter of dispute. In some years they kept the price of food higher than it might otherwise have been, but they could also have had the effect of keeping the supply generally up by allowing land to remain under cereal cultivation that might otherwise have been taken out.[38] So far as the Customs were concerned they added the need to assess and check yet another sort of cargo. Portsmouth was to some extent involved in exporting grain,[39] and, in addition, from time to time the letters mention supervision of unloading and reloading corn from damaged vessels which put into port. If parts of cargoes of corn were spoiled, permission was given for its supervised replacement. The purpose was to prevent abuse of the corn bounty, either by double payment, or by relanding corn which had never in fact been intended for an overseas port.[40]

It was not just a matter of discouraging the export of raw materials which could be worked up abroad, and of disadvantaging foreign manufactures by imposing duties: there was a human dimension. Skill and equipment were to be jealously guarded. Under an Act of 1719 skilled artisans were forbidden to leave the country to work and instruct abroad. In 1749 the London Weavers' Company, who controlled the rapidly developing silk manufacture in Spitalfields, informed the government that several of their artisans had been persuaded to go to Spain and that some, with their families, had already left on board the ship called the

---

[35] See no. 192.
[36] An excellent short account of the economic policies of Sir Robert Walpole's government which lasted from 1721 to 1742 is provided by M. Jubb, 'Economic policy and economic development', in *Britain in the age of Walpole*, ed. J. Black (1984), pp. 121–44.
[37] T.S. Ashton, *An economic history of England: the 18th century* (1955), p.48.
[38] Ibid. pp. 49–50.
[39] See no. 656.
[40] E.g. nos 466, 572, 575.

Dorothy and Mary. An alert was sent out, and on 26 July the Portsmouth Customs reported that they had detained the ship and that besides its crew of 13 it was carrying 28 passengers including women and children. Two days later the Customs were being reminded to detain all the passengers on board, for there were rumours (false as it turned out) that one of them had already been seen back in Spitalfields. The Captain was to be required to put on shore all those whom 'there is any ground's to suspect, to be Manufacturer's or the Wive's, and Children of Manufacturer's' before being allowed to proceed with his voyage to Cadiz and Malaga. A search of the vessel revealed weaving equipment which had been falsely specified as woodworking equipment. In the event twenty persons were delivered by the Captain, including women and children. On 17 August a further letter reminded the Portsmouth Customs officers of the need for vigilance in checking all passengers bound for foreign parts, and, if any were suspected of being artisans, to get a magistrate's warrant to detain not only them but any weaving equipment on board. This latter reminder was needed as the Dorothy and Mary had been allowed to sail with the discovered equipment, because the Portsmouth Customs could find no specific statutory prohibition. In September the detained artisans were examined in London, and prosecutions against seven of them were set in hand. Later that month came an indication that people of some standing were involved in organising the clandestine sending of skilled men, their families and equipment abroad. A man described as 'An eminent factor, in the woollen manufacture' was taken into custody for being 'a principal'. The London weavers were undoubtedly silk-weavers, but the involvement of a woollen merchant may explain why the Portsmouth Customs officers were several times directed to make searches for a contraband cargo of raw wool on the Dorothy and Mary. What sentences the unfortunate weavers received is not recorded. The irony is that the silk manufacture in Spitalfields had only developed from the immigration of Huguenot weavers from France after the revocation of the Edict of Nantes in 1685.[41]

In these examples and in the fuller picture of the business of the Customs provided by the letter books we see a major department of state fulfilling a number of inter-related roles critical for the regulation of the national economy. For the most part these often humdrum activities had none of the drama of clashes with smugglers, but historians have come to appreciate anew the significance of the economic policies that they lump together as 'mercantilism'. As Professor Charles Wilson has put it:

> Walpole's reforms . . . completed a long process. To the abolition of export duties was added a series of bounties to stimulate industry positively: on whale fishing, linen, sail cloth, paper, etc. Protective duties on competing manufactured imports were multiplied. The pattern was consistent. . . .
>
> The relatively ordered framework of duties and laws called by Adam Smith 'the mercantile system' provided the matrix within which continued economic expansion went forward. It was not without anomalies, even scandals, and in due time it would outlive its usefulness. But that it did in time do so does not destroy its claim to have been effective in the early stages of growth. . . . Its fundamental assumption – that the economic plant may be induced to grow in apparently infertile soil – embodied a truly dynamic view of economic growth.[42]

That 'dynamic view' depended for its implementation upon a hierarchy of Customs officers from Collector to tidesman who, even if they hardly shared in any awareness of national purpose as they went about their daily business, are surely misrepresented if they are considered as simply the revenue men.

[41] See nos 404–408, 411, 412, 431. Further developments are reported in *The Gentleman's Magazine*, xix (1749), pp. 377, 426, 473.
[42] C. Wilson, *England's apprenticeship 1603–1763* (2nd edn, 1984), pp. 267, 269.

3 The work of the Customs service

NORMAL PROCEDURES

Where dutiable goods were moved coastwise, then the Customs had to enforce various procedures, involving checking, measuring and taking declarations of intended destination on oath, before vessels could be cleared. It was a cumbersome and time-consuming business, and not one which endeared the Customs to impatient skippers or merchants. The owner of the local salt works was among those irritated by the fact that the masters of the vessels he employed to carry salt to London were bound by it and gave notice 'he will no longer be Subject to give Bond, or take out a Cocquet for sending Salt Coastwise'. London told the Portsmouth officers that they must nevertheless insist.[43]

The one major cargo involved in the coastal trade which did carry a duty even when moved between British ports was coal. Coal was loaded unmeasured, for example onto the colliers sailing with four- or five-man crews from the Tyne and Wear. The master usually paid a deposit of twice his estimate of the duty on his cargo and was granted a warrant which permitted the coal meters to unload and weigh the coal at the port of arrival. Any surplus duty was then returned. It was not a popular duty with the Customs. It required the retention of a number of low-ranking operatives, the coal meters, whose main requirements were strength to unload and an ability to keep a tally, which they were supposed to record properly not, as they sometimes did, with chalk.[44] In 1791 the Customs Commissioners said of the administration of the coal duties, which raised around a third of a million pounds a year, that there was 'not an object in their extensive department which creates greater trouble, or requires more particular attention'.[45]

That was saying something. For most Customs activities were complicated, consuming time and paper. Just what could be involved in collecting due payments, in assessing and checking cargoes and in supervising the loading and unloading of ships can be illustrated by the example of tobacco. Tobacco, a luxury, was reasonably considered a source of tax revenue and accordingly it was covered by an import duty. However, under the navigation laws there could be no direct carriage from the Virginian Chesapeake to Europe. Cargoes had to be first unloaded at British ports. If the duty-paid tobacco was re-exported to Europe within three years, then the duty was refunded in what was known as a drawback. This involved a process of quite extraordinary complexity and a massive use of manpower, time and paper. As soon as a ship from the Chesapeake approached the Solent, she would be met and boarded by the Tidesurveyor. A rummage would follow and several tidewaiters placed on board. The in-coming ship would be constantly guarded on her passage to the moorings, for fear that tobacco would be run ashore in small boats. It was a legitimate fear. It has been calculated that in the 1730's and 1740's one pound in three of the tobacco consumed in England had paid no duty, although this was due more to the relanding of tobacco on which the drawback had been obtained than to the direct smuggling from unentered cargoes. Such relandings tended to be made on less busy shores than those of the Solent, typically in Devon, Cornwall and Dorset, counties which accounted for 60 per cent of all seizures in the years 1732–48.[46]

---

43 Nos 468, 476.

44 See especially nos 68, 650, 654, 677.

45 Hoon, p. 267n.

46 Hoon, pp. 245–56, where there is a full account of procedure on importing goods; R.C. Nash, 'The English and Scottish tobacco trades in the seventeenth and eighteenth centuries: legal and illegal trade', *Economic History Review*, 2nd ser. xxxv (1982), pp. 363, 365.

Once the tobacco-carrying vessel had moored, the captain went to the Custom House to declare the burden of his ship, its cargo, the marks and contents of each hogshead of tobacco, the port of loading, where the vessel had come from, who owned her and how she was manned. He had then to produce a certificate that he had given bond in America to carry his enumerated tobacco only to Britain or another colony. All this information was given on oath. Indeed so many declarations on oath were made in the course of Customs business, that according to one critic in 1732 they had become somewhat devalued:

> as the Multiplicity of Oaths in the Business of the Customs, does, it is to be feared, in a great measure, lessen that Awe and just Regard that ought to be paid to such solemn and sacred Ties; it is much to be wished, that fewer Oaths were necessary.[47]

Once the merchant who owned the cargo had been advised of its arrival, he had either in person or through a nominee to enter the cargo at the Custom House within 30 days of the captain's declaration. When this had been done, a warrant was issued which, signed by the merchant, was the instrument of authorisation and the correct levy of duty was then calculated. With the tobacco officially entered and the duty paid, the landwaiters oversaw its unloading, once the tidewaiter on board had been officially notified of the entry and had released the cargo. If lighters were used, then the landwaiters awaited them on the quays and supervised their unloading and the weighing of the cargo – yet again by sworn weighers. When the last hogshead had gone ashore, the tidewaiters gave the ship a final search before leaving. It was a bothersome process and one prone to all kinds of fraud, especially in the weighing. Under the navigation Acts some major goods, described as enumerated, even if intended for a foreign port, had first to be unloaded in Britain. The duty they thus incurred was repayable, wholly so in the case of tobacco after an Act of 1722. Increasingly the practice of retaining the tobacco in bonded warehouses reduced the need for first claiming and then repaying duty, since the merchant could ultimately make an adjusting sum. If part of the cargo was intended for transhipping to another British port, then the master of the conveying vessel made an entry and applied for a 'sufferance' to clear coastwise. As well as giving a detailed specification of the cargo, he had to declare on oath that duty had been paid and indicate his destination. He would then be issued with a clearance document, generally known as a cocket or cocquet, as well as being required to give a bond which was cancelled only when the cargo had been unloaded under supervision at the port nominated. It can be imagined how enormous was the burden of time and paperwork at a busy commercial port, but even at Portsmouth it must be remembered that, although the volume of dutiable goods coming in and out was small, the range was great and so the knowledge needed by the officers of just what carried duties and at what level was both extensive and in constant need of updating.[48]

PROFESSIONAL SMUGGLING

For the most part the smuggling dealt with by the Portsmouth Customs was not in the fullest sense professional. They rather searched for contraband concealed on ships which had otherwise legitimate sailing purposes, or for the running ashore of a part of the dutiable cargo of a ship even if the greater part had been declared, as was, for example, the case with tobacco from the Friendship from Maryland in 1750.[49] Full-scale smuggling, the running and landing of cargoes by ships committed to the 'fair trade', was a problem to be faced on

---

[47] Hoon, p. 247.
[48] Copies of Acts of Parliament making changes were sent each year to the outports by the Secretary to the Board (nos 61, 374, 634).
[49] Nos 561, 564.

Fig. 3 MURDER OF DANIEL CHATER BY SMUGGLERS 1748, an engraving in W. Jackson, *The New and complete Newgate calendar* (8v., 1818), iii, opp. p. 189

shores more remote and unguarded than those adjacent to a busy naval port.[50] This point was stressed by the extensive inquiry into smuggling by a parliamentary committee which reported in 1746; it concluded that a decreasing level of activity on the southern coasts had been offset by a related increase on the coast of Suffolk.[51] Several of the Portsmouth letters do, however, relate to the aftermath of one of the most notorious of eighteenth-century smuggling episodes: the murder of two men by the infamous Hawkhurst gang.

This gang operated in the border area of Hampshire and west Sussex. Their base was the village of Hawkhurst, where, as the report of 1746 pointed out, '500 can get together, armed, in less than an Hour' and that there was 'not One Person in Ten' in the district, 'but would give them Assistance'.[52] When a cargo of tea they had been awaiting was taken at sea by the Customs in 1747, they marched, between thirty and sixty strong, to the Custom House at Poole where the tea had been stored. They broke open the warehouse and secured the tea. Returning in triumph with the tea the next day, they stopped to breakfast in Fordingbridge where hundreds of people came out to watch the triumphal cavalcade, the episode being seen by the populace as a 'gallant expedition'. One of the gang recognised among the crowd a man named Chater with whom he had once worked. He shook his hand and threw him a pack of tea. Tragically for Chater this drew him to the attention of the authorities and he was taken up by the Customs. After an interval of several months he set out with the Riding Officer for Southampton, William Galley, for examination in Sussex. On the way they were intercepted by the smugglers and, to cut an horrific story short, were brutally tortured and murdered. Those who are inclined to romanticise professional smugglers should perhaps read a contemporary account of this incident which took place in February 1748, the two buried bodies not being found until the autumn. Their discovery galvanised the Duke of Richmond not only into taking personal responsibility for the capture of the murderers, but into a fierce campaign to rid Sussex and the adjoining counties of smuggling gangs. Seven men were taken up for trial before a special Commission of Oyer and Terminer at Chichester. The first to be taken was Richard Mills junior, a colt-breaker, who was taken in Sussex on 16 August. He might have been taken sooner – and perhaps also his brother John – for on 30 July the Portsmouth Customs had informed London that they knew his whereabouts but did not think they could act because their warrant did not distinguish between this smuggler and his father, also Richard and also wanted. Perhaps irritation with this delay explains why Portsmouth's later claim for expenses 'in Endeavouring to apprehend Richard and John Mills Smuglers' was refused. In the following October, Portsmouth was alerted that two other members of the gang still at large were endeavouring to flee the country. On 17 January 1749 it took the jury at Chichester only fifteen minutes to find seven men guilty of murder or of being accessories. The judge considered their crime so heinous that he ordered their execution to take place without delay. Accordingly on 18 January they were hanged 'amidst such a concourse of spectators as is seldom seen on occasion of a public execution'.[53]

---

[50] This aspect of smuggling, the running ashore of goods from legitimate trading vessels, has been neglected in many accounts of smuggling. For an account of similar activities in east Kent see P. Muskett, 'Deal smugglers in the eighteenth century', *Southern History*, viii (1986), pp. 47, 49–50. Obviously when, as there, it was returning East Indiamen in question rather than ships from the Chesapeake area, then it was tea not tobacco that was run.

[51] *C.J.*, xxv, pp.101–10.

[52] *C.J.*, xxv, p. 105.

[53] Nos 91, 109, 167; W. Jackson, *The new and complete Newgate calendar* (8v., 1818), iii, pp. 188–98. John Mills was not among those tried, but was hanged on 12 Aug. 1749 for a subsequent murder (ibid., iii, pp. 223–7). The best account of the gang's activities and of the Chater and Galley murders and their aftermath is C. Winslow, 'Sussex smugglers', in D.Hay et al., *Albion's fatal tree: crime and society in eighteenth-century England* (1975), pp. 119–66.

If Portsmouth's officers more rarely faced armed and determined gangs than did their front-line colleagues further up the coast, they hardly lived without any danger. One murder is recorded in the letters. In December 1749 a tidesman, William May, was murdered by William Kemp, a sailor on the sloop Charming Peggy. Securing a conviction was made difficult by the fact that the second tidesman, John Forrest, who had also been on board the sloop, had been drunk and was unable to recall the details of the incident. However an affidavit was eventually obtained from him. May had been struck over the head and thrown into the sea when trying to prevent Kemp and two others sneaking two casks of brandy ashore in a wherry. May's body was not recovered.[54]

SEIZURES

Goods were seized by Customs officers in precisely defined circumstances which, however, could extend to suspicion of intended smuggling. In making the seizure the officer placed his hands on the goods and declared before witnesses (subsequently if none was present at the time) that he was seizing them for the King and for himself. The goods were placed in the local Customs warehouse, having been measured and listed by the warehouse keeper, and a report was made to the Collector; at Portsmouth the Collector was himself the warehouse keeper. The Collector forwarded the report to the Board of Customs which decided, on its Solicitor's advice, whether the goods were to be discharged, compounded for or prosecuted. If discharged, the goods were returned to their owner who, however, would have to make a payment to the officer who seized them. If the owner compounded to avoid prosecution, the officer would be given a share related to what he would have received if they had been prosecuted successfully. If the goods were prosecuted, the Solicitor sent the Collector a writ of appraisement, whereupon two or more local persons would list and value the goods in an indenture of appraisement; this was first passed to the Register of Seizures, who entered it in his own records, and was then proclaimed in the Court of the Exchequer. There the goods were condemned and could then be sold to the highest bidder. A writ of delivery was passed to the Board of Customs, thence to the Collector, to allow the purchaser to take the goods from the warehouse once the sale was concluded. Provided he himself met the costs of making the seizure the officer who seized the goods would normally, by the mid-eighteenth century, be entitled to one-third of the proceeds. The Board might order goods to be prosecuted not in the Court of the Exchequer but before local Justices of the Peace, following a similar procedure.[55]

The Board might decide against prosecution at the Crown's expense, but leave it open to the officer who made the seizure to prosecute if he wished; this might involve him in heavy outlay but would normally entitle him to half of the proceeds. Usually the prosecution of large cargoes of smuggling staples like tea, tobacco or spirits was undertaken at the King's charge, while the officers took on the prosecution of smaller parcels or smuggled luxuries. For example in May 1750 the officers were invited to undertake prosecution of some silk handkerchieves, while a quantity of tea and brandy was left to the public purse.[56]

---

[54] Nos 533, 545, 552, 557, 560, 566, 578.

[55] Crouch, pp. 279–320; Hoon, pp. 270–80. Many stages of this procedure can be illustrated from the letters edited here, e.g. no. 145 (report of seizure), nos 156, 161, 164 (Board orders discharge), nos 520, 524, 549, 580 (Board orders composition), nos 92, 186, 208 (Board orders prosecution), no. 82 (writ of delivery). See also Appendix I. An interesting account of seizures at three south-coast ports very different from Portsmouth is given by G.J. Davies, 'Incentive payments and the sale of smuggled goods in Dorset in the eighteenth century', *Southern History*, xiv (1992), pp. 29–45.

[56] No. 646.

Not only goods but the ships used to convey them might be seized, prosecuted and condemned, and ships taken up at sea for smuggling were from time to time brought into the port. Sometimes they had been captured by the Customs' own cutters and sometimes by naval boats which had secured 'deputation' to cruise in search of smuggling vessels. Under a system which rewarded those who captured contraband cargoes, it was a licensed activity much sought after by naval captains in peacetime. Previously, smuggling vessels that had been condemned were simply sold. However, the report of 1746 concluded that this too often meant that they were simply repurchased by the smugglers and were soon again about their clandestine business.[57] Accordingly it now became usual to order the destruction of the vessel by burning. Presumably the Customs officers were pleased enough to see this penalty inflicted on large-scale professional smugglers, but they seem to have had a degree of distaste for the disproportionate impact on poorer boat-owners caught up in small-scale smuggling for whom the loss of the vessel was the loss of their livelihood. At least they supported the petition of Samuel Saunders who claimed that his boat, taken in smuggling three casks of rum, had been used by others without his knowledge while he was attending a funeral, 'the same being all your Petitioner had to maintain himself, and poor Family, consisting of a sick wife & three small Children'. It was to no avail. Superiors in London, perhaps removed from the kind of personal knowledge which could exist around the port, instructed: 'Prosecute the said Boat to Condemnation'.[58] Another boatman seems to have been luckier. A sloop under seizure for running seven small casks of brandy and rum was returned to its master, 'in consideration . . . of his having made several Discoveries of Persons concern'd in Smugling'.[59] Local officers' sympathy could also extend to persons in gaol for smuggling, like Jonathan Cole, who 'always supported a good Charactor and was never before concern'd in Smugling . . . he is in mean Circumstances, and . . . he has a large family'. Cole was released upon his bond not to smuggle again.[60]

THE CUSTOMS AND THE NAVY

There was a certain irony in naval captains coming forward so readily to assist in the battle against smuggling. The Customs letter books in fact suggest that it was smuggling by naval crewmen, officers as well as the lower deck, which was the most bothersome aspect of the Portsmouth officers' working lives. London warned them in 1750, that Admiral Boscawen with several men-of-war and other ships had been sighted in the Channel. The warning was not intended to prepare for the kind of reception to which a returning fleet might feel itself entitled. It was to alert the Customs officers, especially those on the waterguard, 'to be very carefull in looking out to prevent the running any Goods from those Ships as they pass the Coast'.[61] The view that 'the generality of the People on the Coasts are better Friends to the Smugglers than to the Custom-house Officers' was just as true of naval crews.[62] Several letters suggest that Customs officers in trying to seize contraband from one naval vessel were quite likely to be assaulted by the crews of others, as well as from the determined resistance of those with whom they were directly concerned. On one occasion the Tidesurveyor received information that one of the boats of H.M.S. Berwick was about to bring in some contraband wine. He was just in time to seize it, then met with the longboat from H.M.S. Monarch

[57] *C.J.*, xxv, p. 110, and, for an example, no. 546.
[58] Nos 209, 217.
[59] No. 588.
[60] Nos 573, 577, 618, 625.
[61] No. 611.
[62] *C.J.*, xxv, p. 104. For a discussion of smuggling as a social crime see J.G. Rule, 'Social crime in the rural south in the eighteenth and early nineteenth centuries', *Southern History*, i (1979), pp. 135–53.

and after a rummage discovered five hampers of wine there too. The next morning, on further information, he set out to search H.M.S. Prince Henry and found seven more hampers of wine. The captain, other officers and the ship's company, 'declared that If my self and the Tidesmen with me insisted upon taking the said Hampers of French Wine out of the Ship, they wou'd knock our Brains out'. This, he added, 'I conceive to be a very unjustifyable behaviour' for if officers of the Customs were treated in such a way by 'the Gentlemen of the Navy', it would become quite impossible for them 'to do their Duty, or prevent Clandestine Practices on board his Majestys Ships of War'.[63] On other occasions things went beyond threats. In 1749 a tidesman was violently assaulted by the bosun's mate of H.M.S. Monarch. The captain at first refused to give him up, but later a warrant was issued and he was gaoled. It was on this occasion that when the Customs boat recovered a cask thrown overboard from one ship it was itself then boarded by sailors from a second warship.[64] An anonymous letter warned the Customs Board that 'great Quantities of Brandy is run ashore at Gosport out of the Men of War', and that captains were involved, including several who had been deputised to seek out smuggling vessels.[65] The smuggling proclivities of the Navy were a long-running sore. In 1752 a seizure of 73 hampers of French wine was made on board H.M.S. Winchelsea and in 1761 it was complained that the Customs officers were 'frequently abused and ill-treated especially in the night time, chiefly from common sailors belonging to some of His Majesty's Ships who we are assured would not attempt it if they were not countenanced by their officers'.[66]

The most serious incident of naval smuggling in the period covered by these letters was that involving Captain Richard Gwyn of H.M.S. Ambuscade in the late summer of 1748. Information had been received that a large quantity of wines and spirits had been run ashore, and taken to Gwyn's local home near Bishop's Waltham. Three Excise and Customs officers with a constable went to his house with a warrant, and with some difficulty got to search his cellar. They attempted to confiscate a large quantity of liquor: 40 gallons of brandy in casks, two hampers containing another 16 gallons, 78 gallons of rum and 44 gallons of arrack. As well as these spirits, there were nearly 400 gallons of wine. This seizure was rescued by a mob of country people, at whose instigation is unclear. The Customs officers thought them to have been employed by Gwyn himself. His counter-accusation that 'far from being a Mobb of mine', they had been given his liquor by the Customs officers, saying, 'they had more right to it than I' and that he meanwhile had sent orders that 'no Person's shoud dare to oppose the King's Officers' is hard to believe. Most likely they were as he suggested 'some Idle People gathered together as spectators', which 'in Country Places is usual on such Occasion's'. But their action is most easily explained by the normal tendency of such people to join in on anyone's side who was contesting with the Customs. The case went as far as the Lords Commissioners of the Admiralty, who clearly considered the matter a delicate one, being 'most desirous of discourageing all in their Power such Clandestine Practices in the Officers of the Navy'. They did however point out that Gwyn had told a very different story from the Customs officers and claimed to have permits for most of the liquor. Hard evidence was difficult to secure, but that Gwyn had been attempting to evade duty on an amount of spirits and wine much in excess of the level permitted naval officers as their 'personal store', is clear from the fact that he eventually 'Compromised' with the Excise Board, its Portsmouth officers being allowed by him 'their

---

[63] No. 612.
[64] Nos 509, 522, 526.
[65] No. 687.
[66] Carson (1974), p. 10.

full share, as if the same had been Adjusted as a Seizure'. Gwyn's lieutenant on the Ambuscade seems to have assumed his guilt for he, having been absent when the seizure had been made, sought return of his own small cask, which he had 'no manner of Intention to Run being my private Stock'. He thought it hard that 'for the Behaviour of my Captain I must Suffer the loss'.[67]

Mostly when naval and Customs officers clashed it was over much smaller amounts. Typically such cases arose when officers being commissioned onto new postings were transhipping their personal shipboard stores. It does seem that on several such occasions the Customs did act somewhat prematurely and gave some substance to a naval view of them as bothersome bureaucrats. Resentment might well be due if their usual tone was that of a letter giving permission for a transfer of the stores of Captain Pott from H.M.S. Norwich to H.M.S. Greenwich in 1748, 'under the care of the proper Officers, taking care that no part of the said stores are landed'.[68] Another captain complained in 1757 that his liquor had been seized en route to his new command at Portsmouth despite the fact that 'it had been customary for officers removed from one ship to another to be permitted to carry their liquor'. Twenty years later that particular officer was to be at the centre of a tragic happening which has permanently linked his name with Portsmouth. As Admiral Kempenfelt he went down along with all the crew of the Royal George.[69]

Officers returning from service in the East were tempted to bring ashore fine china, which was heavily dutiable, claiming it had been purchased for cabin use. Portsmouth's Customs officers seem to have overreached themselves, however, when they seized some of the property of Admiral Griffin in 1749. The resulting letter of protest achieved a remarkable level of indignation.[70]

The Treaty of Aix-la-Chapelle in 1748 had ended the War of Austrian Succession near the beginning of the period covered by these letters. In its aftermath, however, the Customs had to add to their busy portfolio of responsibilities matters connected with prize vessels which had been taken in the war. Some of these were purchased at a fair valuation by the Government, but on those which it did not want a duty of 5 per cent on valuation was payable. The problem was not so much direct evasion of the duty, but the temptation to remove valuable items before the duty was assessed: hence the concern over the origin of 31 brass cannons on H.M.S. Montagu.[71] The Customs had also to take care that any dutiable stores or cargoes from seized vessels were not clandestinely landed. Once again the Customs could have problems with high-ranking officers. Admiral Rodney was notorious in this respect as in other matters of financial concern. In 1755 he seems to have been operating dubiously in respect of prize vessels in collusion with the Collector of Customs at Portsmouth.[72]

QUARANTINE

The Customs were entrusted with a further task which contemporaries would have considered of very great importance, literally vital. They were to keep out the plague. Historians, fascinated by the changing ecologies of rats and fleas, have tended to

---

[67] Nos 113, 118, 120, 122, 123, 133, 137, 140, 142–144, 160, 165, 179, 375, 390, 422. The quotations are from nos 120, 137, 375.
[68] No. 48.
[69] Carson (1974), p. 10.
[70] Nos 433, 437, 441.
[71] Nos 157, 169.
[72] N.A.M. Rodger, *The wooden world: an anatomy of the Georgian Navy* (1986), p. 325; the Collector, William Cooley, was acting as the admiral's prize agent.

underestimate human agency in keeping western Europe free of major plague epidemics after the later seventeenth century. The bubonic plague remained endemic and sporadically epidemic in eastern Europe, the Ottoman Empire and north Africa well into the nineteenth century. So far as the land frontier was concerned the Habsburg Empire performed perhaps its greatest service to its western neighbours by maintaining a *cordon sanitaire* along its long Ottoman boundary. But if the plague was to visit Britain, it would of course have to do so across the sea. In 1720 it reached Marseilles in this way. The French government cut off its northern spread by mobilising a quarter of its cavalry and a third of its infantry to cut off Provence until the danger passed. Just as it had done in 1711 when the plague appeared in the German Baltic ports, the British Parliament responded with quarantine legislation on vessels entering our ports from infected areas.[73] The Act passed in 1720 was the one in force until replaced in 1753 and under it an Order in Council could at any time require the Customs to quarantine ships arriving from nominated ports. During the period of these letter books there was clearly a fear of infection being carried from an outbreak in north Africa ('West Barbary') and the eastern Mediterranean and the Portmouth Customs had on several occasions to deal with the situation. Incoming ships from the plagued coasts were escorted to an isolated anchorage ('stationed') and kept under watch, so that no one could disembark for a period of forty days.[74] When the vessel was on station, a Customs officer held up on the end of a long pole the 'Quarantine Testament', otherwise known as the 'Plague Bible'. On this the ship's master had to give his oath that there was no sickness on his vessel. Concealment was punishable by death. He was to fill in a questionnaire declaring where he had sailed from and where he had called en route, as well as any sickness or deaths which had occurred among his crew or passengers.[75] The following period of quarantine was policed constantly by the Customs to prevent anyone going ashore. Had any crewman or passenger done so, they would have received six months imprisonment and a fine of £200. Clearly it was a duty unpleasant in itself and one which hardly made the enforcing officers popular with the crews. Furthermore it placed great strain on human and other resources. Charges of £612 were claimed for a single period of quarantine in 1750. It was hoped they would be paid promptly, for those awaiting their due were the most worthy employees: 'none but our best and ablest Tidesmen are fit for such Service'.[76] The Ottoman rulers only began to take effective control measures in 1840 and until then western Europe kept watch against the plague. So far as Britain was concerned the port Customs officers were the watchmen.

4 The records

THE ARCHIVES OF THE CUSTOMS 1671–1750

All these operations of the Customs generated an immense quantity of written paper. We get some notion of the amount from the forms set out in Customs officers' manuals for cockets, bills and certificates of every kind,[77] from the returns of statistical information on varied topics regularly demanded by the Board[78] and from the long lists of records sent up by carrier to the Board every quarter from Portsmouth[79] – and from every other outport.

73 For a general discussion of the quarantine responsibilities of the Customs see E.A. Carson, 'The Customs quarantine service', *The Mariner's Mirror*, lxiv (1978), pp. 63–9. The clearest statement of the importance of quarantine in keeping western Europe largely plague-free in the eighteenth century can be found in M.W. Flinn, *The European demographic system 1500–1820* (1981), pp. 58–61.

74 E.g. nos 233, 237, 379, 537, 678.

75 See no. 237.

76 No. 701.

77 As in Crouch, passim.

78 E.g. nos 240, 475, 650.

79 Nos 180, 228, etc.

Taking into account the far greater quantity of records produced by the port of London and by the central organisation itself, it is clear that the London Custom House contained vast numbers of books and papers. How much of this was kept, what series of records were selected for permanent or semi-permanent preservation, we do not know, for most were apparently lost when the London Custom House was destroyed by fire on 12 February 1814. There had been an earlier fire in 1718.[80]

In consequence, for the period between the creation of the Board of Customs in 1671 and the mid-eighteenth century we have mostly no more than fragments of its central archives. Of the Board's minute books there is only one, of 1734–6, from before 1767,[81] though there are three volumes of highly selective notes and extracts from 1696 onwards[82] and six volumes of the Receiver-General's own extracts from the Board's minutes, from 1716 to 1734.[83] None of the Board's own letter books survives, and the only central records of its enormous correspondence are a volume of abstracts of its general orders from 1700 to 1776, arranged by subjects,[84] and another of copies of orders and warrants that the Treasury sent the Board, which apart from two items of 1707 includes nothing earlier than 1789.[85] There are three volumes containing copies or abstracts of the letters patent appointing Customs officers from 1671 to 1719, and from 1727 to 1734,[86] and four volumes of copies of counsel's opinions from 1700 to 1763.[87]

From these few records some scraps of information, but no more, can be gleaned about operations at Portsmouth. Thus, among the extracts from the Board's minutes is one of 1722, reporting the view of the principal officers of Trinity House that a ship taking the normal route from Southampton to Portsmouth could not be held to have gone to open sea; the Solicitor's advice was to be sought.[88] Nor do we learn more from the most considerable series of central records to survive from the eighteenth-century Customs service, the monumental ledgers of imports and exports, a volume for each year (with few gaps) from 1697 onwards; these provide full lists and valuations of goods imported and exported, naming the countries of origin or destination, first for London and then for the outports, but for the outports they give only an amalgamated list that does not distinguish the individual ports, and the original returns that would have told us just what goods passed each year through Portsmouth – or any other port – are lost.[89] However, another remarkable surviving series of records does supply local information: the register of seizures, another all-but-complete series of annual volumes from 1715 onwards, that enters full lists of the seized goods that were ordered to be prosecuted in the Exchequer, identifying the port where each group of seizures was made.[90]

Some of the surviving central records of the eighteenth century had been in the hands of a private person or another government department and were acquired by the Customs service to make good the losses of 1814. The volume of Treasury warrants and orders, 1707–1811, was specifically compiled from copies belonging to William Roe, 'sent by him for the

80 Hoon, p. 293; H. Chamberlain, *A new and compleat survey of the Cities of London and Westminster, the Borough of Southwark, and parts adjacent* [1770], p. 552.
81 P.R.O. CUST 28/1.
82 P.R.O. CUST 29/1, 2, 16.
83 P.R.O. CUST 42/1–6.
84 P.R.O. CUST 31/1.
85 P.R.O. CUST 32/1.
86 P.R.O. CUST 39/183–185.
87 P.R.O. CUST 41/1–4.
88 P.R.O. CUST 29/2, s.v. Portsmouth.
89 P.R.O. CUST 3/1–50.
90 P.R.O. CUST 21/21–54.

purpose of being entered after the Fire at the Custom House'.[91] A list of the patent and established officers on the creation of the Board of Customs in 1671 was bought from a bookseller probably in the late nineteenth century.[92] Most of the surviving establishment lists, our principal source of information about the employees of the Customs service in the eighteenth century, are the copies that were kept at the Treasury; they seem to have been transferred, as Treasury records, to the Public Record Office in 1846, then moved to the London Custom House in 1864, eventually returning to the Public Record Office as Customs records.[93] These lists can be supplemented by others that have had a different archival history – including an important group among the papers of the first Duke of Leeds, now also in the Public Record Office[94] – so that we have a fairly complete sequence of quarterly lists of the Customs establishment from 1671 onwards. These lists, however, exclude the increasing number of minor employees who were not counted as establishment officers and whose salaries were paid from the incidents account; of these we have only a few scattered lists from official and private archives.[95]

The records kept in some individual outports have fared no better than the central records at the London Custom House. Those at Bristol were burnt in a riot in 1831, and the series of letter books from 1711 onwards at Liverpool was destroyed in the Second World War – though here a part copy, part calendar, of selected passages from the letters had been made and was published, edited by R.C. Jarvis, by the Chetham Society in 1954.[96] From many outports, however, substantial series of records survive from before 1750. The Customs records at Portsmouth were at a place of safety during the Second World War, were moved not later than about 1960 to Customs and Excise headquarters in London where they were given their current numeration and a card index to them was made, and were finally transferred to the Public Record Office in 1978.[97]

From Portsmouth the in-letter books – copies of letters received by the local officers from the Board of Customs – survive from 1726 onwards. However, the earliest corresponding out-letter books – copies of letters from the Portsmouth officers to the Board – have disappeared; the first to survive covers two years in 1748–50, and there is then a gap until 1760.[98] The letters tell us much of relations between the Board and its Portsmouth officers, showing what small decisions had to be referred to London, what little scope there was for local initiative – even the purchase of stationery when it ran out met with the Board's disapproval.[99] They relate – often in full and vivid detail – every event out of the ordinary in Customs operations in an outport that the dominating presence of the Navy made far from typical. On the other hand, they reveal curiously little of the day-to-day routine of the Customs service at Portsmouth, of the disposition of its premises or of relations between its personnel.[1]

---

91 P.R.O. CUST 32/1.
92 P.R.O. CUST 39/10.
93 P.R.O. CUST 18. This account of their migrations accords with the notes and stamps in the volumes seen, but according to *Guide to the contents of the Public Record Office* (3v., 1963–8), i, p. 107, 'With the exception of Vol. 1A this series was formerly amongst the Treasury records but was transferred from the Treasury to the Custom House in 1830'; the significant point, however, is that they were not, in origin, Customs records.
94 P.R.O. PRO 30/32/15–29.
95 As detailed in Appendix VI.
96 *Customs letter-books of the port of Liverpool 1711–1813*, ed. R.C. Jarvis (Chetham Soc., 3rd ser. vol. vi; 1954), where outport letter books in general are discussed on p. v.
97 Ex inf. Mr I.F. Wright; Carson (1977), p. 429.
98 The Portsmouth letter books to the end of 1760 are listed in Appendix II.
99 Nos 366, 369, 372.
1 Cf. Carson (1974), Carson (1977).

Something of routine activity appears in the only other Portsmouth Customs record to survive from this period, but it dates from well before the earliest letter book. It is a volume containing accounts of expenses in the quarters ending at Michaelmas and Christmas 1689, then, after a gap of many blank pages, in every quarter from Lady Day 1697 to Christmas 1702. Each quarter's account is divided into separate sections for established salaries, incidents (with subsections including, latterly, salaries paid by incidents), portages (allowances made for declaring cargoes correctly), allowances for damaged goods and for over entries (where duty was overpaid) and debentures. The payments under incidents include not only those made to men employed in boarding ships or other occasional work, but repairs to boats and buildings, casual purchases, costs of travel and other minor expenses.[2]

ARRANGEMENT OF THE TEXT

The first out-letter book, comprising letters written from 16 September 1748 to 22 September 1750, is published here in full, together with the letters for the same period from the in-letter books; these fall within two volumes, covering letters from 19 January 1747/8 to 6 February 1749/50 and from 8 February 1749/50 to 11 March 1752. Also included in the edition are all the earlier letters in the first of these two in-letter books, which serve to introduce and explain matters under current consideration when the two-way correspondence starts to survive. It thus prints the whole of one out-letter book and the whole of one in-letter book and part of a second; or, put another way, both sides of the correspondence for two years from September 1748, together with the letters from the Board to Portsmouth over the previous eight months. Unlike the volume of selected letters from Liverpool, this edition thus presents a tranche of the complete correspondence between outport and Board over a relatively short period.

The letters are printed in full, following conventions set out below (pp.xxxvi–xxxvii), with in-letters and out-letters combined in a single chronological sequence. The alphabetical index at the beginning of each of the two in-letter books is omitted; the out-letter book has no index. The signatories and their address are entered in calendared form at the beginning of each letter. The salutation is omitted unless it departs from the normal form: 'Gentlemen' in the in-letters to the Portsmouth officers, 'Honourable Sirs' in their out-letters to the Board.[3] On nearly all the letters the valediction is in one of five forms, with minor variants, and its number is given as in the following list:

1 We are your loving friends
2 I am, gentlemen, your most humble servant
3 We are, with great regard, your honours' most etc.
4 We are your honours' most etc.
5 With great regard we are your honours' most etc.

On enclosures copied into the letter books the signatories, address, salutation and valediction are all printed in full.

The Portsmouth entries for 1748–50 in the register of seizures, fully calendared in Appendix I, provide a useful supplement to the correspondence. They show, as the letter books do not, that large quantities of goods were regularly seized by the Customs officers at

---

2 P.R.O. CUST 58/349.

3 'Gentlemen' on two out-letters (nos 386, 542), no salutation at all on another (no. 585) and 'Honourable Sirs' on one in-letter (no. 545) are clearly clerical errors.

Portsmouth, prosecuted and condemned as a matter of routine, with no more reference to the Board than was embodied in formal reports and orders. Tables of the Customs establishment at Portsmouth at intervals from 1671 to 1748–50 and of all holders of established posts there from 1671 to 1750, forming Appendices IV and V, also fill in some of the background to the letters. Most of the few surviving lists of employees paid salaries by incidents in this period are calendared in Appendix VI; one dates from 1744, close enough to 1748 to provide a reasonably full picture of the outport's personnel at the time of the published correspondence.

THE LETTER BOOKS OF 1748–50

The Public Record Office's reference for the out-letter book of 1748–50 is CUST 58/1 and the in-letter books of 1748–50 and 1750–2 are CUST 58/149 and 150; henceforth in this section they are all referred to by piece number only. All three volumes are physically alike, and were no doubt supplied to the service at Portsmouth by the Board of Customs; indeed, 150 is probably one of the two letter books ordered from London on 11 November 1748 and received on 9 February following.[4] Each contains twelve gatherings, mostly of twelve leaves approximately 370×240 mm.; there are now 120 leaves in 1, 130 leaves in 149 and 137 leaves in 150.[5] All three have the same watermark, a fleur-de-lis on a crowned shield with 'LVG' below and countermark 'IV'.[6] The first twelve leaves of each volume have been cut for use as an alphabetical thumb-index with initial letters handwritten in black or in black and red, two on each leaf, omitting J and U. Although 149 has been rebound it was probably supplied in the same binding as 1 and 150: parchment over cardboard. On the front cover of 150, written in ink, is the contemporary inscription 'Letters from the Commiss^{rs} Commencing Feb^{ry} 8th 1749/50', with ornamental penwork, and on the spine 'Commi[s]s[ioners] IN-LET[TERS F]ROM Feb[r]y 1749 TO Mar 17[52] N° 10.', probably also contemporary. There are traces on the front cover of 1 of a similar inscription with penwork, now illegible, and on the spine, again probably contemporary, '174[8] to 1750'.

A left-hand margin for the text was marked throughout 149 by folding each page; in 1 the margin was marked by folding until 16 September 1749, then by ruling except on the volume's last three leaves, and in 150 the margin was ruled throughout. The pages of 1 are unnumbered, but the pages of text in 149 and 150 all have numbers that were probably added piecemeal as the letters were entered. Six hands wrote the text published here:

---

4 Nos. 191, 267.

5 The collation of each is as follows,

1: 1^{10} (1 front pastedown), 2^{14} (14 cancelled), 3–7^{12}, 8$^{12?}$ (2–11 cancelled), 9^{12}, 10^{12} (3, 4 cancelled), 11^{14} (1? cancelled), 12^{10} (10 back pastedown).

149: 1^{10} (2, 3, 4 cancelled; 1 front pastedown, six unnumbered leaves), 2^{12} (1 cancelled; six unnumbered leaves, pp. 1–10), 3^{12} (1? cancelled; pp. 11–32), 4–8^{12} (pp. 33–56, 57–80, 81–104, 105–28, 129–52), 9^{10} (pp. 153–72), 10^{12} (pp. 173–96), 11^{12} (12 cancelled; pp. 197–218), 12^{12} (10, 11, 12 cancelled; pp. 219–34, one unnumbered leaf).

150: 1^{12} (4 cancelled; 1 and 2 front pastedown, nine unnumbered leaves), 2^{12} (four unnumbered leaves, pp. 1–16), 3–9^{12} (pp. 17–40, 41–64, 65–88, 89–112, 113–36, 137–59 including two pages numbered 143, 160–83), 10^{12}(12 cancelled; pp. 184–205), 11^{12} (pp. 206–29), 12^{10} (pp. 230–45, one unnumbered leaf, 10 back pastedown).

6 Similar to W.A. Churchill, *Watermarks in paper in Holland, England, France, etc.* (1935), no. 406 (dating from 1733); E. Heawood, *Watermarks mainly of the 17th and 18th centuries* (Monumenta Chartae Papyraceae, vol. i; 1950), no. 1843 (1775). The initials are those of Lubertus van Gerrevink, a firm of papermakers at Egmond in the Netherlands, and of Jean Villedary, a French firm which may have collaborated with them or whose initials may have been added as a mark of excellence (Churchill, op. cit., pp. 14, 21–2).

hand	i:	nos 1–47, 57–60
	ii:	nos 48–56
	iii:	nos 61–756. A single hand, though it changes its character over the two years, becoming successively more relaxed.
	iv:	addition to no. 68
	v:	note on nos 74, 94, 95
	vi:	note on no. 152

The identity of none of the writers is known. However, hands i, ii and iii presumably belonged to the Collector's clerks, whose pay was allowed for in the Portsmouth establishment.[7] Out-letters were presumably copied into the book before despatch, but the entry of in-letters might be delayed up to a week from their receipt. When Pusey Brooke, as Surveyor-General, examined the current in-letter book in inspecting the service at Portsmouth, he signed it on 10 June 1748, after a letter of 3 June had been entered but before one of 4 June, and on 21 June 1750, between letters of 9 and 18 June.[8] Again, a letter of 10 August 1748 had not been entered before one of 13 August arrived to cancel it.[9] Most of the running corrections made in the text suggest that the letters were entered simply by copying,[10] but 'old' corrected to 'whole' in the Surveyor-General's instructions of 1750 implies that this exceptionally long letter was dictated to the clerk.[11] The spelling in a later letter, describing a tidesman as 'Disguish'd in Liquor', may be a solitary touch of humour.[12] Where a page-break occurs in the text of a letter there is normally a catchword, giving at the foot of one page the first word of the next, and this is omitted from the edited text, as also the instructions written at the foot of a few pages: 'carried over' in no. 191, 'carried Forward' in no. 350, 'Bill Carried Forward' in no. 731. The index in both 149 and 150 has been entered in successive stages, by hand iii for all the letters edited here; the index headings are mostly subjects, with some names of persons, places and ships.

The few subsequent annotations in the letter books are entered among the footnotes to the edited text apart from the following marks in the margin, all in pencil, which can be more clearly set out here:

cross: in 149, nos 128 (twice), 137 (twice), 143, 147, 165, 167, 192, 532
in 1, nos 169, 200 (three times), 203, 375, 386, 441, 450, 496, 509, 526, 552, 560, 612, 642, 643, 663, 719, 753

tick: in 149, nos 227, 292, 345, 360, 404, 437 (twice), 474, 493, 522, 545, 557

crossed tick: in 149, no. 533

7 Appendix IV, no. 4.
8 Nos 59n, 662n; cf. nos 68, 677.
9 No. 96.
10 E.g. the corrections to no. 301.
11 No. 677.
12 No. 712.

Probably ten pages, the whole of one gathering except the outer bifolium, have been removed from 1, from the end of a letter of 15 December 1749 to the middle of one of 24 January following.[13] They included the letters first reporting the murder of William May, tidesman, on 21 December,[14] and their removal may be connected with subsequent proceedings or with later interest in the event.

The binding of 1 has, at some time, been partly re-covered, and in the early or mid-twentieth century 149 was entirely rebound in yellow buckram with a black leather label on the spine, lettered, in gold, 'PORTSMOUTH BOARD TO COLLECTOR 19 JAN 1747 TO 6 FEB 1749'; to judge from the wording this was probably done when the book was at Customs and Excise headquarters. On the spine of 150 are two twentieth-century paper labels, one printed '10' with the volume's covering dates added in blue-black ink, the other with '15' written in pencil. All three volumes, besides their current Public Record Office labels, have their reference written in pencil on the first leaf in the form 'Customs 58/1'.

[13] Nos 526, 547.
[14] Cf. nos 533, 545.

Notes on editing

1 In principle the text is an exact copy of the manuscripts, reproducing their spelling, punctuation and use of capital letters. Letters or words that are illegible or lost from the manuscripts are supplied in square brackets. Other editorial additions are in italics.

2 Abbreviated names of persons and places have not been expanded.

3 Nearly all other abbreviations have been expanded except those that are still in current use. All letters supplied are in italics except in expanding the following forms (with capital initial or final *s* if on the manuscript) which occur very frequently:

account	acc^{t}	instant	ins', ins^{t}
certificate	cert, cert', cert., cer^{t}	landwaiter	landw^{r}
collector	coll^{r}	master	m'
commissioner	comm^{r}, $\overline{\text{commr}}$	obedient	obed^{t}
comptroller	comp^{r}	per	p
containing	cont^{g}	quarter	qua, qua^{r}
deputy	d^{y}	quire	qr, $\overline{\text{qr}}$, qre, $\overline{\text{qre}}$
&cetera	&c^{a}	receipt	$\overline{\text{rect}}$, $\overline{\text{rec}}^{t}$
hogshead	$\overline{\text{hhd}}$	servant	serv^{t}
honourable	$\overline{\text{honble}}$	ultimo	ult^{o}
house	h^{o}		

4 Omitted from the text are (i) the indexes in CUST 58/149, 150; (ii) catchwords, giving at the foot of one page the first words of the next, (iii) instructions at the foot of the page, such as 'carried over', (iv) the salutation in letters other than enclosures, and (v) some annotations in the form of marks. These are described on pp. xxxii–xxxiv.

5 Punctuation marks are omitted (i) below superscript letters, and (ii) in a series of stops or dashes, where only the first is reproduced.

6 The signatories, address and valediction (as described on p. xxxii) in letters other than enclosures have been given in calendared form in italics. In these sections and in Appendix I, headed 'Calendared', certain forenames have been abbreviated as follows:

Cha.	=	Charles	Rob.	=	Robert
Edw.	=	Edward	Sam.	=	Samuel
Jos.	=	Joseph	Tho.	=	Thomas
Ric.	=	Richard	Wil.	=	William

7 The hand is noted at the beginning of each entry. Unless otherwise stated any added, inserted or cancelled words are in the same hand as the surrounding text. The work in each hand is listed on p. xxxiv.

8 An asterisk is placed before any word included in the Glossary (pp. 233–5) each time it occurs in the text.

9 It is often doubtful whether a writer intended a capital or small initial letter, a comma or a full stop, a final flourish or separate dash, ‘&c’’ or ‘&c^{a}’, two words or one in such cases as ‘an other’ or ‘another’, ‘New Castle ’ or ‘NewCastle’.

Portsmouth Customs Letter Books 1748–1750

Public Record Office

1

19 January 1747/8

CUST 58/149, p. 1

From Sam. Mead, B. Fairfax, Beaumont Hotham and Wil. Levinz ('Sevine') (Custom House, London). Hand i.

Mr John East having by his Memorial of this date apply'd to us desiring that the Cargoe of the Ship Warwick Jno Wadham Mas*ter* for the West Indies which sprung a Leake and put into your Port may be put on board another Vessell till she is repair'd and made capable to proceed on her intended Voyage, We agree (if the Case be as represented) and there is an absolute ⌜necessity⌝[1] to land the Goods, to your permiting the same to be done, and put into proper Warehouses under the Care of the proper Officers, and under the Kings and Proprietors joint Locks, taking care the Crown be at no Charge for Warehouse room, Officers attendance, or otherwise and that the Goods are all reshipt on board the same Vessell when repair'd, and that there be no Embezlements, transmiting us an Account of your proceedings *valediction 1*

2

21 January 1747/8

CUST 58/149, p. 2

From Sam. Mead, J. Evelyn, Wil. Levinz ('Sevine') and G. Vaughan (Custom House, London). Hand i.

In answer to the Account of Seizures transmited in your Letters of the 14th and 15th Instant We direct you to prosecute the Tea thereinmention'd to Condemnation in the Exchequer at the Kings Charge Corresponding with our Solicitor and the Register of Seizures, Reporting to us the Burden of the Vessell out of which Forty nine pounds & a quarter Tea was Seiz'd with all the Circumstances attending the said Seizure and the nature of the Concealment, for our further Orders. *Valediction 1*

3

21 January 1747/8

CUST 58/149, pp. 2–3

From Sam. Mead, J. Evelyn, Wil. Levinz ('Sevine') and G. Vaughan (Custom House, London). Hand i.

We receiv'd your Letter of the 20th Instant transmiting one from Mr Corbett setting forth that Vice Admiral Schryver has acquainted the Lords Commissioners of the Admiralty, that he has rec*eive*d Advice from the Admiralty at Amsterdam, that a Vessell laden with Stores and Provisions for the use of his Squadron under his Command will soon Sail from Holland, and desir'd that she may be permitted to unload her Stores at your Port. We agree thereto and you are on her arrival to permit the Stores and Provisions to be unloaded accordingly and put into Warehouses under the care of the proper Officers till Vice Admiral Schryver shall have occasion to distribute the same on board the Ships of his Squadron, taking care there be no Embezlements. *Valediction 1*

---

1 MS. 'ncessity'.

4
21 January 1747/8

CUST 58/149, p. 4

From W. Wood (Custom House, London). Hand i.

The Commissioners observing that their Order of the 15th Instant forbidding the Granting of Sufferances for the Shiping of Corn at Unlawfull Keys, meets with great Difficulties in the Execution thereof several Persons having apply'd setting forth that they were under Contract for Exporting Cargoes of Corn and had taken up Ships on *Charter Parties sign'd for that purpose before the said Order was given. The Commissioners therefore agree to suspend that Order for the present, and you may permit the Business to go on, taking Care the Corn is shipt under the Inspection of the proper Officers as the Law Directs. *Valediction 2*

5
23 January 1747/8

CUST 58/149, p. 3

From Sam. Mead, Wil. Levinz ('Sevine'), B. Hotham and G. Vaughan (Custom House, London). Hand i.

We receiv'd your Letters of the 19th and 22d Instant, acquainting us that you have stopt the Loading Corn on board a Forreign Ship at your Port which had taken in the greatest part of her Cargoe before the Receipt of our Order of the 15th Instant directing you not to permit any Corn to be shipt, but from the Lawfull Key. Inclos'd we send you Copy of our Order of the 21st Instant And you are to govern yourselves agreable thereto *valediction 1*

6
29 January 1747/8

CUST 58/149, p. 4

From W. Wood (Custom House, London). Hand i.

The Commissioners direct you forthwith to report to them the Practice at your port and Members with respect to the number of working days Allowed for the discharge of Ships laden with Coals to entitle the Masters when Bonded to the Discount of two ⌜&⌝[2] half Per Cent. *Valediction 2*

7
29 January 1747/8

CUST 58/149, p. 5

From G. Vaughan, J. Evelyn, Ric. Chandler and Sam. Mead (Custom House, London). Hand i.

We receiv'd your Letter of the 15th Instant in return to the Memorial of Mr Wm Garrow Surgeon of his Majestys Ship Gosp*o*rt, relating to two small Cags of Rum under Seizure at your Port as mentiond in your Account of Seizures dated the 14th Instant and the said Garrow having represented that he unship'd the Rum inadvertently without any Intention of Fraud and that he did it openly in the Daytime and not in a Clandestine manner, We agree in this particular Case to its being admitted to an Entry, upon the Proprietors giving the Officers concern'd a moderate Satisfaction, but you are to prosecute the rest of the Goods mentio[n'd] in your said Account of Seizures to Condemnation in the Exchequer at the Officers Charge, Corresponding with our Solictor and Register of Seizures *valediction 1*

8
1 February 1747/8

CUST 58/149, p. 6

From W. Wood (Custom House, London). Hand i.

In pursuance of an Order of the House of Commons dated the 29th Ultimo You are immediately to transmit an Account of the Quantity of pounds and number of Hogsheads of Tobacco Imported & Exported for ten Years past, into and out of your Port, distinguishing each Year, As also the neat amount of the Duty paid and Drawn back thereon within the same Space of time Distinguishing each Year. *Valediction 2*

---

[2] Inserted.

9
5 February
1747/8

CUST 58/149, pp. 6–8

From W. Levinz ('Sevine'), John Evelyn, B. Fairfax and G. Vaughan (Custom House, London). Hand i.

Having advis'd with the Patent and other proper Officers of this Port on your several Letters relating to the Dispute between you and the Agents for the Prizes taken by the ⌜Squadron⌝[3] of his Majestys Ships under the Command of Lord Anson and Sir Peter Warren about the Dutys of the Sails Cordage & *cetera* belonging to the said Ships, they have laid before us a Paper (Copy of which is inclos'd) containing an Inventory of such things as are usually sold with a Ship and esteem'd her Tackle *Apparel and furniture whereby it appears that Stores are properly what are Contain'd in the Ship for her own use in the Voyage, and not for Merchandize or the use of any other Ship. And ⌜having⌝[4] fully consider'd the affair We approve of the distinction which they have made And the Collector is to admit to an Entry at five Per Cent the Value of each ⌜Ship⌝[5], her Tackle *Apparel and Furniture agreable to what is above Specified and if any of the Ships, have more on board than for their own use, ⌜the⌝[6] same are to pay the full Duties, and he must advise with the proper Officers of his Majestys Dock Yard to settle the quantity of each particular, which ⌜are⌝[7] to pass as Stores. *Valediction 1*

A Ship her Tackle *Apparel and Furniture as usualy sold consists generally of the following particula[rs]

The Hull of the Ship –	
Masts –	Tackle
Yards –	Tackle
Bowsprits –	Tackle
Standing & running Rigging	Tackle
Sails and Colours –	*Apparel
Guns, Gunpowder Shott & small Arms	
Anchors –	Furniture
Cables and Hawsers –	Furniture
Spare Cordage & Casks –	Furniture
Stores for Repairs –	Furniture
Victuals and all other Provisions	Furniture

N. B. Stores are properly what is containd in the Ship for her own use in the Voyage, and not for Merchandize or the use of any other Ship

10
6 February
1747/8

CUST 58/149, p. 8

From Wil. Levinz ('Sevine'), J. Evelyn, B. Fairfax and G. Vaughan (Custom House, London). Hand i.

In answer to the Account of Seizures transmited in your Letter of the 28th Ultimo We direct you to prosecute the Goods therein mention'd to Condemnation in the Exchequer at the Kings Charge Corresponding with our Solicitor & the Register of Seizures *valediction 1*

11
13 February
1747/8

CUST 58/149, p. [9]

From J. Evelyn and W. Levinz ('Sevine') (Custom House, London). Hand i.

Mr Thos Whitehorne one of the Landwaiters at your Port having by his Memorial of the 16th Ultimo apply'd to us desiring further leave for a month for Recovery of his Health. We have agreed thereto from the Expiration of his last leave without loss of p[ay] and you are to take Care the Service does not Suffer during his Absence. *Valediction 1*

12
13 February
1747/8

CUST 58/149, p. [9]

From J. Evelyn and W. Levinz ('Sevine') (Custom House, London). Hand i.

It appearing by your last Months Abstract, that there is remaining in the Collectors hands the Sum of Two hundred Eighty three pounds ten Shillings & eleven pence three farthings of the Kings Money We direct you forthwith to remit the same together with what you have since receiv'd to the Receiver General pursuant to the Condition of the Collectors Bond *valediction 1*

---

3 Altered from 'Squdron'.
4 Inserted.
5 Altered from 'Shy(?)'.
6 MS. 'they'.
7 Inserted; 'out' struck out.

13 **13 February 1747/8**

CUST 58/149, p. [10]

From W. Wood (Custom House, London). Hand i.

A Bill having pass'd the House of Commons for granting to his Majesty a Subsidy of twelve pence in the Pound upon all Goods and Merchandize to be Imported into this Kingdom[8] I am directed to acquaint you that the said Duty is to commence on the 1st of the next month, and the Act will be sent you as soon as the same is printed. And you are to take to keep a particular Account of all Ships and their Cargoes which arrive at your Port on or after the first of the Month to the time of your Receiving the Act in Order to the Charging the Importers with the said Duty, and transmit the same to the Board. *Valediction 2*

14 **[...] February 1747/8**

CUST 58/149, p. [10]

From W. W[ood] (Custom House, London). Hand i.

The Commissioners direct you to draw out & transmit them without loss of time an Account of the amount of the *Portage Bills on Tobacco Imported at your Port for seven years last past distinguishing each Year, And if you cou'd transmit the said Account by return of the Post it wou'd be very acceptable. *Valediction 2*

15 **20 February 1747/8**

CUST 58/149, p. 11

From W. Westby, J. Evelyn, Rob. Baylis and W. Levinz ('Sevine') (Custom House, London). Hand i.

In answer to the Account of Seizures transmitted in your Letter of the 15th Instant We direct you to prosecute the Goods thereinmention'd to Condemnation before the Justices of the Peace at the Officers Charge, acquainting us when Condemn'd – *valediction 1*

16 **20 February 1747/8**

CUST 58/149, p. 11

From W. Wood (Custom House, London). Hand i.

Inclos'd I send you by Order of the Commissioners an Act pass'd this present Session of Parliament for granting to his Majesty a Subsidy of twelve pence in the pound upon all Goods & Merchandizes to be Imported into this Kingdom from & after the 1st day of March next[9] to which I refer you for the Government of yourselves & the other Officers at your Port And you are to acknowledge the receipt of the said Act by the return of the Post. *Valediction 2*

17 **20 February 1747/8**

CUST 58/149, p. 12

From W. Westby, Ric. Chandler, Beaumont Hotham and G. Vaughan (Custom House, London). Hand i.

Having granted our Commission and Deputation for Jn° Stretch to be a Weighing Porter and Coalmeter at your Port in the room of Thos Merritt Prefer'd, you are to take Care he be under Oath & Security for the faithfull discharge of the said Employ and Qualifys himself as the Law directs. *Valediction 1*

18 **27 February 1747/8**

CUST 58/149, p. 12

From W. Wood (Custom House, London). Hand i.

His Majesty having been pleas'd by his Proclamation of the 19th Instant strictly to prohibit & forbid all his Subjects from holding any Correspondence or Communication as well by way of Trade or Commerce as otherwise with the French King or his Subjects and enjoin'd all Officers of the Customs to be faithfull & diligent in seeing the same duly observ'd I am directed to transmit you a Copy of the said Proclamation Publish'd in the London Gazette for the Government of yourselves & the rest of the Officers at your Port. *Valediction 2*

P:S I am directed to acquaint you that the Duty granted by the late Act upon all Poundage Goods[10] is to be ⌜distinguished⌝[11] in all your Accounts by the Title of Sub*sidy* 1747 –

---

[8] Statute 21 Geo. II, c.2.
[9] Statute 21 Geo. II, c.2.
[10] Statute 21 Geo. II, c.2.
[11] Altered from 'distinguishing'.

19
1 March
1747/8

CUST 58/149, p. 13

From Ric. Chandler, Sam. Mead, Rob. Baylis and W. Levinz ('Sevine') (Custom House, London). Hand i.

We receiv'd your Letter of the 23d Jan*uary* last transmiting a Certificate whereby it appears that the Greenhill Yatch in the Service at your Port under the Command of Capt Coombs is ⌜in⌝[12] good & sufficient Repair. You may pay[13] him the Sum of Thirty four Pounds, seventeen Shillings & six pence, for keeping the said Yatch in Wear & Tare for the Quarters Ended at Midsummer, Mich*ael*mas & Christmas last, and take Credit for the same in your Account of Incidents annexing this Letter with proper Receipts thereto as Vouchers – *valediction 1*

20
3 March
1747/8

CUST 58/149, p. 13

From W. Wood (Custom House, London). Hand i.

It appearing that you have Charg'd in your Preparatory Account of Incidents for the Quarter Ended at Mich*ael*mas last One pound Eighteen Shillings for a Wainscott Book Case, The Commissioners direct you to transmit them the Size with the Particulars of the said Case for their further Orders *valediction 2*

21
3 March
1747/8

CUST 58/149, p. 19

From Ric. Chandler, B. Fairfax, W. Westby and Beaumont Hotham (Custom House, London). Hand i.

Having granted our Commission for Wm Howells to be an Extra Tidesman and Boatman at your Port in the room of Thos Robinson resign'd You are to take care he be under Oath & Security for the faithfull discharge of the said Employ paying him the like allowance by Incidents as was paid to his Predecessor for w*hi*ch the Collector may take Credit from time to time in his Accou[nts] of Incidents refering therein to the date hereof *valediction 1*

P:S Since Writing the above the said Howells has given Security here

22
5 March
1747/8

CUST 58/149, p. 14

From W. Wood (Custom House, London). Hand i.

I have read to the Commissioners your Letter of the 2d Instant, acquainting them with the Arrival of the Blackett & Fenwick of London chiefly laden with Rice from Carolina desiring to know whether the Cargoe of the said Ship is liable to the New Duty. And haveing advis'd with the proper Officer he has reported that this Duty is not due upon any Goods that arrive before the 2d of this Month, which I am to signify to you for your Government *valediction 2*

23
5 March
1747/8

CUST 58/149, p. 14

From W. W[ood] (Custom House, London). Hand i.

The Commiss*ioner*s receiv'd your Letters of the 2d & 3d Instant acquainting them, that the Ship with French Wines consign'd to Mr James Bucknall Merchant at your Port is arriv'd desiring their Directions how you are to behave with regard to the Importations of French Wine and other French Goods. I am directed to acquaint you that the Case is laid before the Attorney General & when his opinion is receiv'd, the same shall be sent you for your Government *valediction 2*

---

[12] Inserted.
[13] MS. omits 'pay'.

24
8 March
1747/8

CUST 58/149, p. 15

From Beaumont Hotham, B. Fairfax, Wil. Westby and Ric. Chandler (Custom House, London). Hand i.

Colonell Murray having[14] applied to us by his Letter of the 4th Instant relating to some Liquors belonging to him & Collo Talbot (now on board the Scorpion Sloop Captain Bate Commander) You are to Order the said Liquors an Account of which is Inclos'd to be bro*ugh*t to the Warehouse at your Port, and there to remain till you receive our further Directions. *Valediction 1*

An Account of Col: Murray's Liquors on board the Scorpion Sloop of war Capt Bate Commander

	Doz*en*	bottles
1 Hamper No 8 containing 3 dozen & 11 bottles of Brandy –	3:	11
3 Hamper N 9. 10. 11 containing 13 dozen & 3 bottles Jamaica Rum –	13.	3
1 Hamper No 12 containing 4 dozen & two bottles White Wine –	4.	2
In all of Col: Murrays –	21.	4
	doz*en*	bott*les*
2 Hampers of Rum belonging to Conl Talbot containing 7 dozen & six bottles –	7 .	6

25
10 March
1747/8

CUST 58/149, p. 16

From W. Wood (Custom House, London). Hand i.

Captain Loy'd of his Majestys Ship the Invincible and Captain Ballet of the Otter Sloop having applied to the Commissioners in relation to two pipes of Madeira Wine, bro*ugh*t home in his Majestys Ship the Bristol Capt Montague, which they desire may be remov'd from the Bristol into their respective Ships. You are to acquaint them that the Duty must be paid for the said Wine, otherwise the Board cannot comply with their request. *Valediction 2*

26
10 March
1747/8

CUST 58/149, pp. 16–17

From W. Wood (Custom House, London). Hand i.

The Collector & Comptroller of the Customs at Milford having in their Letter of the 19th ultimo represented to the Commissioners that the Cumberland Private Ship of war saild from thence with the Polonan a Dutch East India Ship for Spithead and that eight Chests or boxes suppos'd to contain Papers were deliver'd to Capt Hutton Commander of the said Privateer under the Seals of Office and his receipt taken for the same Copy whereof you will receive Inclos'd. And you are to enquire whether the said Ships arriv'd at Spithead and Report to the Board what became of the Papers *valediction 2*

Custom house Milford 8th Feb*ruary* 1747

I do acknowledge to have this day rec*eive*d of & from Matthew Lord Esqr Collector of the Customs for the Port of Milford in pursuance of an Order from the Honble Board of Customs dated 28th Ultimo (and to him for that purpose directed) Eight boxes or Chests suppos'd to contain Papers taken by me the first day of Jan*uar*y last out of the Polonen a Dutch Ship now lying at Humberston in the said Port and the same day bro*ugh*t up by me to Pembroke and by the said Mr Lord taken & secur'd at the Customhouse w*hi*ch said Boxes are each of them now Seald in my presence with the Seals of Office of the said Customhouse and are in the same State & Condition in ev*e*ry respect as they were in when taken out of the said Ship & bro*ugh*t up by me as aforesaid as witness my hand

Wm Hutton

Witness
James Allen
Nichs Stokes

---

14 'by' struck out.

27
11 March
1747/8

CUST 58/149, p. 18

From W. Wood (Custom House, London). Hand i.

Mr Henry Ehlers having applied to the Commiss*ioner*s by his Memorial of the 7th Instant relating to the Metta Christiana a Neutral Ship, now at your Port with Naval Stores which was brought into the Downs by the Culloden Privateer desiring leave to land the Cargoe and to pay the Duty for such part of it as shall be accepted by the Commissioners of the Navy, and to reship the Remainder if any part is refus'd by that Board. The Commissioners agree to the Goods being landed by sight on sufficient Deposits being made, and the other Requisites perform'd agreable to the Report of the Patent Officers transmitted you in my Letter of the 17th of Sept*embe*r 1746 on a Case of the like nature (upon the petition of Messrs Henry & Peter Muilman) to w*hi*ch I refer you for your Government *valediction 2*

28
11 March
1747/8

CUST 58/149, p. 19

From W. Wood (Custom House, London). Hand i.

It having been represented to the Board that large Quantities of Prize Gunpowder are advertised to be sold at your Port out of the Ships taken by Lord Anson and Sir Peter Warren which it is apprehended is for home Consumption.

You are to acquaint the Board what Quantities of Gunpowder are now under your Locks and intended for Sale, & whether the whole or what part of it is declar'd for Exportation *valediction 2*

29
12 March
1747/8

CUST 58/149, pp. 17–18

From W. Wood (Custom House, London). Hand i.

The Lieutenants and other Officers of his Majestys Ship the Invincible having by their Memorial of the 8th Instant applyd to the Commissioners, desiring that a hogshead of Wine w*hi*ch Capt Montague of his Majestys Ship the Bristol made them a present, may be deliver'd without payment of Duty. You are to acquaint them the Duty must be paid for the said Wine which I am directed to signify to you *valediction 2*

30
16 March
1747/8

CUST 58/149, p. 20–1

From W. Wood (Custom House, London). Hand i.

The Commissioners having lately Order'd their Solicitor, to state a Case for the Opinion of the Attorney and Solicitor General with respect to Goods of the growth or Manufacture of France, Imported from thence, or from any Country ⌜now⌝[15] under the Dominion of the French King. I am directed to send you Copy thereof, with copy of their Opinion thereon, for your Information and Government – *valediction 2*

> Whether the Officers of the Customs will be justified by the Proclamation in refusing to permit any Entry to be made of Goods ⌜of⌝[16] French or any other growth or Manufacture which are Imported from France or any other the Dominions of the French King; Or will be thereby justified in refusing to permit an Entry to be made of Goods of the Growth or manufacture of France Imported from any Country not under the Dominions of the French King.
>
> There being no Act of Parliament to prohibit the Importations of French Commoditys and the Acts that charge them with Dutys being still subsisting and those Dutys being now Due immediately on Importation we are of Opinion the Commissioners are not warranted in denying them an Entry (which is the proper method of charging them with the Duty) whether they are Imported from French Dominions or any other Forreign Country, tho' such Importation if by the means of a Correspondence between any of his Majestys Subjects & his Enemies is a misdemeanor in such Subjects and may be punish'd as such. In this Opinion we take it for granted that there is no other objection to the Entry then what is stated – 12th March 1747
>
> D Ryder
> W Murray

---

[15] MS. 'not'.
[16] MS. 'or'.

31
17 March 1747/8

CUST 58/149, p. 21

From Sam. Mead, B. Fairfax, Beaumont Hotham and Ric. Chandler (Custom House, London). Hand i.

Having consider'd your Letter of the 12th Instant, together with your Preparatory Account of Incidents for the Quarter ended at Mich*ael*mas last amounting to Nineteen Pounds, ten Shillings and eight pence half peny. The Collector may pay the same with the Privity of the Comptroller, and take Credit for it in his Account of Incidents annexing this Letter with proper receipts thereto as Vouchers *valediction 1*

32
17 March 1747/8

CUST 58/149, p. 22

From W. Wood (Custom House, London). Hand i.

His Majesty having been pleas'd by his Letters Patents to appoint the Honble Roger Townshend Esqr to be Receiver General & Cashire of this Revenue in the room of Jno Eckersal Esqr and to appoint the said Mr Eckersall to be Register General of all Trading Ships belonging to Great Britain in the room of Thomas Boothby Skrymsher, I am directed to signify the same to you for your Information, and you are to Correspond with them accordingly. But as Mr ⌜Eckersall will act as⌝[17] Receiver General till Lady=day next, he desires you will not remit any Bills of Exchange to him, but what will reach his Office on or before that day, and the Bills you remit afterwards must be made payable to the Honble Roger Townshend Esqr *valediction 2*

33
18 March 1747/8

CUST 58/149, pp. 22–3

From W. Wood (Custom House, London). Hand i.

Mr Corbett Secretary to the Lords Commissioners of the Admiralty having in his Letter of the 17th Instant acquainted the Commiss*ione*rs that their Lordships have been pleas'd to Order the Polenan Dutch East India Ship to be restor'd to the Owners and all the Papers found in her which are in the Custody of Captain Hutton, to be deliver'd to the Master, which I am directed to signify to you *valediction 2*

34
22 March 1747/8

CUST 58/149, pp. 23–4

From W. Wood (Custom House, London). Hand i.

By Mr Carkesses Letter of the 2d December 1736 you were directed to transmit to the Board within six days after every Chr*ist*m*a*s an Account of all Bounties whatsoever that shou'd be paid at your Port between Christmas & Christmas distinguishing each Commodity for which the Bounties were granted. The Commissioners are hereby pleas[ed] to direct that the said Order be revok'd, and judging it necessary for the Service to have an Account of all Bounties sent quarterly they direct you to transmit the same within 14 days after the Expiration of each Quarter without fail to commence from Christmas last, And you are to take particular Care in the Account of the Bounties on Corn to insert the several Species and Quantities of Corn exported with the Bounties payable thereon distinguishing how much of the Bounties were paid at your Port & how much the Bounties 'mount to for the Debentures sent up to be paid here according to the Inclos'd Specimen. *Valediction 2*

Port of –

An Account of the Quantity of Corn and other Grain exported from this Port which are Entitled to a Bounty for the Quarter ended at Lady=day 1748

	Quarters	Bounty due thereon
Wheat Barley & *cetera* –	.	.
Whereof paid at this Port –		£ . . .
Debentures sent up to be paid in London –		

Other Bounties

The several Species of Goods to be inserted and the Bounties due thereon respectively

[17] Inserted.

35
26 March
1748

CUST 58/149, pp. 24–5

From W. Wood (Custom House, London). Hand i.

Inclos'd you have half a dozen of the Advertisements for apprehending the Persons concern'd in the Murder of Danl Chater and William Galley printed on a Single Paper, which you are to make as ⌜publick⌝[18] as[19] possible by affixing up the same in such places as you shall think proper, And by the first Carryer there will be sent you a further Number of the said Advertisements for the like purpose and to be distributed amongst the Officers and in your Neighbourhood *valediction 2*

36
26 March
1748

CUST 58/149, pp. 25–6

From W. Wood (Custom House, London). Hand i.

His Majesty having been pleas'd to Issue a New Order of Council relating to the Distemper'd Cattle, And there being a Clause inserted therein to prevent the Carrying Hides or Skins Coastways without producing proper Certificates to the Officers of the Customs at the places where ship'd & landed, Inclos'd you will receive one of the said Orders in Council, And you are to take Care that his Majestys Commands be duely and strictly observ'd by yourselves, and all the Officers at your Port. *Valediction 2*

P:S The Commissioners direct you forthwith to prepare & send to them an Account of the names and Tonnage of several Ships belonging to your Port, that have traded to Foreign Parts and Coastwise from Chr*istmas* 1742 to Chr*istmas* 1747, distinguishing each Year in Order to be laid before the Parliam*ent*

37
26 March
1748

CUST 58/149, pp. 26–7

From G. Vaughan, J. Evelyn, Sam. Mead and W. Levinz ('Sevine') (Custom House, London). Hand i.

Having granted our Commission for Francis Fuller to be a Tidesman at your Port in the room of Jno Fivefoot resign'd and he having given Security here, You are to admit him to the said Employ, paying him the like allowance by Incidents as was paid to his Predecessor for which the Collector may take Credit from time to time in his Account of Incidents refering therein to the date hereof. *Valediction 1*

38
29 March
1748

CUST 58/149, p. 26

From W. Levinz ('Sevine'), B. Fairfax, W. Westby and Sam. Mead (Custom House, London). Hand i.

By ⌜our⌝[20] Order of the 8th Instant We directed you to Secure in the Warehouse at your Port the Liquors belonging to Colonel Murray and Colonel Talbot which were on board the Scorpion Sloop Capt Batt Commander, till further Orders You are now to deliver the said Liquors upon Payment of the Dutys. *Valediction 1*

39
14 April
1748

CUST 58/149, p. 27

From Rob. Baylis, Sam. Mead, B. Fairfax and Beaumont Hotham (Custom House, London). Hand i.

In pursuance of a Warrant from the Treasury, We have Issued our Deputation for Chas Markland to be Landsurveyor at your Port in the room of Chas Morgan Deceas'd, and when he has perfected the Inclos'd Bond with two Security[s] whose Sufficiency you are to Certify to M^{r} McSwiny Examiner of Officers Securitys, you may admit him to the said Employ giving him all due Encouragement for his Majestys Service, letting him know he must Qualify himself as the Law directs, reporting to us the day he is admitted. And you are to call in Morgans Deputation & Cancel it, and transmit it to us with your next Accounts by the Carrier. *Valediction 1*

---

18 Inserted.
19 MS. omits 'as'.
20 Inserted.

40
19 April
1748

CUST 58/149, p. 28

From R. Chandler, W. Westby, G. Vaughan and W. Levinz ('Sevine') (Custom House, London). Hand i.

Having consider'd the Collectors Letter of the 15th Instant desiring leave to be absent for twenty days in order to attend his private affairs We agree thereto upon his appointing a proper Person for whom he will be answerable, to carry on the Collection during his absence. *Valediction 1*

41
21 April
1748

CUST 58/149, p. 28

From Ric. Chandler, Rob. Baylis, W. Levinz ('Sevine') and G. Vaughan (Custom House, London). Hand i.

In pursuance of a Warrant of the Treasury We have Issued our Deputation for Thos Merrit to be Landwaiter at your Port in the room of Thos Wiggett deceas'd, And when he has perfected the Inclos'd Bond with two Securities whose Sufficiency you are to Certify to Mr McSwiny Examiner of Officers Securities, You may admit him to the said Imploy giving him all due Encouragement for his Majestys Service, letting him know he must Qualify himself as the Law Directs reporting to us the day he is admitted. And you are to call in Wiggetts Deputation and Cancel it, and transmit it to us with your next Accounts by the Carrier. *Valediction 1*

42
26 April
1748

CUST 58/149, p. 29

From W. Wood (Custom House, London) to the Collector. Hand i.

Sir

Mr George Arnold a Merchant of this City having given Us notice of his Intention to send from hence by Land Carriage to your Port & from thence to export to Affrica One hundred fifty *Niccanees, two hundred *Byrampauts four hundred *Brawley Eighty *Neganepacels two hundred forty *Chelloes, three hundred *Chelloes bleu, one hundred *Carridarries seventy *Taffities, three hundred fifty *Romalls, one hundred fifty *Chints, forty *Copees, forty *Photaes, thirty *Cuttanees.

And having here ⌜given⌝[21] Security for the Exportation thereof according to Law enclos'd I send you the *Cocquet taken out for the above Goods And the Commissioners direct you to demand the said Goods of the Carrier and Cause them to be carried to the King[s] Warehouse and inform them if the Package ⌜thereof⌝[22]be entire agreable to the endorsement on the *Cocket and under the Seals of the Officers and in Case the same does not arrive in Twenty days after this date you are to inform them thereof, and you are to deliver the *Cocket to the proper Officers at your Port who before Shipping are to open & Examine the said Goods to see if they in Quantity & Quality agree therewith reporting your proceedings to the Board and am

Sir Your most humble servant

W: Wood.

43
30 April
1748

CUST 58/149, p. 30

From W. Wood (Custom House, London). Hand i.

The Accounts mention'd in your Letter of the 3d March 1747 for the Quarter ended at Chr*ist*m*a*s last are safe come to hand. *Valediction 2*

44
30 April
1748

CUST 58/149, p. 30

From W. Wood (Custom House, London). Hand i.

The Commissioners observing from the Various & Constant applications almost daily made that Forreign as well as English Goods are frequently sent Coastwise without a Coast Dispatch or *Cocket as the Law requires whereby great opportunitys are given for commiting Frauds to the Prejudice of the Revenue. In Order to prevent the same for the future and that the Traders may not complain of Hardships in not being apprised thereof; You are to affix up notice in Writing in the most publick place

---

21 MS. 'giving'.

22 Inserted.

in the Customhouse, That in case any Goods shall hereafter be carried Coastwise without legal Dispatches accompanying the same that such Goods will be seiz'd on the Vessels arrival at the Port they are intended to be deliver'd at and prosecuted according to Law. *Valediction 2*

Laws relating to Coast Dispatches

3 Henry 7. Cap: 7[23]

13 & 14 Car: 2. Cap 11. Sec: 7[24]

8 Geo: 1. Cap 18. Sec: 18

45
3 May
1748

CUST 58/149, p. 31

From Wil. Levinz ('Sevine'), J. Evelyn, Rob. Baylis and Beaumont Hotham (Custom House, London). Hand i.

Having consider'd your Preparatory Account of Incidents for the Quarter ended at Chr*istmas* last amounting to Twenty one pounds six Shillings & four pence. The Collector may pay the same with the Privity of the Comptroller and take Credit for it in his Account of Incidents annexing this Letter with proper receipts thereto as Vouchers *valediction 1*

In margin: £21.6.4[25]

46
5 May
1748

CUST 58/149, pp. 31–2

From W. Wood (Custom House, London). Hand i.

The Commissioners having advised with the Attorney General on a state of the Case whethe[r] the new Duty of 5 Per C*en*t granted by an Act of 21st Year of his present M*ajes*tie[26] is due by Law at the Port of Delivery notwithstanding the Ship was at any other Port on or before the 1st March[27] last, and Mr Attorney General being of opinion the said Duty is due by the late Act at the Port of Delivery I am directed to signify the same to you for your Government. And in Case any Goods were Imported at your Port from & after the said 1st March, You are to insist on ⌜the⌝[28] said Duty for such Goods notwithstanding the Ships or Vessels might arrive in some other Ports before that Day, and in Case the Importers refuse to pay the same You are to acquaint the Commiss*ione*rs therewith for their further Directions *valediction 2*

47
5 May
1748

CUST 58/149, pp. 32–3

From W. Wood (Custom House, London). Hand i.

The Right Honourable the Lords Commissioners of his Majestys Treasury, having been pleas'd in Compassion to the Inferior Officers of the Customs to authorize the ⌜Commissioners⌝[29] to give directions to the Collectors of the Out Ports to pay the Taxes asses'd upon the Salaries of the Deputed Officers, not exceeding Sixty pounds Per Annum, by the Land Tax granted for this Year; and also to reimburse them the Money paid upon their Salaries by Virtue of that Act;[30] the Commissioners direct me to signify the same to you, and that you yield obedience thereto accordingly refering in your Incidents to the date hereof, and withall taking care that no more be allow'd than has been already paid or shall be paid by the said Officers, and that by Virtue thereof you do not allow the Taxes asses'd upon any Patent Officers; And I am further to acquaint you that all Officers are to be Tax'd were they Execute their Offices and not were they are paid their Salaries; and the Collector is to take care of reminding the Assessors thereof that the Asessments may be made accordingly Which is what I have in Command to signify to you, *valediction 2*

---

[23] I.e. Statute 3 Hen. VII, c.8.
[24] I.e. Statute 14 Cha. II, c.11.
[25] Underlined.
[26] Statute 21 Geo. II, c.2.
[27] 'last', repeated, struck out.
[28] MS. 'the the'.
[29] MS. 'Commmissioners'.
[30] Statute 21 Geo. II, c.7.

48 CUST 58/149, p. 33

6 May 1748

From W. Levinz ('Leivieur'), J. Evelyn, R. Baylis and R. Chandler (Custom House, London). Hand ii.

Captain Pott of his Majestys Ship the Greenwich having applyd to us desiring leave to remove his Stores from the Norwich, into the Greenwich, We agree thereto under the care of the proper Officers, taking care that no part of the said Stores are landed *valediction 1*

49 CUST 58/149, p. 33

7 May 1748

From W. Levinz ('Lievieur'), J. Evelyn, R. Baylis and R. Chandler (Custom House, London). Hand ii.

We receiv'd your Letter of the 1st Instant acquainting us that there is in the Warehouses at your Port under the Kings locks large Quantities of Linnens, landed out of the French Prizes, and it appearing that part are British & Irish on which there is a Bounty allowd on Exportation, We direct you to insist on the said Bounty being repaid *valediction 1*

50 CUST 58/149, p. 34

10 May 1748

From J. Evelyn, W. Levinz ('Lievieur') and R. Baylis (Custom House, London). Hand ii.

In answer to the Account of Seizures transmitted in your Letter of the 5th Instant We direct you to prosecute the Goods thereinmention'd to Condemnation in the Exchequer, the Tea & Brandy at the Kings Charge and the rest of the Goods at the Officers Charge Corresponding with our Solicitor & the Register of Seizures *valediction 1*

51 CUST 58/149, p. 35

10 May 1748

From J. Evelyn, W. Levinz ('Lievieur'), R. Baylis and R. Chandler (Custom House, London). Hand ii.

Having granted our Deputation for Thomas Chadwick to be a Coalmeter at your Port in the Room of Henry Gibbs resign'd, You are to take care he be under Oath and Security for the faithfull discharge of the said Employ and Qualifys himself as the Law Directs *valediction 1*

52 CUST 58/149, p. 34

11 May 1748

From W. Wood (Custom House, London). Hand ii.

Mr Robt Day having apply'd to us by order of the Court of Directors of the United East India Company for leave to tranship Sixty Chests of Treasure out of the Pelham & Somerset now at Spithead on board his Maj*es*tys Ship the Tartar bound to the East Indies, We have agreed thereto & you may permit the same to be done under the care of the proper Officers, taking care the Crown be at no expence on this Account We are

Your Loving Friends

This Letter was prepar'd for the Commissioners Signing but the Board being risen before it was finishd their Commands are signify'd to you by

Gentlemen Your most humble Servant

W Wood

53 CUST 58/149, p. 35

12 May 1748

From W. Wood (Custom House, London). Hand ii.

The Commissioners being informd that it is a practice in some Ports to grant Sufferances for Goods to be ship't and Landed at places not within the Limits of any Ports You are forthwith to report whether any such Sufferances are granted by you and your reasons for so doing *valediction 2*

54 CUST 58/149, p. 36

12 May 1748

From J. Evelyn, R. Baylis, Beaumont Hotham and R. Chandler (Custom House, London). Hand ii.

Mr William Denny having by his Memorial of the 11th Instant apply'd to us desiring that nineteen Bags of Coffee & two small Bags of Indigo on board the Grand Biche a French Privateer, may be reship't on board the Sea Nymph. Inclos'd we send you Copy of the said Memorial, and direct you to report to us whether the said Goods are contain'd in the Report of the Grand Biche Prize, and whether it was Reported for Exportation or to pay the Dutys, for our further Orders *valediction 1*

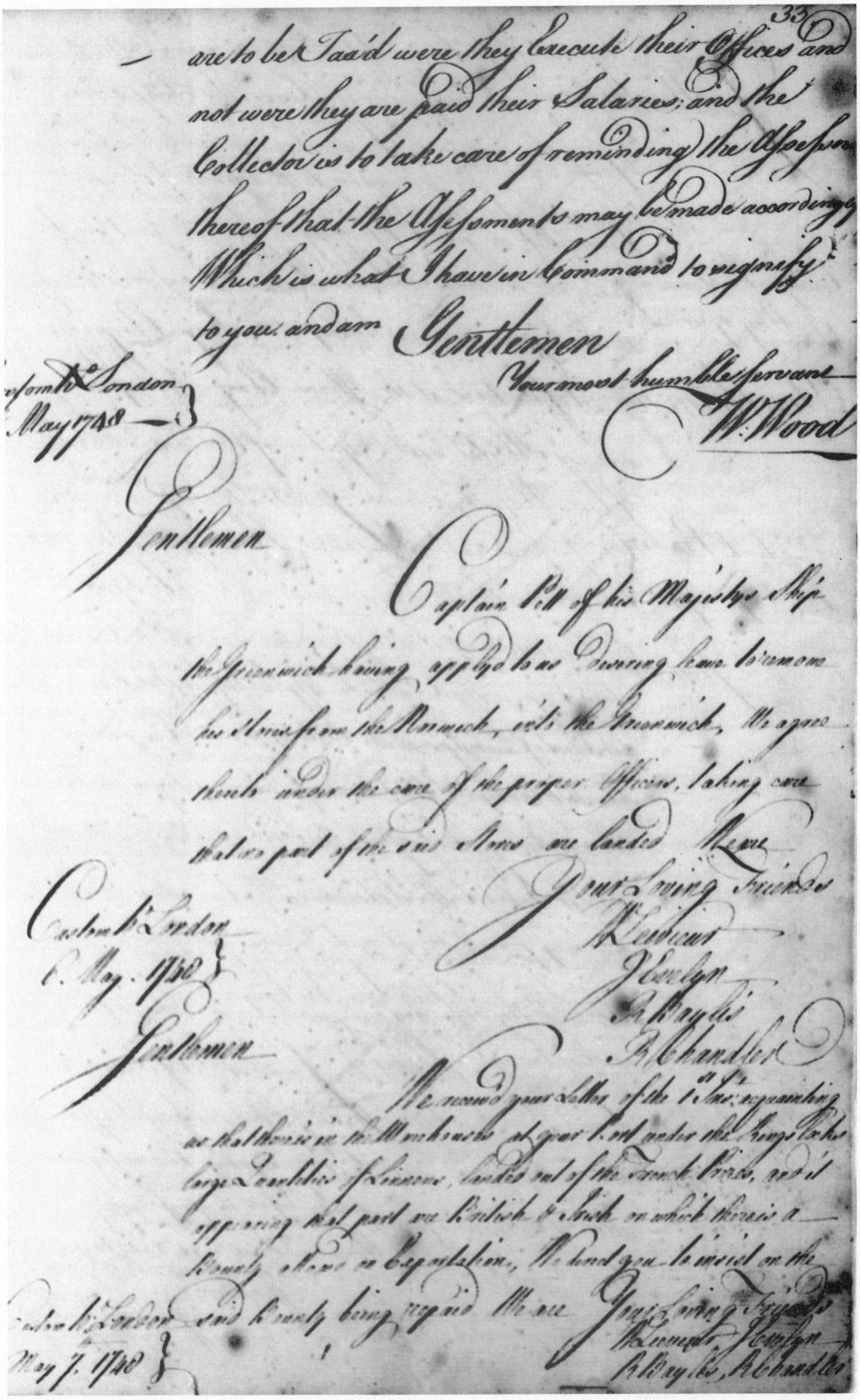
33

are to be Tax'd were they Execute their Offices and not were they are paid their Salaries; and the Collector is to take care of reminding the Assessors thereof that the Assessments may be made accordingly Which is what I have in Command to signify to you and am Gentlemen

Your most humble Servant
W. Wood

[illegible] London
5 May 1748

Gentlemen

Captain [illegible] of his Majestys Ship the Greenwich having applyd to us desiring leave to remove his Stores from the Norwich into the Greenwich, We agree thereto under the care of the proper Officers, taking care that no part of the said Stores are landed We are

Your Loving Friends
[illegible]
J. Evelyn
[illegible] Baylis
[illegible] Chandler

Custom Ho London
6. May . 1748

Gentlemen

We received your Letter of the 1st Inst. acquainting us that there is in the Warehouse at your Port under the Kings Locks large Quantities of Linnens landed out of the French Prizes, and it appearing that part are British & Irish on which there is a Bounty allowed on Exportation, We direct you to insist on the said Bounty being repaid We are

Your Loving Friends
[illegible] J. Evelyn
[illegible] Baylis, [illegible] Chandler

[illegible] London
May 7. 1748

Fig. 4 LETTERS FROM THE BOARD OF CUSTOMS TO THE PORTSMOUTH CUSTOMS OFFICERS 5–7 MAY 1748 (nos 47–49). P.R.O. CUST 58/149, p. 33

May it please Your Honours

There is now on Board the Grand Biche French Privateer at Portsmouth 19 Bags Coffee & 2 small Bags Indigo which were taken out of the Sea Nymph Michael Purse Master bound from S[t] Eustatia to Rotterdam who had been taken by the said Privateer and afterwards retaken by the Bellona man of war, the Recaptors have consented to have the said Coffee & Indigo reship't a board the Sea Nymph, but the Collector at Portsmouth will not suffer it without an Order from your Honours we therefore beg you'l be pleasd to give an Order to that purpose & we are

Your Honours humble Servants for Jonathan Gurnell & C[oy]

W Denny

11th May 1748

55
17 May
1748

CUST 58/149, p. 37

From R. Baylis, J. Evelyn, R. Chandler and W. Levinz ('Leiveur') (Custom House, London). Hand ii.

Admiral Steuart having by his Letter of the 13th Instant acquainted Us that he expects evry day to receive Orders to strike his Flag and desiring that his Sea Store of Liquors on board the Royal George may be admitted to an Entry, We agree thereto, And you may admit them to an Entry as desir'd *valediction 1*

56
20 May
1748

CUST 58/149, pp. 37–8

From W. Wood (Custom House, London). Hand ii.

M[r] John Sarjent, Merchant of this City having given us notice of his Intention to send from hence by land to your Port and from thence to Export to Africa Two hundred *Chelloes blue, two hundred and twelve *Bejutapauts one hundred *Cuttanees two hundred fifty *Musters twelve *Byramputs, twelve *Carridarries, thirty *Brawles, ten *Chelloes, eight *Romalls, eight *Neganepauts, six *Niceanees ten *Guinea Stuffs, And having here given Security for the Exportation thereof according to Law enclosd I send you a *Cocket taken out for the above Goods, and you are to demand the said Goods of the Carrier and cause them to be carried to the Kings Warehouse and inform Us if the Package thereof be entire agreable to the endorsement on the *Cocket and under the Seals of the Officers and in case the same does not arrive in twenty days after this date you are to inform Us thereof, and you are to deliver the *Cocket to the proper Officers at your Port who before Shipping are to open and examine the said Goods to see if they in Quantity & Quality agree therewith reporting your proceedings to the Board *valediction 2*

57
27 May
1748

CUST 58/149, p. 38

From Ric. Chandler, Rob. Baylis, Wil. Levinz ('Levine') and Beaumont Hotham (Custom House, London). Hand i.

Having granted our Commission for Tho[s] Young to be a Tidesman & Boatman at your Port in the room of James Fryar deceas'd you are to take Care he be under Oath & Security for the faithfull Discharge of the said Employ, paying him the like Allowance by Incidents as was paid to his Predecessor for w*hi*ch the Collector may take Credit from time to time in his Account of Incidents refering therein to the date hereof. *Valediction 1*

58
28 May
1748

CUST 58/149, p. 39

From Ric. Chandler, Wil. Levinz, Wil. Westby and Rob. Baylis (Custom House, London). Hand i.

We receiv'd your Letter of the 17th Instant in return to the Memorial of M[r] William Denny desiring that the nineteen bags of Coffee & two small bags of Indigo on board the Grand Biche a French Privateer may be reshipt on board the Sea Nymph. You may upon the Dutys being paid for the Coffee, as Imported after the 1st March last Permit the said Goods to be reshipt on board the Sea Nymph as desir'd.

In answer to the Account of Seizures transmitted in your Letter of the 21st Instant We direct you to prosecute the Goods thereinmention'd to Condemnation in the Exchequer, the Brandy at the Kings Charge, and the rest of the Goods at the Officers Charge, Corresponding with our Solicitor & the Register of Seizures *valediction 1*

59
3 June
1748

CUST 58/149, p. 40[31]

From W. Wood (Custom House, London). Hand i.

The Commiss*ione*rs for Victualing his Majestys Navy having in their Letter of the 1st Instant desird that One Thousand four hundred & forty gallons of Foreign Brandy sent to your Port in the William & Mary Hoy may be issued to any of his Majestys Ships Outward bound, or receiv'd ⌜into⌝[32] his Majestys Stores and Lodg'd under the Kings Locks until such an opportunity shall offer. The Commissioners have agreed thereto, and you are to permit the said Brandy to be transhipt accordingly, or Secur'd in the Warehouse under the Care of the proper Officers, till such time as it shall be put on board other Ships for his[33] Majestys Service, taking Care there be no Embezlements[34] *valediction 2*

60
4 June
1748

CUSY 58/149, p. 40

From Sam. Mead, Rob. Baylis, Wil. Levinz and Ric. Chandler (Custom House, London). Hand i.

In answer to the Account of Seizures transmitted in your Letter of the 27th Ultimo We direct you to prosecute the Brandy therein mention'd to Condemnation before the Justices of the Peace at the Kings Charge acquainting us when Condemn'd *valediction 1*

61
10 June
1748

CUST 58/149, p. 41

From Wil. Wood (Custom House, London). Hand iii.

Inclosed I send you by order of the Commissioners several Acts passed the last session of Parliament relating to the Customs for the Government of yourselves and the other Officers at your Port, Vizt

1 The Malt Act for the Year 1748
2 An Act to prohibit Assurance on Ships belonging to France and on Merchandizes ⌜or⌝[35] Effects laden thereon during the present War with France
3 An Act for permitting Tea to be exported to Ireland & his Majesty's Plantations in America without paying the Inland Duties &cetera
4 An Act for Explaining, Amending and inforcing an Act of the 18 Year of his Present Majesty's Reign for prohibit*ing* the wearing and Importation of *Cambricks and French *Lawns
5 An Act for Encouraging the making of Indigo in the British Plantations in America[36]

Valediction 2

62
14 June
1748

CUST 58/149, p. 41

From Wil. Wood (Custom House, London). Hand iii.

Some Merchants of this City having laid before the Commissioners Papers granted by the Lords of the ⌜Regency⌝[37] for permitting Ships to proceed with their Lading from this and the out Ports for several Ports in France and the Board being given to Understand that Passes have been sent to some Ports without being first imparted to them for their Directions thereupon you are upon return of the Post to Acquaint them if any Passes have been brought to you with the Names of the Ships or Vessels the Masters Name, Burden and Number of Men, and where bound with the Cargo, and what you may have done thereupon, And if any Application should be made to you for the Entry of any Ship with their Lading for France you are to Acquaint the Person Applying that you cannot permit them to do it without producing a Pass for that purpose *valediction 2*

---

31 No. 60 precedes no. 59 in MS.
32 Altered from 'in'.
33 MS. omits 'his'.
34 In the margin is the signature 'June 10th 1748 Pusey Brooke Surv*eyo*r Gen*eral*', presumably on examining the letter book in his inspection of the outport's business (see no. 68 and above, pp. xiii, xxxiv).
35 MS. 'on'.
36 Statutes 21 Geo. II, cc. 1, 4, 14, 26, 30.
37 MS. 'Regeney'.

63
17 June
1748

CUST 58/149, p. 42

From Wil. Wood (Custom House, London). Hand iii.

The Commissioners having received from the Secretary of State's Office a List of such Passes as have hitherto been Granted by their Excellencies the Lords Justices of great Britain for Ships to Sail with their Ladings from several Ports of this Kingdom and Ireland to different Ports in France and the Ships mentioned on the back hereof being accordingly permitted to Sail from your Port with their Cargoes. I am directed to Acquaint you that you may Suffer the said Ships to Lade at your Port for the Port in France mentioned in the passes upon their being produced to you, and likewise all other Ships and Vessels for which regular Passes may be produced for the future according to the tenor of the said Passes. And you are to transmit the Board an Account of the Time when you receive the Passes mentioned on the back hereof and all other Passes, with the Names of the Ships, or Vessels, Master's Name, burden, Number of Men the respective Cargoes and for what place they clear Outwards, *valediction 2*

		Bound	
Ships	Masters	From	To
Friends Goodwill	Edwd Forestall	Portsm^{o}	Havre de Grace
Taunton –	George Tickner –	D^{o} –	Marseilles
Will*iam* & Mary –	William Joad –	D^{o} –	Bourdeaux

64
21 June
1748

CUST 58/149, p. 42

From J. Evelyn, Ric. Chandlor, S. Mead and Wil. Levinz ('Sevine') (Custom House, London). Hand iii.

It appearing by your last Months Abstract, that there is remaining in the Collector's hands the Sum of One hundred and fifty three Pounds, ten Shillings and Nine Pence of the Kings Money, We direct you forthwith to Remit the same together with what you have since received to the Receiver General Pursuant to the Condition of the Collectors Bond. *Valediction 1*
In margin: £153.10s.9d

65
21 June
1748

CUST 58/149, p. 43

From Wil. Wood (Custom House, London). Hand iii.

A Doubt having arisen concerning the manner of Computing the new Duty on Wines and Vinigar imported from and after 25th Mar. 1745 the Commissioners thought proper to advise with his Maj*estys* Att*orney* General and a Case Stated for that purpose whether the Officers of the Customs can by Law oblige the Merchants to enter their Wine for this new Duty as they do for the Old Duty's and agreeable to the Methods always practised in Collecting the *Coinage Duty or whether they are to pay for no more than the Quantity of Wine Actually imported and what shall appear to be contained in the Casks and Mr Att*orney* being of Opinion that "the[38] Merch*ant* cannot make two different sorts of Entrys one for the new and an other for the old Duty and his Entry of so much unfitted for Sale being in effect an Entry for the whole Quantity which the Casks can contain as so much imported concludes him as to the Quantity of which both the old & new Duty are to be Computed and as the Old Duty is subject to the Deduction of 12[39] Per C*ent* leakage and the Duty is not therefore he conceives the Merchant upon such Entry must pay the whole new Duty on that entire Quantity and that this is the stronger as it falls in with the Settled with respect to the *Coinage Duty on Wines" I am directed to signify the same to you and you are to govern your selves accordingly in demanding and Collecting the new Duties beforementioned. *Valediction 2*

[38] Each line of this quotation is introduced by a double quotation mark.
[39] There is an illegible abbreviation above '12'.

66
22 June 1748

CUST 58/149, pp. 43–4

From Wil. Wood (Custom House, London). Hand iii.

Mr John Sone having by his Memorial of the 18th instant, applyed to the Commissioners desiring that a new depenture may be made out for 324 Quarters & 6 Bushels of Flower Shipt at your Port by his Father on board the Theodosia Richard Hunter Master in the room of the former which is lost or mislaid I am directed to send you Copy of the said Memorial & you are to examine into the Allegations therein contained, & Report a State of the Case to the Board with your Opinion *valediction 2*

Honourable Gentlemen

The purport of my Writing is to let you know that my Father Mr Nicholas Sone Shiped on board the Theodosia Richard Hunter Master in the Port of Portsmouth 324 Quarters 6 Bushels of Flower in last September bound to Gibralter my Father going to live a Distance off before the Ship Sailed cou'd not take the Deb*entures* out of the Office & since it has been mislaid in the said Office, I desire the favour of you to give Orders to have a Debenture made out in my Name as my Father lives a great Distance off; I was advised at the Office to Write to you on this Affair

I am Your most Obedient humble Servant

Jno Sone at Havant Hants

Havant
18th June 1748

67
23 June 1748

CUST 58/149, pp. 44–5

From Wil. Wood (Custom House, London). Hand iii.

The Commissioners having received from the Secretary of States Office a List of such Passes as have hitherto been granted by their Excellencies the Lords Justices of Great Britain for Ships to Sail with their Ladings from Several Ports of this Kingdom and Ireland to different Ports in France, and the Ships mentioned on the back hereof being accordingly permitted to Sail from your Port with their Cargoes. I am directed to acquaint you, that you may suffer the said Ships to Lade at your Port for the Port in France mentioned in the Passes upon their being produced to you, and likewise all other Ships and Vessels for which regular Passes may be produced for the future according to the Tenor of the said Passes, And you are to transmit the Board an Account of the time when you receive the Passes mentioned on the back hereof, and all other Passes, with the Names of the Ships or Vessels, Masters Name, burden, Number of Men, the respective Cargoes, and for what Place they clear Outwards *valediction 2*

Ships	Masters	Bound From	To
Sarah –	Selby Waddel –	Portsm^{o}.	Bourdeaux
Tweed –	John Linton –	D^{o} –	D^{o} –
London Pacquet –	Jo^{s} Hume –	D^{o} –	D^{o}

68
27 June 1748

CUST 58/149, pp. 45–8

From Pusey Brooke (Portsmouth) to the Collector, Deputy Customer and Deputy Controller. Hand iii.

Having examined your Books and informed my self as to the manner in which the Bussiness of this Port has been carryed on since the admission of the present Collector I find it necessary to leave the following Directions & Instructions *valediction 2*

Collector Deputy Customer & Deputy Comptroller

That Duplicates are to be taken and kept in the Office of all such Certificates as shall be granted agreeable to the 2^{d} Rule of the Book of Rates where the original Certificate is to be annexed to the Debenture that it may appear upon any Inspection that the requisites of the Law have been duly complyed with

That all Masters Reports Inwards and Outwards are to be Sworne before the Deputy Customer as well as the Collector & ⌜Comptroller⌝[40], and such reports are accordingly to be attested by him.

---

40 MS. 'Cromp^{r}' (for 'Comp^{r}').

Collector & ⌜Comptroller⌝[41]

That agreeable to your Coal Instructions you are frequently to inspect the Coal Meters when employed in *meting of Coals & see that they do diligently & faithfully perform their Duty and you are to be particularly careful not to Suffer them upon any pretence ever to make use of Chalk or to take the Account of *Metage on loose pieces of Paper

That upon the admission of any Officer you are to take care that the Directions, Instructions Books, Acco*un*ts, and other Papers relating to such respective Officer, be then delivered to him, for all which you are to take a Receipt in a Book proper for that purpose

That you are not to pay the Supervisor of the Riding Officers his Salary till such time as he shall have produced to you a Certificate, under my hands whereby it appears that I have received his Journal's together with those of the Riding Officers under his Inspection for the Quarter preceding the date thereof.

Deputy Comptroller

In order that the Comptroller may be a complete Cheque upon the Collector in every branch of his Duty tis necessary that in addition to those in present use he shoud keep the following Books, Viz^{t} of Civil List Receipts and Repayments, Abstracts of Petty Receipts, Superanuation, Sales of Enumerated Goods, together with an Account of Personal Prosecutions

Searcher

That in obedience to the Commissioners Order dated the 1st of November 1726 neither the Searcher nor any other Officer attending the Exportation of Goods do ever receive any Merchants *Cocket or permit any Goods to be Ship'd till the Exporter has endorsed on the back thereof the particular Contents of every Cask Bale or other Package together with the Marks and Numbers

Surveyor

That you are constantly to cast up the Gauges Weights & Contents of all Goods after the Landwaiters, & that upon any Inspection it may appear that you have really performed this so considerable a branch of your Duty you are constantly to sign such Landwaiters Books and to Note the time when you ⌜Signed⌝[42] the same.

That you are to return to the Collector & ⌜Comptroller⌝[43] immediately after the expiration of each Month an account signed by your self of all the Port Entrys standing out in the preceeding Month

Surveyer and Landwaiters

That no such Credit in respect of Port Entrys is for the future to be given as has been allowed by you at this Port and therefore ⌜great Care⌝[44] is for the time to come to be taken, that your general Instructions & repeated Orders from the Board concerning this Branch of Duty are duly observed

Commander of the Greenhill Yatch

Notwithstanding the Commissioners General Orders and my repeated Directions it appears, that you very seldom lye on board the Yatch under your Command, you are hereby reprimanded for the disregard you have shewn to the Orders given you, and likewise for your neglect of Duty, and if this Unworrantable Practice is not for the time to come discontinued you will in consequence of your Misbehaviour be suspended.

Supervisor & Riding Officers

That the coast may be carefully guarded the Riding Officers are not upon any pretence whatsoever to leave their respective Districts and absent themselves from Duty without leave being first obtained from the Supervisor which leave he is constantly to Note in his Journal Booke & therein assign his reason for granting the same.

---

41 MS. 'Cromp^{r}' (for 'Comp^{r}').

42 MS. 'Sirgned'.

43 MS. 'Cromp^{r}' (for 'Comp^{r}').

44 Inserted.

That you are not upon any Account whatsoever to search Coaches and Waggons without a positive Information to which Directions you are to shew yourselves strictly Obedient, the same being given in pursuance of an Order from the Board dated the 22^{d} April 1735

Tide Surveyors

That in pursuance of the Boards Order dated the 20th of August 1726 You are to board all Vessels as well going out as coming into this Port and in all respects diligently & faithfully perform the Duty required by the said Directions.

To the end that each Officer belonging to the Water Guard may be answerable for his own neglects, you are constantly to set the Watch at the time you place Tidesman on board any Ship and to Note the same together with the Officers Name who takes the first Watch in your Boarding Booke

That you do not only use your best endeavours to preserve the Boats under your care and the furniture belonging to them from Damage, but likewise see that the same are constantly kept in perfect repair, clean and in good order.

That no Extramen are to be employed when there are *settled Men ashore Capable of performing their Duty.

⌜These Directions & Instructions are to be entered in your Book of Orders and Copy of so much thereof given to the other Officers as respectively relate to them.⌝[45]

69
28 June
1748

CUST 58/149, p. 48

From Wil. Wood (Custom House, London). Hand iii.

The Commissioners having received from the Secretary of States Office a List of such Passes as have hitherto been granted by their Excellencies the Lords Justices of Great Britain for Ships to Sail with their Ladings from several Ports of this Kingdom & Ireland to different Ports in France, And a Pass having been taken out for the St Ann, [46] Blake Master, to Sail from your Port to Bourdeaux, I am directed to acquaint you that you may Suffer the said Ship to Load her Cargo, upon the Pass being produced to you, and likewise all other Ships, and Vessels, for which regular Passes may be produced for the future, according to the Tenor of the said Passes: And you are to transmit the Board an Account of the time when you receive this Pass, and all other Passes, with the Names of the Ships, or Vessels, Masters Name, Burden, Number of Men, the respective Cargoes, for what Place they clear Outwards. *Valediction 2*

70
30 June
1748

CUST 58/149, p. 49

From W. Wood (Custom House, London). Hand iii.

The Commissioners being informed that notwithstanding their Order of 21st June 1743 some of the Boatman belonging to the Out Ports are not Qualified for their Employments, They direct you in Conjunction with the Surveyor to examine and forthwith report to them whether any of the Boatman belonging to your Port are not Qualified agreeable to the aforesaid Order and incase there are any you are to transmit them a List of their Names and the times of their Appointment. *Valediction 2*

71
2 July
1748

CUST 58/149, p. 49

From Ric. Chandlor, B. Fairfax, Sam. ('W^{m}') Mead and G. Vaughan (Custom House, London). Hand iii.

Application having been ⌜made⌝[47] to us desiring that Jeremiah Fardell Riding Officer at your Port may have leave to be Absent for a Month for the recovery of his health; We have agreed thereto without loss of pay, and you are to take care his Duty be performed by a proper Person during his Absence without any additional Expence to the Crown. *Valediction 1*

---

45 Added (hand iv).
46 Space left blank.
47 Inserted.

72 CUST 58/149, p. 49

4 July 1748

From R. Chandlor, B. Fairfax, Sam. Mead and G. Vaughan (Custom House, London). Hand iii.

In answer to the Account of Seizures transmitted in your Letter of the 17th Ultimo, We direct you to prosecute the Goods thereinmentioned to Condemnation in the Exchequer at the Officers Charge Corresponding with our Solliciter and the Register of Seizures, *valediction 1*

Noted in Seizure Book July 4th 1748

73 CUST 58/149, p. 50

5 July 1748

From Sam. Mead, B. Fairfax, R. Chandlor and G. Vaughan (Custom House, London). Hand iii.

Having considered your Letter of the 11th instant transmitting Samples of two Hogsheads of Wine landed at your Port out of the Vigilant, and it appearing that it is Portugal mixt with some small French Wine, We direct you to Admit it to an Entry as Portugal Wine. *Valediction 1*

74 CUST 58/149, p. 50

5 July 1748

From Sam. Mead, B. Fairfax, R. Chandlor and G. Vaughan (Custom House, London). Hand iii.

We received your Letter of the 22d Ultimo Inclosing a Certificate, whereby it appears that the Greenhill Yatch and Boats belonging to her in the Service at your Port under the Command of Captain Coombs are in good and Sufficient Repair, the Collector may pay the Commander thereof the usual Allowance for keeping the said Yatch and Boats in wear & Tear for the Quarter ended at Lady day last, and take Credit for the same in his Account of Incidents, annexing this Letter with proper Receipts thereto as Vouchers. *Valediction 1*

In margin: ⌜Original transmitted w*i*th the Account of Salarys & Incidents for Mich*ael*mas Q*uarter* 1748.⌝[48]

75 CUST 58/149, pp. 50–1

7 July 1748

From Sam. Mead, B. Fairfax, Rob. Baylis and G. Vaughan (Custom House, London). Hand iii.

We received your Letter of the 29th Ultimo, Inclosing an Estimate of the charge of repairing the Watch Boat in the Service at your Port, amounting to three Pounds twelve Shillings and Seven pence, you may order the said Boat to be forthwith to be repaired in the best and Cheapest Terms you can, taking care the charge does not exceed the Estimate, and when finished to transmit us the Bills of particulars for our further Orders

In answer to the Account of Seizures transmitted in your Letter of the 4th instant, We direct you to prosecute the Goods which were Run to Condemnation before the Justices of the Peace, and the Wine in the exchequer, the Tea, and Brandy, at the Kings Charge, and the rest of the Goods at the Officers Charge Corresponding with our Solliciter and the Register of Seizures. *Valediction 1*

Noted in the Seizure Book July 9th 1748

76 CUST 58/149, p. 51

9 July 1748

From Sam. Mead, W. Levinz ('Sevine'), G. Vaughan and R. Chandlor (Custom House, London) to [W.] Cooley. Hand iii.

Mr Cooley

Having considered your Letter of the 11th Ultimo, setting forth that it has been a Custom of late Years for the Weighing Porter, or one of the Tidesman to be as an Assistant to you, as Warehousekeeper, and John Stretch who was lately appointed Weighing Porter, not being capable of Assisting you, in taking care of the Kings Warehouse. We agree to appoint John Ring as an Assistant to you agreeable to your desire *valediction 1*

[48] Added (hand v).

77
12 July
1748

CUST 58/149, pp. 51–2

From G. Vaughan, B. Fairfax, S. Mead and W. Levinz ('Sevine') (Custom House, London) to [W. Cooley]. Hand iii.

Sir

Mr Robert Burnett a Merchant of this City having given us Notice of his Intention to send from hence by Land to your Port, and from thence to Export to Africa One Hundred twenty *Romaus Fifty *Chints, twenty *Carridarrys ten *Taffaties, five *Cuttanees twenty *Bandannoes forty *Bejutapauts twenty *Neccanees, forty *Brawles ten *Celloes, twenty *Musters and having here given Security for the Exportation thereof according to Law enclosed we send you a *Cocket taken out for the above Goods and you are to Demand the said Goods of the Carrier and cause them to be carried to the Kings Warehouse and inform us if the Package thereof be entire agreeable to the Endorsement on the *Cocket and under the Seals of the Officers and incase the same does not arrive in twenty days after this date you are to inform us thereof and you are to deliver the *Cocket to the proper Officers at your Port who before Shipping are to open and examine the said Goods to see if they in Quantity & Quality agree therewith with sending us an Account of your proceedings herein *valediction 1*

78
14 July
1748[49]

CUST 58/149, p. 52

From G. Vaughan, B. Fairfax, S. Mead and W. Levinz ('Sevine') (Custom House, London). Hand iii.

Captain Dent of His Majesty's Ship Plymouth, having by his Letter of the 10th instant, applyed to us, desiring leave to remove about thirty or forty Dozen Bottles of Rum, & Madera Wine, and it being the remains of his Sea Stores, you may upon the Duties being paid for the same, permit it to be removed, as desired. *Valediction 1*

79
14 July
1748

CUST 58/149, pp. 52–4

From G. Vaughan, B. Fairfax, Sam. Mead, W. Levinz ('Sevine') (Custom House, London). Hand iii.

Mr Fryer a Merchant of this City having by his Letter of the 11th instant, applyed to us desiring that the Free Goods which are on board the Sierraleon Packet now at your Port which Cleared out from hence for Africa, may be taken out and Shipped on board the St Philip John Wade for Africa, Inclosed we send you Copy of the said Letter with an Account of the Goods, and you may permit the Free Goods to be tranship*e*d, as desired under the Inspection of the proper Officers, taking care that no Bounty or drawback Goods are relanded, and that the Crown be at no Charge on this Account giving us an Account of your Proceedings. *Valediction 1*

Honble Sirs

July 11th 1748

Please to give Directions that Orders be sent to the Collector of the Custom house at Portsmouth that he may permit part of the Free Goods on board the Sierraleon Pacquet cleared out from this Port for Africa may be put on board the St Philip John Wade likewise bound to Africa if he find the Sierraleon Pacquet on Account of her deepness in the Water by being Overloaded, unfit to proceed to Africa without being Lightned, I am with great repect

Your Hon*our*s Most humble & most Obedient Servant

Geo: Fryer.

49 MS. '14th July 1747'.

Marks & N^os			Packages	Names Goods	
GF	N°	1 to 9	9 Bales	*Long Ells	
L		9 to 12	4 D°	D°	
		1 to 10	10 D°	D°	
GF		10 to 25	16 D°	*Perpets	
		1 to 32	32 D° –	D°	
		26	1 D° –	*Plains or *Kendall Cottons	
		27	1 D° –	*Long Ells	
GF					
S	N°	1 to 15	15 D° –	Blue *half Says	
G		1 to 2	2 D° –	D°	
		1 to 2	2 Cases	Cutlasses Handles British	
		1 to 12	12 Cases	Cutlasses	
G		300 to 301	2 Bales	*Manchester Stripes	
	N° 100 } D° 25 }		2 Cases	Cheque Linnens British	
		303	a Bale –	Worstead *Monmouth Caps	
G Stores	N°	1 to 8	8 Casks	Gun Flints	
qF	N°	1 to 3	3 Casks –	Earthen Ware British	not to be taken out if the Ship does not absolutely require
			2 Crates –	D°	
	N° 123		5 Casks –	D°	
		126	2 Chests.	Pipes	
	N° 63		4 Casks.	Wrought Iron	
		73	8 Casks.	D°	
GF	N°	1 to 5	5 Casks	Wrought Iron	
			Loose	20 Grapnalls	
G	N° 210		A Chest	Scots Snuff	
		111	A Case	D°	

80

14 July 1748

CUST 58/149, p. 54

From G. Vaughan, B. Fairfax, Sam. Mead and W. Levinz ('Sevine') (Custom House, London). Hand iii.

Application having been made to us, desiring that George Blanckley Esqr Commander of His Majestys Sloop the Porcupine, may have a Commission Impowering him to Seize Prohibited and Uncustomed Goods, We have agreed thereto, And Inclosed you will receive the same, with a Bond to be Executed by him and his Securities, and when done, you may admit him to his Duty, taking care he Qualifies himself as the Law directs, and when he is Admitted, you are to return the Bond to us *valediction 1*

81

16 July 1748

CUST 58/149, p. 55

From W. Wood (Custom House, London). Hand iii.

The Commissioners received your Letter of the 28th May last, desiring the usual Bounty may be allowed to the Widow and Children of James ⌜Fryar⌝[50] late Tidesman at your Port, in consideration that his Death was owing to a fall he received in Execution of his Duty on board the Sea Horse, I am directed to acquaint you that they have considered your said Letter and before they will give any Orders thereon, You must transmit them a Certificate from the Surgeon that Fryars Death was occasioned by the Fall he received in Execution of his Duty, with your reason why you did not represent this Affair when it first happened *valediction 2*

[50] Altered from 'Fryer'.

82 CUST 58/149, p. 55

21 July 1748

From W. Levinz ('H. Sevine'), B. Fairfax, Sam. Mead and G. Vaughan (Custom House, London). Hand iii.

Inclosed you will receive a Writt of Delivery for the Enumerated Goods returned in an Indenture of Appraisment from your Port, and proclaimed in the Exchequer last Term, Amounting to Sixty eight Pounds seven Shillings and three Farthings we direct you to Sell the said Goods, Publickly to the highest bidder putting them up at their Appraisments or such other prices as will be most advantageous to the King and Officers concerned. *Valediction 1*

In margin: Writt Dated the 14th July 1748
£68. 7s. 0¾d'[51]

83 CUST 58/149, p. 56

22 July 1748

From W. Levinz ('Levine'[52]), B. Fairfax, R. Chandlor and G. Vaughan (Custom House, London). Hand iii.

Messrs Leeke and Mason having applyed to us by their memorial of the 13th of April last, desiring leave to pay the five Per Cent on the Cordage landed out of the smaller Ships of War taken by Lord Anson's Squadron, as it appears by Labells fixt to them that they were designed for the use of the Men of War of the same Squadron, and having refered the same to the proper Officers, you may accept of the Duty of five Per Cent on the Value of the Ships their Tackle, *Apparel and Furniture when they are Sold, on the Sum Total of the whole as the same is sold taking care that besides the five Per Cent, the one Penny Per Ell on the Sails be also paid. *Valediction 1*

84 CUST 58/149, p. 56

22 July 1748

From G. Vaughan, W. Levinz ('Levine'[53]), B. Fairfax and Ric. Chandlor (Custom House, London). Hand iii.

Having granted our Commission for William Stubbington to be a Tidesman at your Port, in the room of John Battershell resigned, you are to take care ⌜he be⌝[54] under Oath, and Security, for the said faithful discharge of the said Employ, and Qualifies himself as the Law directs, paying him the like ⌜Allowance⌝[55] by Incidents, as was paid to his Predecessor, for which the Collector may take Credit from time to time in his Account of Incidents referring therein to the date hereof *valediction 1*

85 CUST 58/149, p. 57

23 July 1748

From W. Levinz ('Levine'[56]), B. Fairfax, Ric. Chandlor and G. Vaughan (Custom House, London). Hand iii.

Mr Loyd having by his Memorial of this date applyed to us desiring that a Parcel of Quicksilver Consigned to him from Jamaica by the Plymouth Ship of War may be admitted to an Entry, on giving Bond to produce a Certificate of its Condemnation, We agree thereto, & you may admit the said Quicksilver to any Entry upon Bond being given in the Penalty of Double the Difference between the high and low Duty to produce a Certificate of the Condemnation in twelve Months. *Valediction 1*

86 CUST 58/149, p. 57

23 July 1748

From W. Levinz ('Levine'[57]), B. Fairfax, R. Chandlor and G. Vaughan (Custom House, London). Hand iii.

Mr James Tunlay having by his Memorial of this date, applyed to us by Order of the Court of Directors of the United East India Company for leave to Ship Fifty Chests of Treasure on board the Syren Man of War now at your Port, bound to the East Indies, we have agreed thereto, and you may permit the same to be Shipt as desired under the care of the proper Officers taking care that the Crown be at no Expence on this Account *valediction 1*

---

51 See App. I, no. 2.
52 Altered from 'Sevine'.
53 Altered from 'Sevine'.
54 Inserted.
55 Inserted.
56 Altered from 'Sevine'.
57 Altered from 'Sevine'.

87
26 July
1748

CUST 58/149, pp. 58–9

From B. Fairfax, Sam. Mead and G. Vaughan (Custom House, London). Hand iii.

Mons[r] Schicke, who is charged with the Affairs of Holland during the Absence of Monsieur Hop Envoy Extraordinary from the States General, having applyed to us by his Memorial of Yesterday in relation to the Tea Seized on board the two Brothers Thomas Arnot Master from Rotterdam, with Palatine Passengers for Philadelphia (as mentioned in your Account of Seizures of the 23[d] instant) Inclosed We send you Copy thereof, and you are to Report to us a State of the Case and acquaint us with the Number of Palatines on board and whether they are all to proceed in this Ship, or to be embarqued on another Vessel, as also whether the two Brothers is an English built Vessel, and Qualified and Navigated according to Law *valediction 1*

Hon*ourable* Sirs,

The underwriten Secretary to Monsieur Hop Envoy Extraordinary from the States General charged with the Affairs during Monsieur Hop's absence rec*eiv*ed on Saturday last a Letter from the Dutch Vice Admiral Schryver dated at Portsmouth the 22[d] instant whereby he is informed that the Officers of his Majestys Customs having been on board of a Dutch Vessel called the Twee Gebroeders Captain Thomas Armouth bound from Rotterdam for Philedelphia then lying at Spithead had made Seizure of 2 Chests of Tea Containing near 542 lb's the property of Mathias a Brakel van der Kluyt who is Passenger on board of the said Dutch Vessel with his Wife, two Children & a Nephew in order to go and Settle in Pensilvania for which Passage he is to pay 100 *Pistoles the said Mathias a Brakel van der Kluyt having been assured in Holland even by the Owners of the Vessel that he might without the least difficulty or Risque take the said 2 Chests of Tea over with him and being unacquainted with the Laws of this Land upon that Subject confidently took them on board with his other things whereby it sufficiently appears that this Tea was absolutely designed for Philadelphia and no Fraud intended, which the Proprietor is ready to attest upon Oath The underwritten therefore humbly begs leave to lay this Case before your Hon*our*s and recommend it to you that you will take it into Consideration and as it wou'd be a very great Hardship that the said Mathias a Brakel van der Kluyt shou'd through innocence be so great a Sufferer, order the said 2 Chests of Tea to be restored

F M Schicke

London 25th July 1748

88
27 July
1748

CUST 58/149, pp. 57–8

From Sam. Mead, R. Chandlor, G. Vaughan and W. Levinz ('Sevine'[58]) (Custom House, London). Hand iii.

Having granted our Commission for William Manuel to be a Tidesman, and Boatman, at your Port in the room of Gilbert Stoakes resigned, you are to take care he be under Oath and Security, for the faithful discharge of the said Employ, and Qualifies himself as the Law directs, paying him the like Allowance by Incidents as was paid to his Predecessor, for which the Collector may take Credit from time to time in his Account of Incidents, Refering therein to the date hereof *valediction 1*

89
29 July
1748

CUST 58/149, pp. 59–62

From Wil. Wood (Custom House, London). Hand iii.

M[r] West Secretary to the Right Honourable the Lord Commissioners of his Majestys Treasury having in his Letter of the 28th instant transmitted to the Board a Letter from M[r] Corbett with Copy of one from Admiral Schryver Commander of the Dutch Ships of War at Spithead relating to *Fire Money demanded of him by the Officers of the Customs, Inclosed you will receive Copies of all the said Letters and you are to transmit to the Commiss*ione*rs a State of the Case, acquainting them what was the Practise, on the like occasions during the late War, that they may acquaint their Lordships what is proper to be done in the present Case. *Valediction 2*

[58] Second 'e' underlined.

Gentlemen

The inclosed Letter from John Clevland Esq[r] Secretary to the Lords Commissioners of the Admiralty with the Copy of a Letter from Adm[l] Schryver Com*m*ander of the Dutch Ships of War at Spithead relating to *Fire Money demanded of him by the Officers of the Customs there having been laid before the Lords Commissioners of his Majesty's Treasury their Lordships have directed me to transmit the same to you and desire you will let them know what was the Practice on the like occasions during the late War, with your Opinion what is proper to be done in the present Case I am

Gentlemen Your most humble Servant

J: West

Treasury Chambers
28th July 1748

Admiralty Office 22[d] July 1748

Sir

The Lords Commissioners of the Admiralty having received a Letter from Admiral Schryver Com*mande*r in Chief of the Dutch Ships of War at Spithead relating to *Fire Money demanded of him by the Officers of the Customs, I am commanded by their Lordships to send you inclosed a Copy of a Translation of the said Letter and to desire you will lay the same before the Right Honourable the Lords of the Treasury for their L*ordshi*ps giving such Directions therein as shall appear necessary

I am Sir Your most humble Servant

J. Clevland

Translation of a Letter from Admiral Schryver to M[r] Corbett dated on board the Harlem at Spithead 29th July 1748 N*ew* S*tyle*[59]

Last Year the Officers of the Customs as receiving the *Fire Money pretended to put Waiters on board the French Prize and the latter to receive y[e] *Fire Money for the same.

At that time I demonstrated to those Officers that I had been in the Service 52 Years and never seen any other Practise but that the States Ships are exempted from it. Amongst those Ships of the States were always counted those who are their own Property or in their Service, under that Denomination are Ships of War, Fireships, Bomb-vessels, Advice Yatchs, Storeships, Hospitals, all Ships taken from the Enemy, with that distinction That those taken by Privatiers have always paid, as being considered to be the Property of Private People among the hired Ships and in the Service of the States are Transports as well for Troops as Provisions, And that those Ships may be known, they carry a Pendant.

I have told M[r] Brooks that it was not an Affair for us to have Disputes about that I shou'd acquaint my Lord Sandwich and the Griffier Hagel therewith and if the States was pleased to Alter that Antient Custom I wou'd be his Debtor & take upon me to pay him that he shou'd consider that I coud not take upon my self to treat this Affair otherwise than it was treated in the last War that the Neglect of other Officers was no precedent for me with which M[r] Brooks was contented & the Affair remaind so I have on my Arrival fulfilled the Aforesaid but as yet nothing has followed it.

I desire youll please to acquaint the Lords of the Admiralty herewith that this Affair may be decided in the manner aforesaid to prevent disputes and Threats, which some of the Officers use in a Brutal Manner which is only prejudicial to both Nations I wou'd not fail acquainting you herewith.

90 CUST 58/149, pp. 62–3

2 August 1748

From B. Fairfax, Beaumont Hotham, G. Vaughan and W. ⌜Levinz⌝[60] (Custom House, London). Hand iii.

In answer to the Account of Seizures transmitted in your Letter of the 27th Ultimo We direct you to prosecute the Goods thereinmentioned to Condemnation in the Exchequer at the Kings Charge, Corresponding with our Solliciter and the Register of Seizures *valediction 1*

Noted in the Book of Seizures 4th Aug*us*t 1748

---

59 I.e. 18 July 1748 Old Style.
60 Altered from 'Sevine'.

91
4 August
1748

CUST 58/149, pp. 63–4

From R. Chandlor, B. Fairfax and Wil. Levinz (Custom House, London). Hand iii.

We have received your Letter of the 30th Ultimo acquainting us that Mr John Newnham ⌜the⌝[61] Riding Officer at Fareham, in whose hands a Warrant is lodged for apprehending of Richard Mills concerned in breaking open the Custom House at Poole has received a particular Information where the said Richard Mills resides, but as there are two of the Name of Richard, Father & Son, and as the Warrant does not Specify whether Senior, or Junior, he cannot proceed on his Information, And having referred the same to our Solliciter, he has Reported that the Warrant which has been already obtained against Richard Mills (and sent to Mr Brooke) will authorize the Person possessed of such Warrant to apprehend either Richard Mills Senior, or Junior but as he is informed Richd Mills Junior is the Person meant by that Information, Mr Newnham the Riding Officer should use all possible endeavours to apprehend him, and when apprehended Convey him, with a Sufficient Guard, immediately to London, Which we hereby signify to you, and you are to give the necessary directions accord*ingly* *valediction 1*

92
4 August
1748

CUST 58/149, pp. 64–5

From R. Chandlor, B. Fairfax, Beaumont Hotham and G. Vaughan (Custom House, London). Hand iii.

We received your Letter of the 30th Ultimo transmitting an Account of the Circumstances and manner of Seizure of two Cases of Tea Seized by Mr Charles Markland and other Officers at your Port, out of the two Brothers, as mentioned in your Account of Seizures dated the 23d Ultimo We direct you to keep your hands thereon, till you receive our further Orders; But you are to prosecute the rest of the Goods mentioned in the said Account to Condemnation in the Exchequer at the Kings Charge, Corresponding with our Sollicitor and the Register of Seizures. *Valediction 1*

Noted in the Seizure Book

93
6 August
1748

CUST 58/149, p. 65

From R. Chandlor, B. Fairfax, Beaumont Hotham and G. Vaughan (Custom House, London). Hand iii.

William Hare Tidesman at your Port, having by his Memorial of the 5th instant, apply'd to us desiring leave to be Absent for a fortnight for recovery of his health, We have agreed ⌜thereto⌝[62], without loss of pay, and you are to take care the Service does not Suffer during his absence. *Valediction 1*

94
6 August
1748

CUST 58/149, pp. 65–6

From R. Chandlor, Beaumont Hotham, B. Fairfax and G. Vaughan (Custom House, London). Hand iii.

Having considered your Preparatory Account of Incidents for the Quarter Ended at Lady-day last, amounting to Eighteen Pounds fifteen Shillings & three pence half penny, The ⌜Collector⌝[63] may pay the same with the Privity of the Comptroller, and take Credit for it in his Account of Incidents annexing this Letter with proper Receipts thereto as Vouchers *valediction 1*

⌜N B./ Original sent to London with the Collectors Acco*unts* for Mich*ael*mas Q*uarte*r 1748⌝[64]

---

[61] Inserted.
[62] MS. 'threto'.
[63] MS. 'Colletor'.
[64] Added (hand v).

95
9 August 1748

CUST 58/149, p. 66

From Beaumont Hotham, B. Fairfax, Wil. Levinz and G. Vaughan (Custom House, London). Hand iii.

We received your Letter of the 20th Ultimo transmitting one from Mr Gregory Carlos Surgeon by which it appears that James Fryers Death, was occasioned by a Fall he received in the Execution of his Duty, and having Considered the same, we agree to Allow the Surgeon's Bill, and the usual Bounty to the Widdow, and Six Children, vizt to the Widdow Seven Pounds ten Shillings, and to each Childe One Pound ten Shillings, amounting together to thirty Pounds four Shillings and Seven Pence, and the Collector may pay the same with the Privity of the Comptroller, and take Credit for the same in his Account of Incidents, annexing this Letter with proper Receipts thereto as Vouchers. *Valediction 1*

In margin:

£	s	d
13.	14.	7
7.	10.	0
9.	0.	0.
£30.	4s.	7d

⌜Original Letter was transmitted with the Accounts for Mich*ael*mas Quarter 1748⌝[65]

96
13 August 1748

CUST 58/149, p. 67

From Wil. Wood (Custom House, London). Hand iii.

The Commissioners direct you by return of the Post to transmit them the Commission and Instructions sent to you in their Letter of the 10th instant for John Emberly to be a Tidesman and Boatman at your Port in the room of Wm Howells resigned. *Valediction 2*

P.S. You are also to send up the Commissioners Letter to be cancelled, but you need not send the Bond

97
13 August 1748

CUST 58/149, p. 67

From Wil. Wood (Custom House, London). Hand iii.

The Commissioners having received a Letter from Mr Henry Gibbs Deputy Customer of your Port, dated the 26th Ultimo praying as he is under a necessity of employing an assistant to enable him to perform the Duty, to have an allowance by Incident in consideration thereof, they direct you to report to them what the Fees of the Customer amount to annually for Seven Years, and what allowance is made by the Patentee, to Mr Gibbs, for their consideration. *Valediction 2*

98
13 August 1748

CUST 58/149, p. 68

From W. Wood (Custom House, London). Hand iii.

Sir Peter Warren having represented to the Commissioners that he has Six Cases of Wine in the Warehouse at your Port, which were given him by Admiral Schryver, for his use on board, but did not come from Holland, till after he went out on his Cruize, You are to send up to the Commissioners a State of the Case with an Account of the Quantity, and Quality of the said Wine for their further Directions. *Valediction 2*

99
15 August 1748

CUST 58/149, pp. 68–9

From Wil. Wood (Custom House, London). Hand iii.

Mr Nichol's Sone having by his Memor*ial* of this date applyed to the Commissioners desiring that a Debenture may be made out for Three Hundred and twenty four Quarters Six Bushels of Wheat Meal Shipt at your Port, on board the Theodosia, Richd Hunter Master, I am directed to send you Copy of the said Memorial, and you are to examine into the Allegations therein Contained, and Report to the Board a true State of the Case, with your opinion *valediction 2*

---

65 Added (hand v).

Honourable Sirs

In September last I shiped on board the Theodosia Richard Hunter Master then lying at Portsmouth Harbour and bound for Gibralter, three Hundred and twenty four Quarters Six Bushels Wheat Meal for which a Debenture was made out and finished but as I was obliged to leave the Place, and came to reside at Erith before the Ship Sailed I had not an Opportunity ⌜of⌝[66]then receiving the Money & I now find that the Debenture is lost and that the Collector of that Port does not choose to grant a new one, without having your Honours Order for that purpose which I humbly desire you'll be pleased to grant

N^s^ Sone

15 Aug*ust* 1748

100
15 August 1748

CUST 58/149, pp. 69–70

From W. Wood (Custom House, London). Hand iii.

Mr Moses Lamego having applyed to the Commissioners in relation to twelve Chests of Spanish Prize Quick Silver on board the Plymouth Man of War Capt Dent from Jamaica (for which there is not a proper Certificate that it is Prize) desiring to pay the Duty's for it as Prize on giving Security to produce a Certificate, The Commissioners agree thereto, and you may accept of the Dutys accordingly, on Security being given to produce a Certificate in twelve Months that the Quick Silver is Prize, or to pay the Difference of the Duty's *valediction 2*

101
15 August 1748

CUST 58/149, pp. 70–1

From Wil. Wood (Custom House, London). Hand iii.

Captain Boles of the Deptford Storeship having applied to the Commissioners in relation to two Chests and a Box Containing wearing apparel and a few Trifles, which he left on board His Majestys Ship, Centurion, on coming Post to the Command of the Debtford Storeship, Inclosed you will receive Copy of his Memorial, and you are to send them up to the Warehouse here, giving the Commissioners notice thereof, at the Proprietor's charge and what agreement is made for Carriage, *valediction 2*

May it please your Honours.

Having on board his Majesty's Ship Centurion Two Chests, and a Box Containing wearing Apparel, a few Books, about five Pounds of *Sitteron five Pounds of Coffee, Ten or twelve Bottles of Rum, and a Piece of Sheeting Linnen, which I left on board the said Ship at Portsm^o^ on my coming up Post, to the Command of the Deptford Storeship.

I beg your Honours will be pleased to order them to be sent up to the WareHouse here as they Contain nothing but the Trifles abovementioned & give Directions that they may be delivered to

Honourable Sirs Your most Obedient humble Servant

Jno Boles

15th Aug*ust* 1748

102
16 August 1748

CUST 58/149, pp. 71–2

From Wil. Wood (Custom House, London). Hand iii.

Application having been made to the Board by some of the Officers in the out Ports in relation to the Subsidy of twelve pence Per Pound on the Importation of Foreign Goods & Merchandizes, granted by an Act of the 21st Year of His present Majesty,[67] I am directed to acquaint you, that the said Subsidy is payable upon all Sorts of Goods imported except Wine, Vinegar, Cyder, and such Goods as are imported Duty Free, without any Discompt on the Entry Inwards, & you are to govern your selves accordingly. *Valediction 2*

[66] Inserted.

[67] Statute 21 Geo. II, c.2.

103
17 August
1748

CUST 58/149, p. 72

From G. Vaughan, R. Chandlor, B. Fairfax and Beaumont Hotham (Custom House, London). Hand iii.

Having granted our Commission for James Gutheridge to be an Extra Tidesman at your Port in the room of William Howells resigned, You are to take care he be under Oath and Security for the faithfull Discharge of the said Employ, and Qualifies himself as the Law Directs, paying him the like allowance by Incidents as was paid to his Predecessor, for which the Collector may take Credit from time to time in his Account of Incidents, refering therein to the date hereof *valediction 1*

104
18 August
1748

CUST 58/149, p. 73

From G. Vaughan, R. Chandlor, B. Fairfax and Beaumont Hotham (Custom House, London). Hand iii.

Will[m] Hare Tidesman at your Port having by his Memorial of this date applied to us desiring further leave for a fortnight for Recovery of his health, We have agreed thereto without loss of pay, and you are to take care the Service does not Suffer during his Absence *valediction 1*

105
23 August
1748

CUST 58/149, pp. 73–4

From W. Levinz, Beaumont Hotham, B. Fairfax and G. Vaughan (Custom House, London). Hand iii.

M[r] William Vaughan, having by his Memorial of the 15th Instant applyed to us desiring that the Hogshead of Tobacco, Seized on board his Majesty's Ship Dover, from Ireland, may be admitted to an Entry, Inclosed we send you Copy of the said Memorial, and you are to examine into the Allegations therein contained, and Report a true State of the case to us with your opinion. *Valediction 1*

August 15th 1748

Honourable Sirs

M[r] W[m] Nichol's Purser of his Maj*esty*s Ship Dover being in Necessity for Tobacco for the Men, while on their Station on the Coast of Ireland, was obliged to purchase some at Kinsale but upon her being ordered to Portsmouth Harbour, a Hogshead being left was carried to the Custom House where it now is.

I pray your Honours Directions to the Collector of said Port, that he wou'd admit it to an Entry, & take the Duty on the same

I am Your Honours most Obedient Servant
W. Vaughan.

106
27 August
1748

CUST 58/149, pp. 74–5

From Wil. Wood (Custom House, London). Hand iii.

Their Excellencies the Lords Justices having been pleased by a proclamation, dated the 25th Inst*ant* to take off the prohibitation from Spanish Goods & Merchandizes and granting leave for the Importation thereof on their being first duely entered & paying the Customs, and other Duties due by Law for the same, I am directed to transmit you the said Proclamation, for the Government of your Selves, & the rest of the Officers at your Port. *Valediction 2*

107
1 September
1748

CUST 58/149, p. 75

From B. Fairfax, Sam. Mead, Rob. Baylis and G. Vaughan (Custom House, London). Hand iii.

In Answer to the Account of Seizures transmitted in your Letter of the 27th Ultimo We direct you to Prosecute the Goods therein mentioned to Condemnation before the Justices, of the Peace the Rum at the Kings Charge, and the Candles at the Officer's Charge acquainting us when Condemned, *valediction 1*

Noted in the Book of Seizures.

108 CUST 58/149, p. 76

1 September 1748

From B. Fairfax, Sam. Mead, Rob. Baylis and G. Vaughan (Custom House, London). Hand iii.

Having read your Letter of the 27th June last, in return to the Memorial of Mr John Sone, relating to a Debenture for Flour Shipt at your Port by his father Nicholas Sone, which is lost or mislaid, And the s*ai*d Nichol's Sone having declared here, that he left the said Debenture, in the hands of Mr Charles Markland an Officer at your Port, We direct you to make a strict enquiry, and search for the said Debenture, and Report your proceedings to us for our further Consideration. *Valediction 1*

109 CUST 58/149, pp. 75–6

3 September 1748

From B. Fairfax, Beaumont Hotham, Rob. Baylis and G. Vaughan (Custom House, London). Hand iii.

Having read your Letter of the 29th Ultimo Inclosing the Memorial of Messrs Newnham and Comden Riding Officers praying to be paid their Bill of Charges in Endeavouring to apprehend Richard and John Mills Smuglers and having considered the same, We do not think proper to allow the said Bill this Service being done in the Execution of their Duty. *Valediction 1*

110 CUST 58/149, pp. 77–8

6 September 1748

From Wil. Wood (Custom House, London). Hand iii.

Messrs Lade & Bolton having by their Memorial of the 1st Instant applyed to the Commissioners relating to a Parcel of Shott, Bomb, and *Cohorn Shells, late belonging to the Duke de Chartres Prize, which they bought at a publick Sale, I am directed to send you Copy of the said Memorial, & you are to examine into the Allegations, therein Contained, and report a true State of the Case, to the Board with your opinion *valediction 2*

Honble Sirs

We lately bought at Publick Sale at Lloyds Coffee House, a Parcel of Shott, Bomb, & *Cohorne Shells being Stores late belonging to the Duke de Charters ⌜a French⌝[68] Prize; Your Collector at Portsmouth, Objects against taking the 5 Per Cent Duty, as is paid on Ships Stores, and as the said Stores are loaden on board a Vessel which is detained on them, beg your Honours will please to give Directions that they may be cleared, and brought up to London, We are

Your Honours most Obedient humble Servants

Zeph Lade

Robt Bolton

1st Septemb*er* 1748

111 CUST 58/149, p. 78

6 September 1748

From Rob. Baylis, Beaumont Hotham, B. Fairfax and G. Vaughan (Custom House, London). Hand iii.

We received your Letter of the 26th Ultimo in return to the Memorial of Mr William Vaughan, relating to a Hogshead of Tobacco Seized on board His Majesty's Ship Dover from Ireland; We direct you to examine into the Allegations of the said Memorial and Report to us your Opinion thereon agreeable to our Order of the 23d Ultimo and Whether you have any Objection to what is desired, for our further Orders *valediction 1*

112 CUST 58/149, pp. 78–9

8 September 1748

From Rob. Baylis, Beaumont Hotham, J. Evelyn and Sam. Mead (Custom House, London). Hand iii.

We received your Letter of the 18th Ultimo in return to one from Mr Henry Gibbs Deputy Customer at your Port, praying as he is under a Necessity of Employing an Assistant to Enable him to perform the Duty, that he may have an Allowance by Incidents, in consideration thereof; We have agreed to allow him Ten Pounds Per Annum by Incidents for his Encouragement, in consideration of the good Character he bears, and the Collector may pay him after that rate from time to time, and take Credit for the same in his Account of Incidents, Refering therein to the date hereof. *Valediction 1*

---

[68] Inserted.

113
10 September 1748

CUST 58/149, pp. 79–80

From Rob. Baylis, Sam. Mead, B. Fairfax and G. Vaughan (Custom House, London). Hand iii.

We received your Letter of the 6th Instant acquainting us that the Collector and several other Officers of Excise having an Information, against Captain Gwyn of His Majesty's Ship the Ambuscade for running on shore a large Quantity of Brandy, and other Goods, upon which they Proceeded and found in his house five Casks two Hampers Containing Brandy, four Casks Rum, Eleven large Bottles of *Arrack, one hogshead Spanish, three hogsheads and one Pipe Lisbon Wine, and one Hogshead & 3 Hampers of Claret, but that as the Officers were bringing the Goods away they were obstructed by a Number of People, who rescued the Goods from them after Seizure. We direct you to use your utmost endeavours to discover the Offenders, and you are in Conjunction with the Officers of Excise to send up Affidavits of the Facts, setting forth the Persons Names, with all the Particular Circumstances attending the Case, And you are to take care that all proper and Necessary Steps be taken in Order that the Offenders may be discovered. And that the Commissioners of Excise will by this Post, or the next, give directions to their Officers to the same purpose, with whom you are to Act in Concert for the more effectual performance of this Service. *Valediction 1*

114
10 September 1748

CUST 58/149, p. 80

From Wil. Wood (Custom House, London). Hand iii.

The Accounts mentioned in your Letter of the 1st July 1748 for Lady day Quarter last are safe come to hand. *Valediction 2*

115
10 September 1748

CUST 58/149, p. 81

From Rob. Baylis, B. Fairfax, J. Evelyn and Sam. Mead (Custom House, London). Hand iii.

In answer to the Account of Seizures transmitted in your Letter of the 6th Instant, We direct you to Prosecute the Goods therein mentioned to Condemnation, in the Exchequer at the Kings Charge Corresponding with our Solliciter and the Register *valediction 1*

116
13 September 1748

CUST 58/149, p. 81

From Beaumont Hotham, B. Fairfax, Sam. Mead and G. Vaughan (Custom House, London). Hand iii.

We received your Letter of the 9th Instant, in return to the Memorial of Mr William Vaughan, relating to a Hogshead of Tobacco Seized on board his Majesty's Ship Dover from Ireland, and it appearing that the said Tobacco was taken on board for the Ships use, and not by way of Merchandize, you may admit it to an Entry, *valediction 1*

117
15 September 1748

CUST 58/149, pp. 82–4

From Wil. Wood (Custom House, London). Hand iii.

Mr Thomas Appleford having by his Memorial of the 9th Instant, applyed to the Commissioners Relating to some Cordage under Seizure at your Port, Inclosed you will receive Copy of the said Memorial, and you are to examine into the allegations therein Contained, and Report a true State of the Case to the Board with your Opinion. *Valediction 2*

Portsmouth 9th Septemb*er* 1748

Honourable Gentle*men*

I bought at Publick Sale of French Prize Goods here the 29th & 30th past Sundry Lots of Old Stores Vizt Grease, Rosin Flower Old Cordage Burnt Cable &cetera, the Dutys of £5 Per Cent was promised to me to be clear'd & paid to your Collector here Per Mr Samuel Leeke the Agent, who notified the same to the Collector as he had done in former Sales and debit the Purchasers with the Amount at the Foot of their Bills of Parcels; now a Sloop presenting this Week to load for Bristol I order'd the said Master to hall in a long side of his Majestys Gun Wharf, where the said Old Stores lay, and gave Notice to the s*ai*d Agents to send their Servants and Labourers to Weigh, and delivered the said Old Stores to the said Mast*er* of the Sloop some of which Vizt the Burnt Cable was weighed, and put into the said Sloop, and whilst they were preparing to wheigh the rest the Master of the said Sloop went to the Custom, House to get the proper Dispatches for said Goods: met with Mr Gibbs one of your Officers to whom he applied, and had for Answer he shoud have come before he took in any of the said Old Burnt Cable for that he was then going to the Gun Wharf to Seize the same, and woud Seize his Sloop also and accordingly have taken the said Old burnt Cable on shore, and refuses to deliver the same again notwithstanding the Collector had the Notice from the Agents as above of the Dutys being secured now had their been any Officer attending, or Locks on the said Old Stores, this cou'd not have happened, nor your Honours had all this Trouble but as there was no Intention of any Fraud whatsoever, I humbly pray the said Old burnt Cable may be restored, who am,

Honourable Gentlemen Your Honours most Obedient Servant

Thos Appleford

118

16 September 1748

CUST 58/149, p. 84

From W. Wood (Custom House, London). Hand iii.

Having received directions from the Lords Commissioners of the Treasury for Prosecuting all the Persons Concerned in running, concealing and rescuing the Goods Seized out of the Ambuscade Man of War Captain Gwyn, You are to take care as soon as possible to transmit to the Commissioners the Affidavits required by their Letter of the 10th instant and particular regard must be had that the facts are made out in the Strongest and clearest manner *valediction 2*

119

16 September 1748

CUST 58/1

From W. C[ooley] and R. T[urvin] (Custom House, Portsmouth). Hand iii.

We beg leave to acquaint Your Honours Richard Fitchet late a Tidesman and Boatman at this Port, with the Allowance of £5 Per Annum by Incidents and Coal Meter at Gosport died the 13th Instant, We therefore humbly beg leave to Recommend John Sweet, an Inhabitant of Gosport, a Person who we are to Assure Your Honour's is in all Respects duely well Qualify'd to perform the Duty of a Coal Meter; And we likewise beg leave to Recommend James Burnett to succeed Fitchett at the Allowance of £5 Per Annum said Burnett we Recommended to Your Honours in our joint Letter of the 30th Ultimo he being a good and deserving Officer, hope therefore you will be pleased to take the same into Consideration, *valediction 3*

120

17 September 1748

CUST 58/149, pp. 84–6

From Wil. Wood (Custom House, London). Hand iii.

Mr John Carter Allen having by his Memorial of the 15th Instant applied to the Commissioners relating to a Cask of *Arrack Seized on board the Ambuscade Ship of War as mentioned in your Account of Seizures dated the 6th Instant, Inclosed you will receive Coppy of the said Memorial, and You are to Examine into the Allegations therein Contained and Report to the Board a true State of the Case with all the Circumstances attending the said Seizure and to whom it belongs for their further Orders *valediction 2*

Sir

I make bold to trouble you with this, which probably may be thought an ⌜Intrusion⌝[69] from one who is an intire Stranger to you but the Accident that has happened to me is the occasion, and knowing the Lenity; I am Lieutenant of the Ambuscade, and was sent up with the Merchants Money; in my Absence for the ill Treatment my Captain gave the Customhouse Officers at Portsmouth without any from me, or Officers on board, they went on board and Seized every Individual thing but returned every thing but a small Cask of *Arrack of about 28 Gallons, which I had no manner of Intention to Run being my private Stock, besides the Master haveing my Letters to produce, wherein I mentioned to him to pay Duty for every thing, and that I woud apply my Self for Liberty when the Ship was paid Off, to carry what little Liquor I had on shore, I think its very hard that for the Behaviour of my Captain I must Suffer the loss which the Collector knows I never intended the Running of it, I beg leave to desire you'd consider this, and if it is a thing I ought to lose by such an Accident, after all the World knew my Intention. I am

Sir Your most &cetera

Jno Carter Allen

Thursday September 15th 1748.

---

69 Altered from 'Itrusion'.

121
17 September 1748

CUST 58/1

From W. C[ooley] and R. T[urvin] (Custom House, Portsmouth). Hand iii.

Inclos'd we transmit to Your Honours the Account of Goods Enumerated and Goods not Enumerated lately Seiz'd by the Officers in this Port, to which we beg leave to Refer, *valediction 4*

122
19 September 1748

CUST 58/1

From W. C[ooley] and R. T[urvin] (Custom House, Portsmouth) to W. Wood. Hand iii.

Sir

By your Letter of the 16th Instant, we are Inform'd you have received Direction's from the Lords of the Treasury for Prosecuting all the Person's Concern'd in Running, concealing and Rescuing the Goods Seiz'd out of the Ambuscade man of War Captain Gwyn, we are therefore as soon as possible to transmit the Affidavits required by the Commissioner's Letter of the 10th Instant We are to acquaint you that the Collector, and other Officer's of Excise, who is to Act in Conjunction with the Officers of the Customs, has been from home on Business ever since the Receipt of the Board's Order, but on their Return which will be in a few days time, their Affidavits against such of the People as they can Discover shall with the loss of as little time as possible be transmitted to the Commissioner's, by

Sir &cetera

W: C R: T

P:S: Captn Montagu of his Maj*esty*s Ship Kent, late of the Bristol a few days since wrote to the Board for liberty to remove his Liquor's, beg you will be pleased to Forward the Boards Answer in relation thereto

W: C R: T

123
19 September 1748

CUST 58/1

From W. C[ooley] and R. T[urvin] (Custom House, Portsmouth). Hand iii.

We have Your Honours Order signify'd to us by Mr Wood in his Letter of the 17th Instant, with Copy of the Memorial of Mr John Carter Allen, Inclos'd relating to a Cask of *Arrack Seiz'd on board his Majesty's Ship Ambuscade And by your Honour's said Order we are directed to examine into the Allegation's therein contained, and Report a true State of the Case for Your further Order's, In Obedience thereto we beg leave to acquaint Your Honours, We have called on Mr Threhearne who made the said Seizure from whom we receivd the following Answer Vizt That in the Night before the Tidesmen on Board Seizd a Quarter Cask Contents to them unknown, which some of the People found mean's to throw over board, by which it was Stav'd, and likewise knowing Liquor's to have been run on Shore, belonging to Captain Gwyn, Mr Trehearne by Direction from the Collector, went on board the Ambuscade, and Rummag'd her which he found said Cask of *Arrack, which he Seiz'd & brought to the King's WareHouse, as being Prohibited. The *Arrack may very likely belong to Mr Allen, but at the time Mr Trehearne Seiz'd the same no one own'd it, but the Boatswain of the Ship, said rather than it shou'd go on shore he had a great mind to stave it, on the whole Mr Trehearne therefore hopes he has done no more than his Duty, all which is most humbly submitted to your Honour's Consideration, and whatever further Direction You are pleas'd to send Us in regard thereto, will be duely observ'd *valediction 4*

124
20 September 1748

CUST 58/149, p. 86

From Sam. Mead, Beaumont Hotham, B. Fairfax and G. Vaughan (Custom House, London). Hand iii.

Captain Montagu of his Majesty's Ship the Kent having by his Letter of the 15th instant apply'd to us desiring leave to remove his Stores from the Bristol into the Kent, We agree thereto under the care of the proper Officers, taking care that no part of the said Stores are landed. *Valediction 1*

125
20 September 1748

CUST 58/1

From W. C[ooley] and R. T[urvin] (Custom House, Portsmouth). Hand iii.

We are to acquaint your Honour's, that by the Waggon of George Clarke, which will be at the Whitehart in the Burrough of Southwark on Thursday the 22^d^ Instant, We have this day sent under the Seals of Office directed to your Honours, Two Cases Containing Pictures, landed here out of his Majesty's Ship South Sea Castle, belonging to the Honourable Captn George Townsend, who will apply to Your Honours for delivery thereof, on Payment of the Duty's. *Valediction 3*

126
20 September 1748

CUST 58/1[70]

From W. C[ooley] and R. T[urvin] (Custom House, Portsmouth). Hand iii.

We have your Honours Order signify'd to Us by Mr Wood in his Letter of the 15th Instant Inclosing Copy of a Memorial from Mr Thos Appleford to Your Honours Relating to a Parcel of Old Cordage, and burnt Cable, under Seizure at this Port, and by your said Order we are directed to examine into the Allegation's therein Contained, and Report a true state of the Case, with our Opinion. In Obedience thereto, we are to acquaint your Honour's We have call'd on Mr Henry Gibbs Deputy Customer at this Port who Seiz'd the said old Cordage &cetera from whom we have receiv'd the Inclos'd Answer, to which we beg leave to Refer Your Honour's; In the Memorial of Mr Appleford we take notice he observe's to your Honour's had there been Lock's on the Cordage &cetera the same woud not have been Seiz'd. In answer to which we beg leave to observe it was a thing impossible that so great a quantity of old Cables, ropes &cetera, as have been landed out of the French Prize's at this Port cou'd by no mean's be put into Store House's under the King's Lock's; The Collector therefore having Security from the Agents for the 5 Per Cent Duty due thereon, We permitted the same to be landed at the Gun Wharf together with Gun's Shott &cetera so as the Agents dispos'd of the said Store's they were accountable to the Collector, for the Duty's, such has been the Practice at this Port in Regard to the old Stores, which cou'd not be secur'd under the King's Lock's, which we hope, will not otherwise than be approved of by Your Honour's; In the whole therefore whether Mr Appleford intended a fraud, by Shipping the Cordage, & burnt Cable now under Seizure, before given notice to the proper Officer's or taken out a Syfferance we can not pretend to say[.] We therefore submit the whole Affair to your Honour[']s Consideration and whatever direction's your Honour[']s shall be pleas'd to send us in regard therto shall be duely observ'd *valediction 4*

Gentlemen,

In answer to the Memorial of Mr Thos Appleford transmitted to you by Mr Secretary Wood in his Letter dated the 15th Instant, I am to acquaint you, that on the 8th Instant in the Morning early I receiv'd an Information, that the said Appleford had the day before shipped on board the Marygold John Trick Master for Bristol a large Quantity of French Cordage, without Payment of the Duty, or the Presence of an Officer and that in Pursuance thereof, knowing the same not to be Enter'd even Coastwise, and therefore forfeit'd by the 13th & 14th Car: 2^d^ Chap 11 Sect 7[71] & Strongly suspecting an Intention of Evading the Duty's, I Seiz'd on board the said Vessel Twelve Ton's French Prize Cordage, all which I brought to his Majesty's Warehouse, where it is now secur'd. Mr Appleford has quite Misrepresented the Case in saying that the Agents were to Pay the Duty's for the Condition's of the Sale were, That the Purchasers should pay the Duty's, and since the Sale all of them that have taken away their Goods have paid the Duty's themselves, and the Agents first Clerk is ready to make Oath that Mr Appleford was told by him, that he must pay the Duty's, for the Agents woud not, and Mr Leeke's Declaration to the Collector of his paying the Duty's refer'd to, by Mr Appleford was Void by the Condition's of the Sale, and Mr Leeke did not make a fresh Declaration, till two Day's after the Seizure, at the request of the said Appleford and I verily believe, only to screen him as it is not at all likely, that a particular agreement for paying the Duty of his Good's, should be made with him, as I was going on board to Seize the Cordage, I accidently met the Master, and I told him that I was going

---

[70] The enclosure precedes the letter in MS.
[71] I.e. Statute 14 Cha. II, c.11.

to Seize it, to which he gave me for answer that he was sorry for it, as he shoud thereby lose the freight, and I Possitively Declare that the Assertion of the said Appleford that the Master told me he was coming to the Custom House is false for he never made mention of a Sufferance, till after I had Seiz'd the Cordage, when he told me, that if he had took out a Sufferance, it woud have been for English Cordage, and not French, being so desired by the said Appleford, to the best of your Memorialist['s] Remembrance,

His saying that if there had been an Officer attending, or Lock's on the said Store's, this wou'd not have happen'd, nor their Honour's have had this Trouble is designed as an Invidious Reflection but at the same time makes against himself, as it apparently Imply's that if he had not an OPPortunity of Committing a Fraud he coud or woud not have done it – Mr Appleford sent several Persons to prevail upon me to Restore the Cordage without acquainting the Honourable Commissioner's with the Affair, who offer'd me a handsome Gratuity to consent thereto, but I absolutely refused to receive the same, as I well know the fraudulent Intention from the Master's Declaration to me, and that he coud have no Pretence from Ignorance of the Law, having been a Trader above Forty Year's, and that if I had done so it woud have been contrary to my Duty, all which is submitted by

Gentlemen Your most humble Servant

H^y^ Gibbs[72]

Custom House Portsm^o^ 19th Sep*tembe*r 1748

127
22 September 1748

CUST 58/149, pp. 86–7

From Sam. Mead, R. Chandlor, J. Evelyn and G. Vaughan (Custom House, London). Hand iii.

Having granted our Commission for James Burnett to be a Tidesman, & Boatman at your Port, in the room of Richard Fitchet Deceas'd, You are to take care he be under Oath, and Security for the faithfull Discharge of the said Employ, paying him the like Allowance by Incidents, as was paid to his Predecessor, for which the Collector may take Credit from time to time in his Account of Incidents, refering therein to the date hereof.

Labon Sparrow having been recommended to Us to be a Coalmeter at Gosport, in your Port, in the room of the said Fitchett, We have agreed thereto, & granted him our Deputation accordingly, and you are to take ⌜care⌝[73] he be under Oath, and Security for the faithfull Discharge of the said Employ, *valediction 1*

128
22 September 1748

CUST 58/149, pp. 87–90

From Sam. Mead, J. Evelyn, R. Chandler and G. Vaughan (Custom House, London). Hand iii.

Mr Edward Austin having by his Memorial of the 6th Instant, apply'd to us, relating to a Hogshead of Tobacco Seized at your Port, on board the Richard and Ann Sloop, Inclosd We send you Copy of the said Memorial, and you are to Report to Us when this Seizure was made, with all the Circumstances attending the same, and whether the Officer who made the Seizure, Offer'd to deliver the Tobacco on a Gratification as represented, with Your Observation's and Opinion on the whole, for Our further Consideration.

In Answer to the Account of Seizure's transmitt'd in your Letter of the 3^d^ Ultimo We have no objection to the Officers prosecuting the Sope therein=mentioned to Condemnation before the Justice's of the Peace at their own Charge, acquainting Us when Condemned *valediction 1*

Plymouth Sept*ember* 6th 1748

Honourable Sirs

I beg Pardon for the Freedom of Troubling you with this Letter but the hard usage I meet with obliges me to apply to your Honours for redress, for being Purser of his Majesty's Ship Vanguard & which I expected wou'd have gone a Foreign Voyage, I bought for the use of the said Ship's Company, a Hogshead of Tobacco of one Mr Ralph Kedden of Gosport, but finding we were to go no farther than this Place, and then be reduced to a Guard Ship, I apply'd to the said Mr Kedden to take it again as now shoud have no OPPortunity of Issuing it, which he agreed to do, & I was to

[72] '(Deputy Customer)' added in pencil, 19th or 20th century.
[73] Inserted.

have sent it back ⌜from⌝[74] Spithead, but the Ship Sailing immediately, I had no time to send it ashore there, so refered it till we arrived at this Port when having an immediate Opportunity, I sent it by one Fields Vessel then going to Gosport, and being Ignorant of its being in any Danger as I bought it as Duty paid, I did not apply to the Officers of the Custom's here for a Sufference, which it seems I ought to have done; that when it arrived at Portsmouth it was Seiz'd by the Officers of the Customs, upon which Mr Kedden to whom I directed it acquainted me of it, and said if I wou'd send an Affidavit that I bought it of him, he woud go to the Collector and get it clear'd again, which I immediately did, but the Officer who Seized it, said if I woud not send him 5 Guinea's he wou'd return it a Seizure, I sent for answer that I shou'd not comply with those Demands that if they wou'd accept of a Guinea for their Trouble they[75] were welcome, otherwise I had nothing to fear by his returning it a Seizure, when I shou'd State the Case to your Honours, and from whom I had not the least doubt of having Justice done me, and further shoud desire to know what right he had to Demand 5 Guineas of me, that if through my Ignorance it became a lawfull Seizure in his OPinion why did he not immediately return it as such to your Honours but if not, why has he detained my Property so long, for now Mr Kedden will oblige me to keep it, In Answer to this my Friend acquaints me that he saw the Collector's Clerk (the Collector not being at home) who said he thought it had been given up that the Collector had nothing to do with the Officers demands my Friend then saw one Mr Basterville who is the head of the Officers, and who says he will not take less than 5 Guinea's, and that he says is hurting the Officers of 5 Guinea's for as there was no *Pasport with it, it is a Seizure

I therefore humbly pray your Honours will be so good as to give Orders for an Enquiry into this Affair, that as the Duty has already been paid for the said Tobacco it might be returned to me again & not Suffer me any longer to be deprivd of my Property by an Undesigned Accident and Mistake of mine or to be subject to such Extortion by those under your Honours im*m*ediate Direction's, I am

Honourable Sirs Your most Obedient humble Servant

Edwd Austin

P.S. I have taken the Freedom to send your Honours a Copy of the Affidavit I sent to Portsmouth –

This ⌜Deponent⌝[76] Edward Austin Purser of his Majesty's Ship Vanguard, maketh Oath, that the Hogshead of Tobacco sent by Mr Fields Vessel of Gosport from Plymouth to be returned to Mr Ralph Kedden of Gosport, and said to be Seized by the Offi*ce*rs of the Custom's at Portsmouth was actually the same bought of the said Ralph Kedden, about the 12th day of July last, the reason of the said Hogshead being returned, was by consent, of the said Ralph Kedden his Majesty's said Ship being ordered to be reduced to a Guard Ship at Plymouth & the said Deponent having no Opportunity of issuing it

Edwd Austin

Plymouth 6th day of August 1748 –

Sworn before me Mich^l^ Nichol's Mayor

129
24 September 1748

CUST 58/149, pp. 90–1

From Sam. Mead, Beaumont Hotham and G. Vaughan (Custom House, London). Hand iii.

In answer to the Account of Seizure's transmit'd in your Letter of the 17th Instant, We direct you to prosecute the Enumerated Goods mentioned in the Article's N° 14. 15: 16 & 17 to Condemnation in the Exchequer at the Kings Charge, and We have no objection's to the Officers Prosecuting the Boat, Wine, and Silk, in like manner at the Officers Charge, Corresponding with our Solliciter, and the Register of Seizures, and you are to transmit Us what Proof the Officers have that Bulk was broke of part of the Cargo of the Hope, or that she came into Port with an Intention so to do, with all other Circumstances attending the said Seizure for our further Orders, *valediction 1*

Noted in the Book of Seizures

---

74 Altered from 'to(?)'.

75 MS. omits 'they'.

76 MS. 'Deponet'.

130
27 September 1748

CUST 58/149, p. 91

From G. Vaughan, B. Fairfax, R. Chandlor and Sam. Mead (Custom House, London). Hand iii.

We received your Letter of the 8th instant in return to the Memorial of Messrs Lade and Bolton relating to a Parcell of Shott, *Bumm & *Cohorne Shells, late belonging to the Duke de Chartre's Prize which they bought at a Publick Sale, And they having alledged that the said Shells are for Melting down, We direct you to take care to see they are broken, & rendered unfit for Service, and then you are to take[77] the Duties, as Old broken, *Bushel and Cast Iron, but not otherwise, *valediction 1*

131
27 September 1748

CUST 58/1

From W. C[ooley] and R. T[urvin] (Custom House, Portsmouth). Hand iii.

In Obedience to your Honour's Commands signify'd to us in your Letter of the 24th Instant, Inclos'd we transmit your Honour's what Proof the Officer's have that Bulk was broke of part of the Cargoe of the Hope Paul Greeve Master from St Martin's, bound for ⌜Dronten⌝[78] in Norway, with all other Circumstances attending the said Seizure justly, & truely Stated to which we beg leave to Refer, *valediction 3*

132
27 September 1748

CUST 58/1

From W. C[ooley] and R. T[urvin] (Custom House, Portsmouth). Hand iii.

In our joint Letter of the 30th ⌜Ultimo⌝[79] We acquainted your Honour's that William Manuel a Tidesman & Boatman at this Port, with the Allowance of 5 Per Annum by Incidents, has resign'd his Deputation, and your Honour's not[80] having thought proper to appoint any one to succeed him, We therefore humbly beg leave to Recommend Thos Chadwick, who has been Employ'd in the Service for three Years past & who was recommended to your Honour's in our joint Letter of the 30th June last, and at the same time we believe by Mr Brooke's our Surveyor General, to succeed said Manuel at the Allowance of £5 Per Annum, *valediction 3*

133
27 September 1748

CUST 58/1

From W. C[ooley] and R. T[urvin] (Custom House, Portsmouth). Hand iii.

Obedience to your Honour's Command's signified to us in your Letter of the 10th Instant, We have here Inclos'd The Affidavit of Mr Edward Skeat a Landwaiter at this Port in Conjunction with Edwd Brickitt & Daniel Martin, two of his Majesty's Officer's of Excise, with all the particular Circumstances attending the Obstruction of a Seizure made by the said Officer's at the house of Capt Gwyn at Upham near Bishop Waltham, to which we beg leave to Refer your Honour's, *valediction 3*

134
28 September 1748

CUST 58/149, p. 92

From G. Vaughan, B. Fairfax, R. Chandlor and Sam. Mead (Custom House, London). Hand iii.

We received your Letter of the 20th Instant in return to the Memorial of Mr Thomas Appleford relating to a Parcel of Old Cordage and burnt Cable under Seizure at your Port, as mentioned in the Account of Seizures, transmited in your Letter of the 9th Instant, and as the said Goods are forfeited for being Shipt, to be carried to Open Sea without a Sufference, We have no Objection to the Officers Prosecuting the said Cordage to Condemnation, together with the Wine mentioned in the said Account, in the Exchequer at the Officers Charge, Corresponding with our Solliciter, & the Register of Seizures. *Valediction 1*

135
28 September 1748

CUST 58/149, pp. 92–3

From G. Vaughan, R. Chandlor, B. Fairfax and Sam. Mead (Custom House, London). Hand iii.

We received your Letter of the 19th Instant, in return to the Memorial of Mr John Carter Allen, relating to a Cask of *Arrack, Seized on board his Majesty's Ship Ambuscade, we direct you to go on with the Prosecution of the said *Arrack, agreeable to our Order of the 10th Instant.

We received your Letter of the 1st Instant desiring a new sett of Oar's for the Watch Boat in the Service of the Customs at Hayling, We have agreed thereto, and ordered them to be forthwith provided, and sent you, *valediction 1*

---

77 'care' struck out.
78 Possibly altered from 'Dronton'.
79 MS. 'Ut^{o}' (for 'Ult^{o}').
80 MS. omits 'not'.

136 CUST 58/1

28 September 1748

From W. C[ooley] and R. T[urvin] (Custom House, Portsmouth). Hand iii.

We have your Honours Order of the 22^{d} Instant with Copy of the Memorial of Mr Edward Austin, inclos'd relating to a Hogshead of Tobacco, seiz'd at this Port, on board the Richard & Ann Sloop; And by your Honours said Order, we are directed to Report all the Circumstance's attending the same with our Observation's; In Obedience thereto We beg to acquaint your Honour's we have call'd on Mr William Baskerville one of the Tidesurveyor's at this Port, from whom we have receiv'd the Inclos'd Answer, to which we beg leave to Refer your Honour's; We are to acquaint your Honours the Seizure of the Hogshead of Tobacco was made on the 30th of July last, and brought to the King's WareHouse, as mentioned in Mr Baskerville[']s answer, and an Account thereof was sent in our joint Letter to your Honour's of the 6th Instant[.] The reason of the Account of the Seizure not being immediately sent, was that Mr Kidden desired he might have liberty to write to Mr Austin, which was granted him, and in some time afterwards he produced the Affidavit of Mr Austin, Copy of which is Inclos'd in Your Honour's Letter, but not finding any Application in regard to the said Seizure was made to your Honour's, the Account thereof was transmitted the 6th Instant as beforementioned; We believe the discourse Mr Baskerville had w*i*th Mr Kedden, was as he Represented it, he being an honest and good Officer, having been in the Service upward's of Twenty eight Year's, and his Character not in the least to our knowledge ever call'd in Question, On the whole we are inclinable to believe there was no intention of Fraud, in bringing the said Hogshead of Tobacco, Coastwise without a Dispatch; And Mr Baskerville is ready to submit to whatever Order's your Hon*ou*rs shall be pleas'd to give in Relation thereto, which when receiv'd, will be duely observ'd *valediction 4*

Gentlemen,

In Answer to the Memorial of Mr Edward Austin, in Relation to a hogshead of Tobacco, seiz'd on board the Richard and Ann Sloop, a Copy of which is inclos'd in their Honour's Letter to you of the 22^{d} Instant I take leave to inform you, that on the 30th day of July last, on the arrival of the said Sloop in this Port, from Plymouth, I went on board her & found the said hogshead of Tobacco, whereupon I ask'd the Master of the Vessel, if he had any Certificate, or Sufferance, for bringing the same, who gave me for answer he had none, and that the owner of the Tobacco told him there was no Necessity for having any Dispatch with it for which reason I Seiz'd it, and brought it directly to the King's WareHouse, & made a return of the Seizure.

Mr Ralph Kidden mentioned in the Memorial appearing in the Affair had some Discourse with me about it, and he knowing in some Cases their Honours give relief where the Parties appear clear of Fraud, on satisfying their Officers for their Trouble, ask'd me what we shou'd expect, meaning my self & two Tidesmen concern'd, and I told him five Guinea's, but he very ⌜widely⌝[81] misunderstood me, if he thought I shou'd have accepted of it, without their Honour's ordering satisfaction, and my whole discourse with him was upon that Express Supposition, knowing my Duty too well to be concern'd in such a Transaction as represented in the Memorial, neither did I or is it likely I shou'd say unless Mr Austin wou'd send me five Guinea's, I wou'd return it a Seizure, when I had made a return of it before,

It is unavoidable entering into discourse with Persons that Sollicit on Seizure's, and it is a common case to have it misrepresented as I solemnly, affirm this is, and must appeal to you Gentlemen, from your long knowledge of me; If you think I had any design of acting in this Affair but as consistent with my Duty & hope you will be pleas'd to Report to the Board accordingly

Sep*tember* 26th, 1748

[81] MS. 'ridely', possibly for 'rudely'.

137
30 September
1748

CUST 58/149, pp. 93–6

From W. Wood (Custom House, London). Hand iii.

The Commissioners having received a Letter of the 29th Instant from Mr West transmitting one from Mr Corbett Secretary to the Lords of the Admiralty, with the Memorial of Captn Gwyn, in answer to the Charge against him, by the Collector's of the Custom's and Excise, I am directed to send you Copies of these Papers for your Information, and you are to acquaint the Board whether Captain Gwyn has Stated the Facts right, or any answer or observations which occur to you, *valediction 2*

Memorial in answer to the Charge against Captn Gwyn, by the Collectors of the Custom's & Excise at Portsmouth

Three Officers of the Excise & Custom's came to my house at Upham with a Constable to search for run Goods, but there was no Collector as mentioned in the Letter from the Commissioners of the Customs, I demanded to see their Warrant, but they did not think proper to comply, however they had free access to search the Cellars &cetera, as they pleased.

As to the Quantity of Liquor found in the Cellar I cannot pretend to determine, only must observe that what are denominated Cask's of Brandy, and Rum, in their Complaint dont exceed ten Gallon's each, or thereabouts, and to the best of my Knowledge, there coud not be so many as mentioned.

What Liquor was there that had not paid Duty was the remains of my Sea Stock, and had been brought a shore by my Servants, with other Store's, when the Ship was ordered to be paid off

The Complaint of ⌜my⌝[82] having obstructed the Officers, & wrested a Seizure out of their hands by the Assistance of a Mobb is injurious, and false to the highest degree that there were some Idle People gathered together as spectators is true & in Country Places is usual on such Occasion's, but their being Assembled was neither by my means, or any Person belonging to me to my Knowledge neither did I hear of any Obstruction made by them, & to prevent it I both spoke my self, & sent Orders that no Person's shoud dare to oppose the King's Officers in Executing their Duty, it was so far from being a Mobb of mine, as they are pleased to Term it, that the Officers treated them, by giving my Liquor amongst them saying they had more right to it than I, not to mention several other Irregularities they committed. They had got some Casks out of the Celler in order to carry away upon which I shew'd them Permits from the Custom House at Portsmouth, they Examined them, and were satisfy'd with them, and ordered the Casks to be returned into the Celler, on this I left them, & soon after they were gone away, with regard to what is mentioned of Mr Mossall I know that while the Officer was searching the Cellars a Party of Soldiers came from Waltham who behaved very rudely soon after Lieutenant Mossall came, upon which I asked him if there Duty was to block up the House so that there shou'd be no Passage in or out, he said not, & ordered the Soldiers to retire to the Gate. giving the Serjeant a Charge to see that there was ⌜no⌝[83] opposition made to the Officers, & to take care of whatsoever, shou'd be brought them

Rd Gwynn

In margin: Copy 1st Sep*tember* 1748

Gentlemen

Having laid before the Lords Commissioners of his Majestys Treasury a Letter from Mr Corbett Secretary to the Lords of the Admiralty transmiting Copy of a Memorial presented to their Lordship's by Captain Gwynn, in answer to the Charge against him by the Collectors of the Excise & Custom's, their Lordships have directed me to send you the enclos'd Copies of the said Letter & Memorial for your Information in the Premises, I am

Gentlemen Your most humble Servant

J: West

Treasury Chambers 29th Sep*tember* 1748
Commissioners Customs.

---

82 Inserted.
83 Inserted.

Admiralty Office 27th September 1748

Sir

I receiv'd and laid before the Lords Commissioners of the Admiralty your Letter of the 15th Instant Inclosing Copies of representations from the Commissioners of Excise and Custom's relating to Captain Gwynn of His Majesty's Ship the Ambuscade, upon which he has been examined by their Lordships, who are most desirous of discourageing all in their Power such Clandestine Practices in the Officers of the Navy, but he having made his Defence very contrary to what he is charged with, alledging that he shewed the Officers permits from the Custom's at Portsmouth, which satisfy'd them, & that thereupon they ordered the Cask's to be return'd into his ⌜Cellars⌝[84], I am Commanded to send you a Copy of his Paper of Defence in order to be laid before the Right Honourable the Lords of the Treasury & to desire you to acquaint their Lordships that Captain Gwynn is ordered to attend them if they Judge his appearance necessary, I am

Sir Your most humble Servant

Thos Corbett

John Scrope Esqr

138
1 October
1748

CUST 58/149, p. 97

From Wil. Wood (Custom House, London). Hand iii.

The Accounts undermentioned being wanted from your Port, The Commissioners direct you to transmit the Same to the Board without loss of time, in order to be laid before the Parliament.

I am also to remind you of the Directions contained in my Letter of 11th July 1747 which directs you to transmit to the Board within six days after X'mas an Account of the Money paid for the Bounties on English & Irish Course Linnens Exported, and you are to take care the same be sent accordingly in order to be laid before the Parliament, *valediction 2*

The Account of Prohibited East India Goods for the half Year ending at Michaelmas last.

The Account of Naval Stores Imported from Russia in the Quarters ending at X'mas, Midsummer, & Michaelmas last

139
1 October
1748

CUST 58/149, p. 105

From G. Vaughan, B. Fairfax and S. Mead (Custom House, London). Hand iii.

Mr William Godard Riding Officer at Your Port having by his Memorial of the 18th Ultimo applied to Us desiring further leave to be absent for a Month for Recovery of his health, We have agreed thereto, without loss of pay, & you are to take care the Service does not Suffer during his absence, *valediction 1*

140
2 October
1748

CUST 58/1

From W. C[ooley] and R. T[urvin] (Custom House, Portsmouth). Hand iii.

Inclos'd we transmit your Honours the Affidavit of Robert Bayne's the Younger Inholder & Cunstable of the hundred of Bishop Waltham in the County of South'ton, against several Person's which were Assembled together at the House of Captain Gwynn, at Upham near Bishop's Waltham, in the County aforesaid, at the time the Officer's of Custom's & Excise were obstructed in bringing away a Seizure of Liquor's made by them at the said Captain Gwynn's House, to which Affidavit We beg leave to Refer your Honour's *valediction 3*

141
3 October
1748

CUST 58/149, pp. 96–7

From Wil. Wood (Custom House, London). Hand iii.

Captain Holbourne of his Majesty's Ship Tavistock having applied to the Commissioners by his Letter of the 29th Ultimo, desiring leave to remove his Stores from the Kent into the Tavistock, The Commissioners agree thereto, under the care of the proper Officers, as the Tavistock is bound for the West Indies, and you are to give the Necessary Directions for that purpose, *valediction 2*

84 Altered from 'Cellers'.

142
3 October
1748

CUST 58/1

From W. C[ooley] and R. T[urvin] (Custom House, Portsmouth). Hand iii.

We have your Honours Order signify'd to us by Mr Wood in his Letter of the 30th Ultimo transmitting Copy of a Letter from Mr West & one from Mr Corbett Secretary to the Admi*ral*ty with the Memorial of Captain Gwynn, in answer to the charge against him by the Collector's of the Custom's & Excise. And by your Honour's Order we are directed to acquaint ⌜y*o*u⌝[85] whether Capt Gwynn has Stated the facts right, or any Answer or obstruction's which occur to us, We beg leave to acquaint your Honour's, We have perus'd the Memorial of Captain Gwynn, on which we make the following Observation's as receiv'd from the Officer's concernd; The Collector of Excise did not go to Capt Gwynn's but went w*i*th one of his Officer's, Martin, to Sr William ⌜Gardner's⌝[86] in his way towards Upham to get a search Warrant, which being obtained he gave to Martin & then return'd home, Martin went on with his Warrant to Weekham, about three Miles further, & there met with Mr Skeat, a Landwaiter at this Port, and Mr Brickitt an Excise Officer who went with him to the house of Captain Gwynn; Capt Gwyn never demanded a sight of the Warrant but one William Downton came to the Officers in the Captain's Name & desired that they woud send the Warrant by him to the Capt*ain* upon which Martin one of the Excise Officer's shew'd the Warrant to Downton, and after he had read it, Martin told him, if the Captain wou'd give him leave to wait on him he might see it, but he wou'd not trust it out of his hands to any Servant; The Officer's declare they never gave the Mobb, a drop of Liquor, but they were drinking together in the house, & treated by the Captain's Servant's,

The Captain never shew'd but one Permit, which was only for a hogshead & a half of wine, dated in the Year 1747 The Officer's upon that permit being shewn, never order'd any of the Cask's to be discharged, or returned into the Celler's not believing that Permit to be for any of the Liquor's Seiz'd as is alledg'd by the Captain, for further Circumstances we beg to Refer your Honour's to the Affidavit of the Officers, transmitted in our joint Letter bearing date the 27th Ultimo *valediction 4*

143
5 October
1748

CUST 58/149, p. 98

From Wil. Wood (Custom House, London). Hand iii.

The Commissioners direct You without loss of time to transmit them Affidavits Sworn before a Commissioner in the Exchequer, wherein must be set forth, the Quantity & Quality of the Goods that were Run and Seized by the Officers at Your Port, at the House of Captn Gwynn, with the Names of the Persons concerned in running, Concealing, & Rescuing the Goods, and all other Circumstances attending the same, for their further Order's. *Valediction 2*

144
5 October
1748

CUST 58/1

From W. C[ooley] and R. T[urvin] (Custom House, Portsmouth). Hand iii.

Inclos'd we transmit your Honours the Affidavit of Richard Beckonsfield of Bishop's Waltham in the County of South'ton Labourer against several Person's concern'd in obstructing the Officer's in making a Seizure at the House of Captain Gwyn at Upham near Bishop's Waltham in the County aforesaid, to which we beg leave to Refer your Honour's, *valediction 3*

145
5 October
1748

CUST 58/1

From W. C[ooley] and R. T[urvin] (Custom House, Portsmouth). Hand iii.

Inclos'd we transmit your Honour's two Accounts Viz^{t} of Goods Enumerated & Goods not Enumerated, lately Seiz'd by the Officer's of the Custom's in this Port, to which we beg leave to refer *valediction 4*

---

85 Inserted.

86 Altered from 'Gurdner's'.

146
6 October
1748

CUST 58/149, p. 98

From J. Evelyn, R. Chandlor, B. Fairfax and G. Vaughan (Custom House, London). Hand iii.

The Lieutenants of his Majesty's Ship the Tavistock having acquainted us by their Mem*oria*l of the 29th Ultimo that they are removed into the Anson appointed to be Guard Ship in Your Harbour, and desired leave to remove their Small Stock of Liquors for their own Private Store from the Tavistock into the Anson; We agree thereto, and You may give the necessary Orders for that Purpose taking care it be done under the Care of the proper Officers.

Captain Nut, having also applied to Us, desiring that he may remove his Liquors to the Anson, which he is appointed to Command, We agree thereto under the care of the proper Officers, as ⌜beforementioned⌝[87], *valediction 1*

147
6 October
1748

CUST 58/149, p. 99

From Wil. Wood (Custom House, London). Hand iii.

The Commissioners direct You without loss of time to transmit them an Account of the Christian Name of Lieutenant Moor, or Mose, who was concerned in Obstructing the Officers, and Report whether his Sir Name be Moor, or Mose, *valediction 2*

What is his Right Name

148
6 October
1748

CUST 58/1

From W. C[ooley] and R. T[urvin] (Custom House, Portsmouth). Hand iii.

Inclos'd we transmit your Honours an Account of Goods not Enumerated, lately Seiz'd by the Officer's of this Port, to which we beg leave to refer *valediction 4*

149
6 October
1748

CUST 58/1

From W. C[ooley] and R. T[urvin] (Custom House, Portsmouth). Hand iii.

In Obedience to your Order by Mr Secretary Wood's Letter of the 1st Instant We have here Inclos'd the Accounts, undermentioned to which we beg leave to Refer *valediction 3*

Prohibited East India Good's for the half Year ended Mich*ael*mas last

Naval Store's from Rushia, &cetera, for Christmas Quarter 1747, Midsummer & Mich*ael*mas Quarters last.

150
7 October
1748

CUST 58/149, p. 99

From Wil. Wood (Custom House, London) to [W. Cooley]. Hand iii.

Sir

A Debenture in the Name of William Parsons for One Thousand two hundred & fifty one Quarters of Wheat, Shipt at Your Port, the 19th Ultimo in the Duke of Cumberland David Denham Master for Leghorne, Has been presented to the Commissioners for their Order for Payment, but You having Omitted to send a Duplicate thereof, the same is stopt, You are forthwith to send the said Duplicate, to the Board, which I am directed to signify to You, and am

Sir Your most humble Servant

Wm Wood

151
8 October
1748

CUST 58/149, pp. 99–100

From W. Wood (Custom House, London). Hand iii.

Mr Steevens Agent for the six French Men of War Prizes taken by Sir Edward Hawke, having applied to the Commissioners, desiring that nine hogsheads of Store Vinegar may be delivered on paying the five Per Cent Duty, Inclosed you will receive Copy of his Memorial, & You are to examine into the Allegations therein Contained & Report a State of the Case to the Board, with Your Opinion, *valediction 2*

---

87 Altered from 'before,'.

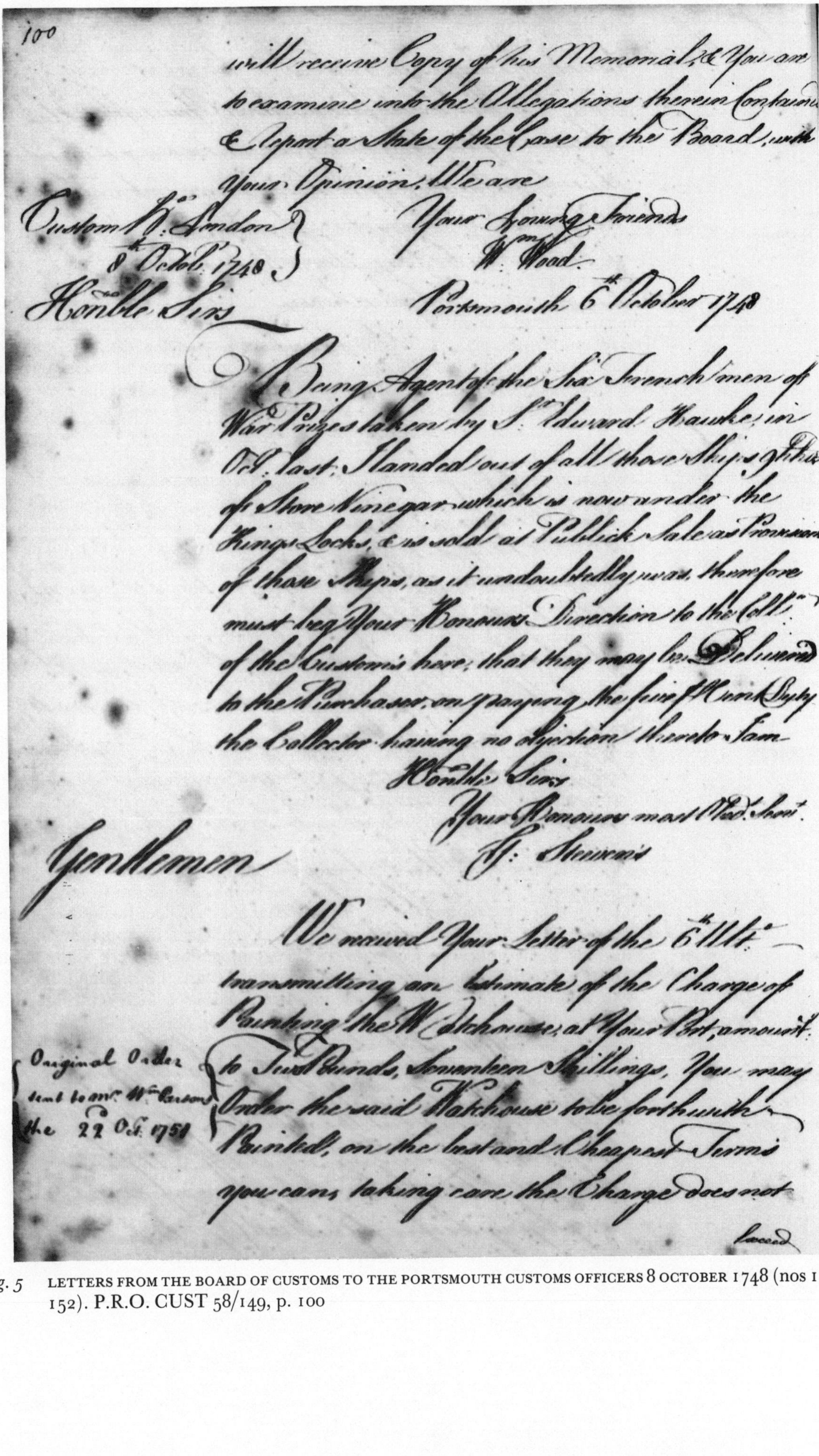
100

will receive Copy of his Memorial, & You are to examine into the Allegations therein Contained & Report a State of the Case to the Board, with your Opinion. We are

Custom Ho. London
8th Octob. 1748

Your Loving Friends
Wm. Wood.

Honble Sirs

Portsmouth 6th October 1748

Being Agent of the Six French men of War Prizes taken by Sr. Edward Hawke, in Oct. last, I landed out of all those Ships 9 [illegible] of Stone Vinegar which is now under the Kings Locks, & is sold at Publick Sale as Provision of those Ships, as it undoubtedly was, therefore must beg Your Honours Direction to the Collr. of the Customs here, that they may be Delivered to the Purchaser, on paying the [illegible] Duty the Collector having no objection thereto. I am

Honble Sirs

Your Honours most Obedt. Servt.
J. Stevens

Gentlemen

We received Your Letter of the 6th Ulto. transmitting an Estimate of the Charge of Painting the Watchhouse at Your Port, amount. to Two Pounds, Seventeen Shillings, You may Order the said Watchhouse to be forthwith Painted, on the best and Cheapest Terms you can, taking care the Charge does not

Original Order sent to Mr. Wm. [illegible] the 22 Oct. 1751

Exceed

Fig. 5 LETTERS FROM THE BOARD OF CUSTOMS TO THE PORTSMOUTH CUSTOMS OFFICERS 8 OCTOBER 1748 (nos 151, 152). P.R.O. CUST 58/149, p. 100

Portsmouth 6th October 1748

Honourable Sirs

Being Agent of the Six French men of War Prizes taken by Sr Edward Hawke, in Oct*obe*r last, I landed out of all those Ships 9 hogsheads of Store Vinegar which is now under the Kings Locks, & is sold at Publick Sale as Provisions of those Ships, as it undoubtedly was, therefore must beg your Honours Direction to the Collector of the Custom's here, that they may be Delivered to the Purchaser, on Paying the five Per Cent Duty the Collector having no objection thereto I am

Honourable Sirs Your Honours most Obedient Servant

G: Steeven's

152
8 October
1748

CUST 58/149, pp. 100–1

From J. Evelyn, B. Fairfax, Beaumont Hotham and G. Vaughan (Custom House, London). Hand iii.

We received Your Letter of the 6th Ultimo transmitting an Estimate of the Charge of Painting the Watchouse, at Your Port, amount*ing* to Two Pounds, Seventeen Shillings, You may Order the said Watchouse to be forthwith Painted, on the best and Cheapest Terms you can, taking care the Charge does not Exceed the Estimate, and when finished, You may Pay the Bill, and take Credit for the same in Your Account of Incidents, annexing this Letter with proper Receipts thereto as Vouchers, *valediction 1*

In margin: ⌜Original Order sent to Mr Wm Parsons the 22d Oct*obe*r 1751⌝[88]

153
8 October
1748

CUST 58/149, p. 101

From B. Fairfax, Rob. Baylis and G. Vaughan (Custom House, London). Hand iii.

We received Your Letter of the 27th Ultimo transmit*ing* Us what Proof the Officers have that Bulk was broke of part of the Cargo of the Hope Paul Greve Mast*er* from St Martin's bound to Norway, And having refer'd the same to our Sollicitor, Inclosed We send You Copy of his Report, and You are to acquaint Us whether the Officers are willing to Prosecute the Brandy Seized on board the said Ship, at their own Risque, and Charge, for our further Orders. *Valediction 1*

In strictness of Law Bulk is broke & consequently a forfeiture incurrd by the two half *Anchors being unshiped, but the Smallness of the quant*ity* unshiped may occasion some difficulty in procuring a Verdict on Trial.

G Mecalfe

154
8 October
1748

CUST 58/1

From W. C[ooley] and R. T[urvin] (Custom House, Portsmouth). Hand iii.

The Inclos'd Letter we receiv'd from Mr George Spry Supervisor of the Riding's Officer's at this Port to which we beg leave to Refer your Honour's, and whatever Order's you shall be pleas'd to send us in relation thereto will be duely Observ'd *valediction 4*

Tuesday last the 4th Instant between the hour's of Six & Seven in the Evening, at Postbridge, I apprehended Richard Broad of Hambledon in this County, Malster, by Virtue of a Warrant under the hand & Seal of Lord Chief Justice Lee, Assisted by the Officer's of Corsham, Fareham, & Titchfield I immediately thereupon dispatch'd the Officer of Corsham, to the Commanding Officer of the Soldier's Quarter'd at Havant, for a Sufficient Guard to secure the Prisoner against any Attempts that might be made to ⌜rescue⌝[89] him, who accordingly came himself with a strong party about Eleven o'clock that same night

Early the next Morning we carried the Prisoner to Fareham, who was committed to the County Goal at Whinchester by Sir William Bart[90] John Gring's Esqr J: New His Majesty's Justice's of the Pease, to which Prison he was accordingly Guarded, by the said Com*mand*ing Officer, and his Soldier's, & the Officer's of Corsham & Titchfield, I am

Gentlemen Your most humble Servant

G: Spry

Stubbington[91] Oct*obe*r 7th 1748

---

[88] Added (hand vi).

[89] MS. 'recue'.

[90] Probably Sir William Gardner.

[91] MS. 'Subbington'.

155
10 October
1748

CUST 58/149, p. 102

From Wil. Wood (Custom House, London). Hand iii.

Mr. Appleford having by his Memorial of the 6th Instant, apply'd to Us, desiring that the Old Cordage, & Burnt Cable's Seized by Henry Gibb's Deputy Customer at Your Port, may be deliver'd and the Duties for the said Goods being paid, You are to deliver them, to the Proprietors upon their Satisfying the Officers Concerned unless they are willing to Prosecute them at their own Risque & Charge, We are

Your Loving Friends

This Letter was prepared for the Commissioners signing but the Board being risen before it was finished, their Commands are signified to You by

Gentlemen Your most humble Servant

Wm Wood

In margin: Noted in the Seizure Book

156
10 October
1748

CUST 58/149, pp. 102–3

From Wil. Wood (Custom House, London). Hand iii.

Messrs James & Godfrey Noke, having by their Memorial of this date applied to the Commissioners, relating to some Empty flower Barrells under Stop at Your Port, I am directed to send You Copy of the said Memorial, and You are to Examine into the Allegations therein Contained, and Report to the Board, by return of the Post, a true State of the Case, with Your Opinion. *Valediction 2*

London 10th October 1748

May it please your Hon*our*s

Having Freighted the Catherine Captain Daverson, the Duke of Dorset Captain Flynn, & the Cumberland Captn Hutton to proceed from hence to Portsmouth, and there take in Corn, or Flour for the Meditarranean we put here on board those Ships, some Corn Bags, and ordered our Cooper Mr Trender & Co', to put on board some empty flour Barrells to be filled with Flour, as usual, our Agent Mr Woodroff Drinkwater of Chichester, advises us the two former are arived, but the barrells all stopt or Seizd for want of a Sufferance, as we were intirely Ignorant, what might be wanted, we left it to our Cooper to do all things necessary in this Case as usual & if he has omitted doing the needfull, We hope your Honours will not permit us to Suffer for an innocent neglect in the Cooper, but will please to Order our Barrells or Casks to be immediately restored to us, as any Delay is of the utmost Importance to us on many occasions, We therefore humbly ask Your Honours Pardon, and are

Your Honours most Obedient humble Servant[s]

James & Godfrey Noke

157
10 October
1748

CUST 58/149, pp. 103–4

From Wil. Wood (Custom House, London). Hand iii.

Inclosed I send you Copy of a Letter from the Board of Ordnance of the 7th Instant representing that You refuse to permit his Majestys Sloop the Montagu to proceed to Woolwich because her Cargo consists in part of some brass Guns, and you are to report to the Commissioners a State of the Case for their Consideration, and further directions, particularly whether the Guns were taken out of or belong to any of the Prize Ships, which have been Purchased by the Government, and paid the Five Per Cent upon the Ship and Furniture, and *Apparrel &cetera, *valediction 2*

Office of Ordnance 7th Oct*obe*r 1748

Gentlemen

Being informed that the Collector of his Majestys Customs at Portsmouth refuses to let his Majesty's Sloop Montagu proceed to Woollwich, because her Cargo consists in part of some Brass Guns, which were Purchased as Old Gun Metal, of the Agents for Lord Anson's Prizes, for his Majesty's Service, untill we have paid a Duty of five Per Cent for the same

As we purchased them by the Kings Command and for his Majesty's Service & can by no means conceive them liable to pay any Duty we desire you'll be pleased to order the said Collector to permit the Montagu Sloop to proceed to Woollwich, & to lodge the said Guns in his Majesty's ⌜Magazine's⌝[92] there, she being very much wanted on further Service immediately, We are

Gentlemen Your most Obedient Servants

Thos Lascelles

Chas Frederick

158
10 October
1748

CUST 58/1

From W. C[ooley] and R. T[urvin] (Custom House, Portsmouth). Hand iii.

Inclos'd we transmit to Your Honours an Account of Seizure's lately made at this Port, to which we beg leave to Refer, *valediction 4*

159
10 October
1748

CUST 58/1

From W. C[ooley] and R. T[urvin] (Custom House, Portsmouth). Hand iii.

We have your Honour's of the 8th Instant with Copy of the Memorial of Mr George Steeven's, Agent for the French men of War Prize's taken by Sr Edward Hawke, Inclos'd desiring that nine hogsheads of Store Vinegar, may be delivered on paying the 5 Per Cent Duty and by your Honour's Order we are directed to Report a State of the Case with our Opinion. In obedience thereto we have Examined into the Allegation's of said Stephen's Memorial, and are ⌜to⌝[93] acquaint Your Honour's there appears to be Nine hogsheads of Vinegar landed out of the six French Men of War Prize's, which are now under the King's Lock's, And it is our Opinion the same were at first taken on board the said Prize's as there Store's, therefore if your Honours think fit we shall have no objection to the said Vinegar being delivered to the Purchaser's on their Paying the 5 Per Cent Duty, all which is most humbly submitted *valediction 4*

160
10 October
1748

CUST 58/1

From W. C[ooley] and R. T[urvin] (Custom House, Portsmouth). Hand iii.

In obedience to your Honour's Command signified to us by Mr Wood in his Letter of the 6th Instant, we are to acquaint your Honour's after having made a strict Enquiry, we find the Lieutenants Name who was concern'd in Obstructing the Officer's in making a Seizure at the house of Captain Gwynn's at Upham near Bishop's Waltham, is Francis Mose, not Moore, *valediction 5*

161
11 October
1748

CUST 58/1

From W. C[ooley] and R. T[urvin] (Custom House, Portsmouth). Hand iii.

In our joint Letter of Yesterday's date, inclos'd we transmitted your Honour's an Account of a Seizure of Empty Cask's, Bags & Old *Matt's, which Mr Baskerville one of the Tidesurveyor's at this Port, Seiz'd, for want of Coast Dispatche's, out of Two Ship's, which came hither from London, to Load with Wheat & Flour and it since fully appearing, there was no intention of Fraud, in bringing the said Bags Casks &cetera without Dispatche's, but that they were to be fill'd with Wheat & Flour, & from hence for Exportation; Mr Baskerville in Consideration thereof has no Objection to Restoring Mr Drinkwater the owner thereof the said Bag's Cask's &cetera, if your Honour's approve thereof; In the mean time we beg to acquaint your Honour's, as not being willing to obstruct the Merchant in going on with Shipping his Corn, We have deliver'd to him part of his Bag's &cetera on his giving Security for the Value thereof, making no doubt but your Honour's will approve of our Proceedings, therefore we hope to receive your Honours Order's in Relation thereto by the return of the Post, *valediction 3*

92 Altered from 'Magazine'.

93 Written only as catchword at foot of page.

162
11 October
1748

CUST 58/1

From W. C[ooley] and R. T[urvin] (Custom House, Portsmouth). Hand iii.

We have Your Honour's Letter of the 8th Instant, with Copy of the Solicitor's Report Inclos'd, in regard to the Seizure of Brandy on board the Hope Paul Greve Master from St Martin's bound to Norway, And in Obedience to your Honour's Order, we have call'd on the Officer's who made the Seizure, to know if they were willing to Prosecute the Brandy, at their own Risque, and Charge, from whom we have received for answer, that they will not by any mean's, We therefore submit the same to Your Honour's, for your further Order's; which when receiv'd will be duely observ'd, *valediction 4*

163
11 October
1748

CUST 58/1

From W. C[ooley] and R. T[urvin] (Custom House, Portsmouth). Hand iii.

Herewith we transmit to your Honour's the Abstract for the Month of September last together with the undermentioned Account's to which we beg leave to Refer, *valediction 4*

Nil List of Bond's
Tea & other Goods Enumerated with Petty rece*ip*ts Endor'sd
Absent Officer's
State of Bond's for Michaelmas quarter last

P:S: From the Book kept in this Office it appears that the Weights, and Beam Coal and Corn Bushels at this Port were tryed the 9th Ultimo by the Surveyor & Landwaiter's & that they found the same to be exact & true and that the Stamp's for marking Hide's, Skin's Linnen's, Seiz'd Good's & ⌜Sail⌝[94] Cloth, are in good & Sufficient Repair, & fit for the use's designed

164
12 October
1748

CUST 58/149, p. 105

From B. Fairfax, Beaumont Hotham, S. Mead and G. Vaughan (Custom House, London). Hand iii.

We received your Letter of the 6th and 10 Instant transmitting two Accounts of Seizures, of Empty Glass Bottles, Casks, Corn bags & *Matts made by the Deputy Customer & Tidesurveyor at your Port, for want of Coast Dispatches, We direct You to deliver them to the Proprietors upon their giving the Officers concerned a Moderate Satisfaction, *valediction 1*

165
12 October
1748

CUST 58/149, p. 105

From Wil. Wood (Custom House, London). Hand iii.

Having laid your Letter of the 8th Instant before the Commissioners, relating to the Goods Seized at the House of Captain Gwynn, They direct you to use your utmost Endeavours to obtain what Proof you can from all the Persons concerned of the Goods being run, and transmit their Affidavits sworn before a Commissioner in the Exchequer, to the Board, taking care that the Quan*tity* and Quality of the Goods that were run be Inserted therein, with all other Circumstances attending the same, in order that Captain Gwynn & the other Persons may be Effectually prosecuted for the said Offence. *Valediction 2*

166
12 October
1748

CUST 58/1

From W. C[ooley] and R. T[urvin] (Custom House, Portsmouth). Hand iii.

We have your Honours Order signified to Us by Mr Wood in his Letter of the 10th Instant, with the Memorial of Messrs Jame's & Godfrey Noke, inclos'd relating to some Empty Cask's, & Flower Barrels under Stop at this Port, & by your Honour's Order We are directed to examine into the Allegations therein contained, & Report a State of the Case with our opinion, In answer to which we beg to Refer your Honour's to our Letter of Yesterday's date, wherein is stated the whole Affair, together with our Proceeding's, in regard to the said Bag's Cask's &cetera which we hope your Honour's will not otherwise than approve of, *valediction 5*

---

94 MS. 'Sail Sail'.

167
13 October 1748

CUST 58/149, p. 106

From Wil. Wood (Custom House, London). Hand iii.

The Commissioners having received Information that John Cobby & Thomas Stringer, who are suspected to have been concerned in breaking open the Warehouse at Poole, & carrying off a large Quantity of Tea, as well as in the Murder of Chater & Gally, are Endeavouring to make their Escape out of the Kingdom the Commissioners direct You to give it in strict Charge to the Commanders of the Sloops, & Officers of the Water Guard to be very carefull in Examining all Passengers going out of the Kingdom, and in case they meet with either the said Cobby, or Stringer, they are to detain them & give the Board an immediate Account thereof, for their further Directions. *Valediction 2*

168
13 October 1748

CUST 58/149, p. 106

From B. Fairfax, Beaumont Hotham, Sam. Mead and G. Vaughan (Custom House, London). Hand iii.

In Answer to the Account of Seizures transmitt'd in Your Letter of the 3^{d} Instant, We direct You to Prosecute the Rum thereinmentioned to Condemnation in the Exchequer at the Kings Charge Corresponding with our Sollicitor & the Register of Seizures, & We have no objection to the Officers Prosecuting the Wine before the Justices of the Peace at their own Charge, acquainting us when Condemned, *valediction 1*

In margin: Noted in the Book of Seizures –

P.S. The Inclosed List of out Law'd Smuglers, You are to cause to be stuck up, in order to be made as publick as possible at Your Port

169
13 October 1748

CUST 58/1

From W. C[ooley] and R. T[urvin] (Custom House, Portsmouth). Hand iii.

We have your Honour's Order signified to us by Mr Wood in his Letter of the 10th Instant, with Copy of one Inclos'd from the Board of Ordnance, acquainting your Honour's, we have refused his Majesty's Sloop Montague to proceed to Woollwich with some Brass Gun's she has on board, And by your Honour's Order, we are directed to Report a State of the Case for your Consideration, & direction and ⌜particularly⌝[95] whether the Gun's were taken out of, or belong to any of the Prize Ship's, which have been Purchas'd by the Government, & paid the 5 Per Cent, upon the Ship, Furniture & *Apparrell &cetera; – In Obedience to your Commands we are to acquaint your Honour's, the Brass Guns (in Number Thirty one)[96], now on board the Ordnance Vessel, were landed out, and belong'd to the Invincible, French Prize Man of War one of the Squadron taken by Lord Anson; The said French man of war was Purchased by the Government, for which we demanded no Duty's, no more than for any other of French Prize's, which were sold to the Government in doing which we followed as a Precedent, the Proceeding's in regard to the Princessa a man of war, which was the first Ship Purchas'd by the Government during the Present war; And for which the Agent's refusing to pay the Duty of 5 Per Cent on the said Ship's, Tackle & Furniture, it was agreed to deliver the Ship with her Tackle, *Apparrel & Furniture, on their giving Bond to pay the said Duty of 5 Per Cent, in case it shoud be determined against them on a Trial, but afterwards the said Bond was deliver'd up, & no Duty was ever paid for the same, And upon this Subject we have several time's wrote to your Honour's desiring your Direction's in our Letter of the 15th June, 15 August & 12th March 1747, and acquainted your Honour's with our Proceeding's as above, desiring if your ⌜Honour's⌝[97] disapproved thereof, you woud signify the same to u's, & give us other Order's, and according we shoud have demanded no Duties for these Gun's as being part of the Furniture of the Invincible, a French Prize, & bought for the use of the Government; Had Mr Eddowe's the Agent apply'd to us & prov'd that they were bought for the Goverment, but he Ship'd the same for Woollwich without either paying the 5 Per Cent or proving on Oath, which we think necessary in such Case's that they were Purchas'd, for the Goverment; If therefore Mr Eddowe's will make Oath that the said Gun's are purchas'd for the Government, we have no objection to their passing Free agreeable to our Practice, which we hope will be approved by your Honour's, but if they are private Property the 5 Per Cent is due, all which we humbly submit *valediction 3*

---

[95] MS. 'particulary'.
[96] MS. omits closing bracket.
[97] MS. 'Hononour's'.

170
14 October
1748

CUST 58/149, pp. 106–7

From Wil. Wood (Custom House, London). Hand iii.

The Master and Wardens of the Wire Drawers Company having represented to the Commissioners that they are informed, large Quantities of Foreign Gold, and Silver Lace and Embroidery is ready made up in France with intent to be very soon run into this Kingdom to the Detriment of his Majesty's Subjects, The Commiss*ione*rs direct you to give it in strict Charge to all the Officers belonging to Your Port to be very Vigilant in their respective Stations to prevent the running thereof as well as all custimable and Prohibited Goods, the Board being determined to Punish severely all such Officers who shall not exert themselves in the Execution of their Duties, *valediction 2*

171
15 October
1748

CUST 58/149, p. 107

From B. Fairfax, Beaumont Hotham and G. Vaughan (Custom House, London). Hand iii.

Mr Ward having by his Memorial of the 1st Instant applied to Us desiring that such Part of the Cargo of ⌜y^e^⌝[98] American Prize as shall be thought Necessary may be Landed at Your Port, till she is fitted and Repaired for the Sea, We agree thereto if you have no Objection, taken care there be no Embezlements, and that the Crown be put to no Charge for WareHouse room, Officers attendance or otherwise, *valediction 1*

172
15 October
1748

CUST 58/149, p. 107

From Wil. Wood (Custom House, London). Hand iii.

Messrs Pritzler and ⌜Amyand⌝[99] having by their Memorial of this date apply'd to Us relating to 2500 Bags & 500 *Matts Shipt on board the Sophia Nicholas Coxen Master, which are under Stop at Your Port, for want of proper Dispatches, We direct You to deliver the said Bags & *Matts to the Proprietors upon their giving the Officers concerned a moderate Satisfaction. We are

Your Loving Friends

This Letter was prepared for the Commissioners signing but the Board being risen before it was finished, their Com*m*ands are signified to You, by Gentlemen

Your most humble Servant

Wm Wood

173
15 October
1748

CUST 58/149, p. 108

From B. Fairfax, Beaumont Hotham and G. Vaughan (Custom House, London). Hand iii.

We received your Letter of the 11th Instant, acquainting Us that the Officers who Seized the Brandy on board the Hope Paul Greve Master from St Martins bound to Norway, are not willing to Prosecute it at their own risque and Charge, We direct You to Prosecute the said Brandy to Condemnation in the Exchequer at the Kings Charge Corresponding with our Sollicitor and the Register of Seizures, *valediction 1*

Noted in the Seizure Book

174
17 October
1748

CUST 58/149, pp. 108–9

From Wil. Wood (Custom House, London). Hand iii.

Mr John Nesham having informed the Commissioners that the Ship Sunderland William Watson Master being under Process of the Court of Adm*iral*ty at his Suit, and their Officers boarded on her in the Port of N'Castle, the Master being apprehensive of being dispossessed; on the Night between the 7 & 8th Instant confined the Admiralty Officers, and put to Sea with only half her Loading, and as is apprehended, without any Dispatches from the Custom House, and when so got to Sea sent the Officers of the Admiralty on shore, and Mr Nesham having reason to beleive that the Ship is gone to some of the Western Ports, but as it is Probable the Master may change the Name of his Ship, as well as his own, On the back hereof you will receive a Description of the said Ship, and incase she puts into Your Port, You are immediately to give the Board an Account thereof, *valediction 2*

The Vessel is Pink Stern'd very black, three Masts, and Carries 16 Keels of Coals has now only 8 on board the Master is a Short Young Man Aged about 23 Years

---

98 Inserted.

99 Altered from 'Amyard'.

175 CUST 58/1
22 October 1748
From W. C[ooley] and R. T[urvin] (Custom House, Portsmouth). Hand iii.
Inclosed we transmit to Your Honours a Plantation Certificate for the Ship Sophia of London Nichola's Coxen Master for Maryland which when Perfected we desire it may be return'd *valediction 4*

176 CUST 58/149, p. 109
25 October 1748
From Beaumont Hotham, Sam. Mead, B. Fairfax and G. Vaughan (Custom House, London). Hand iii.
We received Your Letter of the 10th Inst*ant* in return to the Memorial of Mr George Steephens Agent for the six French Men of War Prizes, taken by Sir Edward Hawke, desiring that Nine hogsheads of Store Vinegar may be delivered, We agree thereto and You may deliver them to the Purchasers upon their paying the 5 Per Cent Duty for the same, *valediction 1*

177 CUST 58/149, pp. 109–10
25 October 1748
From Beaumont Hotham, Sam. Mead, B. Fairfax and G. Vaughan (Custom House, London). Hand iii.
We received Your Letter of the 28th Ultimo in return to the Memorial of Mr Edward Austin, relating to a Hogshead of Tobacco Seized at Your Port on board the Richard and Ann Sloop Richard Field Master from Plymouth, for being brought Coastways without any Dispatch, You may upon Proof being made on Oath from the Entry that the Duties of the said Tobacco have been paid deliver ⌜it⌝[1] to the Proprietor, on his giving the Officers concerned a moderate Satisfaction, *valediction 1*

178 CUST 58/1
25 October 1748
From W. C[ooley] and R. T[urvin] (Custom House, Portsmouth). Hand iii.
Inclosed we transmit to your Honour's, an Account of Seizure's lately made by the Officer's of the Custom's at this Port to which we beg leave to Refer *valediction 4*

179 CUST 58/1[2]
29 October 1748
From W. C[ooley] and R. T[urvin] (Custom House, Portsmouth). Hand iii.
By your Honour's Order signify'd to u's in Mr Wood's Letter of the 12th Instant; We are directed to use our utmost endeavour's to obtain what Proof we can from all the Person's concern'd, of the Goods being run, that were Seiz'd at the house of Captain Gwyn;
In answer to which we beg leave to acquaint your Honour's, in pursuance of your said Order, we have used our best endeavour's, & Inclos'd we transmit your Honour's the Affidavit of Jame's Good, the Person who gave the Original Information to the Collector of Excise, which is all the Proof we can obtain, to which we beg to refer your Honours; The Person whom we and the Officer's most depended on for a Proof of the Good's being run was Mrs Phillpot an Inhabitant of Gosport, in whose house the Goods were lodg'd, before conveyance to the house of Captain Gwyn at Upham, with whom we have talked & used our utmost endeavour's to procure the truth from her, but she absolutely refuses to give us any Information on Oath but told us Captain Gwynn did lodge at her house and at that time had Cask's & other thing[s] brought there, but the content's she knew not, *valediction 5*

180 CUST 58/1
31 October 1748
From W. C[ooley] and R. T[urvin] (Custom House, Portsmouth). Hand iii.
We have here inclos'd a Schedule of Accounts due from this Port, for the Quarter ended Midsummer last, the same being this day forwarded by the Waggon of George Clarke, which Inn's at the Whitehart in the Burrough of Southwark, on Wednesday the 2^{d} November, for the Carriage of which We have agreed that Two Shilling's & Six Pence shall be paid, *valediction 3*

---

[1] Written only as catchword at foot of page.
[2] No. 180 precedes no. 179 in MS.

Portsmouth,

A Schedule of Accounts due from this Port, for Midsummer Quarter last, sent by the Waggon of George Clarke which will be at the Whitehart in the Burrough of Southwark on Wednesday the 2[d] November 1748

Customer & Collector's Quarter Book
Comptrollers Quarter Book
General Incidents with the Establishment, & one Original Order
Eight Debenture's, eight Damage Certificate's, two *over Entry's, & one *Portage Bill
Coal Incidents
Import's & Export's
Wooll brought & carried Coastwise
Civil List Receipt
Repayment D[o]
Corn Exported whereon there is a Bounty
Enumerated Good's
Personal Prosecution's
Preparatory Account of Incident's
An Account of Ship's from the British Plantation's &cetera
Journal's of the Commander & Mate of the Greenhill ⌜Yatch⌝[3]
D[o] – of the Chief Boatman at Hayling

Deputation & Instruction's	of Alex[r] Strahan	Tidesman &cetera
D[o] –	of W[m] Howell's	D[o]
D[o] –	of W[m] Manuel	D[o]
Deputation of Gilbert Stoake's –		D[o]
Copy of Instruction's –	to W[m] Stubbington	D[o]
D[o] –	to Ja[s] Burnet	D[o]
D[o] –	to Labon Sparrow	Coal Meter

181 CUST 58/1

1 November 1748

From W. C[ooley] and R. T[urvin] (Custom House, Portsmouth). Hand iii.

Inclos'd we transmit to your Honours two Accounts viz[t] of Good's Enumerated, and Goods not Enumerated, lately Seiz'd by the Officer's of the Customs in this Port, to which we beg leave to Refer *valediction 4*

182 CUST 58/149, p. 110

3 November 1748

From Wil. Wood (Custom House, London). Hand iii.

The Commissioners having received Information that great Quantities of French *Cambricks & *Lawns continue to be Imported, and vended in the Country; The *Cambricks passing Chiefly under the Denomination of German *Lawns, are made up exactly in shape and Bulk with those German or Selesia *Lawns, commonly known by the Name of *Pistol Lawns, and the French *Lawns are Imported under Colour & Title of Selesia *Lawns, the Pieces are commonly Starch'd blue in imitation of the Selesia's to disguise the Fraud; The Commissioners direct You to give it in strict charge to the Landsurveyors, Landwaiters, or other proper Officers who have the care of discharging Linnens, to be very carefull in the Examination thereof, to detect and prevent the Importation of French *Cambricks & *Lawns Reporting to the Board Your Proceedings *valediction 2*

183 CUST 58/149, pp. 110–11

3 November 1748

From Sam. Mead, Rob. Baylis, Beaumont Hotham and G. Vaughan (Custom House, London). Hand iii.

In Answer to the Account of Seizures transmitted in Your Letter of the 25th Ultimo We direct You to Prosecute the Tobacco thereinmentioned to Condemnation in the Exchequer at the Kings Charge, and the Wooll and Worsted before the Justices of the Peace, at the Officers Charge, acquainting Us when Condemned, And We have no Objection to the Officers Prosecuting the rest of the Goods in the Exchequer at their own Charge Corresponding with our Sollicitor and the Register of Seizures, *valediction 1*

Noted in the Seizure Book –

3 Written over an illegible erasure.

184 CUST 58/149, p. 111

8 November 1748

From G. Vaughan, B. Fairfax, J. Evelyn and Beaumont Hotham (Custom House, London). Hand iii.

In answer to the Account of Seizures transmitted in Your Letter of the 1st Instant, We direct You to Prosecute the Enumerated Goods thereinmentioned to Condemnation in the Exchequer at the Kings Charge, and We have no Objection to the Officers Prosecuting the rest of the Goods at their own Charge Corresponding with our Sollicitor, & the Register of Seizures, *valediction 1*

In margin: Noted in the Seizure Book

185 CUST 58/1

8 November 1748

From W. C[ooley] and R. T[urvin] (Custom House, Portsmouth). Hand iii.

We beg leave to acquaint Your Honour's, we have sent by the Waggon of William Connop which will be at the King's Head in the Burrough of Southwark on Wednesday the 9th Instant, under the Seals of Office directed for your Honour's, in order to be Examined by the proper Officer's, five Case's Containing Book's, belonging to Doctor Lidderdale late Physicion to his Majesty's Fleet in the Mediterranean, *valediction 5*

186 CUST 58/1

8 November 1748

From W. C[ooley] and R. T[urvin] (Custom House, Portsmouth). Hand iii.

By your Honour's Order of the 4th August last, we were directed to keep our hands on a Seizure of Tea, made by Mr Charles Markland, & other Officer's at this Port, till we shou'd receive your further Direction's, We therefore beg to know whether the said Tea is to be Prosecuted in the Exchequer or not, if it is, desire your Honour's immediate direction's thereon, *valediction 5*

187 CUST 58/149, pp. 111–12

10 November 1748

From G. Vaughan, Beaumont Hotham, J. Evelyn and Sam. Mead (Custom House, London). Hand iii.

Mr Charles having applied to Us, in the Name of Sir Peter Warren in relation to some Wine in Bottles in the WareHouse at Your Port, which he desires may be admitted to an Entry, And as it was intended to have been expended at Sea, during Sir Peter Warren's late Command, We agree to its being admitted to an Entry, agreeable to the request of Mr Charles, which we hereby signify to You, *valediction 1*

188 CUST 58/149, p. 112

10 November 1748

From G. Vaughan, Beaumont Hotham, J. Evelyn and Sam. Mead (Custom House, London). Hand iii.

Mr John Waters having by his Memorial of the 9th Instant applied to Us desiring that the 200 Casks of Flour, 559 Bags Wheat and 440 Iron Shott Saved out of the Tuscany, Samuel Webster Master, lately run on shore near Margate, and Secured in the WareHouse there, may be shipt on board a Vessell bound to Your Port in order to be put on board the Tuscany, We have agreed thereto, and given Orders to the Officers at Sandwich accordingly, and on the arrival of the Vessel You are to permit the said Goods to be reshipt on board the Tuscany under the care of the proper Officers at the Proprietors Charge, and when the Corn & Flour is reshipt, You are to transmit Us a Certificate thereof, that We may give Orders for the Debentures to pass, *valediction 1*

189 CUST 58/1

10 November 1748

From W. C[ooley] and R. T[urvin] (Custom House, Portsmouth). Hand iii.

Herewith we transmit your Honour's the Abstract for the Month of October last together with the undermentioned Accounts to which we beg leave to Refer *valediction 4*

Nil List of Bonds
Tea & other Goods Enumerated with Petty Receipts Endors'd
Absent Officers

P:S/ From the Book kept in this Office it appear's that the Weight's and Beam Coal and Corn bushels at this Port were try'd the 7th Ultimo by the Surveyor and Landwaiter's and that they found the same to be exact and true, & that the Stamps for marking Hide's, Skin's, Linnen's, Seiz'd Goods & Sail Cloth, are in good and Sufficient Repair & fit for the use's design'd

190 CUST 58/1

10 November 1748

From W. C[ooley] and R. T[urvin] (Custom House, Portsmouth). Hand iii.

Inclos'd we transmit to Your Honour[s] two Accounts vizt of Goods Enumerated and Goods not Enumerated, lately Seiz'd by the Officer's in this Port, to which we beg leave to refer *valediction 4*

191 CUST 58/1

11 November 1748

From W. C[ooley] and R. T[urvin] (Custom House, Portsmouth). Hand iii.

We have here Inclos'd a List of such Stationary Wares as are much wanted for the Service at this Port with which We beg to be immediately Supply'd, and the same shall be frugally manag'd *valediction 4*

PS/ The last Supply was Crav'd the 8th March 1747/8 and Receiv'd in June following

Portsmouth, A List of such Stationary Wares as are wanted for the Service of his Majesty's Customs at this Port, humbly Crav'd to be allow'd, vizt

2 Leidger's Inwards Ruled for the Collector & Comptroller
4 Quire of Quarter Book Paper Inward's
2 Quire of large *Imperial Unrul'd
4 Rheam's 2^{d} *Pott Paper
3 Rheam's fine *Pott Cutt
6 Quire *Demy Cutt
3 Quire D^{o} Rough
A Book for Entering Letters from the Board
A Book for D^{o} – to D^{o}
A Coast Book Inwards & one D^{o} Outwards
A Sufferance Book
A Ship's Entry Book
A Ship's Register Book
A Book for Ship's, Inwards, Outwards & Coastwise
A Book for Monthly Accounts of Absent Officer's
A Book to Enter all Accounts of Seizures
D^{o} for Indenture's of Appraisement
2 Book's for the Monthly Account's of Petty Receipts
A Incident for the Comptroller
2 Book's for the Account of Personal Prosecution's
2 Dozen *Demy Pocket Book's for Coal Meters &cetera
Blue Book's for the use of the Surveyor & Landwaiters viz

80 – 4 Leaves	20 – 14 Leaves
50 – 2 Leaves	12 – 16 Leaves
60 – 6 Leaves	12 – 20 Leaves
40 – 8 Leaves	12 – 24 Leave's
30 – 10 Leave's	
30 – 12 Leave's	

Two Gallon's Black Ink	½ Pound of *Pounc[e]
A Quart Red Ink	2 Book's 1 Quire *Demy each
4 ⌜Ivory⌝[4] Penknive's	2 Quire *Boarding's
4 horn *Pounce Boxe's	A Report Book Outwards
2 Dozen Pencils	2 Quire D^{o} in Sheets
4 Bodkin's	1 Quire D^{o} Inwards
2 Dozen P*ieces* Tape	A Quire Coal Warrants
3 Bag's of Sand	1500 Quils
A Pound of Wax	3000 Wafer's
	1000 large D^{o}
	2 Dozen Tag's
	12 Pastboard Files

4 MS. 'Iory'.

192
12 November 1748

CUST 58/149, pp. 112–13

From G. Vaughan, J. Evelyn and Sam. Mead (Custom House, London). Hand iii.

Having receiv'd a Warrant of the Treasury on a Report from this Board dated the 5th Instant directing that Nicholas Trant Committed to the Goal of Your Town in October 1746 at the Suit of Pusey Brook late Collector for an Offence by him Committed against the Laws of the Customs, in relation to Exporting Wooll, be discharged out of Prison, We direct you to take care he be discharged from his Confinement agreeable to the said Warrant, *valediction 1*

193
12 November 1748

CUST 58/1

From W. C[ooley] and R. T[urvin] (Custom House, Portsmouth). Hand iii.

Inclos'd we transmit to Your Honour's an Account of Seizure's lately made by the Officer's of the Custom's in this Port, to which we beg to refer *valediction 4*

194
15 November 1748

CUST 58/149, p. 113–14

From Wil. Wood (Custom House, London). Hand iii.

Since my Letter of the 14th Ultimo The Commissioners have received a Letter from Mr West Secretary to the Lords Commissioners of his Majesty's Treasury signifying "That[5] their Lordships having been informed that great quantities of Foreign Gold, and Silver Lace, and also of Lac'd & Embroider'd Cloaths, have been lately Imported, and run into this Kingdom to the Prejudice of those Manufactures here with their Lordships Directions for the Commissioners to give strict Orders to their Officers to use their utmost diligence, in searching for, seizing and preventing the Importation thereof, and where any Seizures have or shall be made of such Gold and Silver Lace, or Lac'd or Embroidered Cloaths, to cause the Persons who have or shall Import run, or Conceal, the same, to be Prosecuted with the utmost Severity of the Law" The Commissioners direct You, to give it in strict charge to all the Officers belonging to Your Port, to be particularly carefull & diligent to carry their Lordships Orders into Execution, & whenever they make any Seizures of such Goods they are to use their utmost Endeavours to discover & find out the Persons who Imported, Run, or Concealed the Goods, Reporting to the Board their Names, Employments & Places of Habitation, as well ⌜as⌝[6] the Proof they can obtain against them for the Boards further Direction's, *valediction 2*

195
17 November 1748

CUST 58/149, p. 114

From W. Wood (Custom House, London). Hand iii.

Mr Nisbitt having ⌜by⌝[7] his Memorial of the 10th Instant applied to the Commissioners desiring leave to Enter ten small Casks of Nails & a few Compound Medicines, Condemned as Prize, Inclosed You will receive Copy of the said Memorial, & You are to examine into the Allegations therein Contained, and Report to the Board a true State of the Case, with Your Opinion, *valediction 2*

Portsmouth 10th November 1748

Honourable Sirs

About two Months since at a Sale of Prize Goods taken by Lord Anson's Squadron, I purchas'd ten small Cask's Nails, & a few Compound Medicines which were actually Stores for the use of the Ships, from whence they were laden, I therefore pray Your Honours woud be pleased to direct that the said Stores may be admitted to an Entry on paying the 5 Per Cent ad Valorem, I crave pardon for troubling Your Honours & am with due respect

Honourable Sirs Your most Obedient humble Servant

Albitt Nisbitt

---

5 Each line of this quotation is introduced by a double quotation mark.
6 MS. 'as as'.
7 MS. 'by by'.

196
17 November 1748

CUST 58/149, p. 115

From Wil. Wood (Custom House, London). Hand iii.

The Commissioners direct You to draw out And transmit them without loss of time a List of the Established Officers belonging to Your Port, to whom any Annual Allowance's are made by Incidents, mentioning in one Column the Amount of the Establish'd Sallary, and in the other the Allowances by Incidents with the Dates of the first Orders for making the Incident Allowances, and they further direct You, to Draw out, and transmit at the same time a Distinct ⌜List⌝[8] of all the Officers, who are paid by Incidents only, mentioning their Allowances with the Dates of the first Orders for making the same, and you are to Distinguish at the foot of the Account such Officers as have been appointed since the Commencement of the War with Spain, and at the same time Report what Services each Officer has Performed on[9] Account of such Allowances as are made by Incidents, with Your Opinion whether it be Necessary for the Service of the Revenue to continue them, and you are carefully to consider and report whether any Saving can be made out of the said Incident Allowances, and how much without any Prejudice to the Service, *valediction 2*

197
18 November 1748

CUST 58/149, p. 115–16

From W. Levinz ('Sevine'), B. Fairfax, Wil. Westby and G. Vaughan (Custom House, London). Hand iii.

In answer to the Accounts of Seizures transmitt'd in Your Letter of the 10th & 12th Instant, We direct You to Prosecute the Tobacco thereinmentioned to Condemnation in the Exchequer at the Kings Charge Corresponding with our Sollicitor and the Register of Seizures, and We have no objection to the Officers Prosecuting the Wine before the Justices of the Peace at their ⌜own⌝[10] Charge, acquainting Us when Condemned, *valediction 1*

Noted in the Seizure book

198
20 November 1748

CUST 58/1

From W. C[ooley] and R. T[urvin] (Custom House, Portsmouth). Hand iii.

We have Your Honour's Order signified to us by Mr Wood in his Letter of the 17th Instant, transmitting us Copy of a Memorial from Mr Albert Nisbitt, desiring leave to enter ten small Cask's of Nails, and a few Compound Medicine's (Condemn'd as Prize)[11], on his paying the 5 Per Cent Advalorem, In obedience to Your Honour's Order we have examined into the Allegation's of said Nisbitts Memorial and we are to acquaint Your Honour's it is our Opinion the said Nails & Compound Medicines were part of the Stores for the Ship's use, which we shall have no objection to passing as such on payment of the five Per Cent Duty, provided it meets with your Honours approbation *valediction 5*

199
22 November 1748

CUST 58/149, p. 116

From J. Evelyn, Sam. Mead, W. Westby and W. Levinz ('Sevinz') (Custom House, London). Hand iii.

Thomas Young Tidesman at Your Port, who had Leave of the Collector to come to London for six Days on his private Affairs, having by his Memorial of the 21st Instant, applyed to Us desiring further Leave for six days to finish the same, We have agreed thereto with the loss of two thirds of his Sallary during the whole time of his Absence, which you are to remit to Mr Harrison Paymaster of Superanuated Officers, to be apply'd towards that Fund, giving notice thereof to the Comptroller General, *valediction 1*

Ret*urn*ed the 26th Nov*embe*r to his Duty

---

8 Inserted.
9 'such' struck out.
10 Inserted.
11 MS. omits closing bracket.

200
23 November 1748

CUST 58/1

From W. C[ooley] and R. T[urvin] (Custom House, Portsmouth). Hand iii.

In obedience to your Order's of the 17th Instant, we herewith send you an Account of such Officers, whose Sallaries are paid by Incident's, or have Additional Allowance's paid by Incidents at this Port, with the Dates of the first Order's for the Payment of the same; In regard to which we crave leave to observe that the Sallaries are paid to Officer's which have been found Necessary to be added to the Number paid by Establishment from time to time as the Service required, by reason of the Increase of Trade and Shipping at this Port, And as the reason for their first Appointment still subsists, & in a greater degree, as we conceive the Trade of the Port is considerably increas'd since the Appointment of these Officer's, we are humbly of Opinion it is for the Good of the Revenue to continue them

The Additional Allowance's are such as your Honour's have thought fit to make to such Officer's whose Sallaries by the Establishment have been deem'd too small when the Business of the Port Increas'd, or else to such as having less on the Establishment, than others who did the same Duty, had such Allowance's made to put them upon a footing with them; Only the Allowance of 5 Per Annum, to Twenty *Preferable Tidesmen was made, about the beginning of the War, and was then not thought barely reasonable but absolutely necessary to encourage able hand's to Enter into the Service, without which by reason of the deerness of House Rent & Provision's, and also of Labour in this Place, we are persuaded we could not have otherwise provided proper hand's to carry on the Business, the truth of which may appear, by several of them having thrown up their Deputation's notwithstanding such Encouragement, and they have been generally our best hands. With regard to this Article we have consulted with the Tidesurveyor's who join with us in Opinion, that tho' your Honour's shou'd think proper to discontinue this Allowance, We shall still have occasion for the whole Number of hand's to carry on the Business, and that therefore it woud be advisable, to continue their Deputation's, which impower's them to Seize Goods, and is thereby some small Encouragement to their continuance in the Service

With regard to the Sallarie's and other Additional Allowance's abovemention'd, as the reason's for their first appointment, are now grown stronger by a still encrease of Business at this Port, we are far from thinking they should be discontinued, or lessen'd; And upon the whole Crave leave humbly to observe to your Honour's in regard to the Officers at this Port, in general, that the particular deerness of Provision's, House Rent, & Labour in this Place, subsists in time of Peace, as well as in War, tho' not in the same degree, insomuch that to speak within Bound's, an Officer may live as well at most other Out Ports, with a Sallary of £40 as here with £50, And the *settle Tidesmen at £30 Per Annum, we are Persuaded must have been very hard put to it to live during the War, and must be still even in time of Peace in Proportion as all necessaries of life, are dearer than at other Ports, We hope your Honours will not impute this Remark, to any undue Bias, on the Contrary if we said less, we should have concealed from your Honours our real & sincere Sentiments on the Subject, and beg leave to assure your Honour's, we shall on all occasion's consult as our Duty is, the true Interest of the Revenue, and manage with the utmost frugality, as the nature of the Case will admit of, *valediction 5*

201
24 November 1748

CUST 58/149, pp. 116–17

From Wil. Wood (Custom House, London). Hand iii.

The Board of Ordnance having acquainted the Commissioners that the Collector refuses to permit some Brass Guns purchased as Old Gun Metal, of the Agents for Sir Edward Hawke's Prizes for his Majestys Service to be shipt on board the Sloop Montagu of Woollwich untill a Duty of five Per Cent is paid for the same; I am directed to inclose You a Copy of the Letter, and you are to Report to the Board a State of the Case for their Consideration, *valediction 2*

Office of Ordnance 23d November 1748

Gentlemen

Being acquainted by your Officer's at Portsmouth that the Collector of his Majesty's Custom's there Refuse's to let them ship on Board his Majesty's Sloop Montagu for Woollwich some Brass Gun's, purchased as Old Gun Metal of the Agents for Sir Edward Hawke's Prize's, for his Majesty's Service, untill we have paid a Duty of five Per Cent for the Same

As we purchas'd the said Gun's by the King's Command and for his Majesty's Service, and cannot possibly conceive them liable to pay any Duty, we desire you will be pleased to Order the said Collector, to permit the Montagu Sloop, to proceed to Woollwich, and lodge the said Gun's in his Majesty's Magazine's there, she being much wanted on further Service immediately, We are

Gentlemen Your most humble ⌜Servant

Thos Lasselle's⌝[12] W. R Earle

Chas Frederick

202
26 November 1748

CUST 58/149, pp. 117–18

From J. Evelyn, Wil. Westby and W. Levinz ('Sevine') (Custom House, London). Hand iii.

Captain Faulknor of his Majesty's Ship the Fox having by his Letter of the 7th Instant, apply'd to Us desiring that a Hogshead of Claret & Twenty Gallons Rum, in the WareHouse at Your Port, may be sent to Plymouth and put on Board the said Ship, We direct You to deliver the said Wine and Rum, ⌜upon⌝[13] his Paying the Duty for the same, *valediction 1*

203
26 November 1748

CUST 58/1[14]

From W. C[ooley] and R. T[urvin] (Custom House, Portsmouth). Hand iii.

Inclos'd we transmit your Honour's a Certificate whereby it will appear that Capt Coombs Commander of the Greenhill Yatch, Employ'd in the Service at this Port, hath duely perform'd his Contract, agreeable to what was transmitted in our joint Letter to your Honour's bearing date the 13th November 1743 Vizt for the Quarter's ended Midsummer and Michaelma's last, and therefore we pray your Honour's Order for paying the said Captain Coombs the Sum of Twenty three Pounds, five Shilling's, being after the Rate of Thirty Shilling's Per Ton Per Annum, for thirty one Ton's Burthen agreeable to the said Contract, *valediction 5*

Port of Portmouth

These are to Certify that upon a carefull Survey made for the half Year ended Mich*ael*mas last, it appear'd to us that the Greenhill Yatch & Boats belonging to her Employ'd in the Service of the Custom's at this Port, together with all the Materials have been duely kept, and are in good and Sufficient repair, and that Capt Coombs Commander thereof hath well and duely perform'd his Contract, and is thereby entituled to half a Year's Allowance Amounting to £23.5.0 Witness our hands, Dated at the Custom House 24th Nov*ember* 1748

W: C Collector Wm Baskerville Tides*urveyo*r

W Read Shipwright

204
27 November 1748

CUST 58/1

From W. C[ooley] and R. T[urvin] (Custom House, Portsmouth). Hand iii.

We have your Honour's Commands signified to us by Mr Wood, in his Letter of the 24th Instant transmitting Copy of a Letter from the Board of Ordnance, in which is alledged that the Collector refuses to permit some Brass Guns, which they bought of the Agents for the Prizes taken by Sir Edwd Hawke to be Shipt on board the Montagu Sloop for Woollwich untill the Duty of five Per Cent is paid for the same, And by your Honour's said Order, we are directed to Report a State of the Case for your Consideration and Direction, In answer to which we are to acquaint Your Honour's the Brass Guns for which the Collector now Demand's the Duty of five Per Cent, are under the same Circumstances, as those Purchas'd of the Agents to the Prize's taken by Lord Anson, for which the Collector before Conveyance of the same to Woollwich, took a Promisary Note of hand for the five Per Cent Duty of Mr Eddowe's Storekeeper of his Majesty's Ordnance at this Port, on Condition if he coud not on an Application to your Honour's procure an Order for the said Gun's not being charg'd with such a Duty, but to pass free as this Affair in regard to the Gun's Purchas'd by the Board of Ordnance of the Agent's to Sir Edward Hawke's Prize's is a Parallel Case, with those Purchas'd of the Agents to Lord Anson's Prizes, on which your Honour's was apply'd to by the

12 Added.
13 MS. 'upon upon'.
14 No. 204 precedes no. 203 in MS.

Board of Ordinance, as appear's by their memorial, dated the 7th of October last, Copy of which was transmitted Us in M[r] Woods Letter, dated the 10th of said Month, We were then directed by Your Honour's Order, to Report a State of the Case for your Consideration & further Direction's, which we did in Obedience thereto, as will appear by our joint Letter dated the 13th, to which we beg leave to Refer your Honour's; – On the whole as we only want your Honour's Approbation to our Proceeding's in regard to the Ship's, as well as the Material's sold to the Government, We have no objection to their passing free of the 5 Per Cent Duty agreeable to our Practice since the Commencement of the War, only we think it necessary that M[r] Eddowe's who Purchas'd the said Gun's for the use of the Government, shou'd make Oath to the same, all which is most humbly submitted *valediction 4*

205
1 December 1748

CUST 58/149, p. 118

From Wil. Wood (Custom House, London). Hand iii.

The Account of Ships and Vessels arriving at Your Port from the Plantations, which by the Commissioner's Orders of the 24th July 1741, were directed to be sent to the Board, within one Week after the end of every Quarter, not having Return'd for Michaelmas last, You are forthwith to transmit the said Account, and strictly observe the said Order's for the future. *Valediction 2*

206
3 December 1748

CUST 58/1

From W. C[ooley] and R. T[urvin] (Custom House, Portsmouth). Hand iii.

Inclos'd we transmit to your Honour's two Accounts viz[t] of Goods Enumerated and Good's not Enumerated, lately Seiz'd by the Officer's of the Custom's in this Port, to which we beg leave to Refer *valediction 4*

207
3 December 1748

CUST 58/1

From W. C[ooley] and R. T[urvin] (Custom House, Portsmouth). Hand iii.

In obedience to your Order's signify'd to us by M[r] Secretary Wood 1st Instant, We have here Inclos'd an Account of all Ship's & Vessel's Discharg'd at this Port, from the British Plantation's in America for the Quarter ended Michaelmas last, to which we beg leave to Refer *valediction 3*

208
8 December 1748

CUST 58/149, p. 118

From R. Chandler, Sam. Mead, J. Evelyn and W. Levinz ('Sevine') (Custom House, London). Hand iii.

We receiv'd Your Letter of the 8th Ultimo Relating to the Tea, Seiz'd by M[r] Cha[s] Markland, and other Officers at Your Port, on board the Two Brothers Tho[s] Arnot Master from Rotterdam, as mentioned in the Account of Seizure's transmitted in Your Letter of the 23[d] July last, We direct You to prosecute the said Tea to Condemnation, in the Exchequer at the Kings Charge Corresponding with our Solliciter, and the Register of Seizures, *valediction 1*

Noted in the Seizure Book –

209
8 December 1748

CUST 58/1

From W. C[ooley] and R. T[urvin] (Custom House, Portsmouth). Hand iii.

Inclos'd we transmit your Honour's a Petition, which we this day receiv'd from Samuel Saunder's relating to a Wherry, lately Seiz'd by M[r] Baskerville, one of the Tidesurveyor's at this Port for running three small Cask's of Rum, an Account of which in the usual Form, was transmitted to your Honour's in our joint Letter bearing date the 3[d] Instant; as we have no reason to believe what Saunder's has alledged in regard to his being Ignorant & unacquainted of his Boat being Employ'd in running the three small Cask's of Rum, but that she was stolen from him as he Alledges in the Inclos'd Petition, on those Circumstances we beg leave to acquaint your Honour's M[r] Baskerville who Seiz'd the said Boat, provided it meets with Your Honour's Approbation, has no objection to restoring said Boat to Saunder's, believing him to be intirely innocent of the Affair, all which is humbly submitted to your Honour's Consideration, *valediction 4*

To The Collector and Comptroller of his Maj*es*tys Custom's at Portsmouth

The Petition of Samuel Saunder's Humbly Sheweth That on the 23^{d} day of November last past, your Petitioner's Wherry & the Material's thereunto belonging was Seiz'd by Mr Baskerville one of the Tidesurveyor's, together with three small Cask's of Rum.

That your Petitioner being then entirely Ignorant, or unacquainted thereof, has sustained great Damage by the loss of his Boat which was actually stollen from him, by an ill dispos'd Person, who took the Opportunity while your Petitioner, was attending a Funeral at Kingston, which Person having ever since absconded, or even was he here present, is he worth a Shilling to answer such Damage, your Petitioner therefore humbly pray's relief, in the Case, hoping that in regard he is clearly Innocent of the thing transacted & is also ready to make Oath accordingly, when required,

The Gentlemen concern'd will be so good to intercede with the Honourable the Commissioner's to restore his said Wherry & Material's, the same being all your Petitioner had to maintain himself, and poor Family, consisting of a sick wife & three small Children, and as in Duty bound your Petitioner will ever pray &cetera –

Samuel Saunder's

Dec*ember* 7th 1748

210 CUST 58/1

9 December 1748

From W. C[ooley] and R. T[urvin] (Custom House, Portsmouth). Hand iii.

Herewith we transmit to Your Honour's the Abstract for the Month of Nov*ember* last, together with the undermention'd Account's to which we beg leave to refer *valediction 4*

Nil List of Bond's

Tea & other Goods Enumerated with Petty receipts Endors'd

Absent Officers

PS From the Book kept in this Office it appear's that the Weights & Beam, Coal & Corn Bushels at this Port were try'd the 7th Ultimo by the Surv*eyo*r & Landwaiters & that they found the same to be exact & true, and that the Stamp's for marking Hides, Skin's Linnen's Seiz'd Goods & Sail Cloth, are in good & sufficient repair, & fit for the uses design'd –

211 CUST 58/149, p. 119

13 December 1748

From Beaumont Hotham, Sam. Mead, J. Evelyn and W. Levinz ('Sevine') (Custom House, London). Hand iii.

We receiv'd Your Letter of the 26th Ultimo Inclosing a Certificate, whereby it appear's that the Greenhill Yatch, and Boats belonging to her in the Service at Your Port, under the Command of Captain Coomb's are in good and Sufficient Repair The Collector may pay the Commander thereof, the usual Allowance for keeping the said Yatch, and Boats, in wear and Tear for the Quarters ended at Midsummer and Michaelma's last, and take Credit for the same in his Account of Incidents, annexing this Letter with proper Receipts thereto as Voucher's, *valediction 1*

In margin: ⌜Original transmitted with the Account of Salarys & Incidents for Christmas Quarter 1748⌝[15]

212 CUST 58/149, p. 119

15 December 1748

From W. Westby, Sam. Mead, Beaumont Hotham and G. Vaughan (Custom House, London). Hand iii.

Having granted our Commission for George Karrington, to be a Tidesman and Boatman at Your Port, in the room of Peter Dunstan resigned, You are to take care he be under Oath & Security, for the faithfull Discharge of the said Employ, and Qualifies himself as the Law directs, paying him the like Allowance by Incident's, as was paid to his Predecesser for which the Collector may take Credit in his Account of Incidents, Referring therein to the date hereof, *valediction 1*

P.S. Since writing the above the said Karrington has given Security here.

[15] Added.

213
17 December 1748

CUST 58/149, p. 119–20

From Beaumont Hotham, R. Chandlor and Sam. Mead (Custom House, London). Hand iii.

Captain Obrien of his Majesty's Ship the Colchester, having by his Letter of the 16th Ultimo apply'd to Us desiring as his Ship is under Order's to be paid off, that his Store of Liquors in Bottle's, may be Entered; We agree thereto, and You are to admit them to an Entry as Desired, *valediction 1*

214
17 December 1748

CUST 58/149, p. 120

From Beaumont Hotham, R. Chandlor, W. Westby and G. Vaughan (Custom House, London). Hand iii.

Having receiv'd Your Preparatory Account of Incidents, for the Quarter ended at Midsummer last, amounting to Twenty Pounds five Shillings & Nine Pence half Penny, The Collector may pay the same, with the Privity of the Comptroller, and take Credit for it in his Account of Incidents, annexing this Letter with Proper Receipts thereto as Voucher's, *valediction 1*

In margin: ⌜Original transmitted with the Account of Salary's and Incidents for Christmas Quarter 1748⌝[16]

215
17 December 1748

CUST 58/1

From W. C[ooley] and R. T[urvin] (Custom House, Portsmouth). Hand iii.

In obedience to your Commands of the 23d of October 1742 we have here inclos'd an Account of all the Officer's of this Port, to whom Annual Allowance's are made by Incident's distinguishing those who are Establish'd with the Dates of the Order's for paying the same, And in pursuance of your said Direction's, we humbly report that the said Officer's have faithfully & diligently perform'd their Duty, And ti's our humble opinion it will be for the Service to continue them at their several Incident Allowance's which have hitherto been paid. We therefore pray an Order for paying the same, *valediction 5*

216
20 December 1748

CUST 58/149, p. 120

From Sam. Mead, W. Levinz ('Sevine'), J. Evelyn and G. Vaughan (Custom House, London). Hand iii.

Having granted our Commission for John Gayton, to be a Tidesman, and Boatman at Your Port, in the room of William Manual, resigned, You are to take care he be under Oath & Security, for the faithfull discharge of the said Employ

We have also granted our Commission for William Pendrill, to be a Tidesman and Boatman in the room of Alexander Strahan resigned, and he having given Security here, You are to admit him to his Duty & you are to pay them the like allowance by Incidents, as was paid to their Predecessor's for which the Collector may take Credit in his Account of Incidents from time to time, Referring therein to the date hereof. *Valediction 1*

P.S Pendrills Commission was deliver'd to him here –

217
20 December 1748

CUST 58/149, p. 121

From Sam. Mead, Beaumont Hotham, W. Westby and G. Vaughan (Custom House, London). Hand iii.

We received Your Letter of the 8th Instant, transmitting the Petition of Samuel Saunder's praying the Delivery of a Wherry lately Seiz'd by Mr Baskervile, one of the Tidesurveyor's at Your Port, for Running three small Cask's of Rum, We direct you to Prosecute the said Boat to Condemnation before the Justice's of the Peace, at the Kings Charge acquainting us when Condemn'd. *Valediction 1*

---

[16] Added.

218 **20 December 1748**

CUST 58/149, p. 121

From Sam. Mead, Beaumont Hotham, W. Westby and G. Vaughan (Custom House, London). Hand iii.

Having taken into Consideration your Letter of the ⌜7th⌝[17] Instant, transmitting an Account of the allowance's made to the Officers at Your Port, by Incidents, We agree to Your Paying the said Officer's their respective Allowances to Michaelma's last, and to their Continuance from that time for Twelve Month's longer, for which the Collector may take Credit in his Account of Incidents, referring therein to the date hereof, and at the Expiration thereof You are to Report to Us the Services performed by the said Officer's with Your Opinion whether it will be for the Interest of the Revenue to continue the said Allowance's, and incase the Collector pays any of the Allowance's without our previous Order for that purpose, he will not have Credit for the same in his Accounts, *valediction 1*

219 **22 December 1748**

CUST 58/149, pp. 121–2

From Sam. Mead, G. Vaughan, R. Chandlor and W. Levinz ('Sevine') (Custom House, London). Hand iii.

In answer to the Account of Seizures transmitted in Your Letter of the 3d Instant, We direct You to Prosecute the Enumerated Goods which were run to Condemnation before the Justice's of the Peace, and the rest in the Exchequer at the Kings Charge, and we have no objection to the Officer's Prosecuting the Non Enumerated Goods before the Justices of the Peace at their own Charge, acquainting us when Condemn'd *valediction 1*

Noted in the Book of Seizures Dec*embe*r 24th 1748

220 **23 December 1748**

CUST 58/149, p. 122

From Wil. Wood (Custom House, London). Hand iii.

Mr Richard Hughes having by his Memorial of the 8th Instant, apply'd to the Commissioners relating to a Butt of *Allowance Wine, on board the Assurance, Inclos'd you will receive Copy of the said Memorial, and You are to Examine into the Allegations therein Contained, & Report a State of the Case to the Board, with Your Opinion, *valediction 2*

Honourable Sirs

I have a Butt of *Allowance wine on board which Your Officers have in their care, I pray the favour that you will give Direction's to the Collector at this Port for the Delivery of it to the Victualling Office here. I am

Honourable Sir's Your most humble Servant

Rd Hughes

Assurance in Portsmouth Harbour
the 8th Dec*ember* 1748

221 **24 December 1748**

CUST 58/149, pp. 122–3

From Sam. Mead, Beaumont Hotham, W. Westby and G. Vaughan (Custom House, London). Hand iii.

Inclos'd You will receive Writts of Delivery for the Enumerated Goods, Returned in Two Indentures of Appraisement from Your Port, and Proclaimed in the Exchequer last Term, The Total amount of which is on the back hereof. We direct You to sell the said Goods Publickly to the highest bidder, putting them up at their Appraised Values, or such other Prices as will be most Advantageous to the King and Officers concerned *valediction 1*

Writt Dated 13th Dec*ember* 1748		£76. 6. 0¾
D° –	13 D° –	65. 14. 9
		£142. 0. 9¾[18]

[17] Correctly '17th'; see no. 215.
[18] See App. I, nos 3, 4.

222
29 December 1748

CUST 58/1

From W. C[ooley] and R. T[urvin] (Custom House, Portsmouth). Hand iii.

Inclos'd is the Deputation & Instruction's &cetera for John Gayton appointed by your Honour's a Tidesman and Boatman at this Port, he having refus'd acceptance thereof, the same is therefore return'd *valediction 4*

223
29 December 1748

CUST 58/1

From W. C[ooley] and R. T[urvin] (Custom House, Portsmouth). Hand iii.

We have your Honour's Order signify'd to us by Mr Wood in his Letter of the 23^d^ Instant, Inclosing Copy of a Memorial from Mr Richd Hughes to Your Honour's, Relating to a Butt of *Allowance wine on board the Assurance man of war, which he requests may be return'd into the Victualling Office at this Port, having agreeable to your ⌜Honour's⌝[19] Order examined into the Allegation's of the said Memorial, We are to acquaint your Honour's there is on board the Assurance, a Butt of *Sower *Allowance wine, belonging to said Hughe's, Purser of the Ship, which we have no objection to the delivery of, in the manner requested, provided it meets with your Honour's approbation, *valediction 5*

224
30 December 1748

CUST 58/149, p. 123

From Wil. Wood (Custom House, London). Hand iii.

Captain Shuldam of his Majesty's Ship Sheerness, having apply'd to the Commissioners, desiring to put his Liquors & China on board a Guard Ship at Your Port, he being removed from the Command of the Sheerness, You may permit his Liquor's and China to be put on board the Hulk under the Seals of Office, and when he is appointed to another Ship, which he acquaints the Commissioners he dayly expects, You are to inform the Board thereof, and whether he is designed for Foreign Service, and you will then receive their further Direction's, in relation to Captain Shuldam's things. *Valediction 2*

225
31 December 1748

CUST 58/149, pp. 123–4

From W. Wood (Custom House, London). Hand iii.

It appearing by a List transmitted from Mr Corbett of the Admiralty Sloop's, Employ'd on the Coast of this ⌜Kingdom⌝[20], that the Porcupine Captain Blanckley is appointed to Cruize between Beachy Head and the Isle of Wight, You and the several Officer's are to keep a Correspondence with Captain Blanckley, and give him an Account from time to time of such Informations that he as well as the Officers of the Custom's may Endeavour to prevent any Frauds, which may be Attempted against this Revenue, *valediction 2*

226
3 January 1748/9

CUST 58/149, p. 124

From W. Levinz ('Sevine'), Sam. Mead, Beaumont Hotham and G. Vaughan (Custom House, London). Hand iii.

We receiv'd your Letter of the 29th Ultimo in return to the Memorial of Mr Richard Hughes Relating to a Butt of *Allowance Wine on Board the Assurance man of War, We agree to Your Delivering the said Wine, to be Return'd into the Victualling Office at Your Port as desired, *valediction 1*

227
4 January 1748/9

CUST 58/149, p. 124

From W. Wood (Custom House, London). Hand iii.

The Commissioner's having directed Mr Sheerer the Collector of Southampton, upon a particular Service, You are to Order the Yatch at Your Port, under the Command of Captain Coomb's, immediately to proceed to Southampton, and the Captain ⌜is on his⌝[21] Arrival there to follow such Order's, as he shall receive from Mr Sheerer *valediction 2*

---

[19] MS. 'Honour'.
[20] MS. 'Kingdon'.
[21] Written over an illegible erasure.

228 CUST 58/1

4 January 1748/9

From W. C[ooley] and R. T[urvin] (Custom House, Portsmouth). Hand iii.

We have here Inclos'd a Schedule of Account's due from this Port, for the Quarter ended Michaelmas last, the same being this day forwarded in a Box directed to your Honour's, by the Waggon of George Clarke, which Inn's at the Whitehart in the Burrough of Southwark on Friday the 6th Instant for Carriage whereof, we have agreed that Two Shillings & six pence shall be paid, *valediction 5*

Portsmouth

A Schedule of Account's due from this Port, for Michaelmas quarter 1748, sent by the Waggon of George Clarke, which will be at the Whitehart, in the Burrough of Southwark on Friday 6th January 1748 vizt

Collectors Quarter Book
Comptrollers – D° –
General Incidents with the Establishment
& three Original Order's –
Nine Debenture's, five Certificates of Damage
& *over Entry
Coal Incidents
One *Portage Bill
Imports & Exports
Wooll bro*ugh*t & carried Coastwise
Civil List Receipt
Repayment of D°
Enumerated Goods
Personal Prosecution's
Preparatory Account of Incidents

31 Reports Inwards
30 Reports Outwards
Journals of the Com*man*d*er* & Mate
of the Greenhill Yatch
D° of the Chief Boatman
at Hayling
R^d Fitchett Deputation
as Tidesman
D° as Coal Meter

229 CUST 58/1

4 January 1748/9

From W. C[ooley] and R. T[urvin] (Custom House, Portsmouth). Hand iii.

In answer to your Honours Order, signify'd to us by Mr Wood in his Letter of the 30th Ultimo We are to acquaint your Honour's the Liquor's & China belonging to Captain Shuldham, late of his Majesty's Ship Sheerness is secur'd under the King's Lock's, and we are to inform your Honour's Captain Shuldam has acquainted the Collector, he is appointed to the Command of his Majesty's Ship Queenborough, which he daily expects from Chatham, and that he is design'd for Foreign Service We therefore shall wait your Honour's further direction's in regard thereto, which when receiv'd shall be duely observ'd *valediction 4*

230 CUST 58/1

6 January 1748/9

From W. C[ooley] and R. T[urvin] (Custom House, Portsmouth). Hand iii.

Herewith we transmit to your Honour's the Abstract for the Month of Dec*embe*r last together with the undermention'd Accounts, to which we beg leave to refer, *valediction 4*

State of Bonds for Christmas Quarter last
Tea & other Goods Enumerated with petty receipts Endors'd
Absent Officer's
Nil List of Bond's
Bounty's on British & Irish Course Linnen, from Christmas 1747 to Christmas 1748

PS From the Book kept in this Office, it appears that the Weights & Beam, Coal & Corn Bushels at this Port were try'd the 9th Ultimo by the Surveyor & Landwaiter's, and that the Stamps for marking Hides, Skin's, Linnen's, Seiz'd Goods & Sail Cloth, are in good and sufficient repair, & fit for the uses design'd

231
7 January
1748/9

CUST 58/1

From W. C[ooley] and R. T[urvin] (Custom House, Portsmouth). Hand iii.

We are to acquaint your Honours last night was drove on shore, at South Sea Beach, within the Limits of this Port, the Ship Over Schie of Delft, Captain Leandert de Bruyn bound for the East Indie's, And there being but little hope's without their immediately unshipping part of her Cargoe, of her ever floating again, We have therefore on the Application of Mr George Huish, the Dutch Agent at this Port, given him Leave to Unship part of the said ship's Cargo; We shou'd not have so Readily granted his request, without an Application first to your Honour's, was not the Ship & Cargoe in the utmost danger of being lost; We therefore hope your Honour's will not otherwise than approve of our Proceeding's, *valediction 3*

232
10 January
1748/9

CUST 58/149, pp. 124–5

From R. Chandler, W. Westby, J. Evelyn and Sam. Mead (Custom House, London). Hand iii.

We receiv'd Your Letter of the 7th Instant, acquainting Us that the over Schie Lendert de Bruyn Master bound for the East Indies, was Stranded at Your Port, & that You have on the Application of Mr Geo: Huish the Dutch Agent, at Your Port, given leave to Unship part of the said Ship's Cargo. We approve thereof, but you are to take care that none of the Goods are Run, or any Embezlement made, and that the Crown be at no Charge for WareHouse Room, Officers attendance or otherwise transmitting Us an Account of what Goods are Landed, *valediction 1*

233
11 January
1748/9

CUST 58/1

From W. C[ooley] and R. T[urvin] (Custom House, Portsmouth). Hand iii.

We beg leave to acquaint your Honour's, on the 10th Instant, arrived at the Motherbank the Ann's, John Dormer from Santa Cruize, And by his Majesty's Order in Council, dated the 18th of June 1747, sent us by your Honour's the 20th of said Month it is directed that all Ship's & Vessel's coming from Santa Cruize, or any other Ports in West Barbary, do make their Quarentine for forty day's, agreeable to the Rules & Instruction's, sent us the 8th & 21st July 1743, We beg leave to acquaint your Honour's, in the absence of the Greenhill Yatch, in the Service of the Custom's at this Port, which at present is attending Mr Sheerer Collector of Southampton by your Order of the 4th Instant, We have given Direction's to the Commander & Mate of the Richmond Cutter, in the Service at Chichester, to attend the Ann's John Dormer from Santa Cruize, and see that shee duely perform's Quarentine, till the Greenhill Yatch shall return; We therefore beg your Honour's will be pleased to send Direction's to the Collector of Chichester, that she may remain here, till your Honour's shall be pleas'd to order the Greenhill Yatch to return to her proper Station; We shou'd have sent Your Honour's the Muster of the Ship's Crew &cetera agreeable to Form, but the Weather ever since her Arrival at the Motherbank has been so bad no Vessel cou'd Attempt going to her, but the first moment the Weather will permit, the Richmond Cutter will proceed to the Motherbank to her, and immediately when we have received the State and Condition's &cetera of the Crew, with all other Particular's the same will be forwarded to your Honour's, We beg to know whether your Honour's are pleas'd we shoud hire a Vessel to attend the Service of Quarentine, in the same manner as was done formerly as it will be impossible the Greenhill Yatch on her return from Southton can strictly attend such Ship's or Vessels, as may arrive from Santa Cruize or any other Ports in West Barbary, as ⌜his⌝[22] whole attendance on that Duty will be detrimental to the Service at this Port, as we have Dayly Ship's of Consequence arrive, which necessarily require his attendance, all which is humbly submitted to your Honours Consideration, *valediction 4*

PS We shou'd not have detained the Richmond Cutter, was it possible any open Boats cou'd attend the Service of Quarentine, but on the contrary we are to assure your Honour's it is quite impracticable

WC RT

---

[22] MS. 'is'.

234
12 January
1748/9

CUST 58/149, p. 125

From W. Wood (Custom House, London). Hand iii.

The Commissioner's direct You to draw out and transmit them as soon as possible, an Account of the Number of Hogsheads and Quantity of Pounds of Tobacco Imported into & Exported from Your Port, with the Neat Amount of the Duty's paid, and Drawback thereon from Christmas 1747 to Christmas 1748 and also an Account of what has been sent Coastwise & to what Ports, for the same time, *valediction 2*

235
12 January
1748/9

CUST 58/149, p. 125

From J. Evelyn, W. Westby, Sam. Mead and W. Levinz ('Sevine') (Custom House, London). Hand iii.

We received Your Letter of the 4th Instant, acquainting Us that the Liquors, and China belonging to Captain Shuldam, late of his Majesty's Ship Sheerness, are Secured under the King's Lock's. We direct You to Report to Us the Quantity & Quality of the said Liquors & China, for our further Orders, *valediction 1*

236
13 January
1748/9

CUST 58/149, p. 126

From J. Evelynn, W. Levinz ('Sevine'), Beaumont Hotham and Edw. Hooper (Custom House, London). Hand iii.

Having granted our Commission for John Allen to be a Tidesman and Boatman at Your Port, in the room of John Gayton, who has Refused to accept of the said Employ, You are to take care he be under Oath & Security for the faithfull Discharge of the said Employ, paying him the like Allowance by Incidents as was paid to his Predecessor, for which the Collector, may take Credit from time to time in his Account of Incidents Referring therein to the Date hereof. *Valediction 1*

237
13 January
1748/9

CUST 58/1

From W. C[ooley] and R. T[urvin] (Custom House, Portsmouth). Hand iii.

Inclos'd we transmit to Your Honour's an Account taken of the Master of Mariner's, belonging to the Ann's from Santa Cruize in Barbary, now performing Quarentine at the Motherbank, to which we beg leave to Refer *valediction 4*

Question's to be put to the Masters of Ship's on their arrival from the Island of Sicily, or other Places in the Mediterranean

		Answers
1st	The Name of the ship or Vessel	The Ann's
2	The Name of the Commander, or other Person having charge of her	Jno Dormer
3	At what Place the Cargoe was taken on board	Santa Cruize in Barbary
4	What Place or Place's the Ship or Vessel touch'd at in her Voyage	None
5	Whether such Place's, or any, and which of them were infected with the Plague	D^o
6	How long such Ship or Vessel has been in her Passage or Voyage –	25 Days Passage
7	How many Person's where on board when the said Ship set Sail –	Ten
8	Whether any & what Person's during the Voyage on board, have been, or now are infected with the Plague, & what number are so	None
9	How many died in the Voyage & of what Distemper –	None
10	What Ship or Vessel's, he or any of his Ship's Company went on board during the Voyage –	None
11	What Person's from other Ship's came on board his, in the Voyage & to what Place such Ship's belong –	None
12	The true contents to the best of his Knowledge,	Bees Wax Almonds, Wooll & Gum

Corn^s Legg

N B You are by the first opportunity, after you have received answer's to the above Questions to transmit the same to the Commissioners

238
14 January
1748/9

CUST 58/149, p. 126–7

From W. Wood (Custom House, London). Hand iii.

Mr Chas Hamilton having by his Memorial of this Date apply'd to the Commissioners Relating to Some Rum & Sugar under Seizure at Your Port Inclosed you will receive Copy of the said Memorial, & you are to Examine into the Allegation's therein Contained, & Report a true State of the Case to the Board ⌜with your Opinion⌝[23], *valediction 2*

Honourable Sir's

I am Gunner of his Majesty's Ship Dragon lately arrived at Portsmouth, from the W*est* Indies, and the Sunderland man of War being then at Portsmouth & bound for Plymouth, where my Family Live, ⌜I⌝[24] inadvertently put 2 Small Cask's q*uantity* in all about Twenty Eight Gallon's Rum into a Boat with a Loaf of Sugar, Part of the Remnant of my Sea Stores, in Order to send it on board the Sunderland to be carried to my Family at Plymouth, and it was seiz'd by Your Honours Officer's, at Portsmouth, and as I had no ill design, not knowing the Necessity of Paying the Duty's of it at Portsmouth, or of getting leave of the Principal Officers of the Port for removing it from Ship to Ship, as it was not to be landed there, I humbly hope Your Honour's will be pleased to consider it, & as it was done thro' Ignorance, that You will be pleased to admit it to an Entry. I am

Your Honour's most Obedient humble Servant

Chas Hamilton

14th Jan*uar*y 1748

239
14 January
1748/9

CUST 58/1

From W. C[ooley] and R. T[urvin] (Custom House, Portsmouth). Hand iii.

Inclos'd we transmit your Honour's the Account of the Muster's of the Passenger's & Mariner's on board the Ann's now under Quarentine at this Port, as taken by Cornelius Leg, Mate of the Richmond Cutter, to which we beg leave to Refer *valediction 4*

240
14 January
1748/9

CUST 58/1

From W. C[ooley] and R. T[urvin] (Custom House, Portsmouth). Hand iii.

In obedience to Your Honour's Commands, signified to us by Mr Wood in his Letter of the 12th Instant, Inclos'd we transmit your Honour's an Account of the Number of Hogsheads & quantity of Pounds of Tobacco Imported into, and Exported from this Port, with the neat amount of the Duty's paid & Drawback thereon from Christmas 1747 to Christmas 1748, And also an Account of what has been sent Coastwise, & to what Ports for the same time, to which we beg leave to refer *valediction 4*

Portsmouth

An Account of the Number of hogshead's & Quantity of Pounds of Tobacco, Imported into & Exported from this Port, with the neat amount of the Duty paid, & Drawback thereon, as also what has been sent Coastwise, and to what Ports, from Christmas 1747 to Christmas 1748

Imported			Exported			Sent Coastwise		
N^{o} of hogsheads	lib's	Neat Amount of the Duty paid	N^{o} of hogsheads	lb's	Neat Amount of the Duty Repaid	N^{o} of hogsheads	Lib's	To what Port's
2	1700	39 14 4½	Cask's 2	1180	Duty Inwards & Drawback paid at London	Nil		

Custom House dated 14th Jan*uar*y 1748

[23] Added.
[24] MS. 'I I'.

241 CUST 58/1
14 January 1748/9

From W. C[ooley] and R. T[urvin] (Custom House, Portsmouth). Hand iii.

Agreeable to your Honour's Order of the 10th of November last, Inclos'd we transmit your Honour's a Certificate signed by the proper Officer's whereby it will appear there has been reshipt on board the Tuscany, which run on shore near Margate, brought from thence in a Vessel by your Honour's Permission, five hundred & sixty nine Bags Containing Two hundred & Seventy five Quarters & five bushel's of Wheat & one hundred & thirty five barrel's Containing Sixty seven quarters & four bush*els* Wheaten Flour, on Account of Mr John Waters, to which Certificate we beg leave to refer, *valediction 3*

Portsmouth

These are to Certify that in Pursuance of a Sufferance under the hands of the Collector Deputy Customer & Deputy Comptroller of this Port, unto us directed bearing date the 31st of December last, We have attended at Spithead, & that in our presence on the 7th & 9th instant the Corn and Wheaten Flour undermentioned was unshipt out of the Ramsgate. John Bayly Master from Sandwich & put on board the Tuscany Saml Webster Master for the Streights, vizt

Five hundred sixty nine bag's Containing Two hundred & Seventy five quarters & five bushels of Wheat, winton mea*sur*e One hundred & thirty five barrels, Containing Sixty seven quarters four bushels of Wheaten Flour winton measure mention'd to be on Account of Mr John Water's, Custom House Certify'd 14th Jan*uar*y 1748

242 CUST 58/149, pp. 127–8
17 January 1748/9

From Wil. Wood (Custom House, London). Hand iii.

The Commissioner's having received Information, that it has been a Practice when Officers of the Custom's, have been permitted to exchange Places, or Resign their Employments, for the Person appointed to succeed thereto, to give the Person who exchanged or Resign'd a Consideration in Money, or to allow them part of the Salary annex'd to such Employ, which Practice is highly detrimental to the Publick Service, & is a great Temptation for the Officer who gives the same, to be Unfaithfull or Negligent, in the Execution of his Office, in order to put a Stop thereto, for the future, the Commissioners direct you to take care, that when any Officers exchange Places, or are permitted to Resign their Employments, that you require such Person's to make Oath, That they have not given, nor will give directly, or indirectly, any Money, Gratuity, or pecuniary Consideration to any Person or Persons whatsoever, for such Appointment, Agreeable to the Practice, in this Port, and you are not to Admit such Person's to their Duty, till you have transmitted such Affidavit to the Commissioner's & received their Direction's thereon, *valediction 2*

243 CUST 58/149, p. 128
19 January 1748/9

From Wil. Wood (Custom House, London). Hand iii.

The Commissioner's received Your Letter of the 11th Instant, acquainting them with the Arival of the Ann's John Dormer Master from Santa Cruize, in West Barbary, and desiring to know whether you may hire a Vessel to attend the said Ship, in the Motherbank, during the time of Performing her Quarentine, I am directed to acquaint you that as the Greenhill Yatch in the Service at Your Port, now attending Mr Sheerer Collector of Southampton, will very soon return to her Station, there is no occasion to hire another Vessel, as proposed by you, *valediction 2*

244 CUST 58/1
19 January 1748/9

From W. C[ooley] and R. T[urvin] (Custom House, Portsmouth). Hand iii.

Inclos'd we transmit your Honour's the Account of the Muster's of the Passenger's, and Mariner's, on board the Ann's, now under Quarentine at this Port, as taken by Captain Coombs Commander of the Greenhill Yatch, to which we beg leave to refer *valediction 4*

245
20 January
1748/9

CUST 58/1

From W. C[ooley] and R. T[urvin] (Custom House, Portsmouth). Hand iii.

Inclos'd we transmit your Honour's agreeable to your Order of the 12th Instant, an Account of the Quantity & Quality of Liquor's belonging to Captn Shuldham, late of his Majesty's Ship Sheerness, under the King's Lock's, to which we beg leave to refer, *valediction 3*

P.S./ We beg leave to acquaint your Honour's, Capt Shuldam has no China as mentioned in our Letter of the 4th Instant,

In the WareHouse. Landed out of the Sheerness man of war belonging to Captain Shuldam

Examined 7 Hamper's as under

N° 1 –	1 Hamper *quantity*	4 Dozen bottles Corsica wine
2 –	1 D^{o}	{ 2 D^{o} – *Arrack 2 D^{o} – & 9 bottles Levant wine
4 –	1 D^{o} –	4 D^{o} & $^{1}/_{2}$ Corsica wine
3 –	1 D^{o} –	4 D^{o} & $^{1}/_{2}$ Spanish wine
5 –	1 D^{o} –	4 D^{o} – Mahone wine
6 –	1 D^{o} –	4 D^{o} –
7 –	1 D^{o}	{ 1 Dozen & 10 Bottles Rum 10 bottles Streights Wine

1 hogshead Spanish wine
1 hogshead Rum

Chas Markland Surv*eyo*r
Thos Merritt

Portsmouth 17th Jan*uary* 1748

246
21 January
1748/9

CUST 58/1 [25]

From W. C[ooley] and R. T[urvin] (Custom House, Portsmouth). Hand iii.

We have your Honour's Order signify'd to us by Mr Wood, in his Letter of the 14th Instant inclosing Copy of a Memorial from Mr Chas Hamilton relating to some Rum & Sugar, under Seizure at this Port, And by your Honour's Order, we are directed to examine into the Allegation's thereincontain'd & Report a State of the Case with our opinion; – Having call'd on the Officer who made the Seizure, Inclosed we transmit your Honour's his answer, which we believe to be just & true, & as such is humbly submitted to your consideration; We beg leave to acquaint your Honour's an Account of this Seizure was transmitted to your Honour's in our joint Letter bearing date the 3 Dec*embe*r last, in the usual Form, & by your Order of the 22^{d} of said Month we were directed to Prosecute the Goods to Condemnation *valediction 5*

Sir

You having been pleased to communicate to me Mr Secretary Wood's Letter bearing date the 14th Instant, inclosing a Memorial of Mr Chas Hamilton, Gunner of his Majesty's Ship the Dragon, lately arriv'd at Spithead, from the W*es*t Indies, wherein the said Hamilton pray's leave of the Honourable the Commissioner's, to admit to an Entry, Two Cask's of Rum & one loaf of Sugar, Seiz'd by me, alledging that he unshipt the same inadvertently & thro' Ignorance, in answer to which Memorial I humbly beg leave to acquaint you, that being place'd as a Guard, on board the Dragon, on the 24th of Nov*embe*r last Mr Hamilton took an Opportunity, to put out of the Port Hole's into a Wherry then lying along side the said Ship, in a private & Clandestine manner, Two Cask's Containing about Twenty three Gall*ons* of Rum, & one Loaf weighing thirty seven Pounds Sugar which was cover'd & Secreted in the said Boat in a very artfull manner, & even without the Privity or consent of the Waterman, in order to have been carried on board the Sunderland by the Gunner of the said Ship if I had not luckily Suspected that there was something more on the said Wherry than what ought to be, whereupon I immediately ⌜stept⌝[26] into her & finding the Goods above mention'd with the utmost difficulty I made a Seizure thereof which I cou'd not have done, had not the first Lieu*tenan*t of the Dragon by the Captain's Order's given me his Assistance being strongly oppos'd,

---

[25] The enclosure precedes the letter in MS.
[26] MS. 'sept'.

both by the Gunner of the Sunderland & M[r] Hamilton, the latter of which Order'd his People to step into the Boat & by force to rescue the said Seizure from me, but finding that he coud not effect the same owing to the kind Interposition of the Lieutenant, he then Denounced Vengeance upon me whenever he met me on shore; I therefore humbly submit it to your Consideration whether this Gentlemen can reasonably hope for any Indulgence from the Honourable Board, after such unwarrantable behaviour, & committing a Fraud, which there is not the least appearance of being done either thro' Inadvertency or Ignorance, but with a downright Intention of Defrauding his Majesty of his Duty's, As I humbly apprehend I have done my Duty, so I hope I shall be supported in my Legall Seizure, With great regard I am

Sirs &cetera

W[m] Brown

Portsm[o]
20th Jan*uary* 1748
To the Collector & Comptroller

247
21 January
1748/9

CUST 58/1

From W. C[ooley] and R. T[urvin] (Custom House, Portsmouth). Hand iii.

Inclosed we transmit your Honour's agreeable to your Order of the 10th of November last, a Certificate whereby it will appear there has been reshipt on board the Tuscany at this Port, under care of the proper Officer's, Sixty five Cask's Containing Thirty two Quarters & four bushel's Wheaten Flour, said to be on Account of M[r] John Waters, to which Certificate we beg leave to Refer, *valediction 3*

Portsmouth

These are to Certify that in pursuance of a Sufferance, under the hands of the Collector, Deputy Customer & Deputy Comptroller of this Port, unto us directed, bearing date the 18th Instant, We have attended at Spithead, & that on the 18th & 19th of this present Month, was unship'd out of the Sloop call'd the Isle of Wight, Edw[d] Jarvis Master from Sandwich & put on board the Ship Tuscany, Cap[t] Samuel Webster Com*mander* for the Streights viz[t]

Sixty five Cask's Containing Thirty two Quarter's and four bushel's of Wheaten Flour winton measure said to be on Account of M[r] John Water's Custom House Certify'd the 20th January 1748

Cha[s] Markland Surv*eyo*r
Rob[t] Alexander, Deputy Sea*rche*r &
Assistant Landwaiter

248
21 January
1748/9

CUST 58/1

From W. C[ooley] and R. T[urvin] (Custom House, Portsmouth). Hand iii.

Inclos'd we transmit your Honour's two Accounts viz[t] of Goods Enumerated, & Goods not Enumerated, lately Seiz'd by the Officer's of the Custom's in this Port, to w*hi*ch we beg leave to refer *valediction 4*

249
24 January
1748/9

CUST 58/1

From W. C[ooley] and R. T[urvin] (Custom House, Portsmouth). Hand iii.

Inclos'd we transmit your Hon*our*s the Account of the Musters of the Passenger's & Mariner's on board the Ann's now under Quarentine at this Port, as taken by Captain Coombs of the Greenhill Yatch, to which we beg leave to refer *valediction 4*

250
26 January
1748/9

CUST 58/149, p. 129

From Wil. Wood (Custom House, London). Hand iii.

You are immediately on receipt hereof to draw out and transmit to the Board An Account of all Tobacco Bonds, Standing out at Your Port, (Exclusive of those that have been, or are in Process, or Older then three Years) with the Names of the Principal's, and the Security's, the Dates of the Bonds, and the Amount of the Duty's for which they are given, as also such Sum's as have been Discharged by Endorsement, on any of the said Bonds, either by Drawback, or Payments, in Money according to the Underwritten Form, *valediction 2*

Date of the Bond	Principals Names	Securitys Names	Amount of the Duty's for which the Bonds are given –	How much has been Discharged of the said Bonds To Distinguish whether in Money or by Debentures –

251
26 January 1748/9

CUST 58/149, p. 129–30

From R. Chandlor, Sam. Mead, Beaumont Hotham and G. Vaughan (Custom House, London). Hand iii.

We receivd Your Letter's of the 14th & 21st Instant, transmitting the proper Officers Certificate's of ⌜the⌝[27] Wheat and Wheaten Flower Reshipt on Board the Tuscany which run on Shore near Margate, and it appearing that there has been Ten Bags of Wheat Reshipt at Your Port, more than the Officer's at Margate, have Certify'd to be taken out of the said Ship, We direct You to call upon the Officer's, and order them to examine the Bag's, and be very exact as to the Number they saw Shipt, and transmit Us a Certificate thereof, *valediction 1*

252
28 January 1748/9

CUST 58/149, p. 130

From Beaumont Hotham, Sam. Mead and G. Vaughan (Custom House, London). Hand iii.

Our Solliciter having acquainted us that there is a Trial to come on this Term upon a Seizure of Brandy in Cask's, under Sixty gallon's, made by William Baskerville Tidesurveyor, We direct you to send up William May, and Foster Perry Tidesman at Your Port, who are the Witnesses, and take care they be here, and Attend our Solliciter by the 9th Febr*uary* next, without fail.

We receiv'd Your Letter of the 21st Instant in return to the Memorial of Mr Chas Hamilton relating to Some Rum & Sugar, under Seizure, at Your Port, and it appearing that the said Goods were run, You are to go on with the Prosecution thereof agreeable to our Order's of the 22^{d} Ultimo *valediction 1*

253
28 January 1748/9

CUST 58/1

From W. C[ooley] and R. T[urvin] (Custom House, Portsmouth). Hand iii.

In obedience to your Honour's Order signified to us by Mr Wood in his Letter of the 26th Instant, We have here Inclos'd, an Account of all Tobacco Bonds standing out at this Port, exclusive of those that have been, or are in Process, or older than three Year's, to which we beg leave to refer *valediction 3*

Portsmouth. An Account of all Tobacco Bond's, standing out at this Port, exclusive of those that have been, or are in Process, or Older than three Year's –

Date of Bonds	Principal's Names	Security's Names	Amount of the Duty's for which the ⌜Bonds⌝[28] are given	How much has been discharged of the said Bonds
– Nil[29] –				

Custom House Dated 28th Jan*uary* 1748

254
28 January 1748/9

CUST 58/1

From W. C[ooley] and R. T[urvin] (Custom House, Portsmouth). Hand iii.

Inclos'd we transmit your Honour's the Account, of the Muster's of the Passenger's & Mariner's, on board the Ann's, now under Quarentine, at this Port, as taken by $Capt^{n}$ Coombs of the Greenhill Yatch, to which we beg leave to refer *valediction 4*

255
28 January 1748/9

CUST 58/1

From W. C[ooley] and R. T[urvin] (Custom House, Portsmouth). Hand iii.

Inclos'd we transmit your Honour's a Plantation Certificate for the Ship Elizabeth of $Portsm^{o}$ Robt Cleeve Master for Boston in N*ew* England, which when Perfected we desire may be return'd *valediction 4*

---

[27] Inserted.
[28] MS. 'Bond'.
[29] Written across all the columns.

256 **31 January 1748/9**

CUST 58/149, pp. 130–1

From Beaumont Hotham, W. Levinz ('Sevine'), J. Evelyn and Edw. Hooper (Custom House, London). Hand iii.

We receivd your Letter of the 20th Instant transmitting an Account of the Quantity and Quality of Liquors belonging to Captain Shuldam late of his Majesty's Ship Sheerness, under the Kings Locks, We agree to Your Delivering ⌜the⌝[30] said Liquors upon the Duty's being paid for the same.

In Answer to the Account of Seizures transmitted in Your Letter of the 21st Instant, We direct You to Prosecute the Enumerated Goods to Condemnation, in the Exchequer, at the King's Charge, and we have no objection to the Officer's Prosecuting the rest of the Goods, in like manner at their own Charge Corresponding with our Sollicitor & the Register of Seizures. *Valediction 1*

257 **31 January 1748/9**

CUST 58/1

From W. C[ooley] and R. T[urvin] (Custom House, Portsmouth). Hand iii.

Inclos'd we transmit your Honour's the Account of the Muster's of the Passenger's & Mariner's on board the Ann's, now under Quarentine at this Port, as taken by Captain Coombs of the Greenhill Yatch, to which we beg leave to refer, *valediction 4*

258 **31 January 1748/9**

CUST 58/1

From W. C[ooley] and R. T[urvin] (Custom House, Portsmouth). Hand iii.

We received your Honour's Letter of the 26th Instant, in which you observe to us that by the Certificates transmitted 14th & 21st Instant it appears there has been Reshipt on board the Tuscany, which lately run on shore at Margate, ten bag's of Wheat, more than the Officer's at Margate have Certify'd to be taken out of the said Ship, and by your Honour's Order, we are directed to call upon the Officer's, & order them to examine the Bag's & to be very exact as to the number they saw shipt, and transmit your Honour's a Certificate thereof, In obedience thereto we immediately call'd on the Officer's from whom we have receiv'd the inclos'd Particular Account, which appear's to us to be very just & true, to which we beg leave to refer your Honour's, *valediction 3*

Gentlemen,

You having communicated to us a Letter from the Honourable the Commissioners bearing date the 26th Instant wherein their Honour's are pleas'd to observe, that by our Certificate dated the 14th, it appear's that there has been ten bags of Wheat Reshipt at this Port on board the Tuscany which run on shore near Margate, more than the Officer's at Margate have Certify'd to be taken out of the said Ship, We beg leave to give you for answer thereto, vizt that in obedience to the Honourable Boards Commands dated the 10th Nov*embe*r last we both attended at Spithead on the 7th & 9th Instant being properly Assisted with a Sworn Meter, with a Standart Bushel & round *strike, in order to take an Account of the number & try the measure of the Bags of Wheat, which were allowed to be unshipt out of the Ramsgate Sloop John Baylay Master from Sandwich & put on board the Tuscany aforesaid Samuel Webster Master for the Streights, and as the Account was not only taken by us, but likewise cheque Tally's of the number of Bags kept by a Mate & ⌜the⌝[31] Boatswain of the said Ship, in which we all agree, vizt that the same amounted to five hundred, sixty eight full, & two *Ullage's, each Containing near two Bushels, amounting in the whole, to Five hundred sixty nine bag's, so there is not the least probability of any mistake, being made by us, & as a further Proof of our being right in this Account, pleas'd to be refer'd to the *Transcire Bro*ugh*t by Bayly from Sandwich dated the 23d of November last, granted in the name of Robt Brooke, sign'd by Wm Jorden for the Collector, the Deputy Cust*omer* & Deputy Comptroller, vizt for five hundred Sixty eight bags of Wheat, Certify'd to be ship'd at Sandwich by Wm Hewett, & this only differ's from our Account one bag, which is occasion'd by the *Ulage's as above observ'd, which Bayly had intended as he himself acknowledg'd to keep for his own use, ⌜thinking⌝[32] that they might be overlook'd by the Officer's

---

[30] MS. 'the the'.
[31] Altered from 'a'.
[32] Inserted.

In Case any Doubt had remain'd with us in regard to the number of Bag's Reshipt, of which we are quite Satisfy'd it wou'd have been entirely out of our Power, to have made a Retrospection, because the Tuscany was Sail'd from Spithead, before their Honour's Order abovemention'd was communicated to u's

On this occasion we have only further to observe that we have discharged our Duty's with the utmost care & exactness in our Power, that the Number of Bag's of Wheat mentioned in our Certificate dated the 14th Instant being five hundred, sixty nine, is the just & true number transhipt at this Port from the Ramsgate Sloop, into the Ship Tuscany the Contents whereof upon the nearest Computation we cou'd possibly make, being Two hundred, Seventy five Quarters five bushel's – vizt Short mea*sure* upon each bag one Gallon, now supposing the Number had been 558 Bagg's at 4 bus*hels* Each

	Quarters	bus*hels*
the *Quanti*ty woud have been	279.	0
The *Quanti*ty Reshipt & Certify'd by us for the Bounty is only	275.	5
vizt less	3.	3

With due respect we are Gentlemen Your most humble Servants
Chas Markland Surv*eyo*r
Rob' Alexander Deputy Sea*rcher* & Ass*istant* Landwaiter

Custom House Portsm^o 31st Jan*uary* 1748
To the Collector & Comptroller

259
2 February 1748/9

CUST 58/1

From W. C[ooley] and R. T[urvin] (Custom House, Portsmouth). Hand iii.

Inclos'd we transmit to your Honour's an Account of Seizures lately made by the Officer's of the Custom's, in this Port, to which we beg leave to refer *valediction 4*

260
3 February 1748/9

CUST 58/149, p. 131

From Beaumont Hotham, Sam. Mead, R. Chandlor and G. Vaughan (Custom House, London). Hand iii.

Mr Farrar having apply'd to us by his Memorial of this date, desiring that the Wheat on Board, the Shoreham *Snow James Boyd Com*mander* may be relanded, the Ship having receiv'd so much Damage, that she is not Able to proceed on her Voyage, We agree thereto, under the care of the proper Officer's, taking care there be no Embezlement[s] and that the Crown be at no Expence, and you are to Report to us the Quantity relanded & reshipped, *valediction 1*

261
4 February 1748/9

CUST 58/149, pp. 131–2

From Beaumont Hotham, Sam. Mead, R. Chandler and G. Vaughan (Custom House, London). Hand iii.

Mr John Waters having by his Memorial of the 3^d Instant apply'd to Us, desiring that the 515 Quarters of Wheat on board the Valencia Pacquet Gabriel Black Master, which has received Damage, may be Relanded, Inclosed we send you Copy of the said Memorial, and if there is an absolute Necessity, and the Case be as Represented you may permit the Wheat to be landed as desired under the care of the proper Officer's, taking care that no part of the Cargo be Embezled, and that the Crown be at no Charge for WareHouse room, Officers attendance, or otherwise, and you are to measure the Quantity of Corn relanded, & Reshipped, & Certify the same to us, having in the mean time ordered the Debenture to be Stopt, *valediction 1*

May it please Your Honours

The Petition of Jno Water's of London Cornfacture Humbly Sheweth That 28th January past the Valencia Pacquet Gabriel Black Master, Wheat Loaden met with a Gale of Wind in the Channel, that has greatly Damaged the Ship, and I apprehend the Cargo has likewise received Damage, by a Quan*tit*y of Water Ship'd, said Ship is put into Portsmouth Harbour, to Refit, & as the Cargoe's proceeding on without its being Examined might occasion a Total Loss, Your Petitioner prays your Honours will grant him Leave to take out into Lighter's, or otherwise that shall be found Necessary, either in Part or the whole, under Inspection of your Officers that same may be searched into & reshipt again & the Ship proceed on her intended Voyage, I am *wi*th great respect

Your Honour's most Obedient Servant

John Waters

London 3^{d} Febr*uary* 1748

In margin: 515 Quarters

262
7 February 1748/9

CUST 58/149, p. 133

From W. Wood (Custom House, London). Hand iii.

The Account of the Bounties paid on the Exportation of British & Irish Course Linnen Exported from Your Port, from Christmas 1747 to Christmas 1748 wanting some Explanation, The Commissioner's direct you to draw out and transmit them by the Return of the Post, if Possible, an Account according to the Enclosed Form, in order to be laid before the Parliament, *valediction 2*

263
7 February 1748/9

CUST 58/1

From W. C[ooley] and R. T[urvin] (Custom House, Portsmouth). Hand iii.

Inclosed we transmit your Honour's an Account of Goods Enumerated, & Goods not Enumerat'd lately Seiz'd by the Officer's in this Port, to which we beg leave to refer, *valediction 4*

264
9 February 1748/9

CUST 58/1

From W. C[ooley] and R. T[urvin] (Custom House, Portsmouth). Hand iii.

Agreeable to Your Honour's Order, signify'd to us, by Mr Wood in his Letter of the 7th Instant We have here Inclos'd an Account of the Bounty's paid on the Exportation of Brit*ish* & Irish Coarse Linnen's, from Christmas 1747 to Christmas 1748, according to the Form sent us in Mr Woods said Letter, to which we beg leave to refer, *valediction 3*

An Account of the Bountie's paid on the Exportation of British and Irish Coarse Linnen's from Christmas 1747 to Christmas 1748

British Linnen				Irish Linnen				
Value under 5 Per Yard	Value 5$^{d'}$ & under 6$^{d'}$ Per Yard	Value 6 & under 12$^{d'}$ Per Yard	Value 12$^{d'}$ & not exceeding 1^{s}.6^{d} Per Yard	Value under 5^{d} Per Yard	Value 5$^{d'}$& under 6$^{d'}$ Per Y'd	Value 6$^{d'}$ & under 12$^{d'}$ Per Y'd	Value 12 & not exceeding 1^{s}.6^{d} Per Y'd	Bounty
Yards	Y'ds	Yds	Yds	Yds	Yds	Yds	Yds	£ s d
Portsmouth								
Nil	Nil	Nil	Nil	Nil	Nil	Nil	420	2 12 6

265
10 February 1748/9

CUST 58/1

From W. C[ooley] and R. T[urvin] (Custom House, Portsmouth). Hand iii.

Inclos'd we transmit your Honour's the Account of the Muster's of the Passenger's & Mariner's on board the Ann's now under Quarentine at this Port, as taken by Captain Coombs of the Greenhill Yatch to which we beg leave to refer *valediction 4*

266
10 February 1748/9

CUST 58/1

From W. C[ooley] and R. T[urvin] (Custom House, Portsmouth). Hand iii.

Herewith we transmit to your Honour's the Abstract, for the Month of January last, together with the undermention'd Accounts, to which we beg leave to refer *valediction 4*

Nil List of Bonds

Tea & other Goods Enumerated with petty receipts Endors'd

Absent Officer's

PS From the Book kept in this Office it appear's that the Coal & Corn bushels at this Port, were try'd the 4th Ultimo by the Surveyor & Landwaiters & that they found the same to be exact & true, & that the stamp's for marking Hide's, Skin's, Linnen's, Seiz'd Goods & Sail Cloth, are in good & sufficient repair, But the Beam's & one Pair of Scales, being very much worn, are not fit for the use's design'd

267 CUST 58/1

11 February 1748/9

From W. C[ooley] and R. T[urvin] (Custom House, Portsmouth). Hand iii.

Inclos'd we transmit your Hon*our*s an Account of such Stationary Ware's, as was lately sent for the use of this Port which was receiv'd the 9th Instant. *Valediction 5*

2 Leidger's Inwards for Collector & Comptroller
2 Quire *Imperial
3 Rheam's fine *pott
2 Book's for Entering Letter's from the Board –
1 Sufferance Book
1 Book for monthly Accounts of Absent officer's –
1 Book to enter Account of Seizures
1 Incident Book for the Comptroller
80 Blue Books 4 Leave's
50 – 2 Leaves
60 – 6 Leaves
40 – 8 Leaves
30 – 10:12 Leaves
20 – 14 Leave's
12 – 16:20:24 Leaves
1/2 Pound *Pounce
1 Quart red Ink
3000 Wafer's

2 Petty Receipt Books
2 Quires *Boarding's
1 Report Book Outwards
2 Quire D^{o} in Sheets
1 Quire D^{o} Inw*ar*ds
1 Quire Coal Warrants

4 Quire Quarter Book Pap[er] Inwards –
4 Reams 2^{d} *Pott
6 Quire *Demy Cutt
3 Quire D^{o} uncutt
1 Coast Book Inwards
1 D^{o} – Outwards
1 Ship's Entry Book
1 Ship's Register Book
1 Book for Ship's Inwards &cetera –
1 Book for Indentures of Appraisement –
2 Doz*en* *Demy Pockett B*oo*k's
3 Ivory Penknive's
3 *Pounce Boxe's
1 Dozen Pencill's
3 Bodkin's
1 Dozen Tape
3 Bags Sand
1 Pound Wax
2 Gallon's Ink
1000 Quills
12 Paistboard files
2 Books 1 Quire *Demy each
⌜3 Quire's *Demy ⌜*V*at* B*lued*⌝[33]⌝[34]

268 CUST 58/1

13 February 1748/9

From W. C[ooley] and R. T[urvin] (Custom House, Portsmouth). Hand iii.

Inclosed we transmit your Honour's the Account of the Muster's of the Passenger's & Mariner's on board the Ann's, now under Quarentine as taken by Captain Coomb's of the Greenhill Yatch, to which we beg leave to refer *valediction 4*

269 CUST 58/1

13 February 1748/9

From W. C[ooley] and R. T[urvin] (Custom House, Portsmouth). Hand iii.

Agreeable to your Honour's Order sent us the 3^{d} Instant, inclos'd we transmit your Honour's an Account taken by the proper Officer's of the Quantity of Wheat, unship'd & reshipt on board the Shoreham *Snow, Ja^{s} Boyd Master for Lisbon, to which Account we beg leave to Refer your Honour's *valediction 3*

Portsmouth

These are to Certify that in pursuance of a Sufferance under the hands of the Collector, Deputy Customer & Deputy Comptroller of this Port unto us directed bearing date the 5th Instant, We have attended in the Harbour on board the Shoreham *Snow, James Boyd Master from Shoreham, bound for Lisbon, laden with Wheat, & that in our presence on the 6th Instant, there were unship'd from the said *Snow, & put on board the John & Grace Hoy John Alley Master lying alongside, One hundred & sixty bag's Containing Eighty Quarters Wheat winton mea*sure* being all Dry, Sound, & Merchantable Corn;

33 Or, possibly, '*Vellum Bound*'.

34 Added.

That on the 7th Instant, there were Landed out of the said *Snow, One hundred & nine bag's Containing upon a strict Admeasurement, Fifty three Quarters seven bushel's & a half of Damaged Wheat

That on the 9th & 10th Instant, the hundred & sixty Bag's of Sound Wheat, put on board the John & Grace Hoy, as also One hundred & nine bag's Containing fifty four Quarters four bushel's of Sound, Dry & Merchantable Wheat, in lieu of the like Number of Bag's of Damag'd Wheat, found to contain only fifty three Quarters seven bushels & a half, were Reshipp'd on board the abovementioned *Snow, vizt the Shoreham James Boy'd Master for Lisbon, Custom House Certify'd 11th February 1748

Chas Markland Surv*eyo*r
Robt Alexander Deputy Sea*rche*r &
Ass*istant* Landwaiter

N B/ The number of Bag's of Damag'd Wheat landed being 109 shoud have Cont*aine*d 54 Quarters. 4 bus*hels* tho' they only Contained 53. 7½ vizt short 4½ bus*hels* which short mea*sure* was made up by shiping 109 bags each Containing 4 bushels making in the whole 54 Qu*arter*s. 4 bus*hels* Winton measure

270
15 February 1748/9

CUST 58/149, p. 133

From W. Wood (Custom House, London). Hand iii.

The Commissioners receiv'd your Letter of the 10th Instant, acquainting them that the Beams & one Pair of Scales, are very much worn & not fit for the uses ⌜design'd⌝[35], if there are others wanting You are to Report to the Board the Sizes of the Beams & Scales, that they may be provided here & sent you, *valediction 2*

271
16 February 1748/9

CUST 58/149, pp. 133–4

From G. Vaughan, J. Evelyn and W. Levinz ('Sevine') (Custom House, London). Hand iii.

In answer to the Account of Seizure's transmitted in Your Letter of the 2^d & 7th Instant We direct you to Prosecute the Enumerated Goods which were run, to Condemnation, before the Justices of the Peace, and the rest in the Exchequer at the Kings charge, and we have no Objection to the Officer's Prosecuting the Boat & *Matts before the Justices of the Peace at their own Charge, acquainting Us when Condemned, *valediction 1*

Noted the 18th Febr*uary* 1748

272
16 February 1748/9

CUST 58/1

From W. C[ooley] and R. T[urvin] (Custom House, Portsmouth). Hand iii.

Inclos'd we transmit your Honour's, the Account of Goods Enumerated lately Seiz'd by the Officer's at this Port, to which we beg leave to refer *valediction 4*

273
16[36] February 1748/9

CUST 58/1

From W. C[ooley] and R. T[urvin] (Custom House, Portsmouth). Hand iii.

Inclos'd we transmit your Honour's the Account of the Muster's, of the Passenger's & Mariners on board the Anns now under Quarentine at this Port, as taken by Captain Coombs of the Greenhill Yatch, to which we beg leave to refer, *valediction 4*

274
18 February 1748/9

CUST 58/1

From W. C[ooley] and R. T[urvin] (Custom House, Portsmouth). Hand iii.

Inclos'd we transmit your Honour's the Size's of the Beam's, & Scale's &cetera, wanting for the Service of this Port, as received from the Surveyor, and Landwaiter's, of which there is great need of, as likewise a new Sett of Gauging Instruments, & several Brass Standart Weights, all which we beg to be supply'd with *valediction 5*

---

35 Inserted.

36 MS. '26th'. This is clearly incorrect, as the quarantine was over by 21 Feb. (no. 277); from the position of the letter in the MS., between nos 272 and 274, it is likely that 16 Feb. is the correct date.

Gentlemen

You having been pleased to communicat to us a Letter from M[r] Secretary Wood, dated the 15th Instant, wherein it is directed that the Size's of the Beam's and Scale's wanting for the Service at this Port, shoud be reported to the Honourable the Commissioner's in order that the same may be provided at London – In obedience to their Honour's said Commands, We humbly report viz[t] that there are wanting

A Small Scale Beam, Two feet six Inche's long with Scale's and Scale Rope's, proper for the same

Another Scale Beam, five feet in length with Scale's two feet & a half wide & Scale Ropes

Beside's which there are likewise wanting a new sett of Gauging Instruments, as likewise the Brass Standart Weight's, undermention'd, with all which we beg to be immediately Supply'd & are with due respect's

Gentlemen Your most humble Servants

Cha[s] Markland Surv*eyo*r
Tho[s] Whitehorne }
Edw[d] Skeat } Landwaiters
Tho[s] Merritt }
Rob[t] Alexander Ass*istan*t D[o] & Deputy Sea*rche*r

Custom House Portsm[o] 17th Febr*uary* 1748

Weights
One half hundred
One quarter of hundred
One fourteen Pound
One Seven Pound
One four Pound
One two Pound
One one Pound

275
18 February
1748/9

CUST 58/1

From W. C[ooley] and R. T[urvin] (Custom House, Portsmouth). Hand iii.

Inclosed we transmit your Honour's the Account of the Muster's of the Passenger's and Mariner's on board the Ann's, now under Quarentine at this Port, as taken by Captain Coomb's of the Greenhill Yatch, to which we beg leave to refer *valediction 4*

276
21 February
1748/9

CUST 58/149, p. 134

From W. Wood (Custom House, London). Hand iii.

The Commissioners direct you to Draw out & transmit to them without Loss of Time, an Account of such Frauds relating to Tobacco, as have come to ⌜Your⌝[37] knowledge, committed either in the Importation, Exportation, relanding, or carrying Coastwise, or by Land in great Britain since Christmas 1732. *Valediction 2*

277
21 February
1748/9

CUST 58/1

From W. C[ooley] and R. T[urvin] (Custom House, Portsmouth). Hand iii.

Inclosed we transmit to your Honou[r's] the dayly Muster, of the Master, Passenger's, and Mariner's, on board the Ann's *Snow, lately under Quarentine, at the Motherbank, and having perform'd the same, for the space of forty day's, We have here Inclos'd a Certificate, under the hand of Charle's Coomb's Commander of the Greenhill Yatch, in the Service at this Port, together with an Oath taken this day, by the Master, Mate & Boatswain, belonging to the said Ship, by which it appear's, that the said Vessel, & every Person on board the same are free from Infection, of any kind whatsoever, *valediction 3*

P.S/ The above ship, being bound for London, in a few day's, intend's to proceed to Stangate Creek, in order to air her Good's, when she does, will take care, to acquaint your Honour's therewith

37 Altered from 'our'.

278
24 February
1748/9

CUST 58/1

From W. C[ooley] and R. T[urvin] (Custom House, Portsmouth). Hand iii.

Inclosed we transmit your Honour['s] the Account of Good's Enumerated, lately Seiz'd by the Officer's at this Port, to which we beg leave to refer *valediction 4*

279
25 February
1748/9

CUST 58/149, p. 134

From W. Levinz ('Sevine'), Edw. Hooper, J. Evelyn and G. Vaughan (Custom House, London). Hand iii.

In answer to the Account of Seizure's transmitted in Your Letter of the 16th Instant We direct you to Prosecute the Goods which were Run to Condemnation before the Justices of the Peace, & the rest in the Exchequer at the Kings charge Corresponding with our Sollicitor & the Register of Seizure's, *valediction 1*

Noted the 27th

280
25 February
1748/9

CUST 58/149, pp. 134–5

From W. Wood (Custom House, London). Hand iii.

The Commissioner's having referr'd Your Preparatory Account of Incidents, for the Quarter ended at Michaelma's last, to the proper Officer's here, I am directed to send you Copy of his Report, for your Answer, *valediction 2*

> In Canes the Carpenter's Bill is charged 5s Each for 12 Foot whole Deals, he shoud set down the Breadth & Thickness of them, as it is a bove Double the Price commonly charged & also the Scantlings of the Timber, his Nails are likewise overcharged, Libscomb the Glazier should send up the measure of his Glass.
>
> Which is humbly Submitted
>
> W. Robinson
>
> 20th Febr*uary* 1748

281
25 February
1748/9

CUST 58/1

From W. C[ooley] and R. T[urvin] (Custom House, Portsmouth). Hand iii.

Inclosed we transmit your Honour's, the Account of Goods Enumerated, lately Seiz'd by the Officer's at this Port, to which we beg leave to refer *valediction 4*

282
25 February
1748/9

CUST 58/1

From W. C[ooley] and R. T[urvin] (Custom House, Portsmouth). Hand iii.

In obedience to your Honour's Command's signified to us by Mr Wood in his Letter of the 21st Instant, Inclos'd we transmit your Honour's, an Account of such Fraud's relating to Tobacco, as have come to our knowledge, committed either in the Importation, Exportation, Relanding, or carrying Coastwise, or by Land in great Britain since Christmas ⌜1732⌝[38], to which Account we beg leave to Refer, *valediction 3*

> Port of Portsmouth
>
> An Account of such Fraud's relating to Tobacco, as have come to our knowledge, either in the Importation, Exportation, Relanding, or carrying Coastwise, or by Land, in this Port, since Christmas 1732 to the 25th February 1748
>
> By the Book of Seizure's in this Port, it appear's that 8886 Pound's Tobacco have been Seiz'd for being illegally Imported
>
> 1309 Lib's for being run
>
> 1030 Do for being brou*gh*t Coastwise ⌜without⌝[39] a legal Dispatch & no other Frauds relating to Tobacco have come to our knowledge
>
> WC RT

283
3 March
1748/9

CUST 58/1

From W. C[ooley] and R. T[urvin] (Custom House, Portsmouth). Hand iii.

We beg leave to acquaint Your Honour's, Yesterday Sailed from this Port, to Stangate Creek, the Ann's *Snow, John Dormer Master, who lately perform'd Quarentine for the space of forty day's, at the Motherbank *valediction 5*

---

38 Altered from '1722'.
39 MS. 'with'.

284
4 March
1748/9

CUST 58/149, p. 135

From Edw. Hooper, R. Chandlor, J. Evelyn and G. Vaughan (Custom House, London). Hand iii.

In answer to Your Account of Seizures dated the 24th Ultimo, We direct you to prosecute the Rum thereinmentioned to Condemnation before the Justices of the Peace, at the Kings Charge acquainting Us when Condemned, *valediction 1*

Noted the 6th March 1748 in the Book of Seizures

285
4 March
1748/9

CUST 58/149, pp. 135–6

From Edw. Hooper, R. Chandler, J. Evelyn and G. Vaughan (Custom House, London). Hand iii.

Mr West Secretary to the Lords Commissioners of his Majesty's Treasury, having in his Letter of the 16th Ultimo signify'd their Lordships Direction's that Mr Richard Temple attend at the Waterside at Your Port, in order to his being Instructed in the Business of a Landwaiter, You are to take care their Lordships Directions be duely comply'd with, and if after Six Months Attendance you find him Sufficiently Qualifyd, you are in Conjunction with the rest of the Principal Officer's to join in a Certificate thereof and transmit the same to Us. *Valediction 1*

286
6 March
1748/9

CUST 58/1

From W. C[ooley] and R. T[urvin] (Custom House, Portsmouth). Hand iii.

Inclosed we transmit your Honour's an Account of Good's not Enumerated, lately Seized by the Officer's at this Port, to which we beg leave to Refer *valediction 4*

287
7 March
1748/9

CUST 58/1

From W. C[ooley] and R. T[urvin] (Custom House, Portsmouth). Hand iii.

Herewith we transmit to your Honour's, the Abstract for the Month of February last, together with the undermention'd Accounts, to which we beg leave to refer *valediction 4*

Nil List of Bond's
Tea & other Good's Enumerated with Petty rece*ip*ts Endors'd
Absent Officer's

P:S/ From the Book kept in this Office it appear's that the Coal & Corn Bushel's, at this Port, were try'd the 4th Ultimo by the Surveyor & Landwaiters & that they found the same to be exact & true, & that the Stamp's for marking Hide's, Skin's Linnen's, Seiz'd Goods & Sail Cloth, are in good & Sufficient repair & fit for the use's design'd

288
8 March
1748/9

CUST 58/149, p. 136

From W. Wood (Custom House, London). Hand iii.

Captain Lloy'd having apply'd to the Commissioner's in relation to his Liquor's which are in the Custom House at Your Port, desiring they may be put on board his Majesty's Ship Phynx, at Spithead, the Board agree thereto, & you are to take care it be under the Inspection of the proper Officer's

Captain John Moore having acquainted the Commissioner's that some of his Liquor's in bottle's is arriv'd in the Hornet Sloop at your Port, which he desire's may be put on board his Majesty's Ship the Anson; The Commissioner's agree thereto, & you are to give the necessary Orders for that purpose, Captain Moore having given it under his hand that there is very little, but what was bought of Merchants, *valediction 2*

289
10 March
1748/9

CUST 58/1

From W. C[ooley] and R. T[urvin] (Custom House, Portsmouth). Hand iii.

We are to acquaint your Honour's that by the Waggon of George Clarke which will be at the Whitehart, in the Burrough of Southwark, on Saturday the 11th Instant Yesterday was sent under the Seal's of Office, directed to your Honour's, a Case Containing a Picture landed here out of his Majesty's Ship Plymouth, Capt Dent from Jamaica, belonging to Mr Thos Thomson who will apply to your Honour's for Delivery thereof, on payment of the Duty's, *valediction 3*

290
14 March
1748/9

CUST 58/149, pp. 136–7

From R. Chandlor, Sam. Mead, Beaumont Hotham and G. Vaughan (Custom House, London). Hand iii.

Inclosed you will receive a Writt of Delivery for the Tea, return'd in an Indenture of Appraisement from Your Port, and Proclaim'd in the Exchequer last Term amounting to One hundred thirty two Pounds, fifteen Shilling's; We direct you to sell the said Tea, Publickly to the highest bidder, putting it up at the Appraised Value, or such other price as will be most Advantageous to the King and Officer's concern'd, *valediction 1*
In margin: Writt dated 28th February 1748⌜£132. 15⌝[40]

291
14 March
1748/9

CUST 58/149, p. 137

From Wil. Wood (Custom House, London). Hand iii.

Captain Shuldham having applied to the Commissioner's desiring that his Liquor's which were lodged in the WareHouse at Your Port on his being removed from his Majesty's Ship the Sheerness, to the Queenborough may be put on board the latter at Spithead, as she is bound on a Voyage to Jamaica; The Board agree thereto under the care of the proper Officer's, & you are to give the necessary directions for that purpose, *valediction 2*

292
16 March
1748/9

CUST 58/149, pp. 137–8

From J. Evelyn, G. Vaughan, Sam. Mead and W. Levinz ('Sevinz') (Custom House, London). Hand iii.

It appearing by the Report of Mr Brooke Your Surveyor General, of his last Survey at your Port, that he has left several Rules, and Instruction's for the better carrying on the Business of the Port for the future, We approve thereof, and expect they are carefully & punctually observ'd by you, and the other Officer's, and incase they are not already enter'd in your Book's of Order's, You must take care it be done without loss of time, And we direct you to give it in strict charge to the Officer's in general to exert themselve's in the due Execution of their respective Employments, and to use their utmost endeavours not only to Seize all Prohibited and Uncustomed Good's, but likewise to get the best Information's they can obtain, against all such Person's, as are either concern'd in running or receiving the same, or are any way's aiding or assisting, in order that such Offenders may be Prosecuted according to Law *valediction 1*

…JST 58/149, p. 138

…n J. Evelyn, G. Vaughan, Sam. Mead and W. ⌜Levinz⌝[41] (Custom House, London). Hand iii.

…e have receiv'd your Letter's of the 13th of October and 26th of November in relation … Gun's Purchas'd by the Board of Ordnance, out of the Prize's taken by the …ron under the Command of Sr Edward Hawke, and having advis'd with the …Officer's here, they agree with you in Opinion that this case is Paralel to that of …cessa Prize, You may therefore permit the Gun's Purchas'd by the board of … to pass free of the five Per Cent, on Mr Eddowe's making Oath that they were … for the use of the Goverment, *valediction 1*

294
16 M…
1748/…

…9/1

…rom W. C[ooley] and R. T[urvin] (Custom House, Portsmouth). Hand iii.

We have here Inclos'd a Schedule of Account's due from this Port, for the Quarter ended Christma's last, the same being this day forwarded by the Waggon of George Clarke, which Inn's at the Whitehart in the Burrough of Southwark, on Saturday the 18th Instant for the Carriage of which we have agreed that Two Shilling's & six pence shall be paid, *valediction 3*

---

40 Underlined; see App. I, no. 7.

41 Altered from 'Sevine'.

Portsmouth

A Schedule of Account's, due from this Port, for Christma's quarter last, sent by the Waggon of George Clarke, which will be at the Whitehart in the Burrough of Southwark on Saturday the 18th March 1748 –

Collector's Quarter Book
Comptroller's – D° –
General Incidents with the Establishment
Two Original Order's
One Damage Certificate, five For*eign* Debenture's,
One *Portage Bill, seven Debenture's for Bounty and two Coal Debenture's –
Coal Incidents
Wooll bro*ugh*t & carried Coastwise
Civil List receipt & repayments
Preparatory Account of Incidents
Personal Prosecution's
Enumerated Goods Per Act 12th Geo 1st[42]
An Account of Ship's & Vessel's which discharged in this Port, from any of his Majesty's Plantation's in America
Journal's of the Commander & Mate of the Greenhill Yatch
D° – of the Boatman at Hayling
Corn Exported whereon there is a Bounty, for Michaelma's & Christmas quarters
Age's & Capacity's of Officer's for the Year 1748
Duplicate's of Certificates from Guernsey & Jersey
Deputation & Instruction's of James Gutheridge Tidesman
Copy of Instruction's to – Idem –
D° – to – Jn° Allen – D°

295
18 March
1748/9

CUST 58/149, p. 139

From R. Chandlor, J. Evelyn, S. Mead and Edw. Hooper (Custom House, London). Hand iii.

Mr Brooke Your Surveyor General having in his Letter of the 14th June last, laid before u's an Account of the Service's of the Riding Officer's belonging to your Port, mention'd on the back hereof, who by our Orders of the 10th July 1744 were continued at the Additional Allowance's set against their Respective Name's to Lady=day 1744, And he being of Opinion it is for the ⌜Interest⌝[43] of the Revenue to continue the said Allow*ances*: We therefore agree to your paying the same accordingly from Lady=day 1744 to Lady=day 1748, for which the Collector may take Credit in his Account of Incidents, annexing Copy of this Letter with proper Receipts thereto as Voucher's, But we have discontinued the said Allowances from Lady=day 1748, and you are not to pay them till further Order's, *valediction 1*

Thos Comden Riding Officer –	From Lady=day 1744 to Lady-day 1748 at £5 Per Annum	20. 0. 0
Jn° Wood – D° –	the like time at £5 Per Annum –	20. 0. 0
Jn° Newnham – D° –	the like time at £5 Per Annum –	20. 0. 0
Geo: Everden – D° –	From Lady=day 1744 to the 8th June 1745 Inclusive – the time of his Dismission at 5 Per Annum –	6. 0. 6
Jeremiah Fardell – D° –	From the 14th Aug*ust* 1745 the time of his Admission to Lady=day 1748 at 5 Per Annum	13. 1. 7
Wm Goddard – D° –	From 23d April 1744 the time of his Admission to Lady day 1748 at £5 Per Annum –	19.12. 7
		£98.14.[8]

[42] Statute 12 Geo. I, c.28
[43] MS. 'Insterest'.

296
20 March 1748/9

CUST 58/149, p. 140

From Wil. Wood (Custom House, London). Hand iii.

Lieutenant Tatton having apply'd to the Commissioner's, in relation to a Quarter Cask of White Wine, and a small box of *Castle Soap, on board his Majesty's Ship Fouguex, which he desire's may be remov'd into the Gloucester bound to Jamaica, to which Ship he is appointed Lieutenant – The Board agree thereto under the care of the proper Officer's, and you are to give the necessary orders accordingly *valediction 2*

297
23 March 1748/9

CUST 58/149, p. 140

From Wil. Wood (Custom House, London). Hand iii.

Mr John Water's having by his Memorial of this date, apply'd to the Commissioners desiring that a Debenture may be pass'd for the Wheat Landed out of the Valentia Packett at Your Port, and Exported, they direct you to Report to them the Exact Quantity actually landed, reshipt, & Exported, *valediction 2*

298
23 March 1748/9

CUST 58/149, pp. 140–1

From Sam. Mead, Edw. Hooper, G. Vaughan and Wil. Levinz ('Sevinz') (Custom House, London). Hand iii.

We receivd your Letter of the 6th Instant, transmitting us an Account of a Seizure of Twelve Spanish Cedar Plank's made by John Noel Waiter and Searcher, on board the John & Elizabeth, Benjamin Miller Master, for want of a Coast Dispatch, and it not appearing there was any Fraud intended, You may deliver them to the Proprietor's on their paying the Officer's a very moderate Satisfaction *valediction 1*

299
23 March 1748/9

CUST 58/149, p. 141

From Beaumont Hotham, Sam. Mead, Ric. Chandlor and G. Vaughan (Custom House, London). Hand iii.

In answer to the Account of Seizures transmitted in your Letter of the 25th Ultimo, We direct you to Prosecute the Tobacco thereinmentioned, to Condemnation before the Justice's of the Peace, at the King's Charge, acquainting us when Condemn'd,

We have order'd the Beam's, Scale's Weights and Gauging Instrument's, Crav'd in your Letter of the 18th Ultimo to be forthwith provided, and sent you, *valediction 1*

300
23 March 1748/9

CUST 58/149, pp. 141–2

From W. Wood (Custom House, London). Hand iii.

Henry Simon Esqr being appointed Receiver of Enumerated Goods as also of Fine's, & Forfeiture's Recover'd before the Justice's of the Peace in the out Port's, in the room of Mr William Hinton deceas'd, I am directed to signify the same to you, And the Commissioner's direct you to Remit the King's share of all Fine's & Forfeiture's, to Mr Simon in like manner you did to Mr Hinton giving advice thereof to the Accomptant of Petty Receipt's, and Mr Hamage the Comptroller, *valediction 2*

301
30 March 1749

CUST 58/1

From W. C[ooley] and R. T[urvin] (Custom House, Portsmouth). Hand iii.

Agreeable to your Honour's Order signify'd to us ⌜by M^r^ ⌝[44] Wood, in his Letter of the 23^d^ Instant, Inclosed we transmit your Honour's, a Certificate under the hands of the proper Officer's of the exact Quantity of Wheat, landed out of the Valencia Pacquet, reshipt & Exported, to which we beg leave to refer, *valediction 3*

[44] Altered from 'in his'.

Portsmouth

These are to Certify that in pursuance of a Sufferance, under the hand's of the Collector, Deputy Customer, & Deputy Comptroller of this Port, unto us directed bearing date the 6th Ultimo We have attended in the Harbour on board the Valencia *Snow, Gabriel Black master from London, bound to Barcelona, laden with Wheat, & that in our presence on the 6th 7th ⌜9th⌝[45] & 10th of February last, there were unship'd out of the said *Snow & landed, One hundred & sixty nine bag's of Damag'd Wheat, & that in lieu thereof on the 14th & 15th of the said Month of February last, the like number of Bag's Containing good sound & Merchantable Wheat of four bushel's each were reship'd on board the said *Snow, called the Valencia as aforesaid in our presence as Witness our hands at the Custom House the 30th March 1749

Chas Markland Surv*eyo*r
Robt Alexander Deputy Sea*rche*r
Thos Merritt Landwaiter

302
30 March
1749

CUST 58/1

From W. C[ooley] and R. T[urvin] (Custom House, Portsmouth). Hand iii.

We beg leave to acquaint your Honour's William Vernon, late a Tidesman & Boatman with the allowance of £5 Per Annum, by Incidents, & Coal Meter at this Port, died the 29th Instant, We therefore humbly beg leave to recommend Jno Chadwick a Tidesman & Boatman at this Port, with the Allowance of £5 Per Annum, to succeed said Vernon as Coal Meter, he being in all respects well qualify'd to perform the said Duty, And we further beg leave to recommend Hy Barn's, who has been Employ'd in the Service of the Custom's as an Extra man upwards of five Year's, to succeed said Vernon, at the Allowance of five Pounds Per Annum, We beg to Assure Your Honour's that Barn's is a good & deserving Officer, & as such he is recommended to Your Honour's consideration *valediction 4*

303
1 April
1749

CUST 58/149, p. 142

From W. Wood (Custom House, London). Hand iii.

The Commissioner's having receiv'd Information's that great Quantities of Muslin and other Good's are intended to be run into the several Ports of this Kingdom; you are to give it in strict Charge, to all the Officer's at your Port, as well those of the Water Guard as Preventive that they exert themselves in preventing the Running either of Muslin's, or any other Customable or Prohibited Commoditie's, at or near your Port, or within your District Reporting to the Board your Proceeding's, *valediction 2*

304
1 April
1749

CUST 58/149, p. 142

From Sam. Mead, Edw. Hooper, Beaumont Hotham and G. Vaughan (Custom House, London). Hand iii.

Having considered your Preparatory Account of Incidents for the Quarter ended at Michaelma's last, amounting to Twenty eight Pound's, one Shilling & six pence half Penny, The Collector may pay the same with the Privity of the Comptroller, and take Credit for it in his Account of Incidents, annexing this Letter with proper Receipt's thereto as Voucher's; But you are for the future to transmit us the Tradesmen's Bill's of particular's, with your Preparatory Accounts *valediction 1*

In margin: £28. 1. 6½[46]

---

45 Inserted.

46 Underlined.

305
1 April
1749

CUST 58/149, p. 143

From Sam. Mead, Edw. Hooper, Beaumont Hotham and G. Vaughan (Custom House, London). Hand iii.

Having receiv'd a Warrant from the Treasury on a Refer'd Petition of Nichol's Sone, praying that a new Debenture may be made out for three hundred, twenty four quarter's & six bushel's Wheaten Flour, Shipt at your Port on board the Theodosia, Richard Hunter Master for Gibralter, in lieu of a former Debenture which is either lost or Mislaid, We direct you agreeable thereto, to make out a Second Debenture for the said Flower, upon Security being given in Duble the Amount of the Bounty, to Indemnify the Crown against any Person, who shall or may be Possess'd of the first Debenture, incase the Money due thereon should hereafter be demanded, noting the same specially in Your Book's, *valediction 1*

306
4 April
1749

CUST 58/149, p. 143

From G. Vaughan, Sam. Mead, Beaumont Hotham and Edw. Hooper (Custom House, London). Hand iii.

Having granted our Deputation for Richard Man to be a Coalmeter at your Port, in the room of Willm Vernon Deceas'd, You are to take care he be under Oath and Security, for the faithful Discharge of the said Employ, and Qualifie's himself as the Law direct's. *Valediction 1*

307
7 April
1749

CUST 58/1

From W. C[ooley] and R. T[urvin] (Custom House, Portsmouth). Hand iii.

Herewith we transmit to your Hon*our*s the Abstract for the Month of March last, together with the undermention'd account's, to which we beg leave to refer *valediction 4*

Nil List of Bond's
Tea & other Goods Enumerated, with Petty receipts Endors'd
Absent Officer's
State of Bonds for Lady=day quarter 1749

P:S/ From the Book kept in this Office, it appear's, that the Coal & Corn bushel's at this Port, were try'd the 4th ⌜Ultimo⌝[47] by the Surveyor & Landwaiter's & that they found the same to be exact and true, & that the stamp's for marking Hide's, Skin's, Linnen's, Seiz'd Goods & Sail Cloth are in good & Sufficient repair & fit for the use's design'd

308
8 April
1749

CUST 58/149, p. 144

From G. Vaughan, Edw. Hooper and Sam. Mead (Custom House, London). Hand iii.

Mr Robert Wilson having by his Memorial of the 31st Ultimo apply'd to us desiring leave to take two Quarter Cask's of Madeira, which are under the King's Lock's at Your Port, on board the Centurion, to which Ship he is appointed Master, We agree thereto upon his paying the Duty for the same. *Valediction 1*

309
10 April
1749

CUST 58/1

From W. C[ooley] and R. T[urvin] (Custom House, Portsmouth). Hand iii.

By the Waggon of George Clark, which will be at the Whitehart, in the Burrough of Southwark, on Wednesday the 12th Instant, we have this day sent directed, to your Honour's, a Case Containing three Picture's, landed here out of the Superbe man of war from the Streight's, belonging to Admiral Forbe's, who will apply to your Honour's, for delivery thereof, on paymen[t] of the Duty's, *valediction 3*

---

47 MS. 'Ullt^{o}' (for 'Ult^{o}').

310
11 April
1749

CUST 58/149, p. 144

From Edw. Hooper, Sam. Mead, Beaumont Hotham and G. Vaughan (Custom House, London). Hand iii.

We receiv'd your Letter of the 30th Ultimo Inclosing a Certificate of the Quantity of Wheat, Landed, reshipt and Exported, on board the Valencia *Snow Gabriel Black Master; whereby it appear's that there was Eighty four Quarter's, and a half Wheat, Reshipt at Your Port; We direct you to pass an Entry for that Quantity and make out a Debenture for the same, having Cancell'd the first Debenture, And order'd another to be made out here for the Remainder *valediction 1*

311
11 April
1749

CUST 58/1

From W. C[ooley] and R. T[urvin] (Custom House, Portsmouth). Hand iii.

Inclos'd we transmit Your Honour's a Memorial which we this day received from Mrs Ann Nixon relating to a Hamper Containing between four & five Dozen of wine, in bottle's sent her as a present from Gibralter, which she reported amongst other Good's, for which the Duty have been paid, but the wine in bottle's being Prohibited to be Imported, we refused Admitting the same to an Entry, without first receiving your Order for that purpose. We therefore beg to refer Your Honour's to the Memorial of Mrs Nixon wherein she requests leave to enter & pay the Duty's for the said Wine, to which we have no objection provided it meets with your Honour's approbation *valediction 5*

Gentlemen

I beg leave to acquaint you that my son who reside's at Gibralter, amongst other Goods for which I have paid the Duty's, sent me as a present, a hamper of Wine, Consisting of between four & five Dozen Bottle's, of which I am inform'd, I cannot be admitted to make an Entry without the Direction's of the Honourable the Commissioners of his Majesty's Custom's (as Wine in bottle's is Prohibited to be Imported, of this I was quite Ignorant) as well as I believe my Son who sent it as a present, was, but as not any Fraud ⌜was⌝[48] intended, since the same was duely reported with my other Good's, brought in the Two Brother's William Hick's Master, & for which I fully intended & hope I shall be permitted, to pay Duty's, I beg therefore that you will be pleased to represent my Case to the Honourable Board, to the end that I may be relieved & admitted to pay the Duty's, in such a manner, as they shall be pleased to direct, I am

Gentlemen Your most humble Servant

Ann Nixon

Portsmouth 10th of April 1749.

312
11 April
1749

CUST 58/1

From W. C[ooley] and R. T[urvin] (Custom House, Portsmouth). Hand iii.

Inclosed we transmit your Honour's an Account of Good's not Enumerated in the Act 12th Geo 1st,[49] lately Seiz'd by the Officer's at this Port, to which we beg leave to refer *valediction 4*

313
11 April
1749

CUST 58/1

From W. C[ooley] and R. T[urvin] (Custom House, Portsmouth). Hand iii.

Inclosed we transmit your Honour's an Account of Good's Enumerated, & not Enumerated, lately Seiz'd by the Officer's at this Port, to which we beg leave to refer, *valediction 4*

---

48 Inserted.
49 Statute 12 Geo. I, c.28.

314
15 April
1749

CUST 58/149, pp. 144–5

From Edw. Hooper, G. Vaughan and Beaumont Hotham (Custom House, London). Hand iii.

We receiv'd your Letter of the 11th Instant transmitting the Memorial of Mrs Ann Nixon relating to a Hamper of wine in bottle's sent her as a present, from Gibralter, And it appearing that the said wine was Reported, and no fraud intended, We agree to your admitting it to an Entry, upon the Proprietor's giving the Officer incase it was stopt or Seiz'd, a moderate Satisfaction,

In answer to the Account of Seizure's transmitted in your Letter of the 11th Instant We have no objection to the Officer's Prosecuting the wine thereinmention'd to Condemnation in the Exchequer, at their own Charge, Corresponding with our Sollicitor and the Register of Seizure's, *valediction 1*

315
18 April
1749

CUST 58/149, p. 145

From J. Evelyn, Wil. Levinz ('Sevinz') and Edw. Hooper (Custom House, London). Hand iii.

In answer to the Account of Seizure's transmitted in your Letter of the 14th Instant, We direct you to Prosecute the Enumerated Goods thereinmentioned to Condemnation, before the Justice's of the Peace, at the King's Charge, and we have no objection to the Officers Prosecuting the Wine in like manner, at their own Charge, acquainting us when Condemn'd, *valediction 1*

316
18 April
1749

CUST 58/149, pp. 228–9

From Beaumont Hotham, J. Evelynn, W. Levinz ('Levine') and Edw. Hooper (Custom House, London). Hand iii.

Application having been made to us desiring that Capt Wyatt of the Fly Sloop may have ⌜a⌝[50] Commission Impowering him to Seize ⌜Prohibited⌝[51] & Uncustomed Goods, & he having given Security here, Inclosed you will receive our Commission accordingly & you may admit him to his Duty taking care he Qualifies himself as the Law directs *valediction 1*

Rec*eive*d the 24th Jan*uar*y 1749

317
19 April
1749

CUST 58/1

From W. C[ooley] and R. T[urvin] (Custom House, Portsmouth). Hand iii.

Inclos'd we transmit your Honour's a Plantation Certificate, for the Ship, Falmouth, of London, whereof Hy Grant is Master bound for Piscatagua, which when perfected we desire your Honour's will be pleased, to return the same, *valediction 5*

318
19 April
1749

CUST 58/1

From W. C[ooley] and R. T[urvin] (Custom House, Portsmouth). Hand iii.

Inclosed we transmit your Honour['s] an Account of Goods Enumerated, in the Act 12th Geo 1st,[52] lately Seiz'd by the Officer's, at this Port, to which we beg leave to refer *valediction 4*

319
24 April
1749

CUST 58/149, p. 146

From Beaumont Hotham, J. Evelyn and Edw. Hooper (Custom House, London). Hand iii.

In answer to the Account of Seizure's transmitted in your Letter of the 19th Instant, We direct you to Prosecute the Good's thereinmentioned, to Condemnation, in the Exchequer, at the King's Charge, Corresponding with our Sollicitor, and the Register of Seizure's *valediction 1*

---

[50] Written only as catchword at foot of page.
[51] MS. 'Prohiblted'.
[52] Statute 12 Geo. I, c.28.

320
24 April
1749

CUST 58/1

From W. C[ooley] and R. T[urvin] (Custom House, Portsmouth). Hand iii.

Inclos'd we transmit your Honour's a Certificate whereby it will appear that Captain Coombs, Commander of the Greenhill Yatch Employed in the Service at this Port, hath duely perform'd his Contract, agreeable to what was transmitted in our joint Letter, bearing date the 13th November 1743, Vizt for the quarter's ended Christma's & Lady=day last, And therefore we pray your Honour's Order, for paying the said Captain Coomb's, the Sum of Twenty three Pound's, five Shilling's, being after the Rate of Thirty Shilling's Per Ton, Per Annum for Thirty one Ton's Burthen, *valediction 3*

Port of Portsmo

These are to Certify that upon a Carefull Survey made for the half Year, ended Lady=day last, it appear'd to us, that the Greenhill Yatch, & Boats, belonging to her, Employ'd in the Service of the Custom's, at this Port, together with all the Materials have been duely kept, & are in good & sufficient repair & that Captain Coomb's Commander thereof, hath well & duely perform'd his Contract & is thereby entituled to half a Year's Allowance, amounting to Twenty three Pounds, five Shilling's, Witness our hands, Dated at the Custom House 24th April, 1749

Wm Cooley Collector
Wm Baskerville Tidesurv*eyo*r
Wm Read Shipwright

321
26 April
1749

CUST 58/149, p. 146

From Sam. Mead, G. Vaughan, Beaumont Hotham and Edw. Hooper (Custom House, London). Hand iii.

Mr Thomas Missing having by his Memorial of the 8th Instant, apply'd to Us desiring to be repaid the Dutie's of a Butt of Spanish wine, which was Stav'd in Landing, and entirely lost, You are to acquaint him it being contrary to Law, We cannot agree to his being repaid the Dutie's, *valediction 1*

322
29 April
1749

CUST 58/149, p. 146

From Sam. Mead, Edw. Hooper, W. Levinz ('Sevinz') and G. Vaughan (Custom House, London). Hand iii.

In answer to the Account of Seizure's transmitted in Your Letter of the 24th Instant, We have no objection to the Officer's prosecuting the Good's thereinmentioned to Condemnation before the Justice's of the Peace, at their own Charge, acquainting us when Condemn'd, *valediction 1*

323
29 April
1749

CUST 58/149, p. 147

From Sam. Mead, Edw. Hooper, W. Levinz ('Sevinz') and G. Vaughan (Custom House, London) Hand iii.

Inclos'd you will receive a Writt of Delivery for the Brandy return'd in an Indenture of Appraisement from Your Port in Michaelma's Term last, which was Seiz'd by William Baskerville, an Officer at your Port, and Appraised at £269. 8. 0,[53] We direct you to sell the same Publickly to the highest bidder, putting it up at the Apprais'd Value or such other Price as the Goodness of the Commodity deserve's;

But the Lord's of the Treasury having been pleas'd by their Warrant dated the 13th Instant, to direct that his Majesty's two thirds of the Money, arising by the Sale of the Brandy be paid to Han's Hornman of Dronthem in Norway Merchant the Claimant, after deducting the Law Charge's, and the Charge's of Condemnation & Sale,

We hereby signify the same to You and direct when the Brandy is Sold, that you transmit us a particular Account of the Produce and Charge's thereof, for our further Direction's, *valediction 1*

[53] See App. I, no. 5.

324
1 May
1749

CUST 58/1

From W. C[ooley] and R. T[urvin] (Custom House, Portsmouth). Hand iii.

Inclosed we transmit Your Honour's an Account of Good's Enumerated, lately Seiz'd by the Officer's, at this Port, to which we beg leave to refer, *valediction 4*

325
3 May
1749

CUST 58/149, pp. 147–9

From G. Vaughan, W. Levinz ('Sevinz'), J. Evelynn and Edw. Hooper (Custom House, London). Hand iii.

Mr Gerritt Van Erven having by his memorial of the 21st Ultimo apply'd to us, relating to the Whale bone, Iron Lock's, Coffee Pott, and Shoemaker's Thread, under Seizure at your Port, Inclos'd we send you Copy of the said Memorial, and if you find the facts as therein represented, and none of the Goods be Prohibited, You may deliver them to the Proprietor's on payment of the Duty, and giving the Officer's concern'd, a moderate Satisfaction *valediction 1*

To the Honourable the Commissioner's of his Majesty's Custom's,

The humble Petition of Gerritt Van Erven Chief Cooper of the Over Schie dutch East India Ship now lying at Spithead Sheweth That whilst the said Ship lay Stranded at Portsmouth, Your Petitioner's Chest was broke open by some of the said Ship's Crew, and 50 Lib's of Whale Bone, 21 Iron Lock's, one Coffee Pott, and Eight Pounds of Shoemaker's Thread, Stolen thereout, without the Knowledge or Privity of Your Petitioner, That the said Good's were Seizd by the Person, or Person's, who committed the said Fact, as they were bringing the said Good's ashore by Mr Baskerville Tidesurveyor in the Port of Portsmouth, who was desired to take care of the said Goods for the concern'd by the Companie's Agent at Portsmouth, but on the said Agent Applying to the proper Officers of that Port to have the said Good's restored, he was told that a Report had been made to Your Honour's of this Seizure, in order for Condemnation, and they cannot be restored without Your Honour's direction's

Your Petitioner therefore humbly hopes that as he was no way's Concern'd in Attempting to bring the said Goods ashore, he shall not Suffer for the faults of other's, but that your Honour's will be so good to consider the Equity of his Case and order his Goods to be restor'd to him, as he is but in mean Circumstance's, and these Goods were intended for a Venture in the Voyage, And your Petitioner as in Duty shall ever pray &cetera

Gerritt Van Ervin

Portsmouth 21st April 1749

326
3 May
1749

CUST 58/149, pp. 149–50

From G. Vaughan, W. Levinz ('Sevinz'), J. Evelynn and Edw. Hooper (Custom House, London). Hand iii.

We receiv'd your Letter of the 24th Ultimo transmitting a Certificate[54] whereby it appear's that the Greenhill Yatch in the Service at your Port, under the Command of Captain Coomb's, is in good & Sufficient repair, You may pay him the Sum of Twenty three Pounds, five Shilling's, for keeping the said Yatch in Wear & Tear for the Quarter's ended at Christmas & Lady=day last, and take Credit for the same in your Account of Incidents, annexing this Letter with proper Receipts thereto as Voucher's,

Mr Brooke Surveyor General, having in his Letter of the 17th March last, transmitted us a Bill of Incident's amounting to £ 7.10s. 3d' Crav'd by Mr Spry Supervisor & other Officer's for apprehending Richard Broad by Virtue of a Warrant from the Lord Chief Justice of the Court of King's Bench, and having considered the same, We agree to allow them the Sum of Four Pounds, four Shilling's, And no more being the usual Allowance in like Case's. And the Collector may pay them the said Sum, and take Credit for it in the manner before directed, *valediction 1*

---

54 'whereby it appear's', repeated, struck out.

327
8 May
1749

CUST 58/149, p. 150

From W. Wood (Custom House, London). Hand iii.

Mr Robert Hardy having in his Memorial of this date apply'd to Us, desiring as Commodore West has paid the Duty for two Pipe's of Madeira, one Pipe of Mahone, & two hogsheads & a half of White wine, that he may be permitted to Enter Nine Dozen of White wine in Bottle's, We have agreed thereto, and you are to Admit the said Wine to an Entry as desired, We are

Your Loving Friends

This Letter was prepared for the Commissioner's signing, but the Board being risen before it was finished, their Commands are signify'd to you by

Gentlemen Your most humble Servant

W Wood

328
8 May
1749

CUST 58/1

From W. C[ooley] and R. T[urvin] (Custom House, Portsmouth). Hand iii.

We are to acquaint your Honour's on the 7th Instant, died Benjamin Summer's, late a Coal Meter, and Extra Tidesman & Boatman at this Port, with the Allowance of £5 Per Annum by Incident's, We humbly beg leave to recommend John Chadwick, who for several Year's, have been a Tidesman & Boatman, (with[55] the like Allowance by Incidents) to succeed Summer's as a Coal Meter, Chadwick having always since an Officer, at this Port, executed the Trust committed to his Charge, with great care & fidelity, on that Account we think he is highly deserving of your Honour's Encouragement, & as it have been a Practice, with your Honour's to supply the Vacancy's of Coal Meter's, at this Port, with such People as are Employed in the Service as Extra Tidesmen, & Boatmen, with the Allowance of £5 Per Annum by Incident's, And it being very Necessary your Honour's so continue your favour to such as are deserving of Encouragement, We therefore earnestly beg you'l be pleased to accept of our Recommendation of Chadwick, & cause a Deputation to be sent us, for his being a Coal Meter at this Port, in the room of Summer's deceas'd *valediction 3*

329
10 May
1749

CUST 58/1

From W. C[ooley] and R. T[urvin] (Custom House, Portsmouth). Hand iii.

Herewith we transmit Your Honour's the Abstract for the Month of April last, together with the undermention'd Account's, to which we beg leave to refer *valediction 4*

Nil List of Bond's
Tea & other Good's Enumerated with Petty receipts Endors'd
Absent Officer's

P.S:/ From the Book kept in this Office, it appear's that the Coal & Corn bushel's, at this Port, were try'd the 7th Ultimo by the Surveyor, & Landwaiter's, & that they found the same to be exact & true, & that the stamps for marking Hide's, Skin's, Linnen's, Seiz'd Good's & Sail Cloth, are in good, and Sufficient repair and fit for the use's design'd.

330
11 May
1749

CUST 58/149, p. 151

From W. Levinz ('Sevinz'), R. Chandlor, J. Evelynn and G. Vaughan (Custom House, London). Hand iii.

Having considered your Preparatory Account of Incident's for the Quarter ended at Christmas last, Amounting to Twelve Pounds, & two Pence, The Collector may pay the same with the Privity of the Comptroller, And take Credit for it, in his Account of Incidents, annexing this Letter with proper Receipts thereto as Vouchers, *valediction 1*

331
11 May
1749

CUST 58/149, p. 151

From W. Levinz ('Sevinz'), R. Chandlor, J. Evelyn and G. Vaughan (Custom House, London). Hand iii.

In answer to the Account of Seizure's dated 4th Instant; We direct you to Prosecute the Goods thereinmentioned to Condemnation before the Justice's of the Pease, at the King's Charge acquainting us when Condemn'd, *valediction 1*

---

55 MS. omits opening bracket.

332 CUST 58/149, pp. 151–2

12 May

1749

From W. Wood (Custom House, London). Hand iii.

The Right Honourable the Lords Commissioners of his Majesty's Treasury, having been pleased in Compassion to the Inferior Officer's of the Custom's to Authorize the Commissioner's to give direction's to the Collector's of the Out Ports to pay the Taxe's Assess'd upon the Salaries of the Deputed Officer's, not exceeding Sixty Pounds Per Annum, by the Land Tax granted for this Year; and also to Reimburse them the Money paid upon their Sallarie's by Virtue of that Act;[56] The Commissioner's direct me to signify the same to you, & that you yield obedience thereto accordingly, refering in your Incidents to the Date hereof, & withall taking care that no more be Allow'd than as been already paid, or shall be paid by the said Officer's, and that by Virtue thereof you do not allow the Taxes Assess'd upon any Patent Officer's, And I am further to acquaint ⌜you⌝[57] that all Officer's are to be Tax'd where they execute their Office's, & not where they are paid their Salaries; & the Collector is to take care of reminding the Assessor's thereof, that the Assessments may be made accordingly, which is what I have in Command to signify to You, *valediction 2*

333 CUST 58/149, pp. 152 (letter), 155 (enclosure)

13 May

1749

From W. Wood (Custom House, London). Hand iii.

Application having been made to Us by Mr Edward Marjoribank's, a Passenger from Spain, in the Crown man of War, lately arriv'd at your Port, Inclos'd you will receive a Copy of his Petition, and if it appears to you to be fact, that the Cloath's have been wore you may deliver them without any further Order's,

We are Your Loving Friends

This Letter was prepar'd for the Commissioners signing but the Board being risen before it was finish'd their Commands are signifyd to You by

Gentlemen Your most humble Servant

W Wood

May it please your Honour's

Being come from Spain, a Passenger in the Crown man of War, lately arriv'd at Portsmouth, the Custom House Officer's there took out of my Trunk, one Coat & three ⌜Wastcoats⌝[58], giving for reason that they were Lac'd, or Embroider'd, tho', all of them have been worn, I beg the favour of your Honour's to give such Order's for their being return'd me as that I may receive them soon being going abroad, I am

Your Honour's most Obedient humble Servant

Edwd Majoribank's

Enterd out of Course thro' mistake, it being Inclos'd in the Boards Order dated 13 May – 1749 –

334 CUST 58/149, p. 153

17 May

1749

From W. Wood (Custom House, London). Hand iii.

Application having been made[59] to the Commissioner's praying the delivery of a Box suppos'd to be Snuff or Tobacco, stopt from Mr John Cockburne at your Port; You are to send up the said Box to the WareHouse here, under the Seal of Office, and acquaint the Commissioners by what Conveyance it is sent & what agreement is made for Carriage, *valediction 2*

335 CUST 58/149, p. 153

18 May

1749

From Beaumont Hotham, Edw. Hooper, W. Levinz ('Sevinz') and G. Vaughan (Custom House, London). Hand iii.

William Hare Tidesman at Your Port, having apply'd to us desiring further leave to be Absent for ten day's, fo recovery of his health, We have agreed to give him leave for six day's, without loss of Pay, and you are to take care the Service does not Suffer during his Absence,

Francis Fuller Extra Tidesman, who had leave of the Collector to come to London, on his private Affair's, having also apply'd to us desiring further leave for six day's, to finish the same, we have agreed thereto, *valediction 1*

---

[56] Statute 22 Geo. II, c.2.

[57] Inserted.

[58] Altered from 'Wascoats'.

[59] MS. omits 'made'.

336
19 May
1749

CUST 58/149, pp. 153–4

From W. Wood (Custom House, London). Hand iii.

M[r] Thomas Farrington Purser of his Majesty's Ship Lynn having by his Memorial of the 28th Ultimo apply'd to the Commissioner's, relating to some Tobacco & Wine under Stop at Your Port, Inclos'd you will receive Copy of the said Memorial, & you are to examine into the Allegation's therein Contain'd, & report to the Board, a true state of the Case with your opinion. *Valediction 2*

Lynn Portsmouth Harbour 28th April 1749

Honourable Sir's

I beg leave to acquaint you I have about 3 Cw[t] of Tobacco, the remain's of what I bought of a Merchant, at Port=mahon for the use of his Majesty's Ship Lynn, which I had no opportunity of Issuing, the Ship being so soon Ordered home, after I made the Purchase, your Officer's of the Custom's here have taken an Account of it, I humbly pray the favour you will be pleased to give direction's that I may be indulg'd with the Exportation thereof, by some Ship bound abroad

I also have about 18 or 20 Dozen of Wine, which is the remain's of my Sea Stock I therefore pray you will be pleas'd to direct the same to be admitted to an Entry, which will greatly Oblige, Honourable Sir's

Your most Obedient humble Servant

Tho[s] Farrington Purser

337
20 May
1749

CUST 58/149, pp. 155–7

From W. Wood (Custom House, London). Hand iii.

The Commissioner's having approv'd the Form of a Certificate, to be granted for allowing the Premium, on the Importation of British Plantation made Indico, direct me to transmit you one of them for your Government, & when you have occasion for any of those Certificate's, you may be supply'd therewith from my Office, taking care when you apply for any, to mention whether the Premium is to be paid at your Port, or in London that proper Form's may be sent you accordingly *valediction 2*

Custom House
17 [60]

These are to Certify, whom it may concern, that the Indico undermentioned, was Imported in the Ship whereof is Master from Consign'd to & Enter'd by Day of viz[t]
which Indico is of the Growth & Produce of as appear's to us by a Certificate under the hands & Seals of
And the Affidavit of the said Master, dated

These are to Certify, that in pursuance of an Act of Parliament, pass'd in the Twenty first Year of his present Majesty, entitle'd an Act for Encourageing the Making of Indico in the British Plantation's in America,[61] we have View'd
And we find the said Indico to be good & Merchantable, free from false Mixture's, & fit for Dyer's use, & of such Quality as to be entituled to the Premium, or Reward, allow'd by the abovesaid Act, being three fourth Parts of the Value of French Indico, or other Indico equal in Goodness to French at the time of Importation

} Land Surveyor's } Landwaiters

⌜Form of a Certificate for the Premium allow'd on Brit*ish* Plantation made Indico⌝[62]

Receiv'd the Day of of the Honourable the Commissioners of his Majesty's Custom's, by the hand's of Collector of the Port of the Sum of in full of this Certificate

[60] Spaces left blank here and throughout the form.
[61] Statute 21 Geo. II, c.30.
[62] Added at foot of page.

338 CUST 58/149, p. 157
20 May
1749
From W. Wood (Custom House, London). Hand iii.

Application's having been made to the Commissioner's, relating to two Quilted Petticoats & a small box of *Sweet Water, belonging to Mrs Rowley, as also two small Pott's of Minorca Honey, two Tyger Skin's, and a Box Containing Six Wastcoats, sent to the Honourable Admiral John Byng Esqr. They direct you without loss of time to send the said things up to the WareHouse here under the Seals of Office, at the Proprietor's Charge, giving the Board an Account when, and by what Conveyance they are sent, and what agreement is made for Carriage, *valediction 2*

339 CUST 58/1
20 May
1749
From W. C[ooley] and R. T[urvin] (Custom House, Portsmouth). Hand iii.

In Obedience to your Honour's Order of the 17th Instant, signify'd to us by Mr Wood, We have this day sent by the Waggon of George Clarke, which will be at the Whitehart in the Burrough of Southwark on Tuesday the 23^{d} Instant, directed for Your Honour's, under the Seal's of Office, a Box suppos'd to be Snuff or Tobacco, which we received from Mr John Cockburne, for the Carriage of which we have agreed that Two Shilling's shall be paid, *valediction 5*

340 CUST 58/149, pp. 157–8
22 May
1749
From W. Wood (Custom House, London). Hand iii.

Mr Robert Man having by his Memorial of this date, apply'd to the Commissioners relating to some Wine & *Arrack, in the WareHouse at your Port, Inclos'd we send you Copy of the said Memorial, and you are to deliver the said Goods, upon the Dutie's being paid for the same

We are Your Loving Friend's

This Letter was prepar'd for the Commissioners signing, but the Board being risen before it was finish'd, their Commands are signify'd to you by

Gentlemen Your most humble Servant

W: Wood

Honourable Sir's

I have lodg'd in his Majesty's WareHouse, at Portsmouth, Six Hamper's Containing a small Quantity of *Arrack, & some Wine's in Bottle's, being the remainder of my Sea Store's, which I brought home with me from the Medditerranean, in his Maj*es*tys Ship Lynn, then under my Command, as also a Damjan of Cyprus Wine, all which I humbly beg you will permit to be deliver'd me on the Payment of the accustomed Dutie's

I am Honourable Sir's Your most Obedient Servant

Robt Man

London 22^{d} May 1749.

341 CUST 58/1
22 May
1749
From W. C[ooley] and R. T[urvin] (Custom House, Portsmouth). Hand iii.

We have your Honour's Order of the 19th Instant, Inclosing the memorial of Mr Thoma's Farrington, Purser of his Majesty's Ship Lynn, relating to some Wine & Tobacco belonging to him, in the King's WareHouse at this Port, And by your Honour's said Order, We are directed to examine into the Allegation's of said Farrington's Memorial, & report a state of the case, with our opinion, In Obedience thereto we beg leave to acquaint your Honour's, at the time his Majesty's Ship Lynn was paid off, there was brought on shore to his Majesty's Warehouse for Security of the Duty's, about Eighteen, or Twenty Dozen of Wine, the remains of his Sea Store's, & about Three hundred w*eigh*t of Tobacco, which he had not an Opportunity of Issuing to the Ship's Company before they were paid Off, Its therefore our Opinion, what Mr Farrington has alledged to your Honour's in his Memorial is just & true, and we think it reasonable his Request should be comply'd with, provided Your Honour's have no objection, all which is humbly submitted *valediction 4*

342
23 May
1749

CUST 58/149, pp. 158–9

From W. Wood (Custom House, London). Hand iii.

Mess[rs] Philip Stephen's & Edm[d] Mason, having by their Memorial of the 19th instant apply'd to the Commissioner's, desiring to be Excus'd from paying the five Per Cent Duty, on the Hull of the Apollo a French Ship of War, taken by Lord Anson's Squadron, I am directed to send you Copy of the said Memorial, and you are to examine into the Allegation's therein Contain'd, and Report to the Board a State of the Case with Your Opinion, for their further Order's, *valediction 2*

Honourable Gentlemen

The Sales of the Hulls & Stores of the French men of war, taken by Lord Ansons Squadron in May 1747 being now compleated & a final Distribution of those Prize's near at hand, We find an objection to our closing those Accounts, by a Demand from the Collector of the Custom's at Portsmouth for Duty on the Hull of the Apollo, one of the smaller French Ship's of War sold to the Government by private Contract with the Navy Board, in like manner as the Invincible & the other larger Ship's were sold

We cannot conceive the least reason for such a Demand, unless from the Vulgar Error of her being a French East India man, freighted with Store's for Foreign Parts, but on the contrary the Ship appears by Copy of Condemnation, to be a French Ship of War, & the Captor's have receiv'd Bounty Money for the Prisoners taken in her as such, and as we have never objected, & are now ready to pay 5 Per Cent, for such Store's landed out of her at the Dock, as were reputed by your Officer's not to be the proper Tackle, *Apparrell & Furniture belonging to her, We hope you will be pleased to give Direction's to your Collector to wave his Demand of 5 Per Cent, on the Ship, for the reason's here before set forth, that we may settle with him out of hand & pay his other Demands for Duty's of Store's, sold at Publick Sale, We are

Honourable Gentlemen Your most Obedient humble Servants

Philip Stephen's   Edm[d] Mason

London 19th May 1749

343
23 May
1749

CUST 58/1

From W. C[ooley] and R. T[urvin] (Custom House, Portsmouth). Hand iii.

We are to acquaint your Honour's that by the Waggon of George Clarke, which will be at the Whitehart, in the Burrough of Southwark on Thursday 25th Instant, We have this day sent under the Seal's of Office, directed to your Honour['s] a Case Containing Picture's, landed here out of his Maj*es*tys Ship Lynn from the Streights, belonging to M[r] Dorrington, who will apply to Your Honour's for delivery thereof on payment of the Duty's, *valediction 3*

344
23 May
1749

CUST 58/1

From W. C[ooley] and R. T[urvin] (Custom House, Portsmouth). Hand iii.

Under the Seals of Office, agreeable to Your Honour's Order signify'd to us by M[r] Wood in his Letter of the 20th Instant, We have this day sent directed for Your Honour's, which will be at the Whitehart in the Burrough of Southwark on Thursday the 25th Instant, Two Boxe's belonging to Admiral Byng & Forbe's Containing Waistcoats & a Quilt, for the Carriage whereof we have agreed that four Shilling's shall be paid, but as to two Quilted Petticoats & a small Box of *Sweet Water belonging to M[rs] Rowley, and also two small Potts of Minorca Honey & two Tyger Skin's, belonging to the Honourable Admiral Byng, has Never been bro*ugh*t to his Majesty's WareHouse at this Port, But we believe there may be such thing's on Board the Crown man of war, from which Ship the Boxe's now sent up to your Honour's, under the Seal's of Office were taken out by M[r] William Baskerville, one of the ⌜Tidesurveyor's⌝ [63], who begs your Honour's will be pleased to Order he may be reasonable rewarded, if the said Waiscoat's & Quilt be not Prosecuted to Condemnation as a Seizure, which he humbly submits to your Honour's Consideration, *valediction 3*

---

[63] MS. 'Tidesuryor's'.

345 CUST 58/149, p. 160
25 May
1749

From R. Chandlor, Edw. Hooper, J. Evelyn and G. Vaughan (Custom House, London). Hand iii.

Having taken into consideration the number of Ship's & Vesels employ'd in the Service of this Revenue, and the great expence they are to the Crown in maintaining them, & being of Opinion that the Additional Allowance of fifteen Pounds Per Annum, over & above their Allowance for Victualling is sufficient Wage's for each Seamen, employ'd on board the said Sloop's & Vessel's, We therefore direct that from & after Midsummer next, the Surplus of three Pounds Per Annum, their present Additional Allowance be taken off & discontinued, And you are to take the necessary care accordingly, *valediction 1*

346 CUST 58/149, pp. 160–1
25 May
1749

From R. Chandlor, Edw. Hooper, J. Evelynn and G. Vaughan (Custom House, London). Hand iii.

We receiv'd your Letter of the 22^d^ instant in return to the Memorial of Mr Thos Farrington Purser of his Majesty's Ship Lynn, relating to some Wine & Tobacco under Stop at your Port, You may deliver the said Goods to the Proprietor, upon his paying the Duty's for the same,

In answer to the Account of Seizure's transmitted in your Letter of the 11th Instant, We have no objection to the Officer's Prosecuting the Velvet thereinmention'd to Condemnation before the Justice's of the Peace, at his own Charge, acquainting us when Condemn'd; And you are to deliver the Coat, and Wastcoats, to the Proprietor's *valediction 1*

In margin: Noted 27th May

347 CUST 58/1
26 May
1749

From W. C[ooley] and R. T[urvin] (Custom House, Portsmouth). Hand iii.

In obedience to Your Order's of the 23^d^ Instant We have examined into the Allegation's contained in the Memorial of Messrs Stephen's & Mason, wherein they claim an Exemption from the Duty of £5 Per Cent, on the Hull of the Apollo, one of the six lesser Ship's of war, taken by Lord Anson's Squadron, in May 1747, on Account of her being sold to the Government by private Contract, with the Navy Board, in like manner as the Invincible and other larger Ship's were Sold; And in relation thereto, we humbly acquaint your Honour's that our insisting on the £5 Per Cent Duty, on the said ship, was in Obedience to your Honour's order dated 22^d^ July 1748, wherein you were pleased to direct us to Demand the £5 Per Cent for the said six Lesser Ship's of War, together with the Spare Store's on Board, without any Provision for such as might be sold to the Government, to exempt them ⌜therefrom⌝[64]; But if the Apollo be sold to the Government and is consequently under the same ⌜Circumstance⌝[65] with the Princessa, & with the other larger Ship's of War, taken by Lord Anson, for which no Duty has been insisted on, And likewise under the same Circumstance, with the Gun's of the said Large Ship's which your Honour's were pleas'd to suffer to pass free of the said Duty of £5 Per Cent, by your Order of the 16th March 1748,

We are humbly of Opinion in Order that we may Act uniformly, that the said Ship should pass free,[66] but we humbly propose that some one of the Agents, may make Oath, of such Sale being made of the Ship, as is alledged, as a proper foundation for such Exemption, as was done by Mr Eddowe's Storekeeper of Ordinance here in relation to the Gun's; And likewise that the same be done in regard to such other of the Ship's, for which the Duty has not been paid, all which is submitted to your consideration *valediction 4*

348 CUST 58/1
26 May
1749

From W. C[ooley] and R. T[urvin] (Custom House, Portsmouth). Hand iii.

Inclos'd we transmit your Honour's an Account of Good's Enumerated, & not Enumerated, lately Seiz'd by the Officer's at this Port, to which we beg leave to refer *valediction 4*

---

[64] Altered from 'from'.
[65] Altered from 'Circumstance's'.
[66] MS. has an opening or closing bracket in place of a comma.

349
27 May
1749

CUST 58/149, p. 161

From Sam. Mead, W. Levinz ('Sevinz'), G. Vaughan and Edw. Hooper (Custom House, London). Hand iii.

Inclos'd you will receive Writts of Delivery for the Enumerated Goods, return'd in an Indenture of Appraisement, from your Port, and Proclaim'd in the Exchequer the last Term, the Total Amount of which, is on the back hereof, We direct you to sell the said Good's publickly to the highest bidder, putting them up at their Appraised Value's, or such other Price's as the Goodness of the Commoditie's deserve's, *valediction 1*

Writt dated the	23^d	May –	£ 91. 12. 2
	24	D° –	90. 6. 10
			£181. 19. 0 [67]

350
30 May
1749

CUST 58/1

From W. C[ooley] and R. T[urvin] (Custom House, Portsmouth). Hand iii.

We have here Inclosed a Schedule of Account's, due from this Port, for the Quarter ended Lady=day last, the same being this day forwarded by the Waggon of George Clarke, which will be at the Whitehart, in the Burrough of Southwark, on ⌜Thursday⌝[68] the 1st June 1749 for the Carriage whereof we have agreed that Two Shilling's & six pence shall be paid, *valediction 5*

Portsmouth

A Schedule of Account's, due from this Port, for Lady=day Quarter last, sent by the Waggon of Geo. Clarke, which will be at the Whitehart in the Burrough of Southwark on Thursday the 1st June 1749

Collector's Quarter Book
Comptroller's – D° –
General Incidents with the Establishment
One Original Order
Two Bounty Debentures } two *over Entry's, one Damage
Two Foreign D° – } Certificate and 2 *Portage's
Coal Incidents
Imports & Exports
Wooll br*ough*t & Carried Coastwise
Civil List receipt & Repayment
Naval Store's from Rushia & Levona
Corn Exported from hence w*i*th the Am*oun*t of ye Bounty due thereon
Preparatory Account of Incidents, with Tradsmen's Bills
Personal Prosecution's
Enumerated Goods Per Act 12th Geo 1st [69]
Ship's &cetera which Discharged in this Port, from any of his Majesty's Plantation's in America –
Loose Reports Inwards & Outwards
Journal's of the Commander & Mate of ye Greenhill Y*a*tch
D° – of the Chief Boatman at Hayling
Deputation & Instruction's of Geo. Karrington Tidesman
Copy of D° – to R^d Mann Coal meter

[67] See App. I, nos 8, 9.
[68] Altered from 'Tuesday'.
[69] Statute 12 Geo. I, c.28.

351
31 May
1749

CUST 58/1

From W. C[ooley] and R. T[urvin] (Custom House, Portsmouth). Hand iii.

We have here Inclos'd a List of such Stationary Ware's, as are much wanted for the Service at this Port, with which we beg, to be immediately supply'd, & the same shall be frugally manag'd *valediction 4*

PS/ The last supply was Crav'd 11th November 1748 –

Portsmouth

A List of such Stationary Ware's, as are much wanted for the Service of his Majesty's Custom's at this Port, humbly Crav'd to be Allow'd – vizt –

4 Quires quarter Book Paper Inward's
2 Quires *Imperial Paper Unrul'd
4 Rheam's fine *pott cutt
5 Rheam's 2^{d} *pott cutt
6 Quire *Demy cutt
3 Quire D^{o} – uncutt
2 Dozen *Demy Pocket Book's for Coal Meters &cetera –
Blue Book's, for the use of the Landsurveyor, and Landwaiters vizt
80 – 4 Leave's
50 – 2 D^{o}
60 – 6 D^{o}
40 – 8 D^{o}
30 – 10 D^{o}
30 – 12 D^{o}
20 – 14 D^{o}
12 – 16 D^{o}
12 – 20 D^{o}
12 – 24 D^{o}
2 Gallon's Black Ink
1 Quart red Ink
4 Ivory Penknive's
4 *Pounce Boxe's
½ Pound *Pounce
2 Dozen Pencils
3 Bodkin's
2 Dozen *Pieces* Tape
3 Bag's Sand
1 Pound Sealing Wax
2 Book's, 1 Quire *Demy each
3 Quire's *Boarding's
2 Quires Reports Inw*ar*ds in sheets
2 D^{o} Outward's
2 Quire Coal Warrant's
1500 Quill's
3000 Wafer's
3 Dozen Tag's
12 Past Board File's
1 Leidg*er* Inw*ar*ds for the Comptroller
1 D^{o} Outwards of Large *Imperial Paper ruled for the Collector
2 Monthly Abstract Book's
2 Quire in sheets for Goods Enumeratd & Goods not Enumerated
1 Quire *Over Entry's
1 Book for Excise Permits
2 Quires Journal Paper
1 Quire Personal Prosecution's
Journal Books for the Commander and Mate of the Greenhill Yatch – and Chief Boatman at Hayling

352
1 June
1749

CUST 58/149, p. 161

From G. Vaughan, W. Levinz ('Levine'), J. Evelynn and Beaumont Hotham (Custom House, London). Hand iii.

In answer to the Account of Seizure's transmitted in your Letter of the 26th Ultimo We direct you to Prosecute the *Arrack thereinmention'd to Condemnation, in the Exchequer, at the King's Charge, And we have no Objection to the Officer's Prosecuting the rest of the Goods at their own Charge Corresponding with our Sollictor & the Register of Seizures, *valediction 1*

In margin: Noted the 1st June 1749

353
2 June
1749

CUST 58/149, p. 162

From G. Vaughan, W. Levinz ('Levine'), Sam. Mead and J. Evelynn (Custom House, London). Hand iii.

Having granted our Commission for James Redstone to be an Extra Tidesman & Boatman at Your Port in the room of Benjn Summer's Deceas'd, You are to take care he be under Oath & Security, for the faithfull discharge of the said Employ, & Qualifies himself as the Law directs, paying him the like Allowance by Incidents, as was paid to his Predecessor, for which the Collector may take Credit from time to time, in his Account of Incidents, annexing Copy of this Letter with proper Receipts thereto as Voucher's, *valediction 1*

354 CUST 58/149, p. 162
3 June
1749

From G. Vaughan, Sam. Mead and W. Levinz ('Levine') (Custom House, London). Hand iii.

In answer to the Account of Seizure's transmitted in your Letter of the 30th Ultimo We have no objection to the Officer's Prosecuting the Boats and Goods thereinmention'd to Condemnation in the Exchequer, at their own Charge Corresponding with our Sollicitor and the Register of Seizure's, *valediction 1*
In margin: Noted the 5th June 1749

355 CUST 58/149, p. 163
3 June
1749

From G. Vaughan, Sam. Mead, J. Evelynn and W. Levinz ('Levine') (Custom House, London). Hand iii.

Messrs Stephen's & Mason, having applied to us for "an [70] Exemption from the Duty of five Per Cent on the Hull of the Apollo, one of the lesser Ship's of War, taken by Lord Anson's Squadron in May 1747, on Account of her being sold to the Government by private Contract with the Navy Board, in like manner as the Invincible, and other large Ship's were sold" – And having refer'd the same, together with your Letter of the 26th Ultimo on this occasion, to the Patent Officer's, and they having reported, that they agree with you in Opinion, We have no objection to this Ships passing free of the 5 Per Cent, provided some one of the Agents make Oath of her being sold to the Government, in like manner as was done by Mr Eddowe's Storekeeper of Ordnance at your Port, in relation to the Gun's, *valediction 1*

356 CUST 58/149, p. 163
3 June
1749

From G. Vaughan, Sam. Mead, J. Evelyn and W. Levinz ('Levine') (Custom House, London). Hand iii.

Having granted our Deputation for William Hare, to be a Coal Meter at Your Port, in the room of Benjamin Summer's, deceas'd, You are to take care he be under Oath and Security, for the faithfull discharge of the said employ *valediction 1*

357 CUST 58/149, p. 164–5
3 June
1749

From Wil. Wood (Custom House, London). Hand iii.

The Commissioner's having taken into consideration the Act of the 21st Year of his present Majesty [71] for allowing the Importer's of British Plantation made Indico, a Præmium of six Pence Per Pound, on the Term's thereinmention'd, And the Board being of Opinion, that it is not thereby intended, there should be any lessenning of the said Præmium or Bounty by a Deduction for Draft, they therefore direct that the Præmium be allowed on the exact net Quantity of Indico, when the quality is of Sufficient Goodness, to entitle the Importer thereto, as it shall weigh at the Scale, And Pursuant to the Direction's in the said Act, the proper Officer's are to take care that every Cask, or other Package of Indico is turn'd quite out, And if different sorts are found therein, they are to take a Sample of each, in Proportion to the quantity, and send the same up to the Board, in order for the Inspection of the proper Officer's here, referring to the Mark's & ⌜numbers⌝ [72] of each Package, and the Officer's are not to grant any Certificate to entitle the Importer to the Præmium, untill you shall receive the Boards Order's for the same, And that in order to prevent Indico which had received the Præmium of six Pence Per Pound from being Exported without Repayment thereof under Pretence of its being Forreign Indico, or British Plantation Indico, which had received no Præmium, the Commissioner's direct the Landsurveyor's & Landwaiter's to Certify before any Indico is Exported whether any Præmium was allowed thereon, at Importation, And the Merchant should also make Oath on the back of the Certificate, that he received no Bounty, and in all Case's where he received a Bounty, You are to take care it be repaid before a Certificate passe's for the Exportation, And you are further to observe that all Indico whatever is to pay the Subsidy Outwards.

In my Letter of the 20th Ultimo I transmitted you the Form of a Certificate to be granted by the Officer's to entitle the Importer's to the Bounty; You are to observe when any such Certificate's shall be deliver'd by you, to be paid by the Receiver General here, You are to send Duplicate's thereof to the Board, in like manner as is done in respect to Corn, Sail Cloth & Linnen Debenture's *valediction 2*

---

[70] Each line of this quotation is introduced by a double quotation mark.
[71] Statute 21 Geo. II, c.30.
[72] Altered from 'number'.

358
7 June
1749

CUST 58/1

From W. C[ooley] and R. T[urvin] (Custom House, Portsmouth). Hand iii.

We have received your Command's of the 3[d] Instant, together with a Deputation, by which W[m] Hare is appointed a Coal Meter, at this Port, On which occasion we conceive it to be our Duty, humbly to acquaint your Honour's, that the said Hare is at this time a settled Tidesman, and if he was likewise to be admitted a Coal Meter, he wou'd possess two inconsistant Employment's, for during the time he Acted as a Coal Meter, the Crown wou'd be at the Expence of paying an Extraman, to do his Duty, as Tidesman, which woud Considerably increase the Incident Charge of the Port, and on this occasion We beg leave further to acquaint your Honour's, that we are so far from having had an Instance of this Kind in the Port, for upward's of fifty Year's, that whenever it has happen'd that an Extraman who was likewise a Coal meter, was promised to be a Tidesman, he was so far from Continuing to enjoy, Coal Deputation of which he was Possess'd that it was constantly resign'd, in order to be given to some other Extra=man, by which mean's the Extra=men have been properly Encouraged, & the Incident Charge of the Port kept low, to which Reason's ti's entirely owing that this humble Representation is made, the same being with the utmost deference,

As we have therefore defer'd Admitting the said Hare till your Honour's further pleasure is known which shall be Oblig'd with the utmost readiness *valediction 4*

359
8 June
1749

CUST 58/149, pp. 165–6

From W. Levinz ('Levine'), Sam. Mead, J. Evelynn and G. Vaughan (Custom House, London). Hand iii.

Captain Harland of his Majestys Ship Monarch, having by his Letter of the 2[d] Instant, apply'd to Us, desiring leave to remove his Store's in the WareHouse at Your Port, on board the said Ship, And they being the remains of his Sea Store's, You may upon the Dutie's being paid for the same permit them to be removed as desired, *valediction 1*

PS We think you highly Blameable for not taking the Dutie's as soon as the Store's were landed –

360
10 June
1749

CUST 58/149, p. 166

From Wil. Wood (Custom House, London). Hand iii.

The Commissioners having received repeated Information's of great Quantities of Good's particularly Muslin, Embroidery work Tea, Brandy &cetera being run on several Parts of the Coast of this Kingdom, notwithstanding their Repeated Order's to prevent the same, and tho', the Number of Sloop's, as well as preventive or Riding Officer's are so great, yet there is little or no effect from their being Employ'd either by preventing the said Fraud's, or Seizing the Goods so clandestinely Run, You are immediately on receipt to give the necessary Direction's to all the Officer's under your Inspection, for putting a stop to Practice's so Prejudicial to the Revenue and fair ⌜Trade⌝[73] for the future, And at the same time to acquaint the Commander's of the Sloop's and Preventive, or Riding Officer's, that unless the Board find much greater Service's render'd the Revenue, by their mean's, than ha's hitherto been done, they shall look upon them as useless person's, consequently no longer deserving any Salary from the Crown. *Valediction 2*

361
10 June
1749

CUST 58/1

From W. C[ooley] and R. T[urvin] (Custom House, Portsmouth). Hand iii.

Herewith we transmit your Honour's the Abstract for the Month of May last, together with the undermention'd Accounts, to which we beg leave to refer *valediction 4*

Nil List of Bonds
Tea & other Goods Enumerated with Petty receipts Endors'd
Absent Officer's

PS/ From the Book kept in this Office, it appear's that the Coal and Corn Bushel's at this Port, were try'd the 7th Ultimo by the Surveyor, and Landwaiter's and that they found the same to be exact & true and that the stamp's for marking Hide's, Skin's, Linnen's Seiz'd Good's and Sail Cloth, are in good & Sufficient repair, and fit for the use's design'd

---

73 MS. 'Trder'.

362
16 June
1749

CUST 58/1

From W. C[ooley] and R. T[urvin] (Custom House, Portsmouth). Hand iii.

We are to acquaint your Honour's on the 16th Instant, William Pendrill a Tidesman and Boatman, with the Allowance of Thirty Pounds Per Annum by Incidents Resign'd his Deputation, And in his room we humbly beg leave to recommend Henry Duncan ju*nio*r an Extra Tidesman & Boatman, with the Allowance of £5 Per Annum Per Incidents, who has been Employ'd in the Service upwards of 14 Year's, and very deserving of your Honour's favour; If your Honour's are pleased to comply with our request, We are to Assure your Honour's no one is more deserving of Preferment, than the Person We have taken the liberty of recommending, he being a very good & Diligent Officer, all which is most humbly submitted to your Consideration *valediction 4*

363
17 June
1749

CUST 58/149, p. 167

From Wil. Wood (Custom House, London). Hand iii.

I have laid before the Board your Letter of the 7th Instant, immediately upon the receipt of it, And the Commissioner's having been since inform'd that several Officer's who are not Extra=men, are employ'd as Coal Meter's, and particularly John Newnham Riding Officer at Fareham, & John Stretch weighing Porter at Your Port, You are by return of the Post to acquaint the Commissioner's whether the said Newnham & Stretch act as Coal Meters, & whether there are other Officer's who have Coal Deputation's beside's Extra men. *Valediction 2*

364
20 June
1749

CUST 58/1

From W. C[ooley] and R. T[urvin] (Custom House, Portsmouth). Hand iii.

We have your Honour's Order of the 17th Instant, signify'd to us by Mr Wood, in which you are pleased to observe of having been inform'd that several Officer's who are not Extra=men are employed as Coal Meter's & particularly, Jno Newnham, Riding Officer at Fareham, John Stretch weighing Porter, at this Port, We are to acquaint your Honour's the two beforemention'd Person's do act as Coal Meter's, but we beg leave to observe to your Hon*our*s that if John Newnham, Riding Officer at Fareham did not execute the Office of Coal Meter, there must be a Person appointed particularly for that Service, & we are to acquaint you that the number of Ship's Discharg'd every Year at Fareham is so small, that we are humbly of Opinion no one wou'd accept of a Coal Deputation,

In regard to John Stretch weighing Porter, with the Allowance of Twenty Pounds Per Annum by Incidents, We are to acquaint your Honour's it has been a Custom ever since the Appointment of a Weighing Porter, at the same time to have a Coal Deputation, without which it wou'd be impossible he cou'd support himself & Family, And we beg leave to observe that his being a Coal Meter is no Obstruction in the Execution of his Duty as Weig*hing* Porter for if at any time he may be Employ'd in Discharg*ing* a Ship with Coal's, and provided it shou'd so happen that he may be wanted at the Scale he has alway's appointed a proper person at his own expence to discharge the said Duty for him,

On the whole we humbly beg leave to observe if your Honour's are inclined to appoint the *Settlemen (those we mean who have £30 Per Annum by Incident's) Coal Meter's, when Vacancy's shall ever happen, it will considerably increase the Incident Charge's of the Port, as we must inevitably employ Extramen to do their Duty, at the time they are Employ'd as Coal Meter's, all which is must humbly submitted to Your Consideration *valediction 4*

365
21 June
1749

CUST 58/1

From W. C[ooley] and R. T[urvin] (Custom House, Portsmouth). Hand iii.

In Obedience to your Order of the 29th April last, Inclosed we transmit your Honour's a Particular Account of the Produce & Charge's of a Parcel of Brandy, Seiz'd out of the Hope, Paul Greve Master from St Martin's, lately sold at this Port to which we beg leave to Refer, *valediction 3*

Portsmouth

An Account of the Produce of the Sale of the Brandy Seiz'd out of the Hope, Paul Greve Master from St Martin's, and return'd in two Indenture's mark'd B & D which was [74] Claim'd by Han's Hornman of Dronthem in Norway, & Condemn'd in the Exchequer Michaelmas Term 1748.

D*ebtor*		Per Contra Cred*itor*	
To 9 *Anchor's & one half *Anchor Containing 76½ Gallon's of Brandy, Return'd in an Indenture Mark'd D Michaelma's Term, being the Seizure of Thomas Trehearne, Apprais'd at £22. 19. 0 Gaug'd at the Delivery 77½ Gallon's & Sold for	25 7 2½	By Charge's on the Sale Viz^{t}	
		Lighter for ⌜bringing⌝[75] the Goods On Contra*ct*, from on board the Hope –	0 4 0
		By two Commissioners each 13.4	1 6 8
		By two Appraiser's each 6. 8	0 13 4
		By Draw*ing* Indenture's & Stamp &cetera	0 10 6
To Thirty one half hogsheads & one *Ulage half hogshead Containing 898 Gall^{s} of Brandy, Return'd in an Indenture mark'd B, Michaelma's Term, being the Seizure of being the Seizure of Wm Baskerville Tidesurveyor, Appraised at £ 269. 8. 0 Gaug'd at the Delivery 897½ & Sold for	281 15 9¼	By the Collectors Allowance of 4^{d} Per Pound on the Sale –	5 2 4½
		By the Comptrollers D^{o} of 3^{d}	3 16 9¼
		By Advertisements & Cryer	0 2 0
		Saml Chandlor as by Bill annexd	2 15 8
			£ 14 11 3¾
		By the Officer's ⅓ of the Am*ount* of the Sale of the Brandy on Contra*ct*	102 7 8
			£116 18 11¾
		By Ballance due –	190 4 0
Total	£307 2 11¾		£307 2 11¾

366
22 June
1749

CUST 58/149, p. 167

From Wil. Wood (Custom House, London). Hand iii.

It appearing that you have Charged in your Preparatory Account of Incidents for Lady=Day Quarter last, the Sum of £4. 0. 10 for Stationary Ware's, The Commissioner's direct you to report to them the reason of your Supplying your selve's therewith without their Order's for that purpose, *valediction 2*

367
23 June
1749

CUST 58/149, p. 167

From Wil. Wood (Custom House, London). Hand iii.

Stephen Moor's being recommended to the Commissioner's to be a Boatman at your Port, They direct you to examine into his Qualification, and if you find him sufficiently Qualified, You are by return of the Post, to transmit the Board a Certificate thereof, in the manner required by my Letter of the 21st June 1743, *valediction 2*

---

[74] 'Pro(?)' struck out.

[75] MS. 'brining'.

368
23 June
1749

CUST 58/149, p. 168

From Wil. Wood (Custom House, London). Hand iii.

The Lord's Commissioner's of his Majesty's Treasury having been pleased to direct an Account to be made out and transmitted to them of the Charge of the Management of the Revenue of the Custom's from Christma's 1732 to Christma's 1748 Annually, You are without loss of time, to prepare and transmit hither the said Accounts for your Port, according to the Form Inclos'd, and you are to take Notice, that the underwritten Article's in the Incident Account are to be Included in the Incident Salarie's viz[t]

The Collectors & Comptroller's Poundage on the Coal Receipt Coastwise

The Collector's Poundage on 4 Pence Per Pound, on the Receipt of the *Coinage Duties, and

The Wages & Victualling of the Crew's of the Sloop's,

Which I have in Command to signify to you, *valediction 2*

Port of [76]

An Account of Salary's & Incident's from Christmas ⌜1732⌝[77] to Christmas 1748 Annually viz.

	Establish'd Salary's	Incident Salary's	Total Salary's	Other Incident Payments	Total Salary's & Incidents
From Christmas 1732 to Christmas 1733					

369
24 June
1749

CUST 58/1

From W. C[ooley] and R. T[urvin] (Custom House, Portsmouth). Hand iii.

You having been pleas'd to Observe that in our Preparatory Account of Incident's for Lady day Quarter last, the Sum of £4. 0.10 for Stationary Ware's is Charged We are therefore directed to Report the reason why we supply'd our selve's therewith, without first obtaining your Order for that purpose, In obedience thereto we beg leave to acquaint your Honour's, it was entirely owing to our not being supply'd with such Stationary Ware's, as was by us Craved the 11th November, which we did not receive till the 9th February following, all which time if we had not provided our selve's with such Stationary ware's, as were wanted, the Business of the Port, cou'd by no mean's have been carried on, The reason therefore for our not applying to Your Honour's for a Particular Order was that we were in dayly Expectation of the Arrival of the Stationary Ware's, from London, and we beg leave further to acquaint your Honour's, we are now under the same Circumstance's, being obliged to provide our selve's at the Stationer's with what is absolutely necessary, to carry on the Business of the Port, untill we receive a supply from London, agreeable to our Crave the 31st Ultimo we therefore beg your Honour's will be pleased to order our being immediately supply'd thereWith, *valediction 5*

370
26 June
1749

CUST 58/1

From W. C[ooley] and R. T[urvin] (Custom House, Portsmouth). Hand iii.

In Obedience to your Honour's Command's signify'd to u's by M[r] Wood in his Letter of the 23[d] Instant, Inclosed we transmit your Honour's a Certificate whereby it will appear that Stephen Moor's, lately recommended to Your Honour's to be a Boatman at this Port, is sufficiently Qualify'd to discharge the said Duty, *valediction 5*

Portsmouth

These are to Certify that upon Examination, we find Step[n] Moor's to be sufficiently Qualify'd for the Management of a Boat, & that he is in every respect, a fit Person to be a Tidesman, & Boatman, in the Service of his Majesty's Custom's, as Witnes's our Hand's, at the Custom House this 26th day of June 1749

W Cooley Collector
R Turvin Deputy Comptroller
Tho[s] Threhearne Tidsurv*eyo*r

---

76 Space left blank.
77 Altered from '1733'.

371
27 June
1749

CUST 58/149, p. 169

From Beaumont Hotham, W. Levinz ('Levine'), J. Evelynn and Sam. Mead (Custom House, London). Hand iii.

Having granted our Commission for Stephen Moor's to be a Tidesman & Boatman at your Port, in the room of William Pendrill removed to be a Boatman here, You are to take care he be under Oath, and Security for the faithfull discharge of the said Employ, paying him the like allowance by Incident's, as was paid to his Predecessor, for which the Collector may take Credit in his Account of Incidents, from time to time, referring therein to the date hereof, *valediction 1*

372
28 June
1749

CUST 58/149, p. 169

From Beaumont Hotham, Sam. Mead, Wil. Westby and G. Vaughan (Custom House, London). Hand iii.

Having considered your Letter of the 24th Instant, together with your Preparatory Account of Incident's, for the Quarter ended at Lady=day last, amounting to fourteen Pounds four Shilling's & eight pence, We agree for this time, to the Collector's paying the said Sum, with the Privity of the Comptroller, & take Credit for it in his Account of Incident's, annexing this Letter with proper Receipts thereto as Voucher's; Butt you are not for the future to provide any Stationary Ware's at the Port without our Order's nor charge for any in your Preparatory Accounts, if you do the samc will be disallowed, *valediction 1*

373
28 June
1749

CUST 58/149, p. 170

From J. Evelynn, Sam. Mead, W. Westby and G. Vaughan (Custom House, London). Hand iii.

Having considered your Letter's of the 7th & 20th Instant, in relation to Wm Hare, John Newnham, & John Stretch, who Act a's Coal Meter's at Your Port, And being of Opinion that it is inconsistent with their other Duty to be Employed as Coal Meter's; We have thought proper to dismiss them the Service as Coal Meter's And you are to call in their Deputation's, & cancell them, and transmit them to us by the Carrier with your next Account's, *valediction 1*

374
28 June
1749

CUST 58/149, p. 170

From Wil. Wood (Custom House, London). Hand iii.

Inclos'd I send you by Order of the Commissioner's, several Acts pass'd the last Session of Parliament, relating to the Custom's for the Government of your selve's & the other Officer's at your Port, to whom you are to communicate the same – Vizt –

1 The Malt Act
2 An Act for the more effectual preventing the Importation & Wear of Foreign Embroidery &cetera
3 An Act for the better Securing his Majesty's Dutie's arising upon Coal, Culm & Cynder's exported beyond Sea
4 An Act for granting to his Majesty the Sum of £1000,000 out of the Sinking Fund &cetera wherein is a Clause for continuing the Bountie's on the Exportation of British & Irish Linnen's, [78]

Valediction 2

---

[78] Statutes 22 Geo. II, cc. 1, 36, 37, 42.

375
28 June
1749

CUST 58/1

From W. C[ooley] and R. T[urvin] (Custom House, Portsmouth). Hand iii.

Inclosed we transmit your Honour's a Memorial, which we this day received from Mr Edward Skeat, a Landwaiter at this Port, who in Conjunction with the Collector and other Officer's of Excise, on the 1st of Sept*embe*r last made a Seizure of a Parcel of Wine, Brandy, Rum, & *Arrack, as mentioned in the Inclosed Memorial, at the House of Captain Richard Gwynn at Upham near Bishop's Waltham, which was afterward forcibly ⌜Rescued⌝[79] from them, In Consequence thereof a Representation of the Case was by us lain before Your Honour's, in our joint Letter dated the 6th September last, since which we are inform'd the Affair has been by the Commissioners of Excise with Captain Gwynn Compromised and the Officer's of Excise have been Allowed by the said Captain Gwynn, their full share, as if the same had been Adjusted as a Seizure, But as no notice in regard to the Wine, Seiz'd at the same time, and rescued as beforemention'd has been taken by your Honour's, We therefore beg to receive your Direction thereon, & hope you'l be pleas'd to take into consideration That Mr Skeat may have a Sutable satisfaction made[80] him, which is most humbly submitted to your Consideration *valediction 4*

Gentlemen

I beg leave to acquaint you, that in Conjunction with the proper Officer's of Excise on the 1st day of September last, in the House of Captain Richard Gwynn, at Upham, near Bishop's Waltham, we Seizd the Good's hereafter mentioned, which having been forcibly rescued from us, a full representation of the Case was laid before the Honourable Board of Custom's & Excise; in consequence whereof, the Officer's of Excise have been Allowed by the said Captain Gwynn, there full share's of all the Brandy, Rum, & *Arrack, so Seiz'd & Rescued as aforesaid, the Value of the Brandy & Rum being computed after the Rate of Eight Shillings Per Gallon, and that of the *Arrack after the Rate of Twelve Shilling's Per Gallon, beside's paying the said Officer's share's of Eight Shilling's Per Gallon, being the Penalty Adjudgd for Harbouring and Concealing all the said Brandy, Rum, & *Arrack, as likewise all their Charge's attending this Seizure, and carrying on the Prosecution against him, but as no Satisfaction has as yet been made, in regard to the Wine Seizd at the same time, and Rescued as aforesaid; I make it my request that you will lay the Case before the Honourable the Commissioner's of the Custom's, being in hope's their Honour's will think it reasonable that the said Captain Gwynn should make a sutable Satisfaction for the Wine's that were legally Seiz'd, & by force rescued from the Excise Officer's, & am

Gentlemen Your most humble Servant

Edward Skeat

Custom House Portsm^o 27th June 1749

5	Casks Containing	40	Gallon's	Brandy
2	Hamper's –	16	D^o	Brandy
4	Cask's, 40 bottle's –	78	Gallon's Rum	
11	Large Bottle's –	44	D^o – *Arrack	
	Total	178		
3	Small Cask's &			
1	Pipe –		Containing 220 Gallon's White Lisbon Wine	
1	hogshead Containing –		60 Gallon's Spa*nish* Wine	
1	D^o 3 Hampers –		Containing 98 Ga*llon*s Clarrett	

376
28 June
1749

CUST 58/1

From W. C[ooley] and R. T[urvin] (Custom House, Portsmouth). Hand iii.

We beg leave to acquaint you that by the Waggon of George Clarke which will be at the Whitehart in the Burrough of Southwark on Friday the 30th Instant, we have this day sent directed to Your Honour's under the Seal's of Office, a Case Containing a Picture which was landed here out of his Majesty's Ship Strafford from Jamaica, the Owner thereof will apply to your Honour's for the Delivery of the same, on payment of the Dutie's, *valediction 5*

---

79 MS. 'Recued'.
80 'by' struck out.

377
29 June
1749

CUST 58/1

From W. C[ooley] and R. T[urvin] (Custom House, Portsmouth). Hand iii.

In obedience to your Honour's Order signify'd to us by Mr Wood, in his Letter of the 23^{d} Instant, Inclosed we transmit Your Honour's an Account of the Charge of the Management of the Revenue of the Custom's from Christma's ⌜1732⌝[81] to Christmas 1748 Annually, And we have agreeable to your Order, Included in the Incident Salary's the Collector & Compt*roller*s Poundage on the Coal receipt Coastwise, and likewise the Coal *Metage, The Collector's Poundage, on the Receipt of the *Coinage Duty's, & the Wage's & Victualling of the Crew of the Sloop's in the Service at this Port to which Account we beg leave to refer your Honour's, *valediction 3*

Port of Portsm^{o}

An Account of Salarie's, and Incidents from Christmas 1732, to Christma's 1748 Annually Viz^{t}

From Xtmas 1732 to	Establish'd Salary's			Incident Salary's	Total Salary's	Other Incident Payments	Total Salary & Incidents
Xtmas 1733	1027	2	8	814 16 7¾	1841 19 3¾	497 1 9¼	2339 1 1
1734	1023	3	5	834 8 0½	1857 11 5½	554 1 11¼	2411 13 4¾
1735	1040	10	4½	820 4 9¼	1860 15 1¾	546 12 6	2407 7 7¾
1736	1051	10	10	837 16 0¾	1889 6 10¾	574 1 4¼	2463 8 3
1737	1053	0	1¾	826 16 9¾	1879 16 11½	408 9 4	2288 6 3½
1738	1028	18	9½	858 16 3½	1887 15 1	585 2 7¼	2472 17 8½
1739	1026	9	4	842 16 4¾	1869 5 8¾	494 15 3¼	2364 1 0¼
1740	1050	3	4	925 18 6¾	1976 1 10¾	831 7 8¾	2807 9 7¼
1741	1127	18	11	846 4 3¼	1974 3 2¼	994 1 10	2968 5 0¼
1742	949	10	9¼	896 0 9½	1835 11 6¾	943 3 5¾	2778 15 0½
1743	1152	6	6½	945 19 9¼	2098 6 3¾	1214 19 4	3313 5 7¾
1744	1140	8	10¾	921 10 9½	2061 19 8¼	1572 18 10¼	3574 18 6½
1745	1139	12	7¾	933 1 3¼	2072 13 11	1353 4 6½	2425 18 5½
1746	1140	⌜19⌝[82]	⌜4⌝[83]	969 3 9¾	2110 3 1¾	1134 17 11¾	3245 1 1¼
1747	1118	⌜13⌝[84]	⌜2½⌝[85]	964 9 2¼	2083 2 4¾	1297 19 2	3381 1 6¾
1748	1133	16	6½	963 1 0¼	2096 17 6¾	1429 9 8½	3526 7 3¼

378
1 July
1749

CUST 58/149, p. 171

From Wil. Whestby, Wil. Levinz ('Levine') and G. Vaughan (Custom House, London). Hand iii.

Mr Brooke Surveyor General having in his Letter of the 27th Ultimo transmitted us one from George Spry, Supervisor of the Riding Officer's, desiring leave to be Absent for a Month, for recovery of his health, We have agreed thereto, without loss of pay, and you are to take care that his districts are guarded by proper Officer's, that the Crown may be put to no expence during his Absence, *valediction 1*

379
1 July
1749

CUST 58/149, pp. 171–2

From Wil. Wood (Custom House, London). Hand iii.

His Majesty having been pleased by his Order in Council, dated the 28th Ultimo, Copy whereof you will receive inclosed, to direct that the Quarentine now subsisting by Virtue of his Majesty's Order in Council of the 18th of June 1747, upon Ship's coming from any of the Ports in West Barbary upon the Atlantick Ocean be continued, and a like Quarentine of 40 Day's laid on all Ship's & Vessel's coming from any of the Ports in the Streights of Gibralter on the Barbary Coast, or any other of the Ports on that Coast in the Mediterranean, lying between the said Streights & Cape de las tres Farcas in the Kingdom of Fez, and that the like Rule's, Regulation's, & Restriction's, be observed by all such Ship's, & Vessel's, as are required to be observ'd, by his Majesty's aforemention'd Order in Council, of the 18th of June 1747.

81 Altered from '1722'.
82 Altered from '18'.
83 Written over an illegible erasure
84 Altered from '12'.
85 Written over an illegible erasure.

The Commissioner's direct that all Necessary care be taken, by your selve's, and the rest of the Officer's at your Port, that his Majesty's said Order in Council be duely comply'd with, taking care to persue the direction's signify'd in my Letter of the 20th of June 1747, in relation to Ship's arriving from the Port of Santa Cruize, or any other Port in West Barbary on the Atlantick Ocean; And you are immediately to acknowledge the Receipt of this Letter to the Board, *valediction 2*

380
1 July
1749

CUST 58/149, pp. 172–3

From Wil. Wood (Custom House, London). Hand iii.

Inclosed you will receive Copy of the Memorial of Mr Jame's Ord, relating to some Chocolate under Seizure at your Port, and you are to examine into the allegation's, therein contain'd & report to the Board, a true State of the Case, with your opinion, *valediction 2*

To The Honourable the Commissioners of his Majesty's Custom's –

The Memorial of Jame's Ord Esqr Sheweth That he, and all his family coming over into England from Jamaica, in the Cornwall man of War, amongst a great Quantity of other Good's, he brought with him some Chocolate for his own private use, and not by way of Merchandize, part of which he used on Ship Board & other part thereof, about Thirty Pounds which he did not use, was Seiz'd by the Officer's of the Custom's at Portsmouth, upon his arrival about a Week ago as not being enterable, tho' your Memorialist had ordered all his Goods to be Enter'd & Duty's paid, which was done accordingly,

Therefore as your Memorialist intended this Chocolate for his own private use, he humbly pray's your Honour's to order the same to be deliver'd to him upon paying the Dutie's

Jame's Ord

381
1 July
1749

CUST 58/149, p. 173

From Wil. Wood (Custom House, London). Hand iii.

The Board having received a Letter from the Treasury, in relation to Captain Harlands Sea Store of Liquor's, which was Lodg'd in the CustomHouse at Portsmouth, out of his Majesty's Ship the Nottingham when she was paid off, You are to acquaint the Commissioner's, what Quantity of Liquor there is and the particular Sort's, & you will then receive their further Order's, *valediction 2*

382
1 July
1749

CUST 58/1

From W. C[ooley] and R. T[urvin] (Custom House, Portsmouth). Hand iii.

In obedience to your Honour's Command's of the 28th Instant, We have call'd in & cancell'd the Deputation's of John Newman & John Stretch Coalmeter's, & there being now three Vacancy's for Coal Meter's We humbly beg leave to recommend, in ⌜the room of Benjamin Summer's Deceas'd, John Chadwick, in⌝[86] the room, of Jno Newman, Richard Lee, & in the room of Jno Stretch Anthony Haswell, Extra Tidesmen at this Port, Person's duely qualify'd & in every respect, highly deserving of Your ⌜H*onour*'s⌝[87] favour, which is most humbly submitted to your Consideration *valediction 4*

---

[86] Inserted.
[87] Inserted.

383 CUST 58/1
1 July
1749

From W. C[ooley] and R. T[urvin] (Custom House, Portsmouth). Hand iii.

Herewith we transmit your Honour's the Abstract for the Month of June last, together with the undermentioned Accounts to which we beg leave to refer *valediction 4*

Nil List of Bond's
Tea & other Good's Enumerated, with Petty receipts Endors'd
Absent Officer's
State of Bonds for Midsummer quarter last

PS/ From the Book kept in this Office it appear's that the Weights & Scale's, Coal and Corn bushel's at this Port were try'd the 5th Ultimo by the Surveyor & Landwaiter's, and that they found the same to be exact & true, and that the Stamp's for marking Hide's, Skin's Linnen's, Seizd Goods, and Sail Cloth, are in good & Sufficient repair & fit for the use's design'd

W. C

384 CUST 58/1
1 July
1749

From W. C[ooley] and R. T[urvin] (Custom House, Portsmouth). Hand iii.

Your Honour's having been pleas'd to order us to call in the Deputation's of Wm Hare, Jno Newnham & Jno Stretch as Coal Meter's, judging them inconsistant with their several Employment's; We have called them in accordingly, But as the Case of Jno Stretch weighing Porter is uncommon, and as we immagine deserving of your Honour's Compassion, we humbly crave leave to recommend him to Your Honours Consideration, he has but £20 Per Annum, and is oblig'd to give constant attendance, at the Scale or at the Custom House, as the Business may require, so that he can have no other recourse, to maintain himself and Family, as therefore it is an Employment of some Trust, and he is really a man fit for the Business, & deserving of Encouragement, We humbly refer it to your Honour's Consideration, since you are pleas'd to take away his Coal Deputation, whether it is not reasonable to make his Allowance equal to a Tidesman, that being the lowest Allowance that is made to any Officer, whose Bussinss requires his whole time & who has nothing besides to help it out, all which is humbly submitted *valediction 4*

385 CUST 58/1
3 July
1749

From W. C[ooley] and R. T[urvin] (Custom House, Portsmouth). Hand iii.

We receiv'd your Honour's Order of the 1st Instant signifyd to us by Mr Wood Inclosing Copy of his Majesty's Order in Council dated the 28th Ultimo, We shall in obedience thereto take care his Majestys said Order in Council be duely observ'd by ourselve's & the rest of the Officer's at this Port, taking care to persue the Direction's signify'd to us by Mr Wood in his Letter ⌜of the 20th ⌝[88] June 1747 in relation to Ship's arriving from the Port of Santa Cruize, or any other Port in West Barbary, on the Atlantick Ocean, *valediction 5*

386 CUST 58/1
4 July
1749

From W. C[ooley] and R. T[urvin] (Custom House, Portsmouth). Hand iii.

Inclos'd we transmit your Hon*our*s a Letter which we this day receiv'd from Mr Charle's Markland Landsurveyor at this Port, who being in a very ill State of Health, and not being able to attend his Duty, is advised by the Physician's to reside in the Country for some time, in order to restore him, to his former health, and as his Case is very Dangerou's, and ever since he has been an Officer has given Constant & Diligent attendance to his Duty, We beg Your Honour's will give him leave to be Absent one Month, without loss of Pay, he having propos'd to us that Mr Skeat one of the Landwaiter's during his Absence may Discharge his Duty ⌜who⌝[89] We are to acquaint your Honour's is in every respect well Qualify'd; and for whose Conduct ⌜M^{r}⌝[90] Markland will esteem himself Answerable, all which is humbly submitted to your Consideration, *valediction 4*

---

[88] MS. 'of the 20th of the 20th'.
[89] Inserted.
[90] Written over 'Mr Markland' erased, followed by 'will' struck out.

Gentlemen

Having for some time been Afflicted with the Rheumatism to such a degree, as to be in danger of losing the use of my Limb's, & being advis'd by the Physicion's to be as much on ⌜Horseback⌝[91] as Possible, I beg the favour of you to apply to the Commissioners that I may have leave of Absence, one month for the Recovery of my Health, and that without loss of Salary, which I presume will be thought the more reasonable, when it shall be known that this is the first application of the kind I ever made, and would not now have been desired but that the Necessity is real, and if the Board is pleas'd to Indulge me, I propose that Mr Skeat ⌜do⌝[92] discharge my Duty, in my Absence, who is every way Qualify'd, & for whose Conduct I shall esteem my self answerable, and this without any Additional Expence to the Crown, I am

Gentlemen Your most humble Servant

Chas Markland

Custom House Portsm^{o} 3^{d} July 1749

387
5 July
1749

CUST 58/1

From W. C[ooley] and R. T[urvin] (Custom House, Portsmouth). Hand iii.

In obedience to your Order signify'd to us by Mr Wood in his Letter of the 1st Instant, Inclosed we transmit your Honour's an Account of the quantity and Particular St*atem*ents of Liquor now in his Majesty's WareHouse at this Port, belonging to Captain Harland, to which we beg to refer Your Honour's *valediction 3*

In the WareHouse Landed out of the Nottingham man of War Capt Harland Examined

Four hogsheads q*uanti*ty 174 gall^{s} Madeira wine
Seven Hamp*ers* q*uanti*ty 7 Dozen & 4 bottle's Clarrett
Two Dozen bottle's Madeira
Four Dozen bottle's Champaingne
One Dozen D^{o} – *Sange's
Four Dozen D^{o} – Port
Six Dozen Minorca Wine w*i*th three Dozen & 3 bottle's *Arrack & 4 bott*les* Spirits

Dated the 4th July 1749

Chas Markland Surv*eyo*r
Edwd Skeat } Landwaiter's
Robt Alexander }

388
5 July
1749

CUST 58/1

From W. C[ooley] and R. T[urvin] (Custom House, Portsmouth). Hand iii.

In Mr Wood's Letter of the 1st Instant, We received Inclos'd Copy of the Memorial, of Mr Jame's Ord, relating to some Chocolate, under stop at this Port, We have examined into the Allegation's therein Contained, and by the Inclos'd Letter, which we received from the Surveyor & Landwaiter's at this Port, who stopt the said Chocolate, & a true state of the Case will appear, to which we beg leave to refer, and what ever Direction's Your Honour's shall be pleas'd to send us in Regard thereto, will be duely observ'd *valediction 4*

Gentlemen

You having been pleasd to communicate to us a Letter from Mr Secretary Wood bearing date the 1st Instant, Inclosing Copy of the Memorial, of Mr Jame's Ord Relating to some Chocolate under Seizure at this Port, in answer thereto, we are to acquaint you, that upon our Examining the Baggage belonging to the said Mr Ord & his Family landed here out of the Cornwall man of war from Jamaica, We found One box ⌜–⌝[93] Containing Fifty Pound's of Chocolate, which we Detained as being Prohibited to be Imported, but did not make a Seizure thereof, because the Gentlemen who had the Key's, & attended the opening of the said Mr Ord's Baggage declar'd to us that this Chocolate was the remain's of the Sea Store's,

[91] Altered from 'Horse'.
[92] MS. 'to'.
[93] Written over an illegible erasure.

belonging to the said Mr Ord, and his Family, & that he woud apply to the Honble Board, not doubting but their Honour's Woud give Direction's for restoring the same, And ⌜notwithstanding⌝[94] the said Chocolate is in strictness of Law Forfeited, yet we are ready to comply with such Order's as the Honourable Board shall think proper, to give on this occasion, and are

Gentlemen Your most humble Servants

Chas Markland
Thos Merritt
Robt Alexander

Custom House Portsm^o 4th July 1749
To The Collector & Comptroller

389
5 July
1749

CUST 58/1

From W. C[ooley] and R. T[urvin] (Custom House, Portsmouth). Hand iii.

We are to acquaint your Hon*ours* the Glorioso Spanish man of War a Prize lately Purchased by some English ⌜ Merchants⌝[95] being now just on Sailing from this Port, And we having agreeable to Practice Demanded the Duty of £5 Per Cent, which we conceive to be due, (as[96] the said Ship was not Purchased by the Government,) Mr Jno Rickman Agent to the Purchaser's, who by their Repeated Order's to him have this Day absolutely refus'd Payment of the said Duty, We therefore beg to know how we are to govern our selve's in this Affair, & that you ⌜will⌝[97] be pleased to send Us Your immediate Direction's thereon, We beg leave to acquaint Your Honour's, for all such Prize Ship's which have been Sold at this Port, otherwise than to the Government, the Duty of £5 Per Cent have been received *valediction 4*

390
6 July
1749

CUST 58/149, p. 173

From Wil. Wood (Custom House, London). Hand iii.

Captain Gwynn of his Majesty's Ship Ambuscade, having by his Memorial of the 8th Ultimo apply'd to the Commissioner's, desiring that his Sea Store's in the WareHouse at Your Port, of four Hamper's of Lisbon Wine, and an *Ulage Cask of Wine, may be deliver'd, They have agreed thereto, and you are to deliver the said Wine, upon the Dutie's being paid for the same, *valediction 2*

391
6 July
1749

CUST 58/1

From W. C[ooley] and R. T[urvin] (Custom House, Portsmouth). Hand iii.

Inclos'd we transmit Your Honour's a Certificate, in order to obtain a Licence to carry Rice to the Southward of Cape Finister, for the ship Edinburgh, of London Jame's Russell Master, together with a Plantation Certificate for the said Ship, and as she is now ready to Sail, We desire the Licence, and the Inclos'd Certificate, may be sent by the return of the Post, *valediction 3*

392
7 July
1749

CUST 58/149, p. 174

From Wil. Levinz ('Levine'), G. Vaughan, Wil. Westby and Edw. Hooper (Custom House, London). Hand iii.

Having granted our Deputation for Rice Ely Diaper, to be a Coal Meter at Your Port, in the room of Benjamin Summer's deceased, You are to take care, he be under Oath, and Security for the faithfull discharge of the said Employ and Qualifie's himself as the Law directs, *valediction 1*

393
8 July
1749

CUST 58/149, p. 174

From Wil. Wood (Custom House, London). Hand iii.

The Commissioner's received your Letter of the 5th Instant, in return to the Memorial of Mr Jame's Ord, relating to some Chocolate under Stop at Your Port; They direct that you send it up forthwith, to the WareHouse here, under the Seal's of Office, at the Proprietor's Charge, giving the Board notice when, and by what Conveyance it is sent, & what agreement is made for Carriage, *valediction 2*

---

94 MS. 'notwithsanding'.
95 Possibly 'Merchant,'.
96 MS. omits opening bracket.
97 Written only as catchword at foot of page.

394
8 July
1749

CUST 58/149, pp. 174–5

From W. Levinz ('Levine'), Wil. Westby, G. Vaughan and Edw. Hooper (Custom House, London). Hand iii.

We receiv'd your Letter of the 4th Instant, transmitting one from Mr Charle's Markland, Landsurveyor at Your Port, desiring leave to be absent for a Month, for Recovery of his health, We agree thereto, without loss of pay, and you are to take care the Service, doe's not suffer during his absence,

In answer to the Account of Seizure's transmitted in your Letter of the 5th Ins*tant* We direct you to Prosecute the Rum thereinmentiond to Condemnation, before the Justice's of the Pease at the King's Charge, acquainting us when Condemn'd *valediction 1*

Noted the 10th of July

395
10 July
1749

CUST 58/1

From W. C[ooley] and R. T[urvin] (Custom House, Portsmouth). Hand iii.

In Obedience to Your Honour's Order of the 8th Instant, we are to acquaint you, by the Waggon of George Clarke, which will be at the Whitehart in the Burrough of Southwark on Wednesday the 12th Instant We have this day sent under the Seals of Office directed for your Honour's, a Box Containing Chocolate belonging to Mr Jame's Ord, for Carriage whereof we have agreed that two Shilling's, and six pence shall be paid, *valediction 5*

396
11 July
1749

CUST 58/149, p. 175

From Edw. Hooper, G. Vaughan, Wil. Westby and W. Levinz ('Levine') (Custom House, London). Hand iii.

Having granted our Deputations for John Chadwick, to be a Coal Meter at Your Port, in the room of Jno Stretch; & Richard Lee in the room of John Newman Dismist, You are to take care they be under Oath, and Security, for the faithful discharge of the said Employ, & Qualifie's themselves as the Law directs, *valediction 1*

397
11 July
1749

CUST 58/149, pp. 175–6

From W. Wood (Custom House, London). Hand iii.

The Commissioner's having receiv'd Information, from several eminent Trader's of this City, that great Quantitie's of Brandy, Tea, Muslin, and other Customable Commoditie's, are daily run into the Neighbourhood of your Port, they direct you to acquaint them what Information you may have from time to time of any Vessel's appearing on your Coast which are suspected of intending to run any Customable, or Prohibited Goods, describing the Vessel, & distinguishing the Place from whence she come's, if you can get an Account thereof, & where the Cargoe is intended to be landed as also what Notice you receive of any such Good's having been landed, & where on your Coast, and of any Smugler's, passing or repassing in Your Parts, & also acquainting them from time to time when any of his Majesty's Ship's which are appointed to Cruize on the *Owler's, & Smugler's, or the Sloop's in the Service of this Revenue, come into or sail out of your Port, *valediction 2*

398
12 July
1749

CUST 58/149, p. 176

From Edw. Hooper, Ric. Chandlor, Wil. Westby and G. Vaughan (Custom House, London). Hand iii.

Mr Russel having by his Letter of the 8th Instant, apply'd to us desiring that his Household furniture, mention'd in the Inclos'd List, may be taken out of the Deptford Lighter at your Port, and put on board the Glorioso, We agree thereto, and you may Suffer them to be taken out of the said Lighter, & Shipt on board the Glorioso as desired, taking care the Crown be put to no Charge on this Account, *valediction 1*

399 CUST 58/149, pp. 176–7
12 July
1749

From Wil. Wood (Custom House, London). Hand iii.

Your Letter of the 8th Instant relating to the five Per Cent, on the Glorioso was immediately read to the Commissioner's, & referr'd to the Patent Officer's & Sollicitor, who have made their report's, but the Board defer coming to any resolution, till they have seen Mr Tovin the Broker, and Mr Warden the Agent, to whom they have sent to attend them, In the mean time they have agreed to permit Mr Russel's thing's to be put on board the said Ship, but to have no relation to the dispute in any shape, *valediction 2*

400 CUST 58/1
13 July
1749

From W. C[ooley] and R. T[urvin] (Custom House, Portsmouth). Hand iii.

Inclosed we transmit your Honour's an Account of such Stationary Ware's, a's was lately sent for the use of this Port, which was received the 9th Instant, *valediction 5*

4 Quires *Imperial Rul'd for
Quarter Book's Inwards –
2 Quires *Imperial
2 Book's 1 quire *Demy in mar*ble*
9 Quires *Demy (6 quires Cutt)
1000 Quill's
3 Dozen Tag's
80 Blue Book's – 4 Leave's
40 D^{o} 8 Leave's
30 D^{o} 12 Leaves
12 D^{o} 16 Leave's
12 D^{o} 24 Leave's
50 D^{o} 2 Leave's
60 D^{o} 6
30 10
3 Bagg's Sand
1 Dozen File's, with Tag's
A Leidger Outward's
3 Quire's *Boarding Bill's
2 Quire's Reports Inward's
2 Quires – Outward's
1 Permit Book
2 Quires Journal's

1 Quart of red Ink & bottle
4 Horn *Pounce Boxe's
1 Dozen Pencil's
1 Dozen Tape
1 Pound of Wax
A Leidger Inwards
4 Rheam's fine *Pott Cutt
4 Rheam's 2^{d}, *Pott
1 Dozen *Demy Pocket B*oo*ks
3000 Wafer's & Box
2 Gallon's Ink & *Rundlet
3 Ivory Penknive's
1/2 Pound of *Pounce
3 Bodkins
20 Blue Book's 14 Leave's
12 D^{o} – 20 Leave's
2 Abstract Book's
1 Quire Quarterly Accounts
Enumerated Goods
One Quire *Over Entry's
One Quire Personal Prosecution's
4 Sloop's Journal's

401 CUST 58/149, p. 177
15 July
1749

From Wil. Wood (Custom House, London) to [W. Cooley]. Hand iii.

Sir

Agreeable to your desire, Inclosed you will receive six Corn Debenture's, and by the next Carrier three Dozen more will be sent you, I am

Sir Your most humble Servant

Wm Wood

402 CUST 58/149, p. 177
20 July
1749

From W. Wood (Custom House, London). Hand iii.

The Commissioner's observing by several Accounts of Seizure's, which have been lately transmitted from diver's Part's, that the Officer's are not so particular, as they ought to be, in explaining the Circumstance's attending the Seizure's[98] of Good's &cetera, they direct that you pay particular regard to Mr Carkesse's Letters of the 1st of April, & the 16th of June 1737, & take care that the Accounts of Seizure's be returnd, & Affidavits transmitted, in the manner thereby directed, which the Commissioner's are of opinion will have a good effect, and be a great mean's of puting a stop to the Smugling, at present carried on in so many Parts of this Kingdom

You are to acknowledge the receipt of this Letter, & acquaint the Board, whether the above Letter's are enterd in your Book of Order's, *valediction 2*

---

[98] 'Seizure's', repeated, struck out.

403
24 July
1749

CUST 58/1

From W. C[ooley] and R. T[urvin] (Custom House, Portsmouth). Hand iii.

We here acknowledge the Receipt of Your Honours' Order, signify'd to us by Mr Wood in his Letter of the 20th Instant, And we are to acquaint Your Honours, we have in our Book of Order's Enter'd Mr Carkess's Letter of the 16th June 1737 (but not of the 1st April) to which we shall pay particular Regard; The Collector begs your Honour's will be Pleas'd to order a Commission for him, to be taken out of the Court of ⌜EXchequer⌝[99] & King's Bench, Impowering him to take Affudavits, *valediction 3*

404
25 July
1749

CUST 58/149, p. 178

From Wil. Wood (Custom House, London). Hand iii.

The Commissioner's have a Letter from his Grace the Duke of New Castle, of this day acquainting them, that having receiv'd Information, that the ⌜Ship⌝[1] Dorothy & Mary, Wm Maguire Commander, bound to Cadiz, Malaga, or some other Port, in Spain, has on board Contraband Good's, & several Artificer's, who has been seduced to leave this Kingdom, in order to Exercise, and teach their Trade, in a Forreign Country, which Ship it is now suppos'd may be in some of the Western Ports of this Kingdom; He was commanded to signify his Majesty's ⌜Pleasure⌝[2], that they should forthwith send direction's to the Officer's of the Custom's, in the several Western Port's, that if the said ⌜Ship⌝[3] Should be in any of those Ports, or come thither, they should stop her, from proceeding on her Voyage, and immediately send Notice of their having so done, for his Majesty's Information, & detain the said Ship till further signification of his Majesty's Pleasure; The Commissioner's direct you to take care that this his Majesty's Pleasure, signify'd by his Grace the Duke of New Castle, be strictly observ'd, and duely comply'd with, & that in case of your stopping the said Ship, You acquaint the Board therewith by Express, with an Account of the Person's which may be found on Board, distinguishing the Number of Passenger's, & Number of Sailor's *valediction 2*

405
26 July
1749

CUST 58/1

From W. C[ooley] and R. T[urvin] (Custom House, Portsmouth). Hand iii.

In obedience to your Honour's Command signify'd to us by Mr Wood, in his Letter of the 25th Instant, We are to acquaint you, as the Ship Dorothy & Mary, Wm Maguire Commander to Cadiz & Malaga, Prov'd to be at this Port. We have in Obedience to your said Order stop the said Ship and Inclos'd we transmit your Honour's an Account of the Person's on Board, distinguishing the number of Passenger's, and Number of Sailor's, to which we beg leave to refer, *valediction 3*

Passenger's on Board the Dorothy & Mary
Wm Maguire Commander
James O'Bryan his Wife & three Children

Thomas Tomlin's & his Wife	
William Gordon & his Wife	
Robert Marshall & his Wife	
An Ryley & her Daughter	
John Godwin & his Daughter	} all for Malaga
Peter Drew	
Samuel Calling & his Wife	
Elizabeth Medcalf	
Thomas Grinsel	

For Cadiz Messrs Dalrymple & Santhill
For Malaga Timothy Macnamara & 3 Servants
For Gibralter Benjamin Roberts
The ⌜N^{o}⌝[4] Mariner's belonging to the said Ship are thirteen Including the Master & Mate

99 Probably altered from 'Xchequer'.
1 Inserted.
2 MS. 'Peasure'.
3 Altered from 'Ship's'.
4 Inserted.

406
27 July 1749

CUST 58/149, pp. 179–80

From W. Wood (Custom House, London). Hand iii.

In consequence of what I wrote you last night, you Will have this put into your hand's by M[r] Brigg's Clerk of the Weaver's Company, upon whose application his Grace the Duke of New Castle was pleased to give direction's for stopping of the Dorothy & Mary; M[r] Brig's bring's with him the necessary Information's, that Wooll, & other Contraband Good's are on board this Ship, which if he prove's to your satisfaction, You will take the most proper measure's to come to the Knowledge of there being such Good's on board, that you may Seize, and Prosecute the same, together with the Ship, according to Law, I recommend this Gentlemen to Your acquaintance, and desire you will do every thing on your Part, to assist him which he can reasonably desire, *valediction 2*

407
28 July 1749

CUST 58/149, p. 179

From Wil. Wood (Custom House, London). Hand iii.

I received this Morning at ten o'Clock by Express your's of Yesterday, which was read to the Board, and immediately after sent to the Duke of New Castle, for his Information, & having this Evening seen M[r] Stone his Secretary; I have reason to believe you will have further direction's, to Morrow, either by the Post, or Express, in the mean time I am to desire you will take particular care, that no Goods be removed Out of the Ship, and that the Person's bound for Malaga, may bc continued on board. But as I was told at M[r] Stone's, that Tho[s] Grinsel, one in your List was seen today in Spittle Field's, I am apprehensive, if this be true, other's may have left the Ship likewise, pray let me hear from you, on Receipt of this in relation to Grinsel, & the other Passenger's for Malaga, & if any attempt has been made to take or throw any Good's out of the said Ship, for it is certain there were Contraband Good's loaden on board, *valediction 2*

408
30 July 1749

CUST 58/149, pp. 180–2

From Wil. Wood (Custom House, London). Hand iii.

Having this Moment almost received a Letter from his Grace the Duke of NewCastle of which the Inclosed is a Copy; I sent for Captain Maguire, and acquainted him with the unwillingness, that his Grace had to detain his Ship, in detriment to the Owner's & Merchant's concern'd, in the Loading, provided there appear'd upon Examination no Wooll, or other Contraband Goods were found on board his Ship, at the same time intimating to him, whether it might not be proper for him, in order to get his ship released the sooner, to proceed to Portsmouth, & give you all the Assistance & Satisfaction in his Power, to convince you, that no such Contraband Goods were on board, to his knowledge; & if there were, to endeavour himself, to find them out, he readily agreed to make the best of his way to your Port, promising to give you all such Assistance and Satisfaction, and to deliver any Letter, I shoud send, into your hand's, likewise promising to put on shore, all the Passengers he had on board, that there is any ground's to suspect, to be Manufacturer's or the Wive's, and Children of Manufacturer's, & to put into your hand's one sett of the Bill of Loading's, he had signed, relating to them, however at the same time desiring for his Security, on his arrival at Malaga that a Certificate may be given him, that he wa's obliged by order from his Majesty, to deliver up such of the Passenger's, as shall be taken out by the King's Messenger's, & deliver'd by him, to you, & also the thing's on board, which shall be taken on shore, and for which he signed Bill's of Loading; as M[r] Brigg's will be with you I desire you will impart the contents, of the Duke of NewCastle's, as well as the contents of this Letter, to him, and advise with him on the subject matter on both, and acquaint the Board by the first Opportunity, of the result of your Conversation's, & of your proceeding's, to the time of your writing, that his Grace the Duke of NewCastle, may have the necessary & most timely Information, & that if his Majesty's Pleasure may be further wanted, it may be given without loss of time, Having only to add in the Absence of the Commissioner's, that you are immediately to cause enquiry to be made, whether the said Ship, has on board any Wooll, or other Contraband Good's, & that after such enquiry, you give direction's, either for permitting the said

Ship's proceeding on her Voyage, or otherwise as shall appear to you, according to Law, referring you to Mr Brigg's, for the making good what is mentioned in the Duke's Letter, to be alledged in the Memorial of the Company of Weaver's, delivered to his Grace the 25th past, *valediction 2*

⌜4 O'clock in the Afternoon⌝[5]

Whitehall 29th July 1749

Gentlemen

Having been inform'd that the Ship, Dorothy & Mary, bound to Cardiz, & Malaga William Maguire, Commander, was stopt at St Helen's, on Thursday last, and that the said William Maguire, has this day made application to you, that the said Ship, may be suffered to proceed on her Voyage, as the detaining of her wou'd be detrimental to the Owner's &cetera, I am to signify to you his Majesty's pleasure, that you should immediately ⌜–⌝[6] cause enquiry to be made, whether the said ship has on board, any Wool, or other Contraband Good's (as was alledged in the Memorial of the Company of Weaver's, deliver'd to me on the 25th past, for which purpose I have ordered Notice to be given, to the Person's concern'd, to lay before you such Informations as they had received, relating thereto, & that after such enquiry, You should give Direction's either for permitting the said Ship to proceed on her Voyage, or otherwise, as shall appear to You, to be according to Law I am

Gentlemen Your most Obedient humble Servant,

Holle's, New Castle

a true Copy Wm Wood

July 30th 1749.

409
31 July
1749

CUST 58/149, p. 183

From Wil. Wood (Custom House, London). Hand iii.

Some time since, was sent you on board the Willingmind, George Danford Mast*er* a Case of Beam's, Weights &cetera, & a bundle of Boards, You are to acknowledge the Receipt thereof, to the Commissioner's, *valediction* 2

410
31 July
1749

CUST 58/1

From W. C[ooley] and R. T[urvin] (Custom House, Portsmouth). Hand iii.

We are to acquaint your Honour's on the 29th Instant, William Hare late a Tidesman, & Boatman, resign'd his Deputation in his room we humbly beg leave to recommend William Brown, who has been Employ'd in the Service of the Custom's at this Port, as an Extra Tidesman, & Boatman, upwards of Eleven Years, all which time he has behav'd himself as a good & Diligent Officer, and worthy of Your Honour's favour, otherwise he wou'd not have been recommended *valediction 4*

411
1 August
1749

CUST 58/1

From W. C[ooley] and R. T[urvin] (Custom House, Portsmouth). Hand iii.

We received your Order of the 30th Ultimo signify'd to us by Mr Wood, together with Copy of his Grace the Duke of New Castle's Letter, And we are to acquaint Your Honour's the strictest rummage have been made after Wooll, or other Contraband Good's, which was suppos'd to have been on Board the Dorothy & Mary, but no such Goods on the Rummage have been found,

There is on board the Utensil's for Weaving which appear to have been Enter'd at the Custom House, and for which the Master has *Cocquets specifying the same to be hand Turnery & Cabinet Ware, We wou'd have stopt those Utensils, but do not find they are by any Act Prohibited to be Exported, – As therefore the King's Messenger's have taken on Shore all the Passenger's which were bound for Malaga, agreeable to the Inclos'd Bill of Lading, which the Master has sign'd relating to them, We have Recleard the Ship, and have given the Master a Certificate that he was Oblig'd to deliver up the said Passenger's in Pursuance of his Majesty's Order, Mr Biggs has agreeable to your Direction's Consulted in every shape which have been taken on this Affair, *valediction 3*

---

5 Follows the letter's date.

6 Written over an illegible erasure.

Port of Portsmouth

These are to Certify whom it may concern, that William Maguire Master of the Dorothy & Mary, now at this Port Bound for Malaga, by Order of Britanick Majesty, did on the 1st of August 1749 deliver up to two of his Majesty's Messenger's, the following Passenger's, for which he had sign'd Bill's of Lading for Malaga, vizt Walter Collin, Mary Collin, Thos Grinson, Jame's OBryan, Bridget OBryan, Mary OBryan, Chas OBryan, & Nich^{s} OBryan, Thomas Tomlin's, Rachael Tomlin's, Peter Drew, Wm Gordon Jno Gowen, Robt Marshall, Bridget Marshall, Ann Ryley & Mary Ryley, Polly Medcalf, Judiah Gordon & Ally Gowen Dated at the Custom House this 1st Day of Aug*ust* 1749

W C R T

412
2 August
1749

CUST 58/149, p. 183

From Wil. Wood (Custom House, London). Hand iii.

I received this morning, your Letter which was sent by Mr Brigg's, who by the Messenger that brought it, sent me word he woud be here to Morrow Morning, I immediately read it to the Board, and am directed to acquaint you, that they approve of your Conduct, on this occasion, I have sent Copy of your Letter, with the Bill of Loading, to Mr Stone, for his Grace the Duke of NewCastle's Information; I suppose as the Wind is fair, this Ship may be Sailed, if not, I wish the Master could be prevailed upon to give you up the Spinning Wheel's &cetera upon the same condition he did the Men, that is by giving him a Certificate for the said Good's, *valediction 2*

413
2 August
1749

CUST 58/1

From W. C[ooley] and R. T[urvin] (Custom House, Portsmouth). Hand iii.

We are to acquaint your Honour's on the 20th June last, we received out of the Willingmind Geo. Danford Master from London, a Case Containing Beam's, Weight's &cetera and a Bundle of Board's, and on the 3^{d} July we receiv'd a Case Containing Gauging Instruments, all for the use of this Port *valediction 5*

414
3 August
1749

CUST 58/149, pp. 183–4

From R. Chandlor, Beaumont Hotham, W. Westby and W. Levinz ('Levine') (Custom House, London). Hand iii.

Mr Bontein having applied to us, by his Memorial of the 27th Ultimo relating to ten, or twelve Dozen Bottle's of Madeira wine, which was landed out of his Majesty's Ship Strafford, and stopt by the Officer's at your Port, If the said wine, was not run, you may deliver it to the Proprietor, upon his paying the Duty for the same, *valediction 1*

415
3 August
1749

CUST 58/149, p. 185

From Wil. Wood (Custom House, London). Hand iii.

The Accounts mentioned in Your Letter's of the 4th January, & the 16th of March 1748, & List for Michaelma's, Christma's, & Lady=day Quarter's last, are safe come to Hand *valediction 2*

416
5 August
1749

CUST 58/149, p. 184

From R. Chandlor, W. Levinz ('Levine'), W. Westby and Edw. Hooper (Custom House, London). Hand iii.

In answer to the Accounts of Seizure's transmitted in your Letter's of the 29th Ultimo & 1st Instant We direct you to Prosecute the Good's thereinmention'd to Condemnation in the Exchequer, at the Officer's Charge, Corresponding, with our Sollicitor, and the Register of Seizure's, *valediction 1*

In margin: Noted the 7th of Aug*ust*.

417
7 August
1749

CUST 58/1

From W. C[ooley] and R. T[urvin] (Custom House, Portsmouth). Hand iii.

Herewith we transmit your Honour's the Abstract for the Month of July last, together with the undermentioned Accounts, to which we beg leave to refer *valediction 4*

Nil List of Bond's

Tea & other Goods Enumerated, with Petty rec*eip*ts Endors'd

Absent Officer's

PS From the Book kept in this Office it appear's that the Weights & Scale's, Coal and Corn Bushel's, at this Port, were try'd the 5th Ultimo by the Surveyor & Landwaiters, & that they found the same to be exact & true, and that the stamp's for marking Hide's, Skin's, Linnen's, Seiz'd Good's & Sail Cloth, are in good & Sufficient repair, and fit for the use's design'd

WC RT

418
7 August
1749

CUST 58/1

From W. C[ooley] and R. T[urvin] (Custom House, Portsmouth). Hand iii.

We are to acquaint your Honour's at the request of Lord Robt & Montagu Barty, we receiv'd into his Majesty's Warehouse at this Port, the Sea Store's of the late Lord Thoma's Barty, Command*er* of his Majesty's Ship the Winchester from East Indie's, amongst which there is four Cask's, one Case, & One Hamper *Arrack, three Case's and two Hamper's of China One Large, & one small Canister of Tea, Their Lordship's intend applying to your Honour's in relation thereto; Notwithstanding which we think it our Duty, to acquaint you, that we have secur'd such Goods into the King's WareHouse, which will remain there till we receive your Honour's Direction's thereon; The Princess Mary Man of war being to be paid off at this Port, and the Officer's &cetera belonging to her having the Remain's of their Sea Store of *Arrack on Board, We beg to know whether your Honour's have any objection to admitting the same to an Entry, which if you are pleas'd to comply with, will prevent their Application to your Honour's on that Account, we shall be glad to receive your immediate Answer, *valediction 3*

419
8 August
1749

CUST 58/149, p. 184

From W. Levinz ('Levine'), W. Westby, J. Evelynn and R. Chandlor (Custom House, London). Hand iii.

Francis Fuller Extra Tidesman at your Port, having by his Memorial of the 7th instant apply'd to us desiring leave to be absent six days, on his private Affair's, We have agreed thereto, & you are to take care the Service does not Suffer during his Absence.

Application having been made to u's desiring that William Tasker, may be appointed a Tidesman & Boatman at your Port, in the room of William Hare resigned, We direct you (in case he is to act as a Boatman) to examine into his Qualification's, & if you find him sufficiently Qualify'd, You are by return of the Post, to transmit us a Certificate thereof, in the manner required by our Secretary's Letter of the 21st June 1743 *valediction 1*

420
10 August
1749

CUST 58/149, p. 185

From W. Levinz ('Levine'), W. Westby, J. Evelynn and Edw. Hooper (Custom House, London). Hand iii.

Application having been made to us, desiring that John Barker Esqr Commander of his Majesty's Sloop, the Wasp, may have a Commission, Impowering him, to Seize Prohibited, and Uncustomed Good's, We have agreed thereto, and Inclosed you will receive our Commission accordingly, and when he has Perfected the Inclosed Bond with two Security's, You may admit him to his Duty, taking care he qualifie's himself as the Law directs, & when the Bond is Executed, You are to return it to us – *valediction 1*

421 10 August 1749

CUST 58/1

From W. C[ooley] and R. T[urvin] (Custom House, Portsmouth). Hand iii.

In Obedience to your order of the 8th Instant, Inclos'd we transmit Your Honours a Certificate whereby it will appear that Wm Tasker, lately recommended to your Honour's to be a Boatman at this Port, is sufficiently Qualify'd to Discharge the said Duty *valediction 5*

Portsmouth

These are to Certify that upon Examination, we find Wm Tasker to be Sufficiently Qualify'd for the Management of a Boat, and that he is a fit Person to be a Tidesman & Boatman in the Service of his Majesty's Customs at this Port, as Witness our hand's, Dated at the Custom House this 10th August 1749

W C R T W Baskerville, Tides*urveyo*r

422 11 August 1749

CUST 58/149, p. 186

From W. Wood (Custom House, London). Hand iii.

The Commissioner's having receiv'd your Letter, of the 28th June last, acquainting them, that Mr Edward Skeat, who was concern'd in making the Seizure of Brandy, Rum &cetera from Captain Gwynn, desire's he may have a suitable Satisfaction, made him as the Affair has been Compromis'd; And as the Warrant from the Treasury of the 21st of March last, directs that upon Captain Gwynn's paying the Duties of the Good's, and all the Charge's of Prosecution, and Satisfying the Officer's, that the Prosecution against him be suspended & discharged, You are to acquaint Mr Skeat, that he must apply to Captain Gwynn for a reward, *valediction 2*

423 11 August 1749

CUST 58/149, p. 186

From W. Levinz ('Levine'), W. Westby, J. Evelynn and Edw. Hooper (Custom House, London). Hand iii.

We have received your Letter of the 7th Instant, in relation to the thing's at Your Port, belonging to Lord Thoma's Bartie, late Commander of his Majesty's Ship the Winchelsea, And Lord Robert Bartie, having applied to us desiring that the *Arrack may be admitted to an Entry, We agree thereto, And the China, & Tea, you are to send up to the WareHouse here, under the Seal's of Office, giving us notice when & by what Conveyance it is sent, & what agreement is made for Carriage

You having represen'ted that the Princess Mary, is to be paid off, & that the Officer's have some remain's of Sea Store's, on Board We agree to your Admitting the same to an Entry Which we hereby signify to you, *valediction 1*

424 12 August 1749

CUST 58/149, p. 185

From Wil. Wood (Custom House, London). Hand iii.

Francis Fuller Extra Tidesman, at Your Port, having apply'd to us, & desired leave to be Absent, from Duty, for Six days longer, We agree to give him leave accordingly, We are

Your Loving Friends

This Letter was prepar'd by the Commissioner's Direction's but the Board being risen before it cou'd be finish'd their Commands are signify'd to You by

Gentlemen Your most humble Servant

Wm Wood

425
12 August
1749

CUST 58/149, pp. 187–9

From W. Levinz ('Levine'), J. Evelynn, W. Westby and Edw. Hooper (Custom House, London). Hand iii.

We receiv'd your Letter of the 21st June last, transmitting, an Account of the Produce, & Charges, of a parcel of Brandy, seiz'd out of the Hope, Paul Greve Master from St Martin's, which Brandy has been Condemn'd, & Sold, And the Lord's of the Treasury, having been pleas'd by their Warrant of the 13th of April last, to direct that his Majesty's $^{2}/_{3}{}^{ds}$ of the 32 half Hogshead's, Seiz'd by William Baskerville, after the deduction of the Charge's of Condemnation & Sale, be paid to Han's Hornman, of Dronthem, in Norway, Merchant, the Claimant, which Amount's to £87. 18. 7¾, as appear's by a State of the Account, laid before us by the Accomptant, of Petty receipts, Copy whereof you will receive Inclosed; We direct you to pay the said Sum of Eighty seven Pounds, eighteen Shilling's & seven Pence, three farthing's, to Han's Hornman, or his lawfull Attorney, pursuant to the Direction's of the Lord's of the Treasury, And Mr Medcalfe our Sollicitor having acquainted us that the Law Charge's, attending the Condemnation of this Brandy, Amount's to £80. 11. 4, You are to remit the same to him, as also £5. 5. 8 to the Accomptant of Petty Receipt's, being the London Officer's Poundage's. But as to the Nine *Anchor's, & one half *Anchor of Brandy, Seiz'd out of the said Ship, by Thomas Trehearne, his Majesty's part of that Seizure is not remitted, You are therefore to pay the Officer his third, & remit the King's part to Mr Simon, in like manner as is done in the Seizure's of Enumerated Good's, which we Signify to you, for your Government, *valediction 1*

In margin: £87. 18. 7¾[7]

Debtors		⌜Creditors⌝[8]		
To the Produce of 32 half hogsheads of Brandy –	£281.15. 9¼	By Officers one third –	93.18. 7	
		Mr Saml Chandlor as by Bill –	2.15. 8	
		Lighterage –	0. 4. 0	
		Two Commission's –	1. 6. 8	
		Two Appraiser's –	0.13. 4	
		Drawing Indenture & cetera –	0.10. 6	
		Poundage to the Collector & Comptroller –	8. 4. 4½	£. s. d.
		Advertisement & Cryer –	0. 2. –	107.15. 1½
		By the Sollicitor's Bill of Law Charges –	80.11. 4	
		Register of Seizure's, fee.	0. 5. 0	
		Poundage to the London officers –	5. 5. 8	86. 2. 0
				193.17. 1½
		By Ballance due to Han's Hornman –		87.18. 7¾
	£281.15. 9¼			£281.15. 9¼

426
12 August
1749

CUST 58/1

From W. C[ooley] and R. T[urvin] (Custom House, Portsmouth). Hand iii.

We are to acquaint your Honour's on the 11th Instant, died R^{d} Gambell late a Coal Meter at Gosport, And in his room we humbly beg leave to recommend Jno Sweet, an Inhabitant of said Place to succeed Gambell, he being in every respect duely well Qualify'd, to execute the Office of a Coal Meter. We beg leave to acquaint your Honour's Sweet was recommended by us the last Vacancy, that was at Gosport. We therefore hope your Honour's will now accept of our Recommendation of him, *valediction 3*

---

7 Underlined.
8 MS. 'C^{rsrs}' (for 'C^{rs}').

427 15 August 1749

CUST 58/149, p. 189

From W. Wood (Custom House, London). Hand iii.

Mr Samuel Earle having by his Memorial of this date, apply'd to the Commissioner's, relating to one Roll of Brocade Silk, one Looking Glass and one Snuff Box, suppos'd to be Gold, & some other triffling Good's, under Stop at Your Port, Inclosed I send you Copy of the said Memorial and you are to report to the Board, a true state of the Case, with all the Circumstances, relating thereto, for their Consideration *valediction 2*

Honourable Sir's

Mr John Gladell formerly Purser of the Deptford man of War, having died in the East Indie's, & there being sent over in the Princess Mary, man of war, now at Portsmouth, one Roll of Brocade Silk, one Looking Glass, one snuff Box, suppos'd to be Gold, with a stone in the Cover, & some other triffling Good's belonging to the ⌜said⌝[9] Gladell, ⌜I⌝[10] humbly desire your Honour's Order, to the Collector of Portsmouth, to deliver the said Good's, or that they may be sent up to London for that purpose, I am

Honble Sir's Your most obedient Servant

Samuel Earle

15th August 1749

428 15 August 1749

CUST 58/149, pp. 189–90

From Edw. Hooper, W. Westby, J. Evelynn and W. Levinz ('Levine') (Custom House, London). Hand iii.

In answer to the Account of Seizure's transmitted in your Letter of the 8th Instant, We direct you to Prosecute the Goods, thereinmention'd to Condemnation, in the Exchequer, the Enumerated at the King's Charge, & the rest at the Officer's Charge, Corresponding with our Sollicitor, & the Register of Seizure's, *valediction 1*

Noted 17th August

429 15 August 1749

CUST 58/1

From W. C[ooley] and R. T[urvin] (Custom House, Portsmouth). Hand iii.

In obedience to your Honour's order of the 11th Instant, We have this day sent by the Waggon of Geo. Clarke, which will be at the Whitehart in the Burrough of Southwark on Thursday the 18th Instant, under the Seal's of Office, Three Case's, & a Chest of China One Box, and one Canister of Tea, for Carriage whereof, we have agreed that [11] shall be paid, *valediction 3*

430 16 August 1749

CUST 58/149, p. 190

From J. Evelynn, Edw. Hooper, W. Levinz ('Levine') and R. Chandlor (Custom House, London). Hand iii.

Having granted our Commission, for William Tasker, to be a Tidesman, & Boatman at Your Port, in the room of William Hare resign'd You are to take care, he be under Oath, & Security, for the faithfull discharge of the said Employ, & qualifie's himself as the Law directs, paying him the like Allowance by Incident's, as was paid to his Predecessor, for which the Collector may take Credit in his Account of Incident's, referring therein, to the date hereof, *valediction 1*

---

9 Altered from 'said's'.
10 Inserted.
11 Space left blank.

431
17 August 1749

CUST 58/149, pp. 190–1

From W. Wood (Custom House, London). Hand iii.

Complaint having been made to the Duke of New Castle, one of his Majesty's Principal Secretaries of State by the Company of Weaver's in London, "that[12] they have receiv'd Information of Sundry Foreigner's, & other's who have endeavour'd to entice & seduce divers of his Majesty's Subject's, Manufacturer's in the Weaving Business, in Spitalfields, & other parts of this Kingdom to go abroad to Spain or other Foreign Parts contrary to the direction's of the 5th Geo 1st Cap 27th and to carry with them Diverie Implement's, and Utensil's belonging to the Weaving Manufacture," And it being of the utmost Importance for the Preservation of the Exportation of the Manufacture's of this Kingdom to foreign part's, that the said Act shou'd be strictly comply'd with, I am to remind you of the Boards Direction's in their Letter of the[13] 20th August 1719 and on this occasion to recommend your calling before you, all the Officer's of your Port, & enjoyn them in the strongest manner, to have a Watchfull Eye what Passenger's are on board all Ship's bound to foreign Parts, and if any of them are Manufacturer's You are immediately to give notice thereof to some Justice of the Peace, in order for his Acting in Pursuance of the said Law, & give it in Charge to the Officer's not to permit any Loom's, or Weaving Utensil's to be ship'd without first acquainting the Commissioner's, and having their Direction's.

You are to cause this Letter to be Enterd in Your Book of Order's, acknowledging the receipt thereof to the Board, *valediction 2*

PS By Order of the Commissioners Inclos'd I send you an Act, passed the last Session, for enlarging & maintaining the Harbour of Ramsgate &cetera,[14] to which I refer you for your Information and Government,

432
17 August 1749

CUST 58/149, pp. 191–2

From Edw. Hooper, W. Westby, J. Evelynn and W. Levinz ('Levine') (Custom House, London). Hand iii.

The Commissioner's for Victualling his Majesty's Navy, having apply'd to u's by their Letter of the 16th Instant, desiring that some remain's of wine, *Arrack, Rice, *Tamarind, & Sugar, furnish'd them by the Agent Victualler, for the Squadron under the Command of Admiral Griffin, on board his Majesty's Ship Princess Mary, at your Port, may be landed & lodg'd in their StoreHouse, till they have an Opportunity of Issuing them to some other Ship Outward bound We agree thereto, and you may permit them to be landed and put into Warehouse's accordingly under the joint Lock's of the Custom's, and the Commissioner's of ⌜the⌝[15] Victualling, *valediction 1*

433
17 August 1749

CUST 58/149, p. 192

From Edw. Hooper, W. Westby, J. Evelynn and W. Levinz ('Levine') (Custom House, London). Hand iii.

Admiral Griffin having applied to u's desiring leave to enter some *Arrack & Wine's, which he has brought over for his own use, & present's for his Friends, You are to report to us the particular's of the store's, & the ⌜quantity's⌝[16] of each sort, for our further Order's, *valediction 1*

434
17 August 1749

CUST 58/1

From W. C[ooley] and R. T[urvin] (Custom House, Portsmouth). Hand iii.

We have your Honour's Order signify'd to us by Mr Wood in his Letter of the 15th Instant, Inclosing Copy of the Memorial of Mr Samuel Earle to your Hon*ou*rs relating to One Roll of Silk, One Looking Glass, & one Snuff Box, suppos'd to be Gold, and some other triffling Good's, said to be under Stop at this Port, In answer to which we beg leave to acquaint your Honour's, we have no such Thing's, under stop at this Port, nor have we heard of any such; In all Probability there may be on Board the Princess Mary such thing's, but no Application in regard thereto, have as yet ever been made to us, *valediction 3*

---

[12] Each line of this quotation is introduced by a double quotation mark.
[13] 'of the', repeated, struck out.
[14] Statute 22 Geo. II, c.40.
[15] Written over 'V' erased.
[16] Altered from 'quantity'.

435 CUST 58/149, p. 192

19 August *From W. Wood (Custom House, London). Hand iii.*

1749 The Commissioner's taking notice that no Account of the Arrival, or Sailing of any of his Majesty's, or Custom House Sloop's, at or from your Port, has been received, since their Letter of the 11th Ultimo, I am to acquaint you that it was the Intention of the Board, by the said Letter, to have an Account from time to time not only when[17] his Majesty's ⌜Ship's⌝[18] of War, but also when the Sloop's in the Service of this Revenue come into, or sail out of your Port, which you are to observe for the future, *valediction 2*

436 CUST 58/1

21 August *From W. C[ooley] and R. T[urvin] (Custom House, Portsmouth). Hand iii.*

1749 In Obedience to your Honour's Command's of the 17th Instant, Inclos'd we transmit your Honour's, an Account of the Store of Liquor's belonging to ⌜Admiral⌝[19] Griffin, now in his Majesty's WareHouse at this Port, to which we beg leave to refer Your Honour's *valediction 3*

437 CUST 58/149, pp. 193–4

23 August *From J. Evelynn, R. Chandlor, W. Westby and W. Levinz ('Levine') (Custom House, London). Hand iii.*

1749 Inclos'd you will receive Copy of a Letter, which we have received from Admiral Griffin, complaining of the behaviour of the Officer's of the Custom's, And we direct you to enquire very ⌜particular⌝[20] into all the matter's represented in the Admiral's Letter, & report to u's a state of the Case, with your Observation's & opinion; And incase the Board of Director's have agreed to the *Arrack's being admitt'd to an Entry, We have no objection, and you are also to receive the Duty for the wine, as desired by Mr Griffin, *valediction 1*

Gentlemen

It is with concern, that I am Constrain'd to make complaints to you, of the Treatment, I daily meet with, from your Officer's; If the Law's of the Custom's are alter'd since I left England, they may be in the right, but if not, I think according to the Old Law's, I have not offended

In the first place I never heard of so triffing a thing, as a patch of *Chint's (for my Wife,) being Seiz'd from an Admiral, with all the Cloath's, and material Paper's in the Trunk, detained most part of the next day, the Trunk unlasht, & open'd when none belonging to me was present, & perhap's my secret paper's read or Copied.

In the next place a dozen of Tea Cup's, and Saucer's, were Seiz'd in my Cabbin, & carried to the Custom House, with my remain's of Tea for Store to bring me home,

In the third Place my House Search'd from top to Bottom, as well as my Cellar, rumag'd under pretence of an Information

In the 4th Place, I have Enterd all my wine's & have permission to Enter my *Arrack, from the Court of Director's of the East India Company, which Letter I have shew'd to your Officer's of the Custom's,

I have paid Duty & Excise, with any other Excise that they may please to put upon me, but still cannot be Allow'd to move any part of my *Arrack; My People who shou'd Assist me are Paying off, so shall have none to help me, but am detain'd by those delay's,

Now I have laid this before you for your Information, and Government, I hope for Redress & that there is no Law's in being, nor reason's subsisting for any Gentlemen to be treated as I have been, I am

Gentlemen Your most Obedient ⌜h*um*ble⌝[21] Servant

Thomas Griffin

⌜Portsm° 21st Aug*ust* 1749⌝[22]

---

[17] One illegible word struck out.
[18] Written over 'of'.
[19] MS. 'Amiral'.
[20] Inserted.
[21] MS. 'hh'ble' (for 'h'ble').
[22] Underlined.

438
23 August
1749

CUST 58/1

From W. C[ooley] and R. T[urvin] (Custom House, Portsmouth). Hand iii.

We receiv'd your Honour's Letter of the 17th Instant, in which you are pleas'd to acquaint us Information have been receiv'd by the Company of Weaver's in London, of Sundry Foreigner's & other's, who have Endeavoured to entice & seduce Diver's of his Majesty Subjects, Manufacturer's in the Weaving Business in Spitalfields & other Parts of this Kingdom, to go abroad to Spain, or other Foreign Parts, contrary to the Direction's of the 5th Geo 1st Cap 27, and to carry with them Diverse Implements & Utensils, belonging to the Weaving Manufacture; In order to put a stop thereto, & that the said Act may be ⌜strictly⌝[23] Comply'd with, We have in Obedience to Your Honour's Order, Recommended to all the Officer's, at this Port, and Enjoyn'd them in the Strongest manner to have a Watchfull Eye, what Passenger's are on Board all Ship's bound to Foreign Parts, and if any of them are Manufacturer's, to give us an immediate Account, And not to permit any Loom's, or Weaving Utensils to be shipt without first obtaining your Honour's order, all which shall be duely observ'd by Ourselve's & the rest of the Officer's at this Port, *valediction 5*

439
26 August
1749

CUST 58/149, p. 194

From W. Westby, R. Chandlor, W. Levinz ('Levine') and Edw. Hooper (Custom House, London). Hand iii.

In answer to the Account of Seizure's transmitted in your Letter of the 23d Instant, We direct you to keep your hand's, on the Brandy, Rum, & *Geneva, thereinmention'd, till You receive our further Order's, But we have no objection to the Officer's Prosecuting the Rice to Condemnation before the Justice's of the Pease, at their own Charge, acquainting us when Condemnd, *valediction 1*

Noted the 28th August 1749

440
28 August
1749

CUST 58/1

From W. C[ooley] and R. T[urvin] (Custom House, Portsmouth). Hand iii.

Inclosd we transmit your Honour's an Account of a Seizure made by Mr Wm Baskerville one of the Tidesurveyor's at this Port, & Inclos'd likewise you'l receive Mr Baskerville Affidavit, relating to the said Seizure, and beg to receive your Honour's Direction's thereon, which when receiv'd will be duely observ'd *valediction 4*

441
29 August
1749

CUST 58/1

From W. C[ooley] and R. T[urvin] (Custom House, Portsmouth). Hand iii.

We have received your Honour's Letter of the 23d Instant, together with Copy of Admiral Griffin's Memorial to your Honour's complaining of the Behaviour of the Officer's of the Custom's to him, In Obedience to your Order we have called on the Officer's who were concernd in Seizing the Patch of *Chints, China &cetera and Rummaging his House from whom we have received the Inclosd Accounts, being in answer to what the Admiral has Alledged, against the said Officer's, to which we beg leave to refer; In regard to detaining the Admiral's Liquor's, we are to acquaint you, that as your Honour's had made a Querry Concerning the quantity, an Account of which we transmitted your Honour's for your further Order's, We thought it proper to defer the delivery of them, till we had received your Honour's Order for that purpose, And as we acquainted the Admiral with the same, we did not expect any complaint wou'd have been made on that Subject, *valediction 3*

Sir's

You having been pleas'd to communicate to me a Letter from the Honourable Board dated the 23d Instant, Inclosing Copy of a Complaint made to their Honour's by Vice Admiral Griffin in relation to the ill Treatment he has met with from the Officer's of the Customs at this Port,

---

[23] MS. 'strícty'.

For my self I give for Answer, vizt That on the 5th Instant on my Rummaging the Princess Mary, in the Larboard Quarter Gallery, under the Lock's of one of the Admiral's People, I found One Canister Containing fourteen Pounds of Tea, & in the Admiral's Cabbin One Box Containing One Dozen & eight Cupp's, One Dozen & eight Saucer's, & one Dozen & seven Cover's, all China, & upon my asking the Admiral's Servant to whom the said Tea & China belong'd, he gave me for Answer that he did not know, for which reason I carry'd the same to the Custom House, at the same time observing to him, that whoever claim'd these Goods might apply at the said Office for the same – In regard to what the Admiral complain's off, of about searching his House, I can only answer that upon an Application made by M[r] Noel the Waiter & Searcher at Gosport for Assistance to Rummage the Admiral's House, he having as he alledg'd seen some Goods Carried thereto, which he suspected to be Run, I was Order'd to go to his Assistance with two Tidesmen, and we accordingly made a Rummage, but in the most Civil manner we Possibly cou'd do Consistant with our Duty, & this I hope I shall not be Blam'd for by the Honourable Commissioners. I am

Sir's Your &cetera

W B Tidesurv*eyo*r

Custom House Portsm[o] 28th Aug*ust* 1749

Gentlemen

In answer to that part of Admiral Griffin's Letter to the Honourable Commissioner's complaining of the Behaviour of the Officer's of the Custom's here, so far as relate to my self and the Watch concerning the Admiral's Trunk, I beg leave to Assure you for Truth, That being on Duty at the Watchouse as Tidesurveyor, Sunday the 30th July last, in which day the Princess Mary, and three other Men of War, under the Command of the said Admiral, arriv'd at S[t] Helen's from the East Indie's We kept a strict look out after the Boats that came into the Harbour, & about 11'O Clock at Night, One being discover'd rowing in, I orderd some Tidesmen in the Watch Boat to chase her (not being able to go my self on Account of a late illness, of which I was not well recover'd) they follow'd her to Gosport Beach, & finding her to be the Princess Mary's Boat, They search'd her and brought away with them, a Trunk and a small Box, which were in her, to y[e] Watchouse, which I took into my Custody till the[24] Morning, when I caus'd them to be carried to the Custom House, & deliver'd them to the WareHouse keeper, About 8 o'Clock the same Morning M[r] Harry Gibb's the Deputy Customer of this Port, inform'd me he had receiv'd a Letter from the Admiral by his Coxswain informing him that the Trunk belong'd to the Admiral, & that it Contain'd his Cloth's, and that without it he cou'd not shift himself, and therefore desired it might be return'd, upon which we proceeded in the Presence of the WareHouse keeper, the Weighing Porter, & two Tidesmen to open the Trunk, which was only Lash'd & the Box in Order to examine the Contents which was perform'd by M[r] Gibb's, with the utmost Decency, & respect to the Admiral as the Trunk at first sight appear'd only to contain his Cloth's, but he finding two Patches Containing Twenty two Yards of *Chints, I Seizd them as Prohibited, & ⌜also⌝[25] a small Parcel of China ware which was in the Box, and the Trunk was immediately Lash'd up, and deliver'd to the Admiral's Coxswain, by 9 o'Clock, or before, who came in whilst that was about, and who might have been present at the Examination, if he had pleas'd, being ask'd so to be by M[r] Gibbs, but he said he had Business to do in Town, & went away about it after he had deliver'd the Letter M[r] Gibbs, and my self are both Positive that we saw no Paper's in the Trunk, and I am ready to verify on my Oath, that the Trunk was not opened whilst it was in my keeping before it was brought to the WareHouse.

As I hope it does appear to you that in the whole of this Affair, my self or any one beside's have done no more than our Duty, I humbly request that you wou'd be pleas'd to report the same accordingly to their Honour's & am

Gentlemen Your most Obedient humble Servant

28th August 1749

---

[24] 'next' struck out.

[25] MS. 'alo'.

442
30 August
1749

CUST 58/1

From W. C[ooley] and R. T[urvin] (Custom House, Portsmouth). Hand iii.

We are to acquaint your Honour's on the 26th Instant Fra^{s} Fuller late an Extra Tidesman & Boatman at this Port with the Allowance of £5 Per Annum, resign'd his Deputation, We humbly beg leave to recommend in his room H^{y} Barn's who have been Employ'd in the Service at this Port upwards of five Year's without any Allowance by Incidents, he being a good & deserving Officer, is therefore recommended, *valediction 4*

443
31 August
1749

CUST 58/149, p. 195

From W. Westby, W. Levinz ('Levine'), J. Evelynn and Edw. Hooper (Custom House, London). Hand iii.

In answer to the Account of Seizure's transmitted in your Letter of the 28th Instant, We direct you to Prosecute the Brandy thereinmention'd to Condemnation, in the Exchequer, at the King's Charge; And we have no Objection to the Officer's Prosecuting the ⌜Vinegar⌝[26], Boat, and Furniture, in like manner, at their own Charge Corresponding with our Sollicitor, and the Register of Seizure's; And you are to take care that Joseph Gilbert, in whose Stable the said Brandy Was Seiz'd, be Prosecuted in the Exchequer, for the Treble Value thereof, Reporting to us whether you are willing to carry on the Prosecution, at your own Charge, or are desirou's it shoul'd be carried on under the Regulation's of the Treasury, signify'd to you in our Secretary's Letter of the 1st Sept*ember* 1736, *valediction 1*

Noted the 5th Sept*ember* 1749

444
31 August
1749

CUST 58/149, p. 195

From Edw. Hooper, W. Levinz ('Levine'), W. Westby and J. Evelynn (Custom House, London). Hand iii.

Having granted our Commission for Jame's Terry, to be an Extra Tidesmen, and Boatman at your Port, in the room of Wm Vernon Deceas'd, You are to take care he be under Oath, and Security, for the faithfull discharge of the said Employ, & Qualifies himself as the Law directs, paying him the like Allowanc[e] of Five Pound's Per Annum by Incidents, as wa's paid to his Predecessor, for which the Collector may take Credit in his Account of Incidents, Referring therein to the date hereof, *valediction 1*

445
1 September
1749

CUST 58/149, p. 196

From R. Chandlor, Sam. Mead, Beaumont Hotham and W. Levinz ('Levine') (Custom House, London). Hand iii.

In answer to the Accounts of Seizure transmitted in your Letter's of the 26th & 29th Ultimo We direct you to Prosecute the Enumerated Good's, thereinmentioned, to Condemnation, in the Exchequer, at the King's Charge, And we have no Objection, to the Officer's Prosecuting the Boat, and wine, in like manner, at their own Charge, Corresponding with our Sollicitor, and the Register of Seizure's, *valediction 1*

Noted the 5th Sept*ember* 1749

446
1 September
1749

CUST 58/1

From W. C[ooley] and R. T[urvin] (Custom House, Portsmouth). Hand iii.

Herewith We transmit your Honour's, an Account of Goods Enumerated, & not Enumeratd lately Seiz'd by the Officer's at this Port, to which we beg leave to refer, *valediction 4*

---

[26] Altered from 'Vingar'.

447
4 September
1749

CUST 58/1

From W. C[ooley] and R. T[urvin] (Custom House, Portsmouth). Hand iii.

We have here Inclos'd a Schedule of Accounts, due from this Port for the Quarter ended Midsummer last, The same being this day forwarded by the Waggon of George Clarke, which will be at the Whitehart in the Burrough of Southwark, on Wednesday the 6th Instant, for the Carriage whereof we have agreed that two Shilling's & six pence shall be paid *valediction 5*

Portsmouth

A Schedule of Accounts due from this Port, for Midsummer quarter last, sent by the Waggon of Geo Clarke, which will be at the Whitehart, in the Burrough of Southwark on Wednesday the 6th Instant.

Collector's quarter Book
Comptrollers – D^{o} –
General Incidents with the Establishment
Two Original Orders
Seven Bounty Debenture's, two *Portage's & 1 *Over Entry
Coal Incidents
Imports & Export's
Wooll brought & carried Coastwise
Civil List Receipt & Repayment
Naval Stores from Rhusia & Levonia
Corn Exported from hence with the Amount of the Bounty due thereon –
Preparatory Account of Incidents & Tradesmens Bills –
Personal Prosecution's
Enumerated Goods P*er* Act 12th Geo 1st – [27]
Ships &cetera which Discharged in this Port, from any of his Majesty's Plantation's in America –
Loose Reports Inwards & Outward's
Journals of the Commander & Mate of the Greenhill Yatch –
Deputation & Instruction's of Jno Newnham Coal meter
D^{o} – & Instruction's of Wm Hare D^{o} & Tidesm*an*
D^{o} – & Instruction's of Wm Pendrill Tidesm*an*
D^{o} – & Instruction's of Fra^{s} Fuller
Copy of Instruction's to { Ja^{s} Redstone & Wm Tasker Tidesmen
R^{d} Lee, Jno Chadwick & Rice Diaper Coalmeters – }
Deputation & D^{o} of Wm Tasker

448
4 September
1749

CUST 58/1

From W. C[ooley] and R. T[urvin] (Custom House, Portsmouth). Hand iii.

We are to acquaint your Honour's this day Thomas Chadwick resign'd his Deputation as a Coal Meter at this Port. We therefore humbly beg leave to recommend in his room Wm Seymore an Inhabitant of this Town he being in every respect very Capable of perform*ing* ye Duty of a Coal Meter, otherwise he woud not have been ⌜Recommended⌝[28], *valediction 4*

449
4 September
1749

CUST 58/1

From W. C[ooley] and R. T[urvin] (Custom House, Portsmouth). Hand iii.

In answer to Your Honour's Letter of the 31st Ultimo wherein we are directed to take care that Joseph Gilbert in whose Stable a Parcel of Brandy was Seiz'd, be Prosecuted for Treble the Value thereof, We are to acquaint your Honour's we have call'd on Mr Wm Baskerville one of the Tidesurveyors at this Port, who made the said Seizure, to know if he is willing to carry on the Prosecution at his own Charge, and he has acquainted us he is not, but is desirous it shou'd be carry'd on under the Regulation's of the Treasury as signify'd in the Secretary's Letter of the 1st Sept*ember* 1736. *Valediction 5*

---

[27] Statute 12 Geo. I, c.28.
[28] Altered from 'recommended'.

450
4 September
1749

CUST 58/1

From W. C[ooley] and R. T[urvin] (Custom House, Portsmouth). Hand iii.

Your Honour's by your Letter of the 11th of July last, were pleasd to Dismiss Jno Stretch weighing Porter, at this Port, from his Place of Coal Meter, as being inconsistant with his Office of Weighing Porter, for which he had an Establish'd Allowance of £20 Per Annum And as we think Stretche's Case to be particular his Sallary being less than that of any other Officer, it being rather an Additional Allowance for Extraordinary Service than a Sallary for a man to live on, for the Person first appointed to the Office, was at the time a Coal Meter and the Sallary of £20 settled as a reasonable Allowance for such further Service, On this occasion as likewise in Compassion to the Man, who has no other mean's to live, and has a family of a Wife and 5 Children, We humbly crave leave to Recommend his Case to your Honour's further Consideration and if your Honour's shall ⌜think⌝[29] fit to consider him, there is now an Opportunity to replace him in his Meters Place, for Jno Chadwick has this day Quitted his Employment of Coal Meter, & left the Port, and tho' he has carried his Deputation with him, it is as he declar'd only to deliver it to Mr Brooke Surv*eyo*r General by whose mean's he obtaind it, We have only to add that as neither of the Employm*en*ts require a Constant Duty, When they Interfere, Stretch hire's one to Act for him, which however doe's not often happen, so that the ⌜Inconsistancy⌝[30] is not near so much in this Case as in that of any other Establish'd Officer, all which is humbly submitted, *valediction 4*

451
5 September
1749

CUST 58/149, p. 196

From Beaumont Hotham, Sam. Mead, W. Westby and R. Chandlor (Custom House, London). Hand iii.

John Chadwick Extra Tidesman at your Port, having by his Memorial of the 3^{d} Instant, apply'd to us desiring leave to be Absent for a Month on his private Affairs, We agree thereto, and you are to take care the Service doe's not Suffer, during his Absence.

In answer to the Account of Seizure's transmitted in your Letter of the 1st Instant, We direct you to Prosecute the Enumerated Good's thereinmentioned to Condemnation in the Exchequer, at the King's Charge, And we have no Objection to the Officer's Prosecuting the *Chints in like manner at his own Charge, Corresponding with our Sollicitor, & the Register of Seizure's, *valediction 1*

Noted the 7th Sept*embe*r 1749

452
5 September
1749

CUST 58/1

From W. C[ooley] and R. T[urvin] (Custom House, Portsmouth). Hand iii.

Inclos'd we transmit Your Honour's an Account of Goods Enumerated, & not Enumerated, lately Seiz'd by the Officers at this Port, & Inclos'd we likewise transmit your Honour's two Information's on Oath, made by Mr Wm Baskerville, one of the Tidesurveyor's at this Port, against Jno Reed Inkeeper at Gosport, for harbouring and Concealing, & the Other, against Richard Champney's Esqr for Running Goods, on which we beg leave to receive your Honour's Order's, which shall be duely observ'd *valediction 4*

453
5 September
1749[31]

CUST 58/1

From W. C[ooley] and R. T[urvin] (Custom House, Portsmouth). Hand iii.

Yesterday we admitted & deliver'd to Captain John Barker, of his Majesty's Sloop Wasp, his Commission, Impowering him to Seize Prohibited and Uncustomed Goods, & Inclos'd we transmit Your Honour's, agreeable to your Order of the 10th Ultimo the Bond duely Executed by him, with two[32] other Securities, to which we beg leave to refer, *valediction 3*

---

[29] MS. 'thing'.
[30] MS. 'Inconstancy'.
[31] MS. '1748'.
[32] 'other', repeated, struck out.

454
6 September
1749

CUST 58/1

From W. C[ooley] and R. T[urvin] (Custom House, Portsmouth). Hand iii.

Inclos'd we transmit your Honour's agreeable to your ⌜Order⌝[33] of the 4th March 1748/ a Certificate sign'd by us, and the rest of the Principal Officer's at this Port, whereby it will appear that Richard Temple is Qualify'd to perform the Duty of a Landwaiter, to which we beg leave to refer your Honours, *valediction 3*

Port of Portsmouth

These are to Certify that in Pursuance of an Order from the Honble the Commissioners of his Majesty's Custom's of the 4th March 1748, Mr Richd Temple hath duely attended the Discharge of Goods at the Keys of this Port, under the Instruction of the proper Officers for Six Months, is able to Gauge, & is otherwise well Qualify'd to perform the Duty of a Landwaiter at this or any other Port. Certify'd at the Custom House this 5th September 1749

Wm Cooley Collector
R Turvin, Deputy Comptroller
Edwd Skeat Landwaiter
Robt Alexander Deputy Patent Sear*cher* & Assi*stant* Landwaiter
Thos Whitehorne }
Thos Merritt } Landwaiter[s]

455
7 September
1749

CUST 58/149, p. 197

From W. Wood (Custom House, London). Hand iii.

The Officer's here having a Suspicion of some Good's which had not paid the Dutie's, were coming up in the Gosport Waggon, and upon its unloading at the Bell Savage Inn, on Ludgate Hill, they found twelve Boxe's, bound with Spun Yarn, Containing a large Quantity of Variou's Drug's, directed to Mr Speed in Absharch Lane, which they have stopt; The Commissioner's direct you to Report to them whether there has been any such Good's, Enter'd at your Port, and what Certificates were granted, for sending them up by Land Carriage, with all other Circumstance's which have come to your Knowledge, relating to this Affair, *valediction 2*

456
8 September
1749

CUST 58/1

From W. C[ooley] and R. T[urvin] (Custom House, Portsmouth). Hand iii.

Herewith we transmit Your Honours the Abstract for the Month of August last, together with the undermentioned Accounts, to which we beg leave to refer, *valediction 4*

Nil List of Bonds
Tea & other Goods Enumerated, with Petty Receipts Endors'd
Absent Officers.

PS/ From the Book kept in this Office it appears that the Weights and Scales Coal & Corn Bushels at this Port, were try'd the 7th Ultimo by the Surveyor & Landwaiters, & that they found the same to be exact & true, and that the Stamps for marking Hides, Skins, Linnens, Seiz'd Goods & Sail Cloth, are in good & Sufficient repair, & fit for the uses design'd.

W. C R. T/

457
9 September
1749

CUST 58/149, p. 197

From Beaumont Hotham, R. Chandlor, W. Westby and Sam. Mead (Custom House, London). Hand iii.

We received your Letter of the 4th Instant acquainting us that William Baskerville, Tidesurveyor at your Port, desires the Prosecution against Joseph Gilbert, for the Penalty of One hundred & three Gallon's of Brandy, may be carried on under the Regulation's of the Treasury, We have agreed thereto, & given Order's to our Solicitor accordingly, *valediction 1*

---

33 Written over 'Ho'.

458
11 September
1749

CUST 58/1

From W. C[ooley] and R. T[urvin] (Custom House, Portsmouth). Hand iii.

We have your Honours Order of the 7th Instant signify'd to us by Mr Wood, by which we are directed to Report, whether a Parcel of Drugs lately stopt on Ludgate Hill which were conveyed to London by the Gosport Waggon directed to Mr Speed in Archurch Lane have been Enter'd at this Port, or whether any Certificates were granted for sending them up by Land Carriage, In answer to which we are to acquaint your Honours no such Goods have been Enter'd here, or permits granted, nor has any Circumstance relating to the Affair ever before come to our Knowledge. *Valediction 5*

459
12 September
1749

CUST 58/149, pp. 197–8

From Sam. Mead, R. Chandlor, Beaumont Hotham and W. Levinz ('Levine') (Custom House, London). Hand iii.

In Answer to the Accounts of Seizure's transmitted in Your Letter of the 5th Instant We direct You to Prosecute the Enumerated Goods thereinmention'd to Condemnation in the Exchequer at the King's Charge, And we have no Objection to the Officer's Prosecuting ⌜the⌝[34] rest of the Good's, and Boat in like manner at their own Charge, Corresponding with our Sollicitor, and the Register of Seizure's, And You are to transmit us an Account of the Value of the Good's Seiz'd in the Boat, and in the House of John Reed, and Report whether he was privy to the Good's being in his House, and in what manner they were found concealed for our further Order's, *valediction 1*

Noted in the Book of Seizure's Sep*tember* 14th 1749

460
14 September
1749

CUST 58/149, pp. 198–9

From W. Wood (Custom House, London). Hand iii.

Messrs Charle's & Edm: ⌜Boehin⌝[35], having by their Memorial of this date, apply'd to the Commissioner's, desiring leave to unload, the Wheat on Board the Neptune, Wm Fowler Master from Stockton, which Sprung a Leak at Sea, and put into Gosport, I am directed to send you Copy of the said Memorial, and you are to examine into the Allegation's therein contained, and Report a true state of the Case to the Board with your Opinion, for their further Order's *valediction 2*

Sep*tember* 14th 1749

Honourable Sir's

The Neptune Captain Fowler from Stockton bound to Marseille's with 840 Quarters Wheat having had the Misfortune to spring a Leak aSea which oblig'd her to put into Gosport, and it having been Represented to us that the said Cargoe is become Damag'd, We pray your Honour's to send an Order immediately to your Collector at Portsmouth to suffer her to be unloaded, and the Damaged Wheat to be replac'd, with good Wheat, so that no Alteration may be in the Debenture, already made for this Cargoe. We are

Honble Sir's Your most humble Servants

Chas & Edm: Boehin[36]

461
14 September
1749

CUST 58/149, p. 199

From W. Wood (Custom House, London). Hand iii.

The Accounts mentioned in your Letter of the 4th Instant, for Midsummer Quarter last, are safe come to hand, *valediction 2*

---

[34] MS. 'the the'.
[35] Altered from 'Boehm'.
[36] 'oe' written over an illegible erasure.

462
16 September 1749

CUST 58/1

From W. C[ooley] and R. T[urvin] (Custom House, Portsmouth). Hand iii.

In Obedience to your Honours Order of the 12th Instant, Inclosed we transmit your Honours an Account of the Value of the Goods Seizd in a Boat from Richard Champneys Esqr of Fareham, and in the House of Jno Reed at Gosport, and we are to acquaint your Honours we have called on Mr Baskerville who Seiz'd the Goods in the House of Jno Reed, who can not pretend to say said Reed was, or was not ⌜privy⌝[37] to the Goods being in his House. Mr Baskerville begs leave to acquaint your Honours, where & in what manner he found the Goods, that it was in a Chamber of the House of said Reed which he Alledges he had lett to Wm Mitchell Master of the Providence then lying in Stoakes Bay ⌜from⌝[38] Bremen Bound to Cadiz, and that part of the Goods was found in the said Room in a Chair which the Masters Wife was then sitting in, & the remaining part which was Tea, was found in the Window of the said room the Curtain being drawn before it, all which is humbly submitted to your Honours & whatever Order you shall be pleased to send us in regard thereto will be duely Observ'd, *valediction 4*

Goods Seizd from Mr Champney Esqr – vizt –		
One large Glass bottle & five stone bottles Containing 17 gallons Brandy at –	0. 6. 3 Per Ga*llo*n –	£ 5. 6. 3
Six Papers Containing Six Pounds *Bohea Tea at –	0. 5. 0 Per lb'	1. 10. 0
Six D^{o} Roasted Coffee –	at 0. 4. 6 Per lb'	1. 7. 0
Eighty Yards *Mendes Holland –	at 0. 3. 0 Per Yd	12. 0. 0
Twelve Yards & half Flour'd Silk –	at 0. 2. 6 Per Yd	1. 11. 3
Seven D^{o} & half Yallow – D^{o} –	at 0. 3. 6 Per Yd	1. 6. 3
Nineteen D^{o} – Blue – D^{o} –	at 0. 5. 0 Per Yd	4. 15. 0
Nineteen D^{o} – Flower'd Cotton –	at 0. 1. 3 Per Yd	1. 3. 9
Thirty nine D^{o} – Strip'd – D^{o} –	at 0. 1. 5 Per Yd	2. 15. 3
Ten D^{o} Silver Lace –		2. 10. 0
Six Gawes Caps –		0. 15. 0
Four *Mead Flours –		0. 5. 0
Two Tipets & two Stomagers –		0. 5. 0
One Embroider'd Handkerchief –		0. 15. 0
One D^{o} –		0. 10. 6
One D^{o} –		0. 12. 0
		37. 7. 3[39]
	Brought Forward	£37. 7. 3
Two Work'd Handkerchiefs –		0. 12. 0
Sixteen Fanns –		0. 13. 0
Four Pair of Necklaces –		0. 4. 0
One Tobacco Box –		0. 1. 0
Three Dozen Buttons –		1. 10. 0
One Pair Ear Rings –		0. 15. 0
Two D^{o} – D^{o} –		0. 6. 0
One Stone Ring –		0. 5. 0
Four Pair Slippers –		0. 10. 0
Twelve Common Spoons – } Twelve D^{o} Tea D^{o} – } One – D^{o} Supe D^{o} – }		0. 6. 0
One Box Containing fishes for Card Playing –		0. 5. 0
	Total	£42. 14. 3

[37] Written over an illegible word.
[38] Written only as catchword at foot of page.
[39] Total drawn at end of page in MS.

Seiz'd in the House of Mr Read at Gosport – vizt –		
Twenty Yards Muslin at 0. 5. 6 Per Yd –		£ 5. 10. 0
Twenty Yards D° – at 0. 3. 3 Per Yd –		3. 5. 0
Two Velvet Shapes –		5. 0. 0
One Remnant Black Velvet –		0. 16. 0
Twelve Pounds & half Green Tea at – 0. 7. 6 Per lb'		4. 13. 9
Eight D° *Bohea Tea –at 0. 5. 0 Per lb'		2. 0. 0
Ten India Silk Handkerchiefs at – 0. 1. 6 each		0. 15. 0
		£21. 19. 9

463
16 September
1749

CUST 58/1

From W. C[ooley] and R. T[urvin] (Custom House, Portsmouth). Hand iii.

We have your Honours Order of the 14th Instant signify'd to us by Mr Wood, together with Copy of the Memorial of Messrs Chas & Edmund Boehem ⌜Inclos'd⌝[40] desiring leave to unload the Wheat on Board the Neptune at this Port William Fowler Master from Stockton she having Sprung a Leak at Sea, In Obedience to your Order we have Examined into the Allegations of said Memorial which we find to be true. As the Cargoe of the said Ship was in danger of Perishing, and any delay in lighting of her may endanger the whole Cargoe We have therefore Ventured, without waiting first for your Honours Order, permitted the Mast*er* (he having made Affidavit before us of his Damage sustained) to begin unloading his Cargoe, under the care of the proper Officers which we hope your Honours will approve of, – With regard to what quantity of Damaged Wheat, that may be taken out and replaced with good, We shall follow such directions as you shall be pleased to send, in regard thereto, *valediction 3*

464
18 September
1749

CUST 58/1

From W. C[ooley] and R. T[urvin] (Custom House, Portsmouth). Hand iii.

Inclos'd we transmit your Honours in the usual Form, an Account of a Seizure made by Mr William Baskerville one of the Tidesurveyors at this Port, and likewise a Memorial which we have received from him, relating to the said Seizure, which we beg leave to refer, *valediction 3*

Sirs

I take leave to acquaint you that Yesterday in the Afternoon upon Visiting the Prosperous Sloop Jn° Watson Master from Southton, in the Harbour I found in the Hold Eight Casks, and upon my asking the said Mr Watson what they Contained or whether he had any thing to Produce for the same from the proper Officers at Southton, he gave me for answer – Vizt that he had no dispatches, I then askd him whether he coud, or woud inform me what the said Casks Contain'd, to which he gave me for answer, that he knew nothing of their Contents, and that I must find that out upon Enquiry, upon which I search'd them & found four

	C*wt*	qr	lb'	
Casks Containing –	3.	1.	20.	Snuff
One Cask Containing –	1.	0.	8.	Raisins
One D° Containing –	0.	2.	6.	Treakle
Two D° Containing –	3.	0.	20.	Refin'd Sug*ar*
	0.	0.	12	Sug*ar* Candy
	0.	0.	6	Pepper
	0.	0.	7	Green Tea
	0.	0.	7	*Bohea D°

40 Written only as catchword at foot of page.

All which Goods I have Seiz'd and brought to his Majestys WareHouse they being neither attended with proper Coast Dispatches from the Officers of the Customs at the Port of Southampton or a permit from the Officers of Excise, for want of which I humbly conceive the said Goods are liable to Forfeiture. I beg leave further to observe to you that the said Watson (in Contempt of the Laws and Orders from the Honourable Board of Customs) [41]told me that he never woud take out a Dispatch, for any Goods that he might bring from Southampton to this Port, & whether this Contempt is well or ill founded is humbly submitted by

Sirs Yours &cetera

W Baskerville Tidesurv*eyo*r

Watch House 16th Sept*ember* 1749
To The Collector & Comptroller

465
19 September 1749

CUST 58/149, p. 199

From Wil. Wood (Custom House, London). Hand iii.

A Debenture in the Name of Thomas Hendy, for One hundred fifty nine Quarters four Bushel's & a half of Wheaten Flour shipt at your Port, the 15th Ultimo in the W*illia*m & Mary for Havre de grace, has been presented to the Commissioners for their Order for Payment, but You having omitted to send a Duplicate thereof, the same is stopt, You are forthwith to send the said Duplicate to the Board, which I am directed to signify to you *valediction 2*

466
19 September 1749

CUST 58/149, p. 200

From W. Levinz ('Levine'), Beaumont Hotham, R. Chandlor and Sam. Mead (Custom House, London). Hand iii.

We received your Letter of the 16th Instant acquainting us that you have permitted the Master of the Neptune from Stockton, which sprung a Leak at Sea, to unload his Cargoe of Wheat, under the care of the proper Officer's, We approve thereof, but you are to take care there be no Embezlement's, or any Goods Run, & that the Crown be at no Charge for WareHouse Room, Officer's attendance, or otherwise sending Us an Account of the exact Quantity landed and Reshipt for Exportation, having in the mean time ordered the Debenture to be stopt, *valediction 1*

467
20 September 1749

CUST 58/149, p. 200

From W. Levinz ('Levine'), Beaumont Hotham, R. Chandlor and Sam. Mead (Custom House, London). Hand iii.

Mr Thoma's Guillaum having by his Memorial of the 7th Instant apply'd to u's relating to four Cask's of Brandy, Rum, & *Geneva Seiz'd by William Baskerville Tidesurveyor at Your Port, on board the Prosperou's Sloop, for want of a proper Dispatch, We direct you to deliver the British Brandy & *Geneva, & also the Foreign Rum, to the Proprietor, on Proof being made that the Dutie's have been paid, & giving the Officer concern'd a moderate Satisfaction *valediction 1*

Noted the 25th Sept*embe*r 1749

---

[41] MS. omits closing bracket.

468 CUST 58/1

20 September 1749

From W. C[ooley] and R. T[urvin] (Custom House, Portsmouth). Hand iii.

By your Honours Letter of the 20th of September 1744 You were pleased in return to a Memorial of Richard Watmore then Agent to the Salt Works at this Port, Complaining that the Masters of Vessels that Load Salt at this Port, were oblig'd to give Bond & take out a *Cocquet for the same, to direct us to insist on a *Cocquet being taken out & a Bond given for every considerable quantity of British Salt sent Coastwise, You being of Opinion that it woud be in the Power of the Masters & others, incase they did not take out a *Cocquet & give Bond, to land the same privately, and take on Board the like quantity of Foreign Salt, and land the same by Virtue of the Coast Dispatches, without being Subject to any Penalty if found out, We have therefore in obedience to your said Order always insisted on a *Cocquet being taken out & Bond given upon the Shipping of every considerable Quantity of British Salt sent Coastwise, But we beg leave now to acquaint Your Honours Mr Reed the Proprietor of the Salt Works at this Port, and who frequently do Ship Considerable quantitys of British Salt for London, has given us Notice he will no longer be Subject to give Bond, or take out a *Cocquet for sending Salt Coastwise, but is determined if your Honours insist thereon, of standing Trial, We therefore beg to know if your Honours think fit of our refusing a *Transcire if demanded, & insisting on *Cocq*ue*t & Bond. We beg to receive your Honours immediate Directions thereon which Will be duely observ'd *valediction 4*

469 CUST 58/149, p. 201

23 September 1749

From W. Levinz ('Levine'), Sam. Mead and Beaumont Hotham (Custom House, London). Hand iii.

It appearing by your last Month's Abstract, that there is remaining in the Collector's hand's, the Sum of Seven hundred thirty Pound's, Nineteen Shilling's & five Pence farthing, of the King's Money, We direct you forthwith to remit the same, together with what you have since received, to the Receiver General, Pursuant to the Condition of the Collector's Bond *valediction 1*

In margin: 730. 19. 5¼[42]

470 CUST 58/149, p. 201

23 September 1749

From W. Wood (Custom House, London). Hand iii.

The Commissioner's direct you to draw out, and transmit them without loss of time An Account of the Number of Hogshead's, and Quantity of Pound's of Tobacco, Imported into and Exported from your Port, with the Net Amount of the Dutie's paid, and Drawnback thereon from Christma's 1748 to this time, *valediction 2*

471 CUST 58/149, p. 202

25 September 1749

From Wil. Wood (Custom House, London). Hand iii.

The Commissioner's for Victualling his Majesty's Navy, having in their Letter of this Date, desired that as much of the Wine as was landed at your Port, from his Majesty's Ship Princess Mary, may be issued to his Majesty's Sloop the Hornett, at Spithead, as the Service may require; The Commissioner's have agreed thereto, & you are to permit it to be shipt on board the Hornett as desired, under the care of the proper Officer's, taking care there be no Embezlements, *valediction 2*

472 CUST 58/1

25 September 1749

From W. C[ooley] and R. T[urvin] (Custom House, Portsmouth). Hand iii.

In Obedience to your Honours Order signify'd to us by Mr Wood in his Letter of the 23d instant We have here Inclosed an Account of the Number of Hogsheads & quantity of Pounds of Tobacco Imported into and Exported from this Port from Christmas 1748 to this Time, to which we beg leave to refer *valediction 3*

Portsmouth, An Account of the Number of hogsheads & quantity of lb's of Tobacco Imported into & Exported from this Port from X'tmas 1748 to this time

– Nil –

Custom House Portsm° Sept*ember* ⌜25⌝[43] 1749

---

[42] Underlined.

[43] Altered from '23d'.

473
26 September
1749

CUST 58/149, pp. 201–2

From R. Chandlor, Sam. Mead, Beaumont Hotham and W. Levinz ('Levine') (Custom House, London). Hand iii.

We received Your Letter of the 18th Instant transmitting an Account of a Seizure, made by William Baskerville, Tidesurveyor at your Port, on board the Prosperou's Sloop, John Watson Master from Southampton, for want of proper Dispatches, And having Referr'd the same to our Sollicitor, he has Reported that "the[44] Tea is Forfeited for want of a permit, but a Coast Dispatch in regard to the other Good's is not Necessary, unless the Ship went out Sea."[45] We signify the same to you for your Government, *valediction 1*

474
28 September
1749

CUST 58/149, pp. 202–3

From R. Chandlor, Sam. Mead, Beaumont Hotham and G. Vaughan (Custom House, London). Hand iii.

We received your Letter of the 16th instant acquainting us that the Officer who Seiz'd the Good's in the House of Jno Reed, cannot say whether the said Reed, was Privy to the Good's being in his House, And having refer'd the same to our Sollicitor, he has Reported that an Information cannot be Enterd against him for the said Good's, as the Officer has no Proof of his Privity, but that Information's may be Enterd against Richard Champney's Esqr for Unshipping & receiving the Good's mentioned in Mr Baskervill's Affidavit. ⌜We⌝[46] have therefore ordered our Sollicitor to send you Process against Mr Champney's accordingly, and to proceed against him. But you are to enquire, and Report to us particularly who Mr Champney's is, and whether the Officer is willing to carry on the Prosecution, at his own Charge, or is desirou's it should be carried on Wholy at the Crown's Charge, or under the Regulation's of the Treasury, signify'd to your Port, in our Secretary's Letter of the 1st of Sept*embe*r 1736. And you are also to wait on Mr Champney's & acquaint him that we have ordered the Prosecution against him to be carried on with all the Civility the nature of the case, will admit, *valediction 1*

475
30 September
1749

CUST 58/149, pp. 203–4

From W. Wood (Custom House, London). Hand iii.

The Account of Prohibited East India Good's, and Naval Store's mention'd on the back hereof, being wanted from Your Port, The Commissioner's direct you to transmit the same to the Board, without loss of time, in order to be laid before the Parliament. I am also to remind you of the Direction's contained in my Letter of the 11th July 1747 for you to transmit to the Board, within six day's after Christma's an Account of the Money paid for the Bountie's on English & Irish Coarse Linnens Exported from your Port, from Christma's 1748 to Christmas 1749, and you are to take care the same be sent accordingly, in the form undermention'd, in order to be laid before the Parliament, And if it shoud happen that no such Linnen's have been Exported from your Port, You are nevertheless to send a Nil Account, *valediction 2*

British Linnen's				Irish Linnen's				
Value – under – 5^{d} Per Yard	Value 5 & under 6^{d} Per Yard	Value 6^{d} & under 12^{d} Per Yd	Value 12^{d} & not exceed*ing* 18^{d} Per Yd	Value und*er* 5d Per Yard	Value 5^{d} & under 6^{d} Per Yard	Value 6^{d} & und*er* 12^{d} Per Yard	Value 12^{d} & not exceed*ing* 18^{d} Per Yard	Bountie's Paid –
Yards	Yards	Yards	Yds	Yards	Yards	Yards	Yards	£ s d

Half Yearly Account of Prohibited East India Good's from Mich*ael*mas 1748 to Mich*ael*mas 1749

Naval Store's Mich*ael*mas 1748 & Mich*ael*mas 1749

---

[44] Each line of this quotation is introduced by a double quotation mark.

[45] MS. omits closing quotation mark.

[46] MS. 'We We'.

476
3 October
1749

CUST 58/149, p. 205

From Beaumont Hotham, Sam. Mead, R. Chandlor and G. Vaughan (Custom House, London). Hand iii.

We received your Letter of the 20th Instant, acquainting us that Mr Reed Proprietor of the Salt work's at your Port, who frequently Ship Considerable Quantities of British Salt for London, has given you notice, that he will be no longer subject to give Bond, or take out a *Cocquet for sending salt Coastwise; We direct you to pursue our Order of the 20th of September 1744, and insist upon Coast Dispatche's being taken out, and Bond given for all British Salt Shipt to go Coastwise, where the Vessel is to go to open Sea, in her Passage, Reporting to Us Your Proceeding's, *valediction 1*

477
3 October
1749

CUST 58/1

From W. C[ooley] and R. T[urvin] (Custom House, Portsmouth). Hand iii.

In obedience to your Honours Commands of the 28th Ultimo. We have acquainted Richard Champneys ⌜Esq.⌝[47]that you have been pleas'd to order a Prosecution against him, for Receiving & Unshipping Goods mentioned in an Affidavit of Mr Baskerville's, one of the Tidesurveyors at this Port, to be carried on with all the Civility the natur[e] of the Case, will admit; We beg leave to acquaint your Honours Mr Champneys is a Gentlemen of very considerable Fortune, & resides at Fareham, within the Limits of this Port, And we are to acquaint your Honours, we have call'd on Mr Baskerville, who Seiz'd the Goods from Mr Champneys, to know if he is willing to carry on the Prosecution at his own, or the Crowns Charge, under the Regulations of the Treasury, from whom we have received for answer, that he is desirous of carrying on the Prosecution at his own Charge, & is therefore desirous of having a Process sent him accordingly, *valediction 3*

478
5 October
1749

CUST 58/149, pp. 205–6

From Wil. Wood (Custom House, London). Hand iii.

The Commissioners for Victualling his Majesty's Navy having in their Letter of the 3d Instant represented to this Board, that the Forrest Transport, lately arrived at Plymouth, with part of the Relieved Regiments from Mahone, and she being ordered to proceed to your Port, to debark the Force's she has on Board there, they desire if there should be any Wine remaining on Board her, that was furnished for the use of the said Forces, in lieu of Beer, that the same may be landed, and Secured in the WareHouse's till an Opportunity ⌜Offer's⌝[48] of issuing it to some of His Majesty's Ship's Outward Bound. The Commissioner's have agreed thereto, and you are to permit it to be landed & secured in the WareHouse's under the care of the proper Officer's, till an Opportunity Offer's of Issuing it to some of His Majesty's Ship's Outward Bound, taking care there be no Embezlements. *Valediction 2*

479
5 October
1749

CUST 58/149, p. 206

From Beaumont Hotham, Edw. Hooper, Sam. Mead and G. Vaughan (Custom House, London). Hand iii.

Having granted our Deputation for Joshua Simpson Extra Tidesman to be a Coal Meter at Your Port, in the room of Thoma's Chadwick Resigned, you are to take care he be under Oath, & Security for the faithfull Discharge of the said Employ, and Qualifie's himself as the Law directs, *valediction 1*

---

[47] Inserted.
[48] MS. 'Officer's'.

480
6 October
1749

CUST 58/1

From W. C[ooley] and R. T[urvin] (Custom House, Portsmouth). Hand iii.

Herewith we transmit your Honours the Abstract for the Month of September last, together with the undermentioned Accounts, to which we beg leave to refer, *valediction 3*

Nil List of Bonds
Tea & other Goods Enumerated, with Petty Receipts Endors'd
Absent Officers
State of Bonds for Mich*ael*mas quarter 1749

PS. From the Book kept in this Office, it appears that the Weights and Scales, Coal and Corn Bushels at this Port were try'd the 7th Ultimo by the Surveyor & Landwaiters, & that they found the same to be Exact & true and that the stamps for marking Hides, Skins, Linnens Seiz'd Goods, and Sail Cloth, are in good & Sufficient repair, and fit for the uses design'd.

481
6 October
1749

CUST 58/1

From W. C[ooley] and R. T[urvin] (Custom House, Portsmouth). Hand iii.

By the Waggon of Geo. Clarke which will be at the Whitehart in the Burrough of Southwark on Saturday the 7th Instant We have sent under the Seals of Office directed to your Honours, Sundry things as mentioned in the Inclosed Account belonging to his Excellency side Mahmud Envoy from Tripoly, *valediction 5*

An Account of the Examination of several Goods belonging to his Excellency Side Mahmud Envoy from Tripoly Landed out of his Majestys Ship the Deptford Storeship Capt Mills Commander from Portmahone, which Goods were put under the Seals of Office, & directed to the Honourable Commissioners of his Majestys Customs – Vizt –

One Chest Containing Horse furniture –
Seven Bags bitter Almonds, not in the Shells –
Three Baskets of Wax –
One Bundle Morocco Skins –
Three Butts Mahone Wine –
One Cask Single Rum –

482
6 October
1749

CUST 58/1

From W. C[ooley] and R. T[urvin] (Custom House, Portsmouth). Hand iii.

In obedience to your Honours Commands of the 19th Ultimo Inclosed we transmit your Honours an Account taken by the proper Officers at this Port, of the exact quantity of Wheat which was taken out of the Neptune from Stockton, which sprung a Leak at Sea, and again reshipt for Exportation, to which we beg leave to refer, *valediction 3*

Custom House Portsmouth

These are to Certify that there were Landed at this Port, out of the Neptune William Fowler Master from Stockton, bound for Marseilles One hundred & Eighty nine Quarters, two bushels of Damagd Wheat & that in lieu thereof the like quantity – Vizt – One hundred, Eighty nine quarters, two bushels of good sound & merchantable Wheat, winton measure As Witness our hands this 5th October 1749

483
7 October
1749

CUST 58/149, pp. 206–7

From W. Wood (Custom House, London). Hand iii.

The Commissioners being call'd upon by the Lord's of the Treasury for an Account of what Sum's have been paid for Bountie's in the Year ending at Mich*ael*mas last, distinguished, under each Quarter, and finding that the Account of Bountie's are wanting from your Port for the Quarter's undermentioned notwithstanding you were directed by my Letter of the 22d March 1747 to send the same within fourteen day's after each Quarter, The Commissioner's direct you to transmit the said Account's by the return of the Post, if it can be done otherwise by the next Post without fail, in the manner directed by my said Letter, and if it[49] should happen that no Bountie's have been paid at your Port, within the said Time, You are Nevertheless to send a Nil Account, and in case you have already sent up any of the said Account's You are to transmit Copy's thereof, *valediction 2*

Christma's Quarter 1748
Lady=day, Midsummer, & Michaelma's Quarters 1749

---

[49] MS. omits 'it'.

484 CUST 58/1
10 October 1749

From W. C[ooley] (Custom House, Portsmouth) to [W.] Wood. Hand iii.
Sir
Inclosed I send you agreeable to your Letter of the 7th Instant in order to be laid before the Treasury an Account of what Sums have been paid for Bountys at this Port, for Christmas quarter 1748, Lady day, Midsummer & Michaelmas ⌜1749⌝[50] to which ⌜I⌝[51] beg leave to refer, being with great regard
Your Honours ⌜&cetera⌝[52]
W C./

485 CUST 58/1
10 October 1749

From W. C[ooley] and R. T[urvin] (Custom House, Portsmouth). Hand iii.
Inclosed we transmit your Honours an Account of a Seizure, in the usual form, made by Charles Coombs Commander of the Greenhill Yatch in the Service of this Port, together with Copy of a Letter which we have from him setting forth the manner & cause of Seizure, to which we beg leave to refer, *valediction 3*

486 CUST 58/1[53]
12 October 1749

From W. C[ooley] and R. T[urvin] (Custom House, Portsmouth). Hand iii.
Inclosed we transmit your Honours a Certificate whereby it appears that Chas Coombs Commander of the Greenhill Yatch, Employ'd in the Service at this Port, hath duely perform'd his Contract, agreeable to what was transmitted in our joint Letter bearing date the 13th Nov*embe*r 1743 Viz. for the Quarters ended Midsummer & Michaelmas last, And therefore we pray your Honours Order for paying the said Captain Coombs the Sum of £23. 5. 0 being after the Rate of Thirty Shillings Per Ton Per Annum, for Thirty one Tons Burthen, *valediction 3*
In margin: £23. 5. 0[54]

Port of Portsmouth
These are to Certify that upon a Carefull Survey made for the half Year ended Michaelmas last, it appear'd to us that the Greenhill Yatch & Boats belonging to her, Employ'd in the Service of his Majestys Customs at this Port, together with all the Materials have been duely kept, and are in good & Sufficient repair, and that Captain Coombs Commander thereof hath well and duely perform'd his Contract, & is thereby entituled to half a Years Allowance, Amounting to Twenty three Pounds, five Shillings, Witness our hands at the Custom House this 4th Oct*obe*r 1749
W Cooley Collector — Wm Baskerville Tides*urveyo*r
R Turvin D*eputy* Comptroller — Wm Read Shipw*righ*t
In margin: £23. 5. 0[55]

487 CUST 58/149, p. 208
13 October 1749

From W. Wood (Custom House, London). Hand iii.
John Forrest being recommended to the Commissioner's to be an Extra Tidesman & Boatman at your Port, they direct you (incase he is to Act as a Boatman) to examine into his Qualification, and if you find him Sufficiently Qualify'd, You are by return of the Post to transmit the Board a Certificate thereof, in the manner required by ⌜My⌝[56] Letter of the 21st of June 1743 and Report whether he doe's not Act at present, as an Officer, *valediction 2*

---

50 Written over 'qua(*?*)'.
51 Possibly inserted.
52 MS. '&' (for '&ca').
53 The enclosure precedes the letter in MS.
54 Underlined.
55 Underlined.
56 Altered to 'by(*?*)'.

488 14 October 1749

CUST 58/149, p. 207

From Sam. Mead, Beaumont Hotham, G. Vaughan and Edw. Hooper (Custom House, London). Hand iii.

Having considered your Preparatory Account of Incident's for the Quarter ended at Midsummer last, Amounting to fifteen Pounds Eleven Shilling's, & Eleven Pence, The Collector may pay the same, with the privity of the Comptroller, and take Credit for it, in his Account of Incident's, annexing this Letter with proper Receipts thereto, as Voucher's, *valediction 1*

In margin: £15. 11. 11[57]

489 16 October 1749

CUST 58/1

From W. C[ooley] and R. T[urvin] (Custom House, Portsmouth) to [W. Wood]. Hand iii.

Sir

In Obedience to the Commissioners Order signifyd to us, in your Letter of the 30th Ultimo we send you here Inclos'd, the Account of Prohibited East Indies Goods for the Year ended Michaelmas quarter 1749 together with the Account of Naval Stores for the last quarter – But we beg leave to acquaint you, that the said Account for Michaelmas quarter 1748, was sent to the Board the 7th October following, We are

Sir ⌜&cetera⌝[58]

W C R T

490 16 October 1749

CUST 58/1

From W. C[ooley] and R. T[urvin] (Custom House, Portsmouth). Hand iii.

Herewith we transmit your Honours an Account of Goods Enumerated, and not Enumerated, lately Seizd by the Officers at this Port, to which we beg leave to refer, *valediction 3*

491 16 October 1749

CUST 58/1

From W. C[ooley] and R. T[urvin] (Custom House, Portsmouth). Hand iii.

By your Honours Order of the 13th instant signify'd to us by Mr Wood, we[59] were directed to examine into the Qualification of Jno Forrest, Recommended to ⌜your⌝[60] Honours to be an Extra Tidesman & Boatman at this Port, and if we find him Sufficently qualifyd to transmit your Honours a Certificate thereof; – We beg leave to inform your Honours Jno Forrest does not act as an Officer at this Port, nor do we know of such a Man, *valediction 5*

492 17 October 1749

CUST 58/149, p. 208

From G. Vaughan, Beaumont Hotham, R. Chandlor and Sam. Mead (Custom House, London). Hand iii.

In Answer to the Account of Seizure's transmitted in your Letter of the 10th Instant We direct you, incase the Good's were Seiz'd within the Limit's of a Port, to send for a Writt of Appraisement, And Prosecute the Ship & Good's to Condemnation, in the Exchequer at the Officer's Charge, Corresponding with our Sollictor, & the Register of Seizure's, *valediction 1*

Noted the 19th Oct*ober* 1749

493 21 October 1749

CUST 58/149, pp. 208–9

From Wil. Wood (Custom House, London). Hand iii.

Having laid before the Board a Letter which I have received from Mr Champney's, in whose House Mr Baskerville, lately Seiz'd a Considerable quantity of Good's, for which he is ordered to be Prosecuted; And Mr Champney's being sensible of his Error in Suffering the thing's to be carried to his House without applying to You, as he is a Gentleman of Fortune and a fair Charactor, and the Goods are already order'd to be Prosecuted, they have no Objection to Wave the Personal Prosecution against him, Provided the Officer's at whose Expence it is Carried on, agree thereto – And you are to Communicate this Letter to him, & Report his Answer to the Board, *valediction 2*

---

57 Underlined.

58 MS. '&' (for '&ca').

59 MS. omits 'we'.

60 MS. 'your your'.

494
24 October
1749

CUST 58/149, p. 209

From W. Wood (Custom House, London). Hand iii.

The quarterly Account of Naval Store's, from Michaelma's to Christma's last, being not yet received, The Commissioner's direct you immediately on Receipt hereof, to transmit it to the Board, *valediction 2*

495
24 October
1749

CUST 58/149, pp. 209–10

From Edw. Hooper, Sam. Mead, R. Chandlor and G. Vaughan (Custom House, London). Hand iii.

We received your Letter of the 12th Instant, Inclosing a Certificate whereby it appear's that the Greenhill Yatch and Boats belonging to her, in the Service at your Port, under the Command of Capt Coomb's, are in good & Sufficient repair, The Collector may pay the Commander thereof the usual Allowance for keeping the said Yatch & Boats in wear & Tear for the quarter's ended at Midsummer, & Michaelmas last, and take Credit for the same, in his Account of Incident's, annexing this Letter with proper receipt's thereto as Voucher's, *valediction 1*

496
24 October
1749

CUST 58/1

From W. C[ooley] and R. T[urvin] (Custom House, Portsmouth). Hand iii.

We have your Honours Letter of the 21st Instant, signify'd to us by Mr Wood, acquainting us of your having received a Letter ⌜from⌝[61] Mr Champneys from whom Mr Baskerville Seiz'd a considerable quantity of Goods, which he was running on shore (& not at his House) for which he was ordered to be Prosecuted, but Mr Champneys being sensible of his Error, in suffering the Goods to be carried on shore without first applying to us. – in consideration thereof, of his being a Gentlemen of Fortune & fair Charactor your Honours have no Objection to wave the Personal Prosecution against him, provided Mr Baskerville at whose Expence it is carried on agree thereto, We are to acquaint your Honours, We have called on Mr Baskerville, and communicated your Letter to him who has assured us that as your Honours seem inclinable to favour Mr Champneys, he shall have no objection to wave the Personal Prosecution against him, but hopes your Honours will order that Mr Champneys make him a Sutable Reward for so doing, *valediction 3*

497
26 October
1749

CUST 58/149, p. 210

From Edw. Hooper, G. Vaughan, R. Chandlor and S. Mead (Custom House, London). Hand iii.

In Answer to the Account of Seizure's transmitted in your Letter's of the 19th & 21st instant, We direct you to Prosecute the Coffee, and Brandy, thereinmentioned to Condemnation, in the Exchequer at the King's Charge, And we have no objection to the Officer's Prosecuting the rest of the Good's in like manner, at their own Charge, Corresponding with our Sollicitor & the Register of Seizure's, *valediction 1*

498
26 October
1749

CUST 58/1

From W. C[ooley] and R. T[urvin] (Custom House, Portsmouth). Hand iii.

In Obedience to your Honours Order signify'd to us by Mr Wood in his Letter of the 24th Ultimo We have here Inclosed an Account of Naval Stores for Christmas Quarter last, to which we beg leave to refer, *valediction 3*

499
27 October
1749

CUST 58/149, pp. 210–11

From Edw. Hooper, G. Vaughan, Beaumont Hotham and S. Mead (Custom House, London). Hand iii.

We received your Letter of the 24th Ins*tant* acquainting us that Mr Baskerville Tidesurveyor, who Seizd a Considerable Quantity of Good's from Mr Champney's has no objection to Wave the Personal Prosecution against him, but Hope's to have a suitable reward for so doing, You are to acquaint him, that we are Surpriz'd, that he shoul'd expect any satisfaction, for Dropping the Personal Prosecution, as there can be no such thing, but he will be sufficiently rewarded by having his share of the Seizure of the Good's, And as it appear's that the Affair was owing to inadvertency, in Mr Champney's, We think it would be unreasonable to commence a Personal Prosecution against him, *valediction 1*

---

[61] Written over 'Mr' erased.

500
28 October
1749

CUST 58/1

From W. C[ooley] and R. T[urvin] (Custom House, Portsmouth). Hand iii.

We beg leave to acquaint your Honours, We have received into the Kings Warehouse, at this Port, from on board the Deptford Storeship, late from Portmahon One Box Containing two Callicoe *Marseilles quilted Petticoats; We beg to know whether the same may be admitted to an Entry, & what Dutys are chargeable thereon, *valediction 5*

501
3 November
1749

CUST 58/149, p. 211

From W. Wood (Custom House, London). Hand iii.

Thomas Hanbury Esqr Com*mand*er of his Majesty's Sloop the Hazard, which is order'd to Cruize on your Station, to prevent Smugling, having apply'd to the Commissioner's desiring to have a Deputation, Impowering him to Seize Prohibited & Uncustomed Good's, You are to call upon him, to know at what Place he Propose's to give Security for the faithfull discharge of his Duty, & Report the same to the Board, *valediction 2*

502
3 November
1749

CUST 58/1

From W. C[ooley] and R. T[urvin] (Custom House, Portsmouth). Hand iii.

Herewith we transmit your Honours the Abstract for the Month of October last, together with the undermentioned Accounts, to which we beg leave to Refer *valediction 3*

Nil List of Bonds

Tea & other Goods Enumerated with Petty receipts Endors'd

Absent Officers

PS/ From the Book kept in this Office it appears that the Weights & Scales, Coal & Corn Bushels at this Port, were try'd the [62] Ultimo by the Surveyor & Landwaiter and that they found the same to be exact & true and that the stamps for marking Hides, Skins, Linnens, Seiz'd Goods and Sail, are in good & Sufficient repair and fit for the uses design'd

WC RT

503
7 November
1749

CUST 58/149, p. 212

From Beaumont Hotham, Sam. Mead, R. Chandlor and G. Vaughan (Custom House, London). Hand iii.

The Collector's Letter of the 3^d instant having been laid before u's relating to the Vessel and Good's Seiz'd by Captain Coomb's Commander of the Greenhill Yatch, ⌜in⌝[63] the Service at Y*our* Port, We direct you incase the ⌜Transaction⌝[64] was within the Limit's of a Port, to Prosecute the Good's to Condemnation in the Exchequer at the King's Charge, And We have no objection to the Officer's Prosecuting the Vessel in like manner, at his own Charge Corresponding with our Sollicitor & the Register of Seizure's, *valediction 1*

504
8 November
1749

CUST 58/149, pp. 212–13

From W. Wood (Custom House, London). Hand iii.

The Commissioner's having receiv'd Information, that there is a large Quantity of Hopp's, bought up at Dunkirk, where the Price is low, with a view to bring them into this Kingdom, in a Clandestine manner, And in order to deceive the Officer's they will be Pack'd in the same manner Our's are to make them Pass as English The Commissioner's direct you to give it in strict Charge to the proper Officer's, to prevent the said Fraud's, Reporting to the Board Your Proceeding's

And you are to give Notice to the proper Officer's, that when any Sufferance's are granted for the Shipping of Hopp's, to be carried from one Port, or Place, of this Kingdom to any other Port, or Place, that they take care to see the Hopp's are Loaded upon the same Ship, or Vessel, which is mention'd in the Sufferance, & that the Hopp's are remaining on board at the time of the Ship, or Vessel's sailing from such Port or place, *valediction 2*

---

[62] Space left blank.
[63] Altered from 'on'.
[64] Altered from 'Transaction's'.

505
8 November
1749

CUST 58/1

From [W. Cooley] and [R. Turvin] (Custom House, Portsmouth). Hand iii.

We are to acquaint your Honours this Morning died Mr Thomas Trehearne, late Tidesurveyor, at this Port, *valediction 3*

506
10 November
1749

CUST 58/149, p. 213

From Beaumont Hotham, Sam. Mead, R. Chandlor and G. Vaughan (Custom House, London). Hand iii.

Having granted our Deputation for Jame's Burnett to be a Coal Meter at your Port, in the room of Jno Chadwick resign'd, You are to take care he be under Oath and Security for the faithfull Discharge of the said Employ, and Qualify's himself as the Law direct's, *valediction 1*

507
10 November
1749

CUST 58/1

From W. C[ooley] and R. T[urvin] (Custom House, Portsmouth). Hand iii.

By your Honours Order of the 13th Ultimo we were directed to Examine into the Qualifications of Jno Forrest recommended to your Honours to be an Extra Tidesman & Boatman at this Port and incase we find him sufficiently qualifyd to transmit your Honours a Certificate thereof. at the time we received the said Order, no such person as Jno Forrest cou'd be heard of, at this Port; We are now to acquaint your Honours said Forrest has been with us & Inclosed we transmit your Honours a Certificate whereby it will appear he is sufficiently qualify'd to act as a Tidesman & Boatman *valediction 5*

Port of Portsmouth

These are to Certify that upon Examination we find Jno Forrest, to be sufficiently qualify'd for the Management of a Boat, and that he is a fit Person to be a Extra Tidesman & Boatman in the Service of his Majestys Customs as Witness our hands. Dated at the Custom House this 10th Day of November 1749

W C   R T   W Baskerville Tidesurv*eyo*r

508
14 November
1749

CUST 58/149, p. 214

From Sam. Mead, G. Vaughan, Beaumont Hotham and Edw. Hooper (Custom House, London). Hand iii.

Having granted our Commission for John Forrest to be an Extra Tidesman & Boatman at your Port, in the room of Francis Fuller resigned, You are to take care he be under Oath and Security for the faithfull discharge of the said Employ, and qualifies himself as the Law directs, paying him the like Allowance of five Pounds Per Annum by Incidents, as was paid to his Predecessor, for which the Collector may take Credit from time to time in his Account of Incidents referring therein to the date hereof, *valediction 1*

509
17 November
1749

CUST 58/1

From W. C[ooley] and R. T[urvin] (Custom House, Portsmouth). Hand iii.

Inclosed we transmit your Honours a Memorial which we this day received from Ja^{s} Burnett a Tidesman & Boatman at this Port, acquainting us of the ill Treatment he have met with, in the Execution of his Duty, which on enquiry we find true, and in justice to the said Officer, we immediately apply'd for a Warrant, to apprehend the Offender, Thos Mac Donal Boatswains Mate of his Majesty's Ship Monarch, but on application to Capt Harland of said Ship he was pleased to refuse delivering up said Mac Donald, without first having an Order from the Lords Commissioners of the Admiralty. We therefore hope your Honours will take Burnetts Case into Consideration, & that your Honours will be pleased to procure an Order from the Adm*iral*ty, that Capt Harland may deliver up said Mac Donald, to be Punished as the Law directs, all which is most humbly submitted *valediction 4*

Gentlemen

I beg leave to inform you, that on Thursday last the 16th Instant, I went on board his Majestys Ship Rippon at Spithead, with an Order from the Office as an Extra Tidesman for bringing on Shore to the WareHouse, Six Pipes, & Two Hogsheads of Wine, in order for payment of the Dutys, which was accordingly put into his Majestys Ship the Berwicks Longboat which went off for that purpose, during my attendance in her alongside ⌜ye⌝[65] Ship, Wm Tasker one of the Tidesmen on board the said Ship, saw a Cask thrown overboard, on which he call'd to me, and Richard Chambers another Tidesman, who was come off to the said Ship for other Goods, to assist him, & by getting into a small Boat, that happen'd to be by the said Ship, we got it out of the Water, and on Examining it, found its Contents to be Rum, quantity about ten Gallons, which was put into the Longboat, for immediate conveying it to the WareHouse; When the Wine was got into the Longboat & she was putting off, several Sailors that did not belong to her, suddenly jump'd into her, and I being at that time near the helm, and intending to Steer her into the Harbour it being very dark and a thick Fogg coming on, & there being but three Young Men in her, belonging to her, besides her Patron, who was hurt and incapable of doing any thing, and my self being well acquainted with the Coast, by being bred a Fisherman here, and one of them taking the helm, I asked him what Business he had with it, upon which he immediately struck me several Violent blows with his Fist, in the Face, which knock'd me down, from which I recovered with Difficulty, when strugling with him, he struck me on the Cheek bone, with the Boats Tiller, and Knock'd me down into the bottom of the Boat senceless, I also at the same time received a Bruise on my right hand, by putting it up to save my head by which I am deprived of the use of my Thumb, & I have the greatest reason to think that the Blow had Kill'd me, if part of its force had not been broke in that manner, and that I had afterwards been otherwise killd if Assistance had not come into the Boat; On my Complaint to the Commanding Officer on Board the said Ship, the Offender was found out & put into Irons, he is named Thomas Mac Donald, & belongs to his Majestys Ships Monarch. As I received this Injury as I was attending the Execution of my Duty, and as there is reason to believe the Strange Sailors coming into the Boat, was by some means to get away the Cask of Rum, which was my apprehension when I spoke to Mac Donald, & as you perceive the greatness of my hurt & abuse, I hope you will be pleased to lay my Case before the Honourable Board, & take measures for bringing the Offender to Justice, as he has confessd himself to be the Person & Makes no Excuse for it but he was Drunk, I am

Gentlemen Your most humble Servant

James Burnett

17th Nov*ember* 1749

To The Collector & Comptroller.

510
21 November 1749

CUST 58/149, p. 214

From G. Vaughan, Beaumont Hotham, J. Evelynn and Edw. Hooper (Custom House, London). Hand iii.

We received your Letter of the 28th Ultimo acquainting us that you have received into the WareHouse at Your Port, from on Board the Deptford Storeship from Portmahone, a Box Containing two Callicoe *Marseilles Quilted Petticoats, We direct you to keep your hands on them till you receive our further Orders *valediction 1*

511
21 November 1749

CUST 58/1

From W. C[ooley] and R. T[urvin] (Custom House, Portsmouth). Hand iii.

Inclosed we transmit Your Honours an Account of Goods Enumerated, & Goods not Enumerated lately Seizd by the Officers in this Port, to which we beg leave to refer, *valediction 4*

---

65 Written over an illegible erasure.

512
22 November
1749

CUST 58/1

From W. C[ooley] and R. T[urvin] (Custom House, Portsmouth). Hand iii.

We are to acquaint your Honours that in Obedience to your Order of the 3^{d} Instant, signify'd to us by Mr Wood, We have called upon Thos Hanbury Esqr Commander of his Majestys Sloop, Hazard, who apply'd to your Honours for a Deputation, Impowering him to Seize Prohibited & Uncustomed Goods, to know at what Place he proposes to give Security, for the faithfull Discharge of his Duty, in answer to which he has acquainted us he proposes giving Security in London *valediction 5*

513
25 November
1749

CUST 58/149, p. 215

From G. Vaughan, Sam. Mead, J. Evelynn and Edw. Hooper (Custom House, London). Hand iii.

In answer to the Account of Seizures transmitted in your Letter of the 21st Instant We direct you to Prosecute the Enumerated Goods thereinmentioned to Condemnation, before the Justices of the Peace, at the Kings Charge, And we have no objection to the Officers Prosecuting the rest of the Goods in like manner at their own Charge, acquainting us when Condemn'd, *valediction 1*

Noted the 27th Nov*ember* 1749

514
25 November
1749

CUST 58/1

From W. C[ooley] and R. T[urvin] (Custom House, Portsmouth). Hand iii.

We have here Inclosed a List of such Stationary Wares as are much wanted for the Service at this Port, with which We beg to be immediately, Supplyd and the same shall be frugally managed *valediction 4*

PS The last Supply was Crav'd the 31st of May 1749 –

Portsmouth

A List of such Stationary Wares as are much wanted for the Service of his Majestys Customs at this Port, humbly Crav'd to be allow'd. Viz^{t}[66]

4 Quire quarter Book Paper Inwards
2 Quire *Imperial Paper Unrul'd
4 Rheams fine *pott Cutt
6 Rheams 2^{d} *pott Uncutt
6 Quire *Demy Cutt
3 Quire D^{o} Uncutt

80	Blue Books –	4 Leaves
50 –		2
60 –		6
40 –		8
30 –		10
30 –		12
20 –		14
12 –		16
12 –		24
12 –		20

1 Dozen *Demy Pocket Books
2 Gallons Black Ink
1 Quart red Ink
4 *Pounce Boxes
1 Dozen Lead Pencils
4 Penknives
1 Dozen Tape
2 Journal Books for the Commander and Mate of the Greenhill Yatch
1 Book *Imperial Paper Unruld

3 Bags Sand –
2 Books 1 Quire *Demy in Marb*le*
3 Quire *Boardings
3 Quire Report Inwards in Sheets, –
2 D^{o} Outwards
2 D^{o} Coal Warrants
1500 Quills
3000 Wafers
1000 large D^{o} for *Cocq*ue*ts &cetera
12 Past board files & 3 Dozen Tags for D^{o}
1 Report Book Inwards
1 large Book *Imperial Paper rul'd for Remittances to the Rec*eiver* General
1 D^{o} large *Imperial Paper Ruld for Indentures of Appraisement –
2 Quire Paper Rul'd for Wooll bro*ught* & Carried Coastwise
1/2 Pound *Pounce
3 Bodkins
1 Pound Sealing Wax
2 Letter Books
2 Books Personal Prosecutions
1 Book for Enumerated Goods

[66] There is a red tick before each item except 2 reams of fine pot cut, 6 reams of second pot uncut, 1000 large wafers and four penknives; this last is followed by a red dash.

515
28 November
1749

CUST 58/149, pp. 215–16

From Sam. Mead, G. Vaughan, J. Evelynn and W. Westby (Custom House, London). Hand iii.

Having received a Letter from Mr H^y^ Gibbs Deputy Customer of your Port, dated the 2^d^ Instant relating to a Cargoe of Coals landed there, out of the Dutchess of Scabro, William Trott Master from Sunderland, together with Copy of a *Cocquet granted there the 14th August last, for 54 Chal*drons* ⌜of⌝[67] Coals which the said Trott alledges he was forced to proceed with to Rotterdam, But that he has since paid the Oversea Duty at your Port, and the Collector & Comptroller of Sunderland to whom we referr'd the same, having represented to us that the *Cocquet shou'd have been Dated the 14th October, instead of the 14th August last, and that they have sent a rectify'd *Cocquet to your Port, you may grant the Master a Certificate to Discharge his Coast Bond, there being no appearance of any Fraud in the Master, and take care the Dutys be bro*ugh*t to Account as for Coals Exported from Sunderland *valediction 1*

516
28 November
1749

CUST 58/1

From W. C[ooley] and R. T[urvin] (Custom House, Portsmouth). Hand iii.

Inclosed we transmit your Honours an Account of Goods Enumerated & Goods not Enumerated, lately Seizd by the Officers, in this Port to which we beg leave to refer, *valediction 4*

517
1 December
1749

CUST 58/1

From W. C[ooley] and R. T[urvin] (Custom House, Portsmouth). Hand iii.

Inclosed we transmit your Honours an Account of Goods Enumerated lately Seiz'd by the Officers in this Port, to which we beg leave to refer *valediction 4*

518
5 December
1749

CUST 58/149, p. 216

From J. Evelynn, Beaumont Hotham, Sam. Mead and G. Vaughan (Custom House, London). Hand iii.

In answer to the Account of Seizures transmitted in your Letter of the 28th Ultimo We direct you to Prosecute the Rum & Brandy, thereinmentioned to Condemnation in the Exchequer at the Kings Charge, and we have no Objection to the Officers Prosecuting the Sloop and Materials in like manner at their own Charge, Corresponding with our Sollicitor & the Register of Seizures *valediction 1*

Noted the 7th Dec*ember* 1749

519
6 December
1749

CUST 58/1

From W. C[ooley] and R. T[urvin] (Custom House, Portsmouth). Hand iii.

Herewith we transmit your Honours the Abstract for the Month of November last, together with the undermentioned Accounts, to which we beg leave to refer, *valediction 3*

Nil List of Bonds
Tea and other Goods Enumerated with Petty Receipts Endors'd
Absent Officers

PS From the Book kept in this Office, it appears that the Weights and Scales, Coal & Corn Bushels at this Port, were try'd the 3^d^ Ultimo by the Surveyor & Landwaiters, and that they found the same to be exact & true, and that the stamps for marking Hides, Skins, Linnens, Seiz'd Goods and Sail Cloth, are in Good & Sufficient repair and fit for the uses design'd

WC RT

[67] MS. 'of of'.

520
7 December
1749

CUST 58/149, pp. 217–18

From J. Evelynn, R. Chandlor, W. Westby and Sam. Mead (Custom House, London). Hand iii.

Inclos'd you will receive Copy of the Referrd Petition of Jos. Gilbert who is under Prosecution for the Treble Value of 95 Gallons of Brandy, praying that the Sum of Twenty two Pounds Sixteen Shillings, & the Charges of Prosecution may be accepted as a Composition for the said Offence. We direct you to ⌜Communicate⌝[68] the same to Mr Baskerville, & transmit us his Report, whether he has any Objection to what is desired, *valediction 1*

To The R^t Honble the Lords Commissioners of his Maj*es*tys Treasury

The Humble Petition of Jos. Gilbert of Gosport in the County of Hants' Sheweth That your Lordships Petitioner is under Prosecution at the Suit of the Crown, on an Information that hath been given against him for having been concern'd in Harbouring & Concealing in a Stable belonging to him Nineteen half *Anchors of Brandy Containing about Seventy six Gallons, on which Account your Petitioner hath been arrested & given Bail for the Sum of £95

Your Petitioner begs leave to assure your Lordships that he was intirely Ignorant of any Law that cou'd lay a Penalty on him for Harbouring or Concealing of Goods that were not his Property which is actually the present Case, & not being desirous or willing to put the Crown to any Trouble or Expence on this Affair humbly submits himself to your Lordships & is willing to pay as ⌜a⌝[69] Composition for the Offence alledg'd against him, the Sum of Twenty two Pounds Sixteen Shillings, being after the rate of 6^s Per Gallon, for the quantity your Petitioner is charg'd with, at the Rate of four Gallons to the half *Anchors, the same being the usual Rate at which you have been pleased to permit others to Compound & likewise paying all Charges.

Your Petitioner therefore most humbly begs your Lordships to take the Hardships of ⌜his⌝[70] Case into Consideration & be pleased to accept the said Composition & to grant your Lordships Warrant to the Honourable Commissioners of His Majestys Customs for their approving thereof & your Lordships Petitioner as in Duty bound will ever pray &cetera

21st Nov*embe*r 1749

521
7 December
1749

CUST 58/149, pp. 218–19

From J. Evelynn, R. Chandlor, W. Westby and Sam. Mead (Custom House, London). Hand iii.

In Answer to the Account of Seizures transmitted in your Letter of the 1st Instant, We direct you to Prosecute the Brandy & Rum thereinmentioned to Condemnation before the Justices of the Peace at the Kings Charge, acquainting us when Condemn'd, *valediction 1*

522
7 December
1749

CUST 58/149, pp. 219–20

From J. Evelynn, W. Westby, R. Chandlor and Sam. Mead (Custom House, London). Hand iii.

We received your Letter of the 17th Ultimo transmitting the Memorial of James Burnett Tidesman and Boatman at your Port, setting forth that he has been Violently Assaulted & Abused in the Execution of his Duty, by Thomas Mac. Donald Boatswains Mate of his Majestys Ship Monarch, and Mr Corbett Secretary to the Lords Commissioners of the Admiralty, having by his Letter of the 5th Instant, acquainted us that the Captain is directed to deliver up the said Mac. Donald, to be proceeded against according to Law, which we signify to you, & you are to carry him before some Justice of the Peace for the Borough of Portsmouth who will commit him to Prison till the next quarter Sessions, & on the Information of Burnett the Justices will set a fine upon him, and he must then remain in Prison, untill the Court of Exchequer discharges him of the Fine & Imprisonment Report*ing* to us your Proceedings, *valediction 1*

---

68 MS. 'Commicate'.
69 Inserted.
70 MS. 'the his'.

523
9 December
1749

CUST 58/1

From W. C[ooley] and R. T[urvin] (Custom House, Portsmouth). Hand iii.

In Obedience to your Commands of the 23^{d} ⌜of October⌝[71] 1742 We have here Inclos'd an Account of all the Officers at this Port, to whom Annual Allowances are made by Incidents, distinguishing those who are Establish'd, with the Dates of the Orders for paying the same. And in pursuance of your said Directions, we humbly Report that the said Officers have faithfully & Diligently perform'd their Duty, And tis our humble Opinion it will be for the Service, to continue them at their several Incident Allowances, which have hitherto been paid, We therefore pray an Order for paying the same, *valediction 3*

524
9 December
1749

CUST 58/1

From W. C[ooley] and R. T[urvin] (Custom House, Portsmouth). Hand iii.

We have received your Honours Letter of the 7th Instant, together with Copy of the Referr'd Petition of Joseph Gilbert, who is under Prosecution for Treble the Value of Ninety five Gallons of Brandy praying that the Sum of Twenty two Pounds, Sixteen Shillings, & the Charges of Prosecution may be accepted as a Composition for the said Offence, We have in Obedience to your Honours Commands communicated the same to Mr Baskerville who has no objection to a Composition, but is humbly of Opinion as the same will be an Indulgence to said Gilbert, and as the Quantity of Brandy is really One hundred Gallons that he shoud pay the Sum of Thirty Pounds, which Sum it will Amount to at six Shillings Per Gallon & likewise all Charges of Prosecution, however Mr Baskerville humbly submits the same to your Honours Determination, *valediction 5*
In margin: £22. 16. 0[72]

525
14 December
1749

CUST 58/149, p. 220

From W. Wood (Custom House, London). Hand iii.

A Debenture in the Name of Thos Bensted for three hundred & nine quarters four Bushels Malt Shipt at your Port the 25th Oct*obe*r last, in the Willingmind Jno Moorey master for Dublin, has been presented to the Commissioners for their Orders for Payment, but you having omitted to send a Duplicate thereof the same is stopt, You are immediately on Receipt hereof to transmit the said Duplicate to the Board, which I am directed to signify to you *valediction 2*

526
15 December
1749

CUST 58/1

From W. C[ooley] and R. T[urvin] (Custom House, Portsmouth). Hand iii.

We are to acquaint your Honours by Virtue of a Warrant from Mr Samuel Chandlor one of his Majestys Justices of the Peace for this Borough, is committed to Prison Thos Mac Donald Boatswains Mate of his Majestys Ship Monarch for Violently Assaulting & abusing Ja^{s} Burnett a Tidesman & Boatman at this Port. As soon as we know what fine the Justices are pleased to set on said Mac Donald, We shall Report the same to your Honours, with our Proceedings *valediction 5*[73]

527
16 December
1749

CUST 58/149, pp. 220–1

From W. Westby, J. Evelynn, Beaumont Hotham and Edw. Hooper (Custom House, London). Hand iii.

Having taken into consideration your Letter of the 9th December 1749 transmitting an Account of the Annual Allowances made to the Officers at your Port, by Incidents, We agree to your paying the said Officers their respective Allowances to Michaelmas last, & to their Continuance from that time to Christmas next, for which the Collector may take Credit in his Account of Incidents, referring therein to the Date hereof; And at the Expiration thereof, you are to report to us the Services perform'd by the said Officers with your Opinion whether it will be for the Interest of the Revenue to continue the said Allowances by Incidents *valediction 1*

---

71 Altered from 'Ultimo'.
72 Underlined.
73 'Pages missing here' added in pencil, 19th or 20th century (see above, p. xxxv).

528
19 December
1749

CUST 58/149, pp. 221–2

From R. Chandlor, W. Westby, J. Evelynn and Edw. Hooper (Custom House, London). Hand iii.

The Commissioners for Victualling his Majestys Navy having in their Letter of the 18th Instant apply'd to us desiring that such part of the Wine as is in his Majestys Victualling Stores at your Port may be Issued to his Majestys Ship the Garland which is ordered to be Victualld for Foreign Service, we have agreed thereto, & you may permit so much of the Wine to be Issued on board the said Ship, under the care of the proper Officers, as shall be found necessary, ⌜taking⌝[74] care there be no Embezlements, *valediction 1*

529
20 December
1749

CUST 58/149, p. 222

From R. Chandlor, W. Westby, J. Evelynn and Edw. Hooper (Custom House, London). Hand iii.

We received your Letter of the 6th Oct*obe*r last, acquainting us that there was landed at your Port, out of the Neptune Wm Fowler Master from Stockton 189 quarters two Bushels of Damag'd Wheat, Winchester measure, and that in lieu thereof the like quantity of good Sound & Merchantable Wheat winton mea*sure* was Shipt for Exportation, We direct you to make out a Debenture for the said Wheat *valediction 1*

530
20 December
1749

CUST 58/149, pp. 222–3

From R. Chandlor, Beaumont Hotham, J. Evelynn and Sam. Mead (Custom House, London). Hand iii.

Inclosed you will receive Writts of Delivery for the Enumerated Goods returnd in four Indentures of Apraisement from your Port, & Proclaim'd in the Exchequer last Term, which have been Condemn'd, The Total Amount of which is on the other side.

We direct you to sell the said Goods Publickly to the⌜highest⌝[75] bidder, putting them up at such Prizes as the Goodness of the Commodity deserves, *valediction 1*

Writt dated	13th	Dec*embe*r 1749	–	94. 15. 0.
Do –	13	Do	–	72. 5. 0.
Do –	13	Do	–	83. 4. 0.
Do –	13	Do	–	72. 9. 8.
				£322. 13. 8.[76]

531
22 December
1749

CUST 58/149, pp. 223–4

From Sam. Mead, Beaumont Hotham, W. Westby and G. Vaughan (Custom House, London). Hand iii.

Having Issued our Commission to John Mc Cloud to be an Extra Tidesman & Boatman at Your Port, in the room of Wm Tasker Preferr'd, and he having given Security here, We direct you to admit him to his Duty, giving all due Encouragement for the Service, acquainting him that he must take the Oaths enjoyn'd by Law, and Certify to us the day he is admitted, And you are to Pay him the like Allowance, as was paid to his Predecessor, & take Credit for it in your Account of Incidents referring therein to the date hereof – *valediction 1*

532
27 December
1749

CUST 58/149, p. 223

From W. Wood (Custom House, London). Hand iii.

Your Letter to the Commissioners relating to the Murder of an Officer I directly sent to the Sollicitor, as soon as I hear from him you shall have the necessary directions, *valediction 2*

---

[74] MS. 'taking taking'.
[75] MS. 'highes'.
[76] See App. I, nos 14, 15, 18, 20.

533
29 December
1749

CUST 58/149, p. 224

From Beaumont Hotham, W. Westby, R. Chandlor and G. Vaughan (Custom House, London). Hand iii.

We received your Letter of the 23[d] instant acquainting us that W[m] May late Tidesman at your Port, was on the 21st Murdered in the Execution of his Duty by W[m] Kemp a Mariner belonging to a Sloop called the Peggy whereof W[m] Hunter is Master, from Bourdeaux bound for North Bergan, & that upon the Informations of Alexander Akin & Frederick Bailey, you have found out & secured the said Kemp. We direct you to use your utmost Endeavours, to procure what further Evidence can be got, in order that all the Circumstances attending the Murder may be set forth, & transmit their Affidavits to us, in the mean time you are to employ M[r] Chandlor the Attorney, to get the Prisoner committed to winton' Goal, giving our ⌜Solicitor⌝[77] from time to time an Account of your Proceedings, *valediction 1*

534
30 December
1749

CUST 58/149, p. 225

From Beaumont Hotham, R. Chandlor, Sam. Mead and G. Vaughan (Custom House, London). Hand iii.

We received your Letter of the 28th Instant transmitting an Account of Seizures made by the Officers at your Port. We direct You to Prosecute the Enumerated Goods thereinmentioned to Condemnation, in the Exchequer at the King's Charge; And the Sollicitor being of Opinion that the Tea should be Prosecuted, but with regard to the Vessel he is in great Doubt of Success, as the quantity is but small, & she is not liable to Seizure on Account of any of the Soap Lace or *Cambricks being found Concealed, You are therefore to deliver her unless the Officers will Prosecute her at their own Risque & Charge. The Soap *Cambricks & Lace are not Forfeited for being concealed, unless the Master had made a Report at the Custom House before they were found & they were not comprisd therein *valediction 1*

535
4 January
1749/50

CUST 58/149, pp. 225–6

From Beaumont Hotham, R. Chandlor, W. Westby and G. Vaughan (Custom House, London). Hand iii.

Application having been made to us desiring that Edward Pratton Esq[r] Commander of his Majestys Ship the Blanford may have a Commission Impowering him to Seize Prohibited & uncustomed Goods, We have agreed thereto & Inclosed you will receive the same, with a Bond to be Executed by him, & when done you may admit him to his Duty, taking care he qualifies himself as the Law directs & when he is admitted you are to return the Bond to us *valediction 1*

536
5 January
1749/50

CUST 58/149, p. 226

From Sam. Mead, Beaumont Hotham, W. Westby and G. Vaughan (Custom House, London). Hand iii.

Our Sollicitor having laid before us a Certificate of the Condemnation of a Sloop with her Tackle *Apparell & Furniture, Seiz'd by Charles Coombs, Apprais'd at £14. 14. 0 in the Exchequer last Term, We direct you to Report to us the Burthen, Age & Condition of the said Sloop & if fit for the Service

And you are to remit the Sum of £1. 6. 8 to our Sollicitor, being the Charges of Condemning y[e] Sloop with her Tackle, *Apparrel & Furniture *valediction 1*
In margin: £14. 14. 0[78]

---

[77] MS. 'Solictor'.
[78] Underlined.

537
9 January
1749/50

CUST 58/149, p. 227

From G. Vaughan, Beaumont Hotham, W. Westby and Sam. Mead (Custom House, London). Hand iii.

Mr Jno Mc Cloud for whom we sent you our Commission the 22d Ultimo to be an Extra Tidesman & Boatman at your Port, being recommended to us as a fit Person to succeed Richard Corker late a Tidesman & Boatman at your Port, with the Allowance of Thirty Pounds Per Annum by Incidents We have agreed thereto, & the Collector may pay the said Mc Cloud the above Allowance from the Date hereof, & take Credit for the same from time to time, in his Account of Incidents, annexing this Letter with a proper Receipt thereto as Vouchers *valediction 1*

PS We have this day Received a Letter from the Collector & Comptroller of Bristol signifying that their is no manner of foundation for the Report lately spread abroad of a Ship arriv'd there with the Infection on Board –

538
17 January
1749/50

CUST 58/149, p. 227

From W. Wood (Custom House, London). Hand iii.

The Commissioners direct you without loss of time to Report to them, what Services have been perform'd by the Boatmen at Langstone Harbour, & the Charge of the Boat for three Years Past *valediction 2*

539
17 January
1749/50

CUST 58/149, p. 228

From W. Wood (Custom House, London). Hand iii.

The Commissioners having received a Letter from Captain Montagu of the 15th Instant desiring that his Stores may be removed from the Mermaid to the Kent, which he is appointed to Command, You are by the return of the Post, to acquaint the Board, whether the Mermaid & Kent are both at Portsmouth, & whether the latter is going on a foreign Voyage, or is to lye as a Guardship, *valediction 2*

540
17 January
1749/50

CUST 58/149, p. 228

From [W.] Wood (Custom House, London). Hand iii.

Application having been made to the Commissioners in relation to a Box on board the Hornett Sloop, Capt Hollwell directed for Lady Bolingbroke, You are on Receipt hereof immediately to send it up to the WareHouse in this Port, under the Seals of Office, giving the Board notice when & by what Conveyance it is sent & what agreement is made for Carriage, *valediction 2*

541
18 January
1749/50

CUST 58/149, p. 232

From W. Wood (Custom House, London). Hand iii.

The Commissioners direct you to transmit to Mr Simon the Solicitor within a Week after the Receipt of this Letter, all the Bonds taken for the Dutys on Tobacco, on which the 18 Months are Expired & not discharged in order to their being put into Process, & you are to observe it as a Rule for the future in sending up from time to time all Tobacco Bonds to the Sollicitor, which remain unpaid at the Expiration of 18 Months, *valediction 2*

542
22 January
1749/50

CUST 58/149, p. 229

From W. Wood (Custom House, London) to [W. Cooley]. Hand iii.

Sir

I have your Letter of the 19th Instant & Inclos'd I send you the Commission for Capt Wyatt of his Majestys Sloop Fly, with a set of Instructions & the Commissioners Letter to you on the Occasion, I am

Sir Your most humble Servant

W Wood

543
22 January
1749/50

CUST 58/149, pp. 229–30

From W. Wood (Custom House, London). Hand iii.

We have received your Letter of the 19th Ins*tant* in return to the Application of Capt Montagu desiring his Stores may be removed from his Majestys Ship Mermaid, to the Kent, & it appearing by your Letter that the Mermaid & Kent are both at your Port, & that the latter is to lye as a Guardship, & the Mermaid to Sail with the first fair Wind You may permit the Stores to be removed as desired under the care of the proper Officers, We are

Your Loving Friends

This Letter was prepared for the Commissioners Signing, but the Board ⌜being⌝[79] risen before it was finished their Commands are signifyd to you by

Gentlemen Your most humble Servant

W Wood

544
24 January
1749/50

CUST 58/149, p. 230

From Edw. Hooper, Sam. Mead, Beaumont Hotham and G. Vaughan (Custom House, London). Hand iii.

We received your Letters of the 20th & 22d Instant, acquainting us that Clatw. Thackstone Master of the Molly from OPorto & Vigo, Reported with Wine &cetera for your Port, & Chichester, & as he intends to proceed with his Cargoe to Guernsey notwithstanding he has Reported part for your Port. You desire to know whether you are to insist on the Dutys being paid for the Wine. We direct you to take care that the Dutys be paid for all the Goods reported to be delivered at your Port, & that the Tidesmen remain on Board the said Ship, untill the Wines Reported for Chichester shall be Landed there, *valediction 1*

545
24 January
1749/50

CUST 58/149, p. 231

From Edw. Hooper, Beaumont Hotham, Sam. Mead and G. Vaughan (Custom House, London). Hand iii.

We received your Letter of the 13th Instant acquainting us that you have used your utmost Endeavours to procure a further Evidence in relation to the Murder of Wm May late Tidesman at Your Port, but without Success: And it appearing by your Letter of the 21st Ultimo that Jno Forrest the other Tidesman who was on board the Peggy when May was Murder'd and at that time in Liquor, was not possitive, on a Rexamination, when perfectly Sober, in regard to several things which he before related. And as this is an affair of great Consequence, we direct you to call all the Parties before you again, and interrogate in a very particular manner, as to what they know of the Murder of May, and transmit Affidavits thereof, which must be very full in all the Circumstances, and then we shall be able to judge when we see the Evidence, in what manner it will be proper to proceed, in order to bring Kemp to Justice. *Valediction 1*

546
24 January
1749/50

CUST 58/149, p. 232

From Edw. Hooper, Beaumont Hotham, Sam. Mead and G. Vaughan (Custom House, London). Hand iii.

We received your Letter of the 12th Instant, in relation to the Sloop thereinmentioned which has been Condemn'd for Importing Brandy, & direct you to burn the Hull thereof, sell the Iron & Materials Publickly to the highest bidder, remitting the Kings part to Mr Simon, giving advice thereof to the Accomptant of Petty Receipts & Mr Simons Comptroller. *Valediction 1*

See no. 316 (letter from the Customs Board, 18 Apr. 1749, received 24 Jan. 1749/50).

---

79 MS. 'be'.

547
24 January
1749/50

CUST 58/1

From W. C[ooley] and R. T[urvin] (Custom House, Portsmouth). Hand iii.

[. . .][80] joint Letter bearing date the 13th November 1743 Vizt for the quarter ended Christmas last, And therefore we pray your Honours Order for paying the said Capt Coombs the Sum of Eleven Pounds twelve Shillings & six pence being after the Rate of Thirty Shillings Per Ton Per Annum for Thirty one Tons Burthen *valediction 3*

Port of Portsmo

These are to Certify that upon a carefull Survey made for the Quarter ended Christmas last it appeared to us that the Greenhill Yatch & Boats belonging to her Employed in the Service of his Majestys Customs at this Port, together with all the Materials have been duely kept, & are in good & Sufficient repair; And that Capt Coombs Commander thereof hath well & duely perform'd his Contract, and is thereby entituled to a Quarter of a Years Allowance, amounting to Eleven Pounds twelve Shillings & six pence. Witness our hands at the Custom House this 24th January 1749

W Cooley Collector — Wm Baskerville Tidesurv*eyo*r
R Turvin D*eputy* Comptroller — Wm Read Shipw*right*.

In margin: £11. 12. 6[81]

548
24 January
1749/50

CUST 58/1

From W. C[ooley] and R. T[urvin] (Custom House, Portsmouth). Hand iii.

We are to acquaint your Honours Yesterday died James Mason who Executed his Employment as a Tidesman at Langston within the Limits of this Port, but was paid his Salary at the Port of Chichester. *Valediction 3*

549
25 January
1749/50

CUST 58/1

From W. C[ooley] and R. T[urvin] (Custom House, Portsmouth). Hand iii.

By your Honours Order of the 7th Instant we were directed to Report whether Mr Baskerville had any objection to Compounding with Joseph Gilbert who was then under Prosecution for Treble the Value of Ninety five Gallons of Brandy, said Gilbert praying that the Sum of Twenty two Pounds Sixteen Shillings & the Charges of Prosecution may be accepted as a Composition for the said Offence, to which Mr Baskerville agreed; as therefore your Honours have been since pleased to accept of said Gilberts Composition, Mr Baskerville hopes your Honours will order us to pay him One Third part of the Composition, agreeable to the Rules of the Treasury, as signify'd by the Secretarys Letter bearing date the 1st Sept*ember* 1736. *Valediction 5*
In margin: £22. 16. 0[82]

550
29 January
1749/50

CUST 58/149, p. 233

From W. Wood (Custom House, London). Hand iii.

By my Letter of the 30th September last, you were directed to transmit to the Board within six days after Christmas last, an Account of the Money paid for the Bountys on British & Irish Coarse Linnens, exported from your Port, from Christmas 1748 to Christmas 1749 according to the form sent in my said Letter in order to be laid before the Parliament, which Account not being yet received; the Commissioners are greatly surpriz'd thereat, & direct me to acquaint you that unless you send the same by return of the Post, they will take other measures for the Service, and incase you have already sent the same you are to transmit a Duplicate thereof, *valediction 2*

551
29 January
1749/50

CUST 58/149, p. 233

From Edw. Hooper, W. Westby and G. Vaughan (Custom House, London). Hand iii.

In answer to the Account of Seizures transmitted in your Letter of the 20th Instant, We direct you to prosecute the Rum thereinmentioned to Condemnation, in the Exchequer at the Kings Charge Corresponding with our Sollicitor & the Register of Seizures *valediction 1*

Noted the 1st Feb*ruary* 1749

---

80 The beginning of this letter was on a page lost from the MS. (see above, p. xxxv).
81 Underlined.
82 Underlined.

552
29 January
1749/50

CUST 58/1

From W. C[ooley] and R. T[urvin] (Custom House, Portsmouth). Hand iii.

In obedience to your Honours Commands of the 24th Instant We have called the Parties before us and Interrogated them in a very particular manner, as to what they know of the Murder of May, having so done in Pursuance of your said Order, Inclosed we transmit your Honours the Affidavit of Jno Forrest, the Tidesman who was boarded on the Peggy when May was Murder'd, in which he has now ⌜related ⌝[83] with Certainty all the Circumstances he know of the Affair, to which we beg to Refer your Honours, We have likewise further Examined Alexander Aiken & Frederick Bailey who cannot depose any thing more relating to the Murder than what they have already done, which was transmitted your Honours in our joint Letter of the 21st Ultimo *valediction 5*

Borough of Portsmouth

Jno Forrest an Officer of his Majestys Customs in the Port of Portsmouth, Maketh Oath that on the 21st day of December last, being St Thomas's day, about 6'oClock in the Evening he this Deponent was carried in a Wherry by one Fred. Bailey on board a Sloop called the Charming Peggy, of which Wm Hunter was then Master, which lately came from France as this Deponent was informed, & was then Loaden with Brandy, & lying in Portsmouth Harbour, that he was boarded on the said Sloop as an Officer of the Customs, and when he came on board he found there also boarded on her Wm May another Brother Officer in the Same Service, That the said Wm May when this Deponent went on board was walking the Quarter Deck, and this Deponent took several turns with him there, for the space of six or seven Minutes, then went down below, where in about a quarter of an hour after, hearing a Noise or Scuffle on board, or alongside the said Sloop, he this Depon*ent* immediately went on Deck were he saw two Men in a Wherry alongside, one of which he afterwards found to be Wm Kemp, but who the other was this Deponent doth not know, however suspecting the said two Men were going to run Brandy, this Deponent then made an Effort to get into the said Wherry which the said Kemp observing asked this Deponent where he was coming, to whom this Deponent answered, on board the said Wherry, but the said Kemp Swore that he shoud not, and this Deponent insisted that he would, and while this Deponent was getting into the said Wherry, the said Kemp attacked this Deponent with a *Stretcher, or some other Wooden Weapon laying this Deponent on with it, with great Violence on his Shoulder, That this Deponent when he came on board the said Wherry, found in her two Vessels Vizt an *Anchor & an half *Anchor Containing as this Deponent believes Brandy; and notwithstanding the said Strokes given by the said Kemp this Deponent immediately took the half *Anchor out of the said Wherry, and return'd it back again into the said Sloop, & as this Deponent immediately afterwards was attempting to do the same by the *Anchor, the said Kemp attacked this Deponent again, with the said *Stretcher, or other Weapon, by the force of which he gave him a Violent blow on the head, knockd him down and then took hold of him by the Breeches, making an Attempt to Shove him into the Water, Head-foremast, whereupon this Dep*onen*t desired him not to drown him; And this Deponent further Saith that he the said Kemp prevented this Deponent from returning the said *Anchor into the said Sloop, but did not further assault him this Deponent; And this Deponent further Saith that on his being so ill treated as aforesaid by the said Kemp this Deponent being then within hearing of the Watchouse, cried out aloud for Assistance, but no Assistance came to him, that immediately after this Deponent return'd from the said Wherry, on board the said Sloop,[84] and the said Kemp together with the said two Wherry Men, Alexr Aiken & Frederick Bailey immediately afterwards went on Shore with the said *Anchor in her; And this Dep*onen*t further Saith that he never saw his Partner the said May after he left him walking on the said Deck as aforesaid, but hath heard and believes that he was basely Murdered & Drown'd by the said Kemp, while this Deponent Stayed in the said Vessel as aforesaid

The Mark of Jno X Forrest

Sworn at the said Borough the 27th Jan*uary* 1749 before me Sam Chandlor D*eputy* Mayor

---

83 Altered from 'lated'.
84 MS. has an opening or closing bracket in place of a comma.

553
31 January 1749/50

CUST 58/1

From W. C[ooley] and R. T[urvin] (Custom House, Portsmouth) to [W. Wood]. Hand iii.
Sir

Inclosed we transmit you, an Account of the Money paid for Bountys on British and Irish Course Linnens, Exported from this Port from Christmas 1748 to Christmas 1749 agreeable to the form sent us in your Letter of the 30th September last, but we beg to observe that this Account was before sent you in our joint Letter of the 6th Ultimo agreeable to the appointed time after Christmas *valediction 4*

554
31 January 1749/50

CUST 58/1

From W. C[ooley] and R. T[urvin] (Custom House, Portsmouth). Hand iii.

In our joint Letter of the 25th of November last we transmitted your Honours an Account of such Stationary Wares as were much wanted for the use of this Port; not having received the same We beg your Honours will be pleased to give Orders that we may be immediately supply'd therewith, otherwise ⌜we⌝[85] must be obliged (that the Service may not Suffer) to[86] supply our selves at this Port, with such Stationary Wares as is absolutely necessary *valediction 5*

555
2 February 1749/50

CUST 58/1

From W. C[ooley] and R. T[urvin] (Custom House, Portsmouth). Hand iii.

In answer to our joint Letters of the 20th & 22^{d} Ultimo acquainting you that Clat. Thackstone of the Molly from OPorto & Vigo had Reported with Wine &cetera for this Port, and Chichester, notwithstanding which he intended Proceeding to Guernsey; at the same time desiring to know whether we were to insist on the Dutys being paid for the same; Your Honours were pleased to direct us to take care that the Dutys be paid for all the Goods to be delivered at this Port, & that the Tidesmen shoud remain on board the Ship, untill the Wines Reported for Chichester were landed there; We are to acquaint your Honours the said Ship is still remaining in this Harbour, and as yet no Entry for the Wine have been made notwithstanding the twenty days from the time of the Masters Report is Expired, we have therefore in Obedience to your Honours Order signify'd by Mr Carkess' in his Letter of the 16th October 1731 Represented the same to your Honours for your further Directions, which when received will be duely observ'd *valediction 4*

556
6 February 1749/50

CUST 58/149, p. 234

From W. Westby, J. Evelyn, Wil. Levinz ('Levine') and Edw. Hooper (Custom House, London). Hand iii.

Application having been made to us desiring that Captain Thomas Hanbury of his Majestys Sloop Hazard now at your Port, may have a Commission Impowering him to Seize Prohibited and Uncustomed Goods, We have agreed thereto, and Inclosed you will receive our Commission accordingly, & when he has perfected the Inclosed Bond, with two Securitys, you may admit him to his Duty, taking care he qualifies himself as the Law directs, & when his Bond is Executed, you are to return it ⌜to⌝[87] us, *valediction 1*

557
6 February 1749/50

CUST 58/149, p. 234

From W. Westby, W. Levinz ('Levine'), J. Evelynn and Edw. Hooper (Custom House, London). Hand iii.

We received your Letter of the 29th Ultimo transmitting the Affidavit of Jno Forrest Tidesman at your Port, who was Boarded on the Peggy at the time that May was Murdered, and having referr'd the same to our Sollicitors, We direct you still to use your utmost endeavours to get further & more possitive proof against Kemp, as it doth not at present appear that May was knock'd overboard by the Blows which he received from the said Kemp. And you are to take care that Forrest, Bailey & Aiken & such other Persons as may be necessary to give Evidence against Kemp, are bound over to appear at the next Sizes to be held for the County of Hants, at the Trial of Kemp for the said Murder, *valediction 1*

---

[85] MS. 'be'.
[86] MS. omits 'to'.
[87] Inserted.

558
6 February
1749/50

CUST 58/1

From W. C[ooley] and R. T[urvin] (Custom House, Portsmouth). Hand iii.

Herewith we transmit your Honours the Abstract for the Month of January last, together with the undermentioned Accounts, to which we beg leave to refer, *valediction 3*

List of Bonds
Tea & other Goods Enumerated with Petty Receipts Endorsd
Absent Officers

PS/ From the Book kept in this Office it appears that the Weights and Scales Coal & Corn bushels at this Port, were tryed the 9th ⌜Ultimo⌝[88] by the Surveyor and Landwaiters, and that they found the same to be exact and true, and that the Stamps for marking Hides, Skins, Linnens, Seizd Goods, & Sail Cloth, are in good & Sufficient repair, and fit for the uses design'd.

WC RT

559
8 February
1749/50

CUST 58/150, p. 1

From W. Westby, W. Levinz ('Levine'), J. Evelynn and Edw. Hooper (Custom House, London). Hand iii.

Having considered your Preparatory Account of Incidents, for the quarter ended at Michaelmas last, amounting to Seventeen Pounds Eight Shillings and ten Pence; The Collector may pay the same with the Privity of the Comptroller, and take Credit for it, in his Account of Incidents, annexing this Letter with proper receipts thereto as Vouchers, *valediction 1*
In margin: £17. 8. 10[89]

560
10 February
1749/50

CUST 58/1

From W. C[ooley] and R. T[urvin] (Custom House, Portsmouth). Hand iii.

In Obedience to your Honours Orders of the 6th Instant, we have again called on Aiken, and again Examined him, with respect to the facts relating to Mays Murder, and have sent Inclosed another Affidavit of said Aiken, taken by Mr Chandlor wherein the Principal fact seems somewhat stronger Express'd, which is all we can possibly do, & are in hopes will be Satisfactory. We beg leave to assure your Honours that from first to last, no Care nor Diligence has been wanting on our part in procuring such Evidence as could possibly be procured on this occasion; at the first when the fact was committed, we examined with the utmost care, and exactness, every Person that was aboard the Vessel separately & apart, and by all other Accounts, we cou'd not find there was any Witness to any part or Circumstance of the Affair, except Aiken Bailey and Forrest whose Affidavit have been transmittd by our Honours and whom ⌜we⌝[90] and likewise Mr Chandlor have Examined & Rexamined with all the exactness Possible, so that unless some thing new and unexpected should ⌜offer⌝[91] to us, we see no possibility of adding any thing to the Evidence already procured, and if any thing should occur we shall take particular care to make the best use of it, and acquaint your Honours therewith

The Three Witness's abovementioned are all bound over to appear at the Sessions, *valediction 3*

Borough of Portsmouth

Alexander Aiken of Portsea within the Limits of the said Borough Waterman, Maketh Oath, that on the 21st day of December last, While Wm May deceased was standing on the Bow of this Deponents Boat, which then lay near a Sloop called the Charming Peggy, then in Portsmouth Harbour, this Deponent saw Wm Kemp give the said Wm May on his head, two or three hard Strokes with a large Stick, or Weapon, in his hand, by which Blows, or some or one of them (but this Deponent believes by the last) the said Wm Kemp knock'd the said Wm May overboard into the Sea, between the said Boat & Sloop, where the said May immediately Sank and was

---

88 Inserted.
89 With line above and below.
90 Inserted.
91 MS. 'ofter'.

Drown'd as this Deponent believeth his Body having never been Descovered since, though great care has been taken by Dragnets or Grapples & other means to fish it up or discover it if possible

Alexander Aken

Sworn 8th February 1749 before me Samuel Chandlor Deputy Mayor

561
12 February
1749/50

CUST 58/150, p. 1

From W. Wood (Custom House, London) to [W. Cooley]. Hand iii.

Sir

The Commissioners having received Information, that severall quantities of Tobacco, have been lately run on shore at your Port, ⌜particularly⌝[92] out of the Friendship, Anthony Marshall Master from Maryland, and that the same has been sent by Land Carriage to London; – You are to acquaint the Board by return of the Post, what ⌜Entrys⌝[93] have been made on the said Ship for Tobacco, in what Names, and the quantities, and also Endeavour to discover whether any part of the said Ships Cargoe has been run on shore, I am

Sir Your most humble Servant

W Wood

562
13 February
1749/50

CUST 58/150, p. 2

From W. Wood (Custom House, London). Hand iii.

The Commissioners direct you forthwith to prepare and transmit them, in order to be laid before the Parliament, an Account of the Bonds taken for *Cambricks Imported in order to be Exported, Pursuant to an Act of the 18th Geo 2d for Prohibiting the Wearing and Importation of *Cambrick & French *Lawns;[94] with an Account of such Bonds for which it appears to you the *Cambricks have been Exported respectively, distinguishing which of the said Bonds (if any) for which the *Cambricks have been Exported, have been demanded to be delivered up, and why the same have not been delivered up accordingly; And you are also to lay before the Board an Account of the Quantity of *Cambricks remaining not Exported after the Expiration of three Years from the date of the Bonds, *valediction 2*

⌜The above Account transmitted the 15th February 1749 to Mr Wood.⌝[95]

563
14 February
1749/50

CUST 58/1

From W. C[ooley] and R. T[urvin] (Custom House, Portsmouth). Hand iii.

On the 6th Instant, arrived here the Bolton Richard Hunter Master Laden with Nine hundred Quarters Wheat, taken in at London & bound for Marseilles, the occasion of coming in here was on Account of some Damage the Cargoe had received by bad Weather at Sea; and as the Master hath made Affidavit to the said Damage alledging ⌜a ⌝[96] necessity for taking out such part of the Corn as hath received Wet, in order for its Preservation we have granted him a Sufferance, that it may be[97] done accordingly, under the Inspection of the proper Officers; he proposes puting such Bags as are found to be Wet into a Vessel alongside, and incase they are not very much Damaged to put them back into the Vessel again but if they shoud be so bad as to be unfit to be replaced amongst the sound Wheat, he begs leave to Land the same and Ship as much sound Wheat in room of it; to all which we have no objection if your Honours approve of it, & beg to receive your Directions concerning the same which shall be duely observ'd *valediction 4*

---

92 MS. 'particulary'.
93 MS. 'Entys'.
94 Statute 18 Geo. II, c.36.
95 Added.
96 Inserted.
97 MS. omits 'be'.

564
14 February
1749/50

CUST 58/1

From W. C[ooley] (Custom House, Portsmouth). Hand iii.

By Mr Woods Letter of the 12th Instant, am inform'd, your Honours have received Information that several Quantities of Tobacco have been lately run on shore at this Port, particularly out of the Friendship Anthony Marshall from Maryland, & that the same has been sent by Land Carriage to London, I am therefore directed to acquaint your Honours what Entries have been made on the said Ship for Tobacco, in what Names & the Quantities; In obedience to your said Order I do humbly report that three Entrys was made on the said Ship, by Mr Peter Fearon for Two hundred & three hogsheads agreeable to the Masters Report, quantity One hundred & Seventy four Thousand, six hundred & sixty Pounds, all which has been ⌜regularly⌝[98] Enter'd & Landed, and taken Account of by the Landwaiters as appears by their Books, & I am to acquaint your Honours since which Mr Fearon has pass'd an Entry Outwards on the said Ship Friendship, which is Sailed for Holland for One hundred & Eighty nine Hogsheads, quantity One hundred & Seventy one Thousand, two hundred & Ninety seven Pounds, the quantity thereof unexported being three Thousand, three hundred ⌜&⌝[99] Sixty three Pounds of Tobacco, I am to acquaint your Honours was sent to London the 10th Instant by Land Carriage, On the whole, I must beg leave to acquaint your Honours, its my humble opinion there was not any Tobacco Run on shore, having Examined every Officer who had any concern with the said Ship, therefore whosoever gave your Honours such an Information must have done it without any foundation With great regard, I am

Your Honours &cetera

W C

565
15 February
1749/50

CUST 58/150, p. 3

From R. Chandlor, Sam. Mead, Beaumont Hotham and G. Vaughan (Custom House, London). Hand iii.

We received your Letter of the 24th Ultimo transmitting a Certificate, whereby it appears that the Greenhill Yatch, in the Service at your Port, under the Command of Capt Coombs, is in good and Sufficient repair, You may pay him the Sum of Eleven Pounds twelve Shillings & six Pence, for keeping the said Yatch in Wear and Tear, for the quarter ended at Christmas last, and take Credit for the same in your Account of Incidents, annexing this Letter with proper receipts thereto as Vouchers, *valediction 1*

In margin: £11. 12. 6[1]

566
15 February
1749/50

CUST 58/150, pp. 3–4

From R. Chandlor, Sam. Mead, Beaumont Hotham and G. Vaughan (Custom House, London). Hand iii.

We received your Letter of the 10th Instant transmitting the Affidavit of Alexander Aken with respect to the facts relating to Wm May late Tidesman who was Murdered in the Execution of his Duty by Wm Kemp, and it appearing that his Evidence is very sufficient to charge the said Kemp with the Murder; We have ordered our Sollicitor to Prosecute him at the next Winton Assizes accordingly, and you are to persue such directions as you shall from time to time receive from him in the said Prosecution *valediction 1*

---

98 MS. 'regulary'.
99 MS. '& &'.
1 With line above and below.

567
15 February
1749/50

CUST 58/150, pp. 4–5

From W. Wood (Custom House, London). Hand iii.

His Grace the Duke of New Castle his Majestys Principal Secretary of State having by his Letter of this date inform'd the Commissioners that three Smuglers Eaton Forrest, Thos Kingsford and Richard Parsons Committed to Newgate on Actions for Debt, have last night broke Goal, and signifying his Majestys Pleasure that the Commissioners should send immediate Orders to the Custom House Officers, in the several Ports, for preventing the said Persons, or any of them from going out of the Kingdom, and give Directions to the said Officers to use their utmost Endeavours to discover and apprehend the said Persons, a Description whereof you will receive Inclosed; The Commissioners direct you to take care that his Majestys Commands be duely and strictly comply'd with, for which Purpose you are to give immediate directions to the Commander of the Sloop, and all the Officers at your Port, diligently to look out for the said Persons, and incase they meet with them to keep them in safe Custody till you have acquainted the Commissioners therewith, and received his Majestys Pleasure concerning them, *valediction 2*

568
17 February
1749/50

CUST 58/150, pp. 5–6

From R. Chandlor, W. Levinz ('Levine'), J. Evelynn and Edw. Hooper (Custom House, London). Hand iii.

It appearing by your last Months Abstract that there is remaining in the Collectors hands, the Sum of One hundred & Twenty one Pounds, five Shillings & a farthing of the Kings Money, We direct you forthwith to Remit the same, together with what you have since received to the Receiver General, pursuant to the Condition of the Collectors Bond.

Mr Walter Plunkett having apply'd to us relating to a Box containing two Quilted Petticoats stopt out of the Deptford Storeship from Portmahone, and Secured in the WareHouse at your Port, We direct you to deliver them to the Proprietor, if he can make proof of their being condemn'd as Prize. *Valediction 1*

In margin: £121. 5. 0¼[2]

569
17 February
1749/50

CUST 58/150, pp. 6–7

From R. Chandlor, Beaumont Hotham, W. Westby and Sam. Mead (Custom House, London). Hand iii.

In pursuance of a Warrant from the Treasury, we have Issued our Deputation to Thomas Garrett, to be a Tidesman at your Port, in the room of Wm May deceased, and when he has perfected the Inclosed Bond, with two Securities, ⌜whose⌝[3] Sufficiency you are to Certify to Mr Mc Swiney Examiner of Officers Securities, you may admit him to the said Employ, giving him all due Encouragement for his Majestys Service, letting him know he must qualify himself as the Law directs, reporting to us the day he is admitted; And you are to call in Mays Deputation and cancel it, and transmit it to us with the next Accounts by the Carrier, *valediction 1*

570
17 February
1749/50

CUST 58/150, pp. 7–8

From R. Chandlor, Beaumont Hotham, W. Westby and Sam. Mead (Custom House, London). Hand iii.

We received your Letter of the 2^{d} instant acquainting us that notwithstanding our Order of the 24th Ultimo directing you to take care that the Duties were paid for all the Goods on board the Molly, Clatworthy Thackstone Master from OPorto, and Vigo, which were to be delivered at your Port, and that the Tidesmen should remain on board the Ship untill the Wines reported for Chichester were landed there, the said Ship still remains in your Harbour and no Entrys made for the Wine, though the Twenty days from the time of the Masters Report are expired, and having referrd the same to our Sollicitor, Inclosed we send you Copy of his Report, and unless the Goods are forthwith Entered, and the Duties paid, you are to take care they are brought to the Kings Warehouse, and proper notice given that they are taken ashore for the Security of the Duties, and not for Forfeiture reporting to us your Proceedings *valediction 1*

---

[2] Underlined.
[3] MS. 'who'.

Your Honours may if you please, Order these Goods to the Kings Warehouse, as they have been in Port Twenty days, but as the quantity is very large, you may file Informations for the Duties, if you think it more adviseable; if the Goods are brought to the Ware House care must be taken, that proper Notice be given that they are taken ashore for securing the Dutys, and not for forfeiture, and that is I think the safest way

G. Medcalfe

571
17 February
1749/50

CUST 58/150, pp. 8–9

From R. Chandlor, W. Levinz ('Levine'), J. Evelynn and Edw. Hooper (Custom House, London). Hand iii.

In pursuance of a Warrant of the Treasury, We have issued our Deputation to Jn° Mears to be Waiter and Searcher at your Port, in the room of Thomas Trahearne deceas'd, and when he has perfected the Inclosed Bond with two Securities, whose sufficiency you are to Certify to Mr Mc Swiney Examiner of Officers Securities, you may admit him to the said Employ, giving him all due Encouragement for his Majestys Service, letting him know he must apply to the Surveyor General, for Instructions, and Qualify himself as the Law directs, reporting to us the day he is Admitted, And you are to call in Trahearne's Deputation and Cancel it, and transmit it to us with your next Accounts by the Carrier; And we have agreed to appoint the said Mears to Act as Tidesurveyor in the same manner his Predecessor did, with the like Allowance of five Pounds Per Annum by Incidents, till further Order to make up his Salary fifty Pounds Per Annum, and the Collector may pay the same from time to time, and take Credit for it in his Account of Incidents referring therein to the date hereof *valediction 1*

572
20 February
1749/50

CUST 58/150, p. 10

From Beaumont Hotham, Sam. Mead, W. Westby and G. Vaughan (Custom House, London). Hand iii.

We received your Letter of the 14th instant acquainting us that you have granted Richd Hunter Master of the Bolton, bound for Marseilles, a Sufferance to take out such part of the Wheat as hath received Damage, under the Inspection of the proper Officers, We approve thereof, and you are to take particular care to admeasure the Corn relanded, and reshipt, reporting to us the exact Quantity of Bags, and Quarters, having in the mean time ordered the Debenture, to be stopt *valediction 1*

573
22 February
1749/50

CUST 58/150, pp. 10–11

From W. Wood (Custom House, London). Hand iii.

John Cole who is under Prosecution for being concern'd in unshipping Brandy & Rum, for which Offence he was lately taken up having by his Memorial of the 3^d^ instant apply'd to the Commissioners praying to be releas'd out of Goal, They direct you to enquire into his Charactor and Circumstances and Report the same to the Board for their further Consideration, *valediction 2*

574
24 February
1749/50

CUST 58/1

From W. C[ooley] and R. T[urvin] (Custom House, Portsmouth). Hand iii.

In Obedience to your Honours Orders of the 17th Instant, we are to acquaint you Mr Mears for whom we received a Deputation to act as Tidesurveyor, was admitted to his said Employ the 21st Instant, as was this day Thos Garrett as Tidesman & Boatman, in the room of Wm May deceas'd. We are to acquaint your Honours since the Receipt of your Letter of the 17th Instant, directing us forthwith to cause the Wine on board the Molly, Clatw^y^ Thackstone from OPorto & Vigo, to be taken ashore into the Kings Warehouse for Security of the Duties, the owners thereof have thought proper to enter & pay the Dutys for the same, *valediction 3*

575
24 February
1749/50

CUST 58/1

From W. C[ooley] and R. T[urvin] (Custom House, Portsmouth). Hand iii.

We received your Honours Letter of the 20th Instant, by which it appears you approve of the Steps taken by us, in permitting the Damaged Corn on board the Bolton, Richard Hunter for Marseilles, to be taken out; In obedience to your Honours Order, Inclosed we now transmit you a Certificate from the proper Officers, of the exact quantity of Bags, and quarters of Wheat, relanded & reshipt, on board the said Ship, to which we beg leave to refer, *valediction 3*

Portsmouth

These are to Certify that in pursuance of a Special Sufferance unto us directed, bearing date the 13th Instant, We have permitted to be unship'd out of the Bolton of London, Richd Hunter Master for Marseilles, and put into the Ruby in this Harbour Vizt Five hundred & Ninety eight Bags Containing Two hundred & ninety nine quarters winton measure of Damaged Wheat, and that in lieu thereof, we have seen and attended the Shipping of the like quantity, Vizt Five hundred & Ninety eight Bags Containing Two hundred & Ninety nine Quarters winton measure of good Sound & Merchantable Wheat, on board the said Ship Bolton, of London, Richard Hunter Master for Marseilles, as Witness our hands at the Custom House the 24th February 1749

Chas Markland Land Surv*eyo*r
Robt Alexander Deputy Sea*rche*r
Thomas Merritt Landwaiter

576
27 February
1749/50

CUST 58/150, p. 11

From Sam. Mead, G. Vaughan, W. Whestby and Edw. Hooper (Custom House, London). Hand iii.

The Collector & Comptroller of the Customs at Exeter, having in their Letter of the 24thInstant, acquainted us that the Goodintent Richard Field Master, laden with Wheat from your Port, has received Damage, and put in there, in order to land part of the Cargoe till she is repaired; We direct you to ⌜stop⌝[4] the Debenture till you receive our further Orders, *valediction 1*

577
1 March
1749/50

CUST 58/1

From W. C[ooley] and R. T[urvin] (Custom House, Portsmouth). Hand iii.

In Obedience to your Honours Commands signify'd to us by Mr Wood in his Letter of the 22d Ultimo We have enquired into the Character & Circumstances of Jno Cole, who is under Prosecution for being concernd in unshipping Brandy, and Rum, and find that said Coles Circumstances are but indifferent, having a large family to support, as to his Charactor we hear from his Neighbours that he has always supported a good one, & that they believe he never was before concernd in Smugling, *valediction 5*

578
2 March
1749/50

CUST 58/150, pp. 11–12

From Sam. Mead, W. Levinz ('Levine'), W. Westby and Edw. Hooper (Custom House, London). Hand iii.

Mr Simon the Sollicitor having acquainted us that the Assizes at Winton' open on Wednesday next, you are to take care that the Witnesses for the Crown, against Kemp for the Murder of May, do attend at Winchester by that time in order to give Evidence against the said Kemp. *Valediction 1*

579
2 March
1749/50

CUST 58/150, p. 12

From Sam. Mead, W. Westby and Edw. Hooper (Custom House, London). Hand iii.

Mr Woodroff Drinkwater having by his Memorial of the 2d Instant apply'd to us desiring that One hundred & fifty quarters Wheat Shipt at NewHaven, on board the Race Horse, Edward Fogden Master, now at your Port, may be relanded, We agree thereto, under the care of the proper Officers, taking care that the Crown be at no Charge for WareHouse room, Officers attendance, or otherwise, having ordered the Debenture to be Cancelled, *valediction 1*

4 MS. 'stopt'.

580
3 March
1749/50

CUST 58/150, pp. 12–13

From Sam. Mead, R. Chandlor, W. Westby and W. Levinz ('Levine') (Custom House, London). Hand iii.

We received your Letter of the 25th of January last, acquainting us that Mr Baskerville Tidesurveyor at your Port, has no objection to the Composition offer'd by Joseph Gilbert, who was prosecuted for the Treble Value of Ninety five Gallons of Brandy, amounting to Twenty two Pounds, Sixteen Shillings, And the said Sum having been paid into the hands of our Sollicitor, The Collector may draw on him for the Officers share, being one third part thereof who has our Orders to pay the same, *valediction 1*

581
5 March
1749/50

CUST 58/1

From W. C[ooley] and R. T[urvin] (Custom House, Portsmouth). Hand iii.

Inclosed we transmit your Honours an Account of Goods Enumerated, lately Seiz'd by Captain Barker, of his Majestys Sloop the Wasp together with[5] Copy of a Letter which the Collector received from him, to which we beg leave to refer, *valediction 3*

Wasp at Spithead the 2^d March 1749

Sir

The 24th Past, being off Dungeness, I saw a Cutter standing in for the Shore, I chased and took her, and found on board her forty four half* Anchors of Brandy, and Eight Bags of Tea, about eight Pounds in each Bag; The Master & People Confess'd they were bound to Selsea, from Dunkirk where they had been with a Cargoe of Oysters, and bought the Brandy with them, he own'd that six of the Bags of Tea belong'd to a Smugler now in Prison at Dunkirk, for Smugling Prohibited Goods there, & that he was to have run them for him, & therefore I made a Seizure of her Cargoe, which I send to you, & I have sufficient Proof to Condemn it, I am

Sir Your most humble Servant

Jno Barker

To The Collector

582
6 March
1749/50

CUST 58/150, p. 13

From W. Wood (Custom House, London). Hand iii.

The Debentures mentioned on the back hereof, having been presented to the Commissioners for their Order for Payment, but you omitting to send Duplicates thereof the same are stopt, You are immediately on receipt hereof to transmit the said Duplicates to the Board, which I am directed to signify to you, *valediction 2*

1749

26 Jan*uary* $Wood^{ff}$ Drinkwater, Genoa Galley Thos Ellis Marseilles 1200 Whe*at*

9th Feb*ruary* R^d Briant, Three Brothers Jno Turner Bourdeaux 484 quarters Wheat

583
6 March
1749/50

CUST 58/150, p. 14

From W. Wood (Custom House, London). Hand iii.

The Account of Enumerated Goods for Christmas quarter last being wanted from your Port, I desire the same may be forthwith transmitted to the Board in order that the Ballance if there is any due thereon may be paid into the Exchequer before Ladyday next, *valediction 2*

---

5 'a' struck out.

584
6 March
1749/50

CUST 58/150, pp. 14–15

From G. Vaughan, Beaumont Hotham, W. Westby and Sam. Mead (Custom House, London). Hand iii.

Having taken into consideration your Letter of the 10th January last, transmitting an Account of the Annual Allowances made to the Officers at your Port, by Incidents, We agree to your paying the said Officers their respective Allowances to Christmas last, and to their Continuance from that time, to Midsum*m*er next, for which the Collector may take Credit in his Account of Incidents, referring therein to the date hereof; And at the expiration of that time, you are to report to us, the Services performd by the said Officers, with your Opinion whether it will be for the Interest of the Revenue to continue the said Allowances, and incase the Collector pays any of the said Allowances without our previous Order for that purpose, he will not have Credit for the same, *valediction 1*

585
7 March
1749/50

CUST 58/1

From W. C[ooley] and R. T[urvin] (Custom House, Portsmouth). Hand iii.

Herewith we transmit your Honours the Abstract for the Month of February last, together with the undermentioned Accounts, to which we beg leave to refer, *valediction 4*

List of Bonds
Tea & other Goods Enumerated with Petty receipts Endors'd
Absent Officers

PS From the Book kept in this Office it appears that the Weights and Scales, Coal and Corn Bushels at this Port, were tried[6] the 3d Ultimo by the Surveyor and Landwaiters, and that they found the same to be exact and true, and that the stamps for marking Hides, Skins, Linnens, Seiz'd Goods and Sail Cloth are in good and Sufficient repair and fit for the uses design'd

W C R T

586
8 March
1749/50

CUST 58/150, p. 15

From W. Wood (Custom House, London). Hand iii.

Mr James Worsley having by his Memorial of the 3d Instant, apply'd to the Commissioners relating to the Carteen Jn° Dore Master, under Seizure at your Port, for Importing Rum & Brandy, and as you have not sent for a Writt of Appraisement for the said Ship, They direct you without loss of time, to report to them what has been done with regard to the Ship, *valediction 2*

587
10 March
1749/50

CUST 58/150, pp. 15–16

From G. Vaughan, R. Chandlor, W. Whestby and Sam. Mead (Custom House, London). Hand iii.

Inclosed you will receive Writts of Delivery for the Enumerated Goods return'd in two Indentures of Appraisement from your Port, & Proclaim'd in the Exchequer the last Term which have been Condemn'd, The Total Amount of which is on the back hereof; We direct you to sell the said Goods Publickly to the highest bidder putting them up at such Prizes as the Goodness of the Commodities deserves *valediction 1*

Writt Dated	27th Feb*ruary* 1749 –	78. 2. 0
D° –	27th D° –	71. 3. 6
		£149. 5. 6[7]

---

[6] MS. omits 'tried'.
[7] See App. I, nos 22, 23.

588
12 March
1749/50

CUST 58/1

From W. C[ooley] and R. T[urvin] (Custom House, Portsmouth). Hand iii.

Mr Wood in his Letter of the 8th instant (by your Honours Order) having acquainted us that Mr James Worsley has apply'd to your Honours Relating to the Carteen Sloop, John Dore Master, under Seizure at this Port, for Importing Brandy, & we not having sent for a Writt of Appraisement for the Sloop, We are directed to report to your Honours what has been done with regard to the said Sloop; In Obedience to your Order we humbly beg leave to acquaint your Honours, the said Sloop is now in our Custody and by your Honours Order of the 5th of December last, to be Prosecuted to Condemnation in the Exchequer, at the Officers charge, for Importing seven small Casks of Brandy & Rum, but the quantity being so small, for which the Officers Seizd the Vessel, and they having no objection to the delivery of her, provided Jno Dore the Master thereof cou'd on his application to your Honours get her restored him, and in consideration likewise of his having made several Discoveries of Persons concern'd in Smugling, an Account of which was transmitted your Honours by the Collector in his Letter of the 1st December last; We did not send for a Writt of Appraisement for the said Vessel, in order to Condem her the last Term, not knowing whether your Honours wou'd not take Dore's Case into Consideration; We shall take care to send for a Writt of Appraisement for the Vessel (provided we do not receive Orders from your Honours to the Contrary) in order for her being Condemn'd the next Term *valediction 5*

589
13 March
1749/50

CUST 58/150, pp. 18–20

From W. Wood (Custom House, London). Hand iii.

The Commissioners having advised with Persons of Experience relating to the Admeasurement of Ships, intended for the Greenland Trade, and Whale Fishery, in order to entitle them to the Bounty; Who are of Opinion that the Rule or Method Practis'd in the River Thames, to ascertain the Tonnage of Ships, built either for the Service of the Crown, or Merchant, as well as all such as are hired by the Government shou'd likewise be observed in the admeasurement of Ships Employ'd in the Greenland Trade, and Whale Fishery; Vizt "The[8] Length to be taken on a strait Line at the uper edge of the Keel of the Ship from the back of the Main Stern Post, to a Perpendicu*la*r Line from the fore part of the Main Stem under the Bowspritt which is the extream Length, from which Substract 3/5 of the Breadth and the Remainder is esteem'd the just Length of the Keel to find the Tonnage; The Breadth is to be taken from the Outside of the Outside Plank in the Broadest place of the Ship, be it either above or below the *Main Whales exc*lusive* of all manner of Doubling Planks that may be wrought upon the sides of the Ship; By this Breadth the Tonnage is cast by Multiplying the Length of the Keel by the Breadth & that Product by 1/2 the Breadth & then divide by 94 which gives the Tons & parts of a Ton required." The Commissioners direct you to give it in strict Charge to the proper Officers carefully to observe the said Rule, in Admeasuring Ships Employ'd in the Greenland Trade and Whale Fishery either Outward or Homeward bound, *valediction 2*

590
14 March
1749/50

CUST 58/1

From W. C[ooley] and R. T[urvin] (Custom House, Portsmouth). Hand iii.

Inclosed we transmit your Honours a Schedule of Accounts due from this Port for Christmas quarter last, the same being this day forwarded by the Waggon of Geo. Clarke which will be at the Whitehart in the Burrough of Southwark on Friday the 16th Instant, for the Carriage whereof we have agreed that two Shillings & six pence shall be paid, *valediction 5*

Portsmouth

A Schedule of Accounts due from this Port for Christmas quarter last, the same being sent by the Waggon of Geo. Clarke which will be at the Whitehart in the Burrough of Southwark on Friday the 16th March 1749

---

[8] Each line of this quotation is introduced by a double quotation mark.

	Coal Incidents
Collectors Quarter Book	Imports & Exports
Comptrollers D°	Wooll br*ough*t & Carried Coastwise –
General Incidents with the Establishment & two Original Orders –	Civil List receipt & Repayment
Debentures, Damages, *Over ⌜Entrys⌝[9] &cetera –	Preparatory Account of Incidents & Tradesmens' Bills

Personal Prosecutions
Enumerated Goods Per Act 12th Geo 1st [10]
Reports Inwards & Outwards
Journals of the Commander & mate of the Greenhill Y*a*tch
D° – of the Chief Boatman at Hayling
Ages and Capacitys of Officers
Securities of D° –
Duplicates of Certificates from Guernsey & Jersey
Naval Stores from ⌜Rushia⌝[11] & Levonia
Ships &cetera which Discharged in this Port from any of his Majestys Plantations in America
Bountys on Corn & other Grain
D° on British & Irish Coarse Linnens
} transmitted the Honourable Board the 15th Feb*ruar*y 1749

591
14 March
1749/50

CUST 58/1

From W. C[ooley] and R. T[urvin] (Custom House, Portsmouth). Hand iii.

The Stationary Wares of which the Inclosed is an Account was received at this Port the 1st Instant, and which shall be frugally managed, with the greatest Frugality *valediction 4*

Allow'd Portsmouth

3 Rheams fine *pott		1 Book 3 quire *Imperial ⌜*V*at* B*lued*⌝[12] unruld –
2 Quire *Imperial		2 Sloops Journal Books
1/2 Pound *Pounce		3 quire Reports Inwards
3 Bags of Sand		2 quire Coal Warrants
1000 Quills		2 quire Personal Prosecutions
1 Dozen files with Tags		4 Rheams 2d *Pott
2 Gallons Ink & *Rundlett		9 quire *Demy
4 *Pounce Boxes		3 Bodkins
3 Ivory Penknives		6 Books 1 quire *Demy each in marble
1 Dozen Pieces of Tape		
4 Round Ink stands		
80 Blue Book	4 Leaves	3000 Wafers & Box
40 –	8 D° –	1 Dozen *Demy Pocq*ue*t Books
20 –	14 D°.	
50 –	2 D°.	1 Q*ua*rt red Ink
60 –	6 D°.	1 Dozen Pencils
30 –	10, 12	2 Dozen Tags
12 –	16, 20, 24	1 lb' fine Wax
2 Letter Books 3 quire *Demy ⌜*V*at* B*lued*⌝[13] & Alpab*e*ts		A Remittance Book 3 quire *Imperial ⌜*V*at* B*lued*⌝[14] ruled
4 Quire *Imperial Ruled for q*uarter*ly paper Inwards		An Indenture Book 3 quire D° –

2 quire *Royal rul'd for Wooll brought & Carried Coastwise
3 quire *Boarding Bills
2 quire reports Outwards
1 report Book Inwards
1 Q*uarte*rly Book of Enumerated Goods

---

9 MS. 'Entys'.
10 Statute 12 Geo. I, c.28.
11 Altered from 'Rhushia'.
12 Or, possibly, 'V*ellum* B*ound*'.
13 Or, possibly, 'V*ellum* B*ound*'.
14 Or, possibly, 'V*ellum* B*ound*'.

592 CUST 58/150, pp. 16–17
15 March 1749/50
From W. Levinz ('Levine'), W. Westby, Beaumont Hotham and G. Vaughan (Custom House, London). Hand iii.

We received your Letter of the 5th instant transmitting an Account of Goods Seiz'd by Captain Barker, of his Majestys Sloop the Wasp, And having refer'd the same to our Sollicitor, he has Reported "that[15] on the Hovering Clause the Goods may be forfeited, altho' the Ship is not",[16] which we signify to you, but the Officer is at Liberty to Prosecute the Goods to Condemnation in the Exchequer, at his own risque & Charge, Coresponding with our Sollicitor and the Register of Seizures, *valediction 1*

Noted the 17th March 1749.

593 CUST 58/150, p. 17
15 March 1749/50
From W. Levinz ('Levine'), W. Westby, Beaumont Hotham and G. Vaughan (Custom House, London). Hand iii.

Having considered the Collectors Letter of the 14th Instant, desiring leave to be Absent from his Duty for fourteen days, to attend his private Affairs, We agree thereto, upon his appointing a proper Person, for whom he will be answerable to carry on the Collection during his absence, *valediction 1*

594 CUST 58/150, pp. 17–18
17 March 1749/50
From W. Levinz ('Levine'), Edw. Hooper, J. Evelynn and G. Vaughan (Custom House, London). Hand iii.

We received your Letter of the 24th Ultimo Inclosing a Certificate of the quantity of Wheat, relanded and reshipt on board the Bolton of London, Richard Hunter Master for Marseilles, whereby it appears that there was Two hundred ninety nine quarters of good sound & Merchantable Wheat reshipt on board the said Ship, at your Port, We direct you to pass an Entry for that Quantity, and make out a Debenture for the same having cancelled the first Debenture, and ordered another to be made out here for the remainder *valediction 1*

595 CUST 58/1
17 March 1749/50
From W. C[ooley] and R. T[urvin] (Custom House, Portsmouth). Hand iii.

Inclosed we transmit your Honours an Account of Goods Enumerated, and Goods not Enumerated, lately Seiz'd by the Officers in this Port, to which we beg leave to refer *valediction 4*

596 CUST 58/150, p. 20
21 March 1749/50
From Edw. Hooper, G. Vaughan, W. Levinz ('Levine') and Sam. Mead (Custom House, London). Hand iii.

Having granted our Deputation for James Terry Extra Tidesman at your Port to be a Coal Meter there, in the room of Richd Gambell Deceas'd, You are to take care he be under Oath and Security for the faithfull Discharge of the said Employ, and Qualifies himself as the Law directs. *Valediction 1*

597 CUST 58/1
22 March 1749/50
From W. C[ooley] and R. T[urvin] (Custom House, Portsmouth). Hand iii.

We are to acquaint your Honours that on Sunday the 18th Instant, died Jno Ring a Tidesman & Boatman at this Port, in whose room we humbly beg leave to recommend H^y Duncan the Sen*io*r Extraman on the £5 List, who is an Able hand understands the Management of a Boat, & is every way Qualify'd to succeed the said Ring in his Employment, *valediction 5*

---

[15] Each line of this quotation is introduced by a double quotation mark.

[16] Under Statute 5 Geo. I, c.11, sec.8, the master of any vessel under 50 tons burden 'laden with customable or prohibited Goods' that was 'found hovering on the Coasts of this Kingdom, within the Limits of any Port, and not proceeding on her Voyage, . . . Wind and Weather permitting' might be required to enter into a bond of three times the value of the goods, the condition being that he should continue the voyage as soon as possible and land the goods at a foreign port; failure to execute the bond or to meet its condition rendered the goods liable to forfeiture. Statute 6 Geo. I, c.21, sec.31, extended this to any such vessel containing brandy 'found at Anchor or hovering within Two Leagues from the Shore'. These provisions were continued by successive Acts, latterly (until 1 June 1754) by Statute 20 Geo. II, c.47.

598 CUST 58/150, pp. 20–1

24 March 1749/50 *From Edw. Hooper, W. Westby, W. Levinz ('Levine') and G. Vaughan (Custom House, London). Hand iii.*

We received your Letter of the 12th instant acquainting us that the Officers concern'd in the Seizure of the Carteen Sloop Jno Dore Master decline prosecuting the said Sloop at their own Charge, and that the said Dore is a poor man has a large family, and the Quantity of Brandy ⌜&⌝[17] Rum Seiz'd on board being so small, they have no Objection to the Delivery of the Vessell, and the Sollicitor to whom we referr'd the same having reported that there are some favourable Circumstances in the Case; We agree upon considering the whole to the Delivery of the Vessel for the present, upon the said Dores giving Security for the Value of the Boat, provided the Officer concern'd have no further Objection but you are to go on with the Prosecution of the Goods as was before directed, *valediction 1*

599 CUST 58/150, pp. 21–2

29 March 1750 *From J. Evelynn, W. Levinz ('Levine'), Sam. Mead and Edw. Hooper (Custom House, London). Hand iii.*

The Collector and Comptroller of the Customs at Exeter having in their Letter of the 17th Ultimo acquainted us that the Two hundred Baggs Containing One hundred Quarters Wheat Unshipt there into a Lighter out of the Goodintent Richd Field Master from your Port, are reship'd on board the said Ship, you are to take off the ⌜stop⌝[18] on the Debenture, if you have no further Objection.

In answer to the Account of Seizures transmitted in your Letter of the 17th Instant We direct you to Prosecute the Goods thereinmentioned to Condemnation before the Justices of the Peace, the Tea at the Kings Charge, & the Cotton at the Officers Charge, acquainting us when Condemn'd, *valediction 1*

600 CUST 58/1 [19]

30 March 1750 *From W. C[ooley] and R. T[urvin] (Custom House, Portsmouth). Hand iii.*

The Officers concern'd in the Seizure of the Carteen Sloop, Jno Dore Master having no objection thereto, We have Pursuant to your Honours Letter of the 24th Instant delivered her up to the said Dore, and taken his Security for her Value, *valediction 5*

601 CUST 58/1

31 March 1750 *From W. C[ooley] and R. T[urvin] (Custom House, Portsmouth). Hand iii.*

Herewith we transmit your Honours the Abstract for the Month of March last, together with the undermentioned Accounts to which we beg leave to refer *valediction 4*

Nil List of Bonds
Tea & other Goods Enumerated with Petty receipts Endors'd
Absent Officers
State of Bonds for Lady day Quarter 1750

PS/ From the Book kept in this Office it appears that the Weights and Scales Coal and Corn bushels at this Port were try'd the 16th Instant by the Surveyor & Landwaiters and that they found the same to be exact and true and that the stamps for marking Hides, Skins, Linnens, Seiz'd Goods & Sail Cloth are in good & Sufficient repair and fit for the uses design'd

602 CUST 58/1

3 April 1750 *From W. C[ooley] and R. T[urvin] (Custom House, Portsmouth). Hand iii.*

Herewith we transmit your Honours, the undermentioned Accounts, the same being due from this Port, for Lady, day Quarter 1750 to which we beg leave to refer, *valediction 3*

Ships &cetera which Discharged in this Port from the British Plantations,
Naval Stores
Corn Exported with the Amount of the Bounty due thereon

---

[17] Written only as catchword at foot of page.
[18] MS. 'stopt'.
[19] No. 601 precedes no. 600 in MS.

603
4 April
1750

CUST 58/150, pp. 22–3

From J. Fremantle (Custom House, London). Hand iii.

The Commissioners of the Sick and Hurt Office for Seamen, having by their Letter of the 2d Instant apply'd to this Board, desiring that four Cases of Elizir of Vitrol, brought to your Port in his Majestys Sloop the Tryal from Portmahone, may be deliver'd, I am directed to send you Copy of the said Letter & you are to examine into the Allegations therein Contain'd & report to the Board a State of the Case without loss of time. I am in the Absence of the Secretary

Gentlemen Your most humble Servant

J: Fremantle

Office for Sick & Hurt Seamen
2d April 1750

Gentlemen

His Majestys Sloop the Tryal, lately arrived at Portsmouth from Port Mahone, brought with her, four Cases of Elizir of Vitrol Remains of our Stores of that kind, sent from hence to Mahone, for the Service of his Majestys fleet in the Mediterranean, during the late War; This Elizir Mr Porter our Surgeon and Agent for Sick and Hurt Seamen at Gosport, had our Orders to receive from the said Sloop, but he having acquainted us that your Officers at Portsmouth had carried it to the Custom house at that place and refus'd to let him have it without Your Directions for so doing, we desire you will be pleas'd to give them Directions accordingly, & are

Gentlemen Your most humble Servants

W Bell Vale Hills

604
4 April
1750

CUST 58/1

From W. C[ooley] and R. T[urvin] (Custom House, Portsmouth). Hand iii.

Inclosed we transmit your Honours an Account of Goods Enumerated lately Seiz'd by an Officer in this Port, to which we beg leave to refer *valediction 3*

605
6 April
1750

CUST 58/1

From W. C[ooley] and R. T[urvin] (Custom House, Portsmouth). Hand iii.

The four Cases of Elixir of Vitrol belonging to the Commissioners of Sick and Wounded concerning which your Honours by your Secretarys Letter of the 4th instant require our Report, were brought to this Port by his Majestys Sloop the Tryal from Portmahone, & Conveyed to the Custom House for Security of the Duties; With regard to the Allegations of the said Commissioners that they are Stores formerly carried out of England, and now return'd, they may be very true for ought we know to the Contrary, & therefore taking Leave to refer them to your Honours. We humbly wait your Direction in this Affair *valediction 3*

606
7 April
1750

CUST 58/150, p. 24

From W. Westby, W. Levinz ('Levine') and J. Evelynn (Custom House, London). Hand iii.

In Answer to the Account of Seizures transmitted in your Letter of the 4th Instant We direct you to Prosecute the Brandy thereinmentioned to Condemnation in the Exchequer at the Kings Charge, Corresponding with our Sollicitor and the Register of Seizures *valediction 1*

Noted the 9th April 1750

607
10 April
1750

CUST 58/1

From W. C[ooley] and R. T[urvin] (Custom House, Portsmouth). Hand iii.

On the 5th Instant arrived here the Redbridge Sloop William Living Master Laden with Sundry Sorts of Goods on Debenture taken in at London & bound for Dublin, the occasion of his coming in here was on Account of his having Sprung a Leak at Sea whereby his Cargoe have received much Damage and as the Master hath made Affidavit to the said Damage alledging a necessity for taking out such part of his Cargoe as to enable him to repair his Damage, & putting it on board a Ship alongside, We Yesterday granted him a Sufferance, that it may be accordingly done under the Inspection of the proper Officers, the Crown to be at no expence for their attendance or otherwise, all which we hope will meet with your Honours Approbation, and beg to receive your Honours Directions concerning the same which shall be duely observ'd *valediction 4*

608 CUST 58/150, pp. 24–5

12 April 1750

From Beaumont Hotham, G. Vaughan, W. Westby and W. Levinz ('Levine') (Custom House, London). Hand iii.

We received your Letter of the 10th Instant acquainting us that you have granted a Sufferance for taking out such part of the Cargoe on board the Redbridge Sloop, William Lewing Master, which has received Damage, till the said Sloop is repaired, We approve thereof, but you are to take care there be no Embezlements, & that the Crown be at no Charge, for Officers attendance or otherwise, and that the Goods be reshipt on board the same Vessel when repaired, Reporting to us your Proceedings, *valediction 1*

609 CUST 58/150, pp. 25–7

12 April 1750

From Beaumont Hotham, G. Vaughan, W. Westby and W. Levinz ('Levine') (Custom House, London). Hand iii.

Mr George Huish having by his Memorial of the 21st January last, apply'd to us relating to the Whale Bone, Iron Locks Coffee Pott & Shoe makers thread under Seizure at your Port, Inclosed we send you Copy of his Memorial, and if you find the facts to be as therein represented, and none of the Goods are Prohibited, You may deliver them to the Proprietor on Payment of the Duty, & giving the Officers concern'd a moderate Satisfaction *valediction 1*

Sir

When the Overschie Dutch East India Ship lay stranded near this place in January 1748 some of her Crew stole £50 [20] of Whalebone, 21 Iron Locks, One Coffee Pott and 8 lb' Shoemakers Thread from the Cooper of the Ship, but being detected the Goods were Seiz'd and brought to the Custom House here, upon which the Owner Petitioned the Honourable Commissioners of his Majestys Customs for their being restored which was granted, but before the Order come he was Sailed in the Ship to the East Indies; since which I (as Agent to the Dutch East India Co at this Port) have apply'd to the Collector here that I might send these goods to the Companys proper Officer at Delft, in Holland, but am told such Liberty cannot be granted without a second Order from the Board, because the first extended no farther, ⌜than to ye⌝[21] Suffering these Goods to be Exported to the East Indies; now as I have the Opportunity of a Homeward bound Dutch East India Ship which lyes at Spithead, I beg the favour that you will please to mention this Affair to the Board & desire their Honours to give Directions to the proper Officers at this Port to suffer me to send these Goods back ⌜to⌝[22] Holland by this Conveyance which will greatly oblige me; I ask pardon for troubling you on ⌜so⌝[23] triffling an occasion, but hope you will be[24] good enough to excuse it, as I am told there is no other way to come at these goods, I am

Sir Your most Obedient humble Servant

Geo. Huish

Portsmouth

21st January 1749/50

610 CUST 58/150, p. 27

14 April 1750

From W. Wood (Custom House, London). Hand iii.

Captain Bonfoy of his Majestys Ship the Berwick having apply'd to the Board in relation to One Hamper of Clarrett, and One of Champaygne, under Seizure at your Port, And he having represented that it was only intended to be Consumed on board of his Ship and no part of it to be landed, You are to Report to the Board a State of the Case without loss of time for their Consideration & further Directions *valediction 2*

---

20 I.e. 50 lb. in weight (no. 325; App. I, no. 24).

21 Written over an illegible erasure.

22 Written only as catchword at foot of page.

23 Written over an illegible erasure.

24 'so' struck out.

611 16 April 1750

CUST 58/150, p. 28

From W. Wood (Custom House, London). Hand iii.

The Commissioners having received advice of the Arrival of Admiral Boscawen at Portsmouth, with some men of war from the East Indies, and that he left several other Men of War, and East India Ships in the *Chopps of the Channel; They direct you to excite the several Officers within the District of your Port, especially those on the Water Guard to be very carefull in looking out to prevent the running any Goods from those Ships as they pass the Coast reporting to the Board your Proceedings *valediction 2*

612 16 April 1750

CUST 58/1

From W. C[ooley] and R. T[urvin] (Custom House, Portsmouth). Hand iii.

Inclosed we transmit your Honours an Account of a Seizure made by Mr William Baskerville one of the Tidesurveyors at this Port, together with a Memorial which we this day received from him setting forth the Circumstances attending the said Seizure, and the Obstruction said Baskerville met with on board his Majestys Ship Prince Henry under the Command of Captain R^d Jasper, to which we beg leave to refer; As Captain Jasper is under Orders for Sailing, we shall be glad to receive your Honours immediate Directions thereon which will be duely observ'd *valediction 4*

Sirs

I beg leave to acquaint you that on the 12th Instant, I receiv'd an Intimation that the Berwick Boat, one of the Guard Ships in this Harbour, was sent out in order to bring in some Goods in a Clandestine manner upon which I kept a look out for her, and upon her Entering the Harbours Mouth, I mann'd a Boat & gave Chase to her, but was not able to come up with her before she got on board the Berwick, into which Ship she had put one Hamper and the other was on the Ladder in order to be Shipt; upon Examining the said Hampers I found they Contained French Wines, which I immediately Seiz'd & Securd in His Majestys WareHouse. As I was returning from the Berwick, I met with and Rummaged the Monarch's long Boat, wherein I found five Hampers of French Wine, which I Seiz'd & Secur'd in his Majestys WareHouse as abovementioned

The same Evening a hint was given to me that there were several Hampers put on board the Prince Henry Man of War at Spithead, in a Clandestine manner, upon which the next Morning I went on Board, made a Rummage & found Seven Hampers of the like sort as those that I had Seiz'd from the Berwick & Monarch's long boat, of which I Endeavour'd to make a Seizure, but therein was prevented by Captain Jasper, the Commander, the other Officers and Ships Company, who declared that If my self and the Tidesmen with me insisted upon taking the said Hampers of French Wine out of the Ship, they wou'd knock our Brains out and as this I conceive to be a very unjustifyable behaviour both in Captain Jasper and his Quarter Deck Officers, so I thought it my Duty to acquaint you therewith to the end that the Honourable Commissioners may have the Case properly laid before them, for if Officers of the Customs are to meet with such Treatment from the Gentlemen of the Navy, it will be out of their Power to do their Duty, or prevent Clandestine Practices on board his Majestys Ships of War, which is humbly submitted by

Sirs Your most Obedient Servant

Wm Baskerville

Watch House Portsm^o 16th April 1750

To The Collector & Comptroller

613 21 April 1750

CUST 58/150, pp. 28–9

From Sam. Mead, W. Levinz ('Levine'), W. Westby and G. Vaughan (Custom House, London). Hand iii.

Mr Frederick Bull having by his Memorial of the 18th Instant apply'd to us desiring that the Sagoe Salved out of the Redbridge Wm Living Master lately Sprung a Leak & put into your Port, may be Dry'd by a Malt Kiln or otherwise as shall be most proper, in order to it being reshipt, We agree thereto, under the care of the proper Officers, taking care to prevent Embezlements, & that the Crown be at no Charge for WareHouse room, Officers attendance, or otherwise. And you are to Weigh the Quantity relanded, and actually reshipt, & report the same to us for our further Orders, *valediction 1*

614 CUST 58/1

21 April 1750 *From W. C[ooley] and R. T[urvin] (Custom House, Portsmouth). Hand iii.*

Inclosed we transmit your Honours an Account of Goods Enumerated & Goods not Enumerated lately Seiz'd by the Officers in this Port, to which we beg leave to refer *valediction 4*

615 CUST 58/150, pp. 29–32

24 April 1750 *From W. Wood (Custom House, London). Hand iii.*

Captain Pawlett having by his Letters of the 21st & 22^{d} Instant apply'd to the Commissioners desiring that his Sea Stores of Liquor and China may be deliver'd, I am directed to send you Copies of the said Letters, and you are to examine into the Allegations therein Contained, and Report to the Board a true state of the Case, with an Account of the Quantity & Quality of the Liquor for their further Orders. *Valediction 2*

Gentlemen

I beg the favour the Collector of the Customs here may have an Order to let me take out of the Ship such remains of Wine as I carried out with me on that Voyage to the East Indies; I have already applied to the said Collector for Leave to bring on shore my Cabbin Furniture about Six or Seven Dozen of China Plates, which I have had in Constant use a great while & such triffling things; every thing has been permitted to pass that is Chairs, Tables, and such things but the Collector informs me he cant lett the China pass without an Order from you, if it is not unreasonable Gentlemen I shall be Oblig'd to you for such an Order; when they please to look over them they'll find about such a Number as I have mentioned tho' of Different Sorts, with some few Dishes &cetera which I believe ⌜wont⌝[25] be thought more than a Captain of a Man of War must always have in use – The Duty of such a Number wou'd have been so triffling that I shou'd not have [26] thought of troubling you about, had not the Collector inform'd me he cou'd not admit it to an Entry, which had I known before I shou'd have ask'd of you (as I now do) the Order without sending them to the Custom House – I am

Gentlemen Your most Obedient Servant

Henry Powlett

Exeter at Portsm° 21st April 1750

Portsmouth 22^{d} April 1750

Gentlemen

I wrote to you Yesterday to desire an Order for the Delivery of a few China Plates for my own use which the Collector of this Place had stopp'd till I cou'd procure such an Order and likewise to desire I might take out of the Ship such remains of Bottled Liquor as I carried out of England when I went to the East Indies three Years ago

I likewise beg the favour that I may be Indulg'd with what *Arrack I have in Bottles, I believe it wont amount to a ⌜Hogshead⌝[27] or if that is thought unreasonable I'll beg of you to suffer it to be enter'd, because I am told without your Indulgence Liquor in Bottles can neither be brought on shore Duty free nor be paid the Duty for. I am

Gentlemen Your most humble Servant

H^{ry} Powlett

616 CUST 58/150, p. 32

24 April 1750 *From W. Levinz ('Levine'), G. Vaughan, Sam. Mead and M. Stapylton (Custom House, [London]). Hand iii.*

We received your Letter of the 6th instant relating to four Cases of Elizir of Vitrol belonging to the Commissioners of Sick and Hurt Seamen which were brought to your Port by his Majestys Sloop the Tryal from Portmahone; & they having Certify'd that they are Stores formerly carried out of England and now return'd you may deliver the said Cases, if you have no further Objection, *valediction 1*

---

[25] MS. 'want'.
[26] MS. omits 'have'.
[27] MS. 'H'd'd' (for 'H'h'd').

617 **26 April 1750**

CUST 58/150, pp. 32–3

From W. Levinz ('Levine'), R. Chandlor, J. Evelynn and M. Stapylton (Custom House, London). Hand iii.

Having considered your Preparatory Account of Incidents for the Quarter ended at Christmas last, amounting to Eighteen Pounds six Shillings & three farthings, The Collector may pay the same with the privity of the Comptroller and take Credit for it in his Account of Incidents, annexing this Letter with proper receipts thereto as Vouchers, *valediction 1*

In margin: £18. 6. 0¾[28]

618 **26 April 1750**

CUST 58/150, pp. 33–4

From W. Levinz ('Levine'), R. Chandlor, J. Evelynn and M. Stapylton (Custom House, London). Hand iii.

We received your Letter of the 1st Ultimo acquainting us that you have enquir'd into the Charactor and Circumstances of John Cole, who is under Prosecution for being concern'd in Unshipping Brandy & Rum and find they are but indifferent and that he always supported a good Charactor and was never before concern'd in Smugling, And having considered the same as you have Reported that he is in mean Circumstances, and that he has a large family, and bears a good Charactor, We have agreed to the Sollicitors consenting to a *Supersedeas to discharge him from his Confinement upon his giving his own Bond not to be concern'd in Smugling for the future, if you have no further Objection thereto, *valediction 1*

619 **26 April 1750**

CUST 58/150, pp. 34–5

From W. Levinz ('Levine'), R. Chandlor, J. Evelyn and M. Stapylton (Custom House, London). Hand iii.

We received your Letter of the 16th[29] Instant transmitting an Account of Seizures of Wine made by Wm Baskerville Tidesurveyor of your Port, with his Memorial setting forth the Circumstances attending the said Seizure's & the obstruction he met with, on board his Majestys Ship Prince Henry under the Command of Captain Richard Jasper, We direct you to Prosecute the said Wine to Condemnation in the Exchequer at the Officers Charge, Corresponding with our Sollicitor & the Register of Seizures, And you are to call upon Mr Baskerville for an Account on Oath of this matter wherein must be set forth, all the particular Circumstances both as to the Wine on board the Prince Henry, and the Obstruction he met with on board the said Ship, and transmit the same to us for our further Orders *valediction 1*

Noted the 2d May 1750

620 **27 April 1750**

CUST 58/1

From W. C[ooley] and R. T[urvin] (Custom House, Portsmouth). Hand iii.

We received your Honours Order signify'd by Mr Woods Letter of the 24th Instant to report what Quantity of Liquors & China belonged to Captain Powlett of his Maj*e*stys Ship the Exeter, with a State of the Case, and beg leave to acquaint your Honours that with regard to the Liquor in Bottles mentioned in his Memorial, he has since acquainted us he will use it on board, The China we have sent an Account off Inclosed, & likewise of a pretty large quantity of *Arrack sent on shore to the WareHouse here by Captain Powlett.

With regard to the China which the Captain thinks is no more than might be pass'd as his Cabbin Furniture, We beg leave to refer the same to your Honours & shall wait your Directions concerning it – And as to the *Arrack tho' we have permitted several Entries to be made of smaller Quantities being the remainder of the Stores of the Commanders & other Officers belonging to his Majestys Ships lately arrived from the East Indies, as being agreeable to the Indulgence which has formerly been given in like Cases to the Gentlemen of the Navy by your Honours Approbation; This of Captain Pawletts being an unusual large Quantity, We thought it our Duty to send your Honours an Account thereof, and beg your Honours Order for admitting it to an Entry, or otherwise as you shall think proper, which shall be duely observ'd *valediction 4*

---

28 With line above and below.

29 MS. omits '16th'.

An Account of Liquor and China belonging to Capt Pawlett, landed here out of his Majestys Ship the Exeter from the East Indies, April 24th 1750

Twelve Casks Containing 469 gallons *Arrack
One Case containing Eleven Dozen China Plates
Eight China Dishes
Two China Basons and one China Cover

Custom House Portsm° 26th April 1750

621 CUST 58/150, p. 35

28 April 1750

From W. Wood (Custom House, London). Hand iii.

Admiral Boscawen having by his Letter of the 26th Instant apply'd to the Commissioners Relating to Six Leopard & Tyger Skins which were sent with his Baggage to the Custom House at your Port in ⌜order⌝[30] to be Enter'd, They direct you forthwith to send them up to the WareHouse here at the proprietors Charge giving the Board an Account when & by what Conveyance they are sent & what agreement is made for Carriage, *valediction 2*

622 CUST 58/150, pp. 36–7

30 April 1750

From W. Wood (Custom House, London). Hand iii.

Captain Lloy'd of his Majestys Ship the Sphinx having by his Letter of the 27th inst*ant* apply'd to the Commissioners desiring he may be permitted to send a board a Pipe of Madeira Wine Duty free, Inclosed you will receive extract of the said Letter, and you are to Examine into the Allegations therein Contained and report to the Board a true State of the Case with your Opinion, *valediction 2*

Extract of a Letter from Captain Lloy'd of his Majestys Ship the Sphinx, dated Spithead 27th April 1750

I beg you will let the Commissioners know that when I arrived here in his Majestys Ship under my Command, about Two Months past from the Madeira's & Lisbon, I landed some Pipes Hogsheads & Quarter Casks of Wine, for my Friends & Gentlemen who I purchas'd them for ⌜aboard⌝[31], and some for my self, at the Custom House here in order to pay Duty which they have all done, excepting One Pipe of Madeira of my own, which when the proper Officers were Gauging, was found to be so bad, as not to be worth the Dutys therefore I must beg the favour of the Board that they will be so kind as to permit me to send it aboard Duty free as the Wine will not be Landed again

623 CUST 58/150, pp. 37–8

30 April 1750

From W. Wood (Custom House, London). Hand iii.

Mr John Sherwood having by his Memorial of the 28th Instant apply'd to the Commissioners desiring that a Parcel of Prohibited East India Goods which he Bought in Michaelmas Term last, in the Court of Exchequer may be sent up, They have agreed thereto, and you are to send them up to the Warehouse here under the Seals of Office at the Proprietors Charge, giving the Board Notice when & by what Conveyance they are sent, and what agreement is made for Carriage, *valediction 2*

624 CUST 58/150, p. 38

30 April 1750

From W. Wood (Custom House, London). Hand iii.

Inclosed I send you by Order of the Commissioners an Act pass'd the last Session for preventing Frauds and Abuses in the Duties arising from Candles, Soap & Starch[32] wherein you will find several Directions to be observ'd by the Officers of the Customs & Excise and you are to take care that the same be duely observ'd by your Selves & the rest of the Officers at your Port, as far as you are respectively concern'd, *valediction 2*

---

[30] MS. 'order'd'.
[31] Possibly in mistake for 'abroad'.
[32] Statute 23 Geo. II, c.21.

625 CUST 58/150, pp. 38–40

3 May 1750

From J. Evelynn, Sam. Mead, Beaumont Hotham and W. Levinz ('Levine') (Custom House, London). Hand iii.

We received your Letter of the 27th Ultimo transmitting an Account of Liquor & China belonging to Captain Pawlett, Landed at your Port out of his Majestys Ship the Exeter from the East Indies, We direct you to secure the China in the WareHouse, and admit the *Arrack to an Entry. And you are to wait on Captain Powlett & acquaint him that his Ship having finish'd the Voyage the Wine on board must pay the Dutys, unless he can shew any just cause for the contrary, and you are to give Directions, incase it be brought to the WareHouse in a Civil manner, for the Duties to be paid accordingly

We received your Letter of the 30th Ultimo acquainting us that you have no Objection to Jno Cole, who is under Prosecution for Unshipping Brandy & Rum, being Discharged out of Jail on his paying the Sum of Five Pounds Eight Shillings & One Penny, being the Charges of apprehending him at Lymington, & carrying him from thence to the County Jail at Winchester, We agree thereto and upon your acquainting our Sollicitor that he has paid the said Charges, he has Orders to consent to a *Supersedeas to Discharge the said Cole from his Confinement agreeable to our Order of the 26th Ultimo *valediction 1*

In margin: £5. 8. 1[33]

626 CUST 58/1

3 May 1750

From W. C[ooley] and R. T[urvin] (Custom House, Portsmouth). Hand iii.

Inclosed we transmit your Honours an Account of Goods Enumerated and Goods not Enumerated lately Seiz'd by the Officers in this Port, to which we beg leave to refer *valediction 3*

627 CUST 58/1

4 May 1750

From W. C[ooley] and R. T[urvin] (Custom House, Portsmouth). Hand iii.

We have your Honours Order signify'd to us by Mr Wood in his Letter of the 30th Ultimo together with Copy of a Memorial to your Honours, from Captain Lloy'd of his Majestys Ship Sphinx Relating to a Pipe of Madeira Wine, which he has landed at this Port, and Secured in the Kings WareHouse desiring as the same is so bad as not to be worth the Dutys your Honours wou'd give him leave to take on board the same again without payment of the Dutys; In Obedience to your Order, we have Examined into the Allegations of Captn Lloyds Memorial & we are to acquaint your Honours a Pipe of Madeira Wine belonging to him about two Months since was landed at this Port, and on the Officers Gauging the same it was found to be but very indifferent & Scarce worth the Dutys, We have therefore no Objection to Capt Lloyds having the said Pipe of Wine again without Payment of the Dutys provided your Honours approve thereof, *valediction 3*

628 CUST 58/1

4 May 1750

From W. C[ooley] and R. T[urvin] (Custom House, Portsmouth). Hand iii.

In Obedience to your Order signify'd to us by Mr Wood in his Letter of the 30 Ultimo We have this day sent directed to your Honours under the Seals of Office, by the Waggon of Geo. Clarke which will be at the Whitehart in the Burrough of Southwark on Monday the 7th instant a Box Containing a Parcel of Prohibited East India Goods which was bought by Mr John Sherwood in Michaelmas Term last, in the Court of Exchequer for the Carriage of which we have agreed that four Shillings shall be paid, *valediction 5*

---

33 With line above and below.

629 CUST 58/150, p. 40

5 May 1750

From J. Evelynn, Sam. Mead, Beaumont Hotham and W. Levinz ('Levine') (Custom House, London). Hand iii.

In answer to the Account of Seizures transmitted in your Letters of the 21st & 28th Ultimo We direct you to Prosecute the Enumerated Goods thereinmentioned to Condemnation in the Exchequer at the Kings Charge, And we have no Objection to the Officers prosecuting the rest of the Goods in like manner at their own Charge, Corresponding with our Sollicitor & the Register of Seizures, *valediction 1*

In margin: Noted the 7th May 1750

630 CUST 58/150, p. 41

5 May 1750

From J. Evelynn, Sam. Mead, Beaumont Hotham and W. Levinz ('Levine') (Custom House, London). Hand iii.

Messrs Isidore Lynch & Co and other Merchants here, having by their Memorial of the 2d Instant, apply'd to us desiring as the Ship Redbridge lately Sprung a Leak at Sea, is incapable of proceeding on her intended Voyage, that the Goods taken out of her and put on board the Ruby Man of War, may be Shipt on board the Northbrooke, Robert Salter Master by Virtue of the Old *Cocquets; We have agreed thereto, and you may permit the said Goods to be reshipt on board the Northbrooke as desired, transmitting us an Exact Account thereof, and take care to Endorse on the back of the Duplicates of the Ship Redbridge, the Goods reshipt in the Northbrooke, mentioning them to be the Goods Saved, and also the Goods lost, *valediction 1*

631 CUST 58/1

6 May 1750

From W. C[ooley] and R. T[urvin] (Custom House, Portsmouth). Hand iii.

Herewith we transmit Your Honours the Abstract for the Month of April last together with the undermentioned Account[s] to which we beg leave to refer *valediction 4*

Nil List of Bonds
Tea & other Goods Enumerated with petty receipts Endors'd
Absent Officers

PS/ From the Book kept in this Office it appears that the Weights & Scales Coal & Corn bushels at this Port were try'd the 4th Ultimo by the Surveyor & Landwaiters & that they found the same to be exact & true & that the Stamps for marking Hides, Skins, Linnens Seiz'd Goods & Sail Cloth, are in good & Sufficient repair & fit for the uses design'd.

W C R T

632 CUST 58/150, p. 42

8 May 1750

From W. Westby, W. Levinz ('Levine'), Beaumont Hotham and M. Stapylton (Custom House, London). Hand iii.

In Answer to the Account of Seizures transmitted in your Letter of the 3d Instant, We direct you to Prosecute the Brandy thereinmentioned to Condemnation in the Exchequer, at the Kings Charge, And we have no Objection to the Officers Prosecuting the rest of the Goods in like manner, at their own Charge Corresponding with our Sollicitor & the Register of Seizures, *valediction 1*

633 CUST 58/150, pp. 42–3

8 May 1750

From W. Westby, Edw. Hooper, J. Evelynn and M. Stapylton (Custom House, London). Hand iii.

The Commissioners for Victualling his Majestys Navy, having by their Letter of the 7th Instant apply'd to us desiring that some remains of Rice, Sugar, and *Tamarinds, on board his Majestys Ship the Exeter, now at your Port, with which she was supply'd for Victualling her Company, may be Landed & Lodg'd in his Majestys Stores, till they have an Opportunity of Issuing them to some other Ship Outward bound; We have agreed thereto, and you may permit them to be landed and put into WareHouses accordingly under the joint Locks of the Customs, & the Commissioners of the Victualling, *valediction 1*

634
8 May
1750

CUST 58/150, pp. 43–4

From W. Wood (Custom House, London). Hand iii.

Inclosed I send you by Order of the Commissioners several Acts pass'd the last Session of Parliament, relating to the Customs for the Government of your selves and the other Officers at your Port, to whom you are to communicate the same – Viz^{t} –

1 The Malt Act
2 An Act for the Effectual Punishment of Persons convicted of Seducing Artificers out of the Dominions of Great Britain &cetera
3 An Act for Encouraging the Growth & Culture of Raw Silk in his Majestys Colonies or Plantations in America
4 An Act for the Encouragement of the British White Herring Fishery –
5 An Act for continuing a former Act for permitting Rum or Spirits of the British Sugar Plantations to be landed before the Duties of Excise are paid –
6 An Act for Encouraging the Importation of Pig & Barr Iron, from his Majestys Colonies in America &cetera –
7 An Act for granting to his Majesty certain Duties upon such Species of Sail Cloth as are thereinmentioned which shall be imported from Ireland &cetera –
8 An Act for permitting raw Silk of the Growth of Persia to be Imported into this Kingdom &cetera [34]

Valediction 2

635
8 May
1750

CUST 58/150, pp. 44–5

From W. Wood (Custom House, London). Hand iii.

It appearing by your Account of Ages and Capacitys of the Officers at your Port for Christmas last, that Thomas Billson Boatman remains ill, and not Capable of performing his Duty; The Commissioners direct you to report to them whether he is in every respect entituled to the Superanuation Allowance agreeable to the Rules sent to your Port the 22^{d} March 1743, *valediction 2*

636
10 May
1750

CUST 58/150, p. 45

From W. Wood (Custom House, London ('Portsm^{o}')). Hand iii.

Herewith you will receive Copy of an Order of his Majestys in Council dated the 29th of March last for altering the form of Mediterranean Passes, after the time thereinmentioned, and for delivering up of Old Passes, And you are to take care that his Majestys Pleasure thereinmentioned, be strictly & duely comply'd with, by your selves and the rest of the Officers at your Port, so far as you & they are respectively concern'd, *valediction 2*

637
10 May
1750

CUST 58/150, p. 46

From W. Westby, Sam. Mead, Beaumont Hotham and W. Levinz ('Levine') (Custom House, London). Hand iii.

Having granted our Commission for Thomas Gorden (who has given Security here) to be a Tidesman and Boatman at your Port, in the room of Jno Mc Cloud Prefer'd, You may admit him to his Duty, taking care he qualifies himself as the Law directs, and pay him the like Allowance of five Pounds Per Annum by Incidents, as was paid to his Predecessor, for which the Collector may take Credit from time to time in his Account of Incidents referring therein to the Date hereof, *valediction 1*

638
11 May
1750

CUST 58/150, pp. 46–7

From W. Westby, Beaumont Hotham, J. Evelynn and Sam. Mead (Custom House, London). Hand iii.

Captain Pawlett of his Majestys Ship Exeter from India, having apply'd to us again by his Letter of the 5th Instant in relation to his Liquors & China, now in the WareHouse at your Port; We have considered his Case, and in regard to the very long Voyage he has been, We agree in this particular Instance, to your Delivery of the China, and such part of the Wine as he carried out of England with him, but the remainder of it, & the *Arrack must pay the Duty, & you are to admit it to an Entry accordingly, agreeable to our Orders in our Letter of the 3^{d} Instant, *valediction 1*

---

[34] Statutes 23 Geo. II, cc.3, 13, 20, 24, 26, 29, 32, 34.

639 CUST 58/150, pp. 47–8

12 May 1750

From W. Westby, Sam. Mead, J. Evelynn and Edw. Hooper (Custom House, London). Hand iii.

We received your Letter of the 4th instant in return to the Memorial of Capt Lloyd of his Majestys Ship Sphinx, relating to a Pipe of Madeira Wine, Secured in the WareHouse at your Port, desiring leave to take it on board again without Payment of the Duties, And having considered the same, you are to acquaint Capt Lloyd, that as such a President might be attended with bad Consequences to the Revenue, And as the said Wine is landed, and the Duties due, if he does not Chuse to pay them, the Wine must be Sold for the Duties according to Law, *valediction 1*

640 CUST 58/150, pp. 48–9

12 May 1750

From W. Wood (Custom House, London). Hand iii.

The Commissioners observing by the Accounts laid before them of Foreign Gold & Silver Coin & Bullion enter'd for Holland, Hambro' Ostend & Callais that much larger Quantities are Enter'd Outwards than are Exported, and having given Directions by their Minute of the 12th Ultimo to the proper Officers in this Port, to prevent this Practice for the future, which may be attended with ill consequences to the Revenue & Publick; I am directed to acquaint you that you are to be particularly carefull to examine & see whether the whole Quantity & Quality of Gold & Silver Coin, or Bullion mentioned in the *Cocquets sent from hence be actually ship'd on board the Ship, & Exported from your Port, And you are every first Monday in the Month to transmit an Account thereof to the Board, agreeable to the Form Inclosed, & incase no Coin or Bullion shou'd be Ship'd you are nevertheless to send a Nil Account. *Valediction 2*

641 CUST 58/150, pp. 49–50

15 May 1750

From W. Wood (Custom House, London). Hand iii.

Gentlemen[35]

I received your Letter of the 14th Instant and agreeable to your desire, Inclosed you will receive Copy of the Rules referr'd to in[36] my Letter of the 22d March 1743 which entitles the Officers to the Superanuation Allowance, and you are to report to the Board whether Thomas Bilson is entituled thereto agreeable to the said Rules, I am

Sir Your most humble Servant

W Wood

Gentlemen

The several Warrants from the Treasury relating to Superanuated Officers requiring that all Pensioners shou'd be qualify'd according to the Rules following

1 Whether such Officers were full Seven Years in the Service of the Customs
2 Whether by any and by what extraordinary Accident he was sooner Disabled
3 Whether he had well behaved himself during the time of his said Service
4 Whether he has at present any other means of Subsistance from the Government or otherwise
5 Whether he is Capable of getting a Subsistance any other way

We direct you carefully to examine & faithfully to Report to us whether such Persons so applying are within the said Qualifications according to the said 5 Rules &cetera

J S, W Y, J P T W[37]

23d July 1721

642 CUST 58/1

17 May 1750

From W. C[ooley] and R. T[urvin] (Custom House, Portsmouth). Hand iii.

In obedience to your Honours Commands of the 8th Instant, signify'd to us by Mr Wood; We do humbly report that Thomas Billson Boatman at this Port, is Aged Seventy Years and has been Employed in the Service upwards of Twenty two Years, and that during the time of his Service, he has behaved himself honest & Well; has not any other means of Subsistance than from the Government, nor is he capable of getting a Subsistance any other way, being very infirm, We therefore think he is in every respect entituled to the Superanuation Allowance, agreeable to the Rules sent by your Honours the 23d July 1721 which is submitted to your Honours consideration *valediction 4*

---

35 In view of the valediction, however, the letter may be addressed to Cooley alone.

36 MS. omits 'in'.

37 I.e. Sir John Stanley, Sir Walter Young, John Pulteney and Thomas Walker.

643
18 May
1750

CUST 58/1

From W. C[ooley] and R. T[urvin] (Custom House, Portsmouth). Hand iii.

In our joint Letter of the 23^d^ December 1749 we acquainted your Honours with the Murder of William May (late a Tidesman and Boatman at this Port) on board a Sloop called the Peggy laden with Wine and Brandy from Bourdeaux, for North Bergon on which Sloop was likewise Boarded Jno Forrest a Tidesman with the Allowance of five Pounds Per Annum by Incidents who we at the same time acquainted your Honours, had been[38] Suspended for being Drunk on his Duty; Your Honours not having given Directions whether he shou'd be Dismiss'd out of the Service or not; We beg now to receive your Direction thereon, We are to assure your Honours Forrest is by no means a fit Person to be Employ'd in the Service, being almost continually Drunk, We have therefore not since the time of our suspending him, Employ'd him Which your Honours, we hope will approve of, *valediction 5*

644
19 May
1750

CUST 58/1

From W. C[ooley] and R. T[urvin] (Custom House, Portsmouth). Hand iii.

Inclosed we transmit your Honours an Account of Goods Enumerated and Goods not Enumerated lately Seiz'd by the Officers in this Port, to which we beg leave to refer *valediction 4*

645
22 May
1750

CUST 58/150, pp. 50–2

From W. Wood (Custom House, London). Hand iii.

The Right Honourable the Lords Commissioners of his Majestys Treasury, having been pleas'd in Compassion to the Inferior Officers of the Customs to Autherize the Commissioners to give Directions to the Collectors of the Out Ports to pay the Taxes assessd upon the Salaries of the Deputed Officers, not exceeding Sixty Pounds Per Annum, by the Land Tax granted for this Year; and also to Reimburse them the Money paid upon their Salaries by Virtue of that Act;[39] The Commissioners direct me to signify the same to you, and that you yield obedience thereto accordingly, referring in your Incidents to the Date hereof, and withall taking care that no more be allowed than has been already paid, or shall be paid by the said Officers, and that by Virtue thereof you do not allow the Taxes Assess'd upon any Patent Officers; And I am further to acquaint you that all Officers are to be Taxed where they execute their Offices, and not where they are paid their Sallaries, and the Collector is to take care of reminding the Assessors thereof, that the Assessments may be made accordingly, which is what I have in Command to signify to you, *valediction 2*

646
22 May
1750

CUST 58/150, pp. 52–3

From Sam. Mead, W. Levinz ('Levine'), J. Evelyn and Edw. Hooper (Custom House, London). Hand iii.

We received your Letter of the 17th instant acquainting us that Thomas Bilson Boatman at your Port, is in every respect entitled to the Superanuation Allowance agreeable to the Rules, We have agreed thereto, & order'd him to be placed on the List of Superanuated Officers accordingly

In Answer to the Account of Seizures transmitted in your Letter of the 19th Instant We direct you to Prosecute the Tea and Brandy thereinmentioned to Condemnation in the Exchequer at the Kings Charge, And we have no Objection to the Officers Prosecuting the Silk Handkerchiefs in like manner at their own Charge, Corresponding with our Sollicitor and the Register of Seizures, *valediction 1*

Noted the 24th May 1750

---

38 MS. omits 'been'.

39 Statute 23 Geo. II, c.2.

647 CUST 58/150, p. 53

23 May[40] *From W. Wood (Custom House, London). Hand iii.*

1750 The Commissioners direct you to transmit them ⌜without⌝[41] loss of time an Account of all Bountys whatsoever that shou'd be paid at your Port, between Christmas and Christmas for Five Years past, distinguishing each Commodity for which the Bountys were granted, as also how much of the said Bountys were paid at your Port, and how much ⌜ye Bountys amount⌝[42] to for the Debentures sent up, to be paid here, agreeable to the Speciman sent you in my Letter of 22^d^ of March 1747 distinguishing each Year *valediction 2*

648 CUST 58/1

24 May *From W. C[ooley] and R. T[urvin] (Custom House, Portsmouth). Hand iii.*

1750 In Obedience to your Honours Order of the 5th Instant, Inclosed we transmit you an exact and particular Account, of the Goods taken out of the Redbridge, which Sprung a Leak at Sea, and Reshipt on board the Northbrook, Robert Salter Master for Dublin, to which we beg leave to refer; And we are to acquaint your Honours an Endorsment was made on the back of the Duplicates, of the Ship Redbridge, the Goods reshipt, in the Northbrooke, mentioning the Goods Saved & also the Goods lost, *valediction 5*

649 CUST 58/1

25 May *From W. C[ooley] and R. T[urvin] (Custom House, Portsmouth). Hand iii.*

1750 Inclosed we transmit Your Honours a Schedule of Accounts, due from this Port for Lady day Quarter last, the same being this day forwarded by the Waggon of Geo, Clarke, ⌜which will⌝[43] be at the Whitehart in the Burrough of Southwark, on Monday the 28th Instant for the Carriage whereof we have agreed that Two Shillings & six pence shall be paid, *valediction 4*

Portsmouth

A Schedule of Accounts due from this Port for Lady day Quarter last, sent by the Waggon of George Clarke which will be at the Whitehart in the Burrough of Southwark on Monday the 28th May ⌜1750⌝[44]

Collectors Quarter Book
Comptrollers Ditto
General Incidents with the Establishment
2 Original Orders
Civil List receipt and Repayment
Preparatory Account of Incidents & Tradesmens Bills
Personal Prosecutions
Enumerated Goods Per Act 12th Geo' 1st[45]
Prohibited East India Goods for the half Year ended Lady day last
Reports Inwards & Outwards
Debentures, Damages,
*Over Entry & Discounts
Coal Incidents
Imports & Exports
Wooll brought & Carried Coastwise
Journals of the Com*mande*r & Mate of the Greenhill Yatch
Ditto of the Chief Boatman at Hayling
Copy of Instructions to James Terry Coal Meter
Ditto to Thos Garrett Tidesman

N B/ The undermentioned Accounts for said Quarter was sent the Honourable Commissioners the 3 Ultimo Viz^t^ –

Naval Stores from Rushia & Levonia
Corn Exported whereon there is a Bounty
Ships &cetera which Discharged in this Port from any of his Majestys Plantations in America

---

[40] MS. 'March'. That this is incorrect is shown by the position of the letter in the MS. and by no. 656.
[41] Altered from 'with'.
[42] Written over an illegible erasure.
[43] MS. 'will will'.
[44] Altered from '1748'.
[45] Statute 12 Geo. I, c.28.

650
26 May
1750

CUST 58/150, pp. 54–5

From W. Wood (Custom House, London). Hand iii.

The Commissioners having caus'd to be prepared the necessary Forms of Certificate, Oaths, Bond, Licence, &cetera pursuant to an Act of the 23^d Year of his Majestys Reign for the Encouragement of the British White Herring Fishery,[46] direct me to transmit you Copys of the said Forms for your Government Viz^t

1 Form of a Certificate of the Qualification of a Ship going on the White Herring Fishery
2 Form of the Oath of an Owner of a Ship going on the White Herring Fishery
3 Form of the Oath of the Master of a Ship going on the White Herring Fishery
4 Form of a Bond for a Ship going on the White Herring Fishery, to be given by the Master Owner ⌜or⌝[47] Agent with two Sufficient Securities.
5 Form of the Oath to be taken by the Master on his return from the Herring Fishery
6 Form of a Licence for a Ship to proceed on the White Herring Fishery –

You will observe by the said Act that besides the Forms beforementioned, The proper Officer of the Customs is on the return of the Vessel immediately to repair on board the same, and View the Condition of such Vessell, and her Lading, and Certify the same together with their observations thereon &cetera which you are to take care, be done accordingly as well as see that the Conditions of the Act is duely and strictly comply'd with in all respects *valediction 2*

The Commissioners direct you to transmit them an Answer to the following Querries by the return of the Post

1 The Name & form of the Coal Measure.
2 The exact Diameter of the Top from Out to Out
3 What Quantity of Liquid Winton measure it contains
4 In what method the Meters keep their Accounts of the Quantities Deliver'd, & whether they are Chequed by any & what Officer.

651
26 May
1750

CUST 58/1

From W. C[ooley] and R. T[urvin] (Custom House, Portsmouth). Hand iii.

Inclosed we transmit your Honours an Account of Goods Enumerated & Goods not Enumerated latly Seiz'd by the Officers in this Port, to which we beg leave to refer *valediction 4*

652
28 May
1750

CUST 58/1

From W. C[ooley] and R. T[urvin] (Custom House, Portsmouth). Hand iii.

We are to acquaint your Honours on the 27th Instant, in the Evening arrived at the Motherbank the James Dutch *Dagger Christian Stilau Master from Santa Cruize in S*outh* Barbary, bound for Amsterdam, which Ship we are to acquaint your Honours was immediately put under Quarentine by Captain Coombs Com*mande*r of the Greenhill Yatch in the Service at this Port; Inclosed we transmit your Honours the Questions put to the Master of the said Ship, on his Arrival, by Captain Coombs with answers thereto, and likewise inclosed we send your Honours the Account of the Musters of the Passengers & Mariners on board the said Ship, to which we beg leave to refer; The Master has inform'd us that he intends Sailing for Amsterdam, the first fair Wind to which we shall have no Objection being agreeable to our former Orders, *valediction 5*

653
29 May
1750

CUST 58/1

From W. C[ooley] and R. T[urvin] (Custom House, Portsmouth). Hand iii.

Inclosed we transmit your Honours an Account of Goods Enumerated & Goods not Enumerated lately Seiz'd by the Officers in this Port to which we beg leave to refer *valediction 4*

---

[46] Statute 23 Geo. II, c.24.
[47] Inserted.

654
29 May
1750

CUST 58/1

From W. C[ooley] and R. T[urvin] (Custom House, Portsmouth). Hand iii.

In Obedience to your Honours Commands signifyed to us by Mr Wood in his Letter of the 26th Instant, Inclosed we transmit your Honours the Answers to the several Querries mentioned therein to which we beg leave to refer *valediction 3*

Answers to the Querrys mentioned in Mr Woods Letter dated the 26th instant

	Querrys	Answers
1	The Name & Form of the Coal Measure	Coal Measure is call'd a Coal Bushel made round with a Plain even Bottom, and fill'd with Iron –
2	The Exact Diameter of the Top from Out to Out –	$19^1/_2$ Inches from Outside to Outside
3	What Quantity of Liquid winton mea*sure* it contains –	A Bushel Contains One Winchester Bushel and one Quart Water –
4	In what method the Meters keep their Account of the Quantitys Deliver'd & whether they are Chequed by any & what Officer	The Meter has a Book in which he Tallys every Bushel deliver'd out of the Ship to which he is appointed, to which Account an Affidavit of Truth thereof is made by the Meter who is Chequed by the Land Surveyor

655
30 May
1750

CUST 58/1

From W. C[ooley] and R. T[urvin] (Custom House, Portsmouth). Hand iii.

Inclosed we transmit your Honours an Account of the Musters of the Passengers and Mariners on board the James, now under Quarentine at this Port as taken by Captain Coombs of the Greenhill Yatch to which we beg leave to refer *valediction 4*

656
31 May
1750

CUST 58/1

From W. C[ooley] and R. T[urvin] (Custom House, Portsmouth). Hand iii.

In Obedience to your Honours Commands signify'd to us by Mr Wood in his Letter of the 23^d^ Instant, Inclosed we transmit your Honours an Account of all Bountys whatsoever that shou'd be paid at this Port, between Christmas and Christmas for five Years past distinguishing each Commodity for which the Bountys were granted, as also how much of the said Bountys were paid at this Port, and how much of the said Bountys Amount to for the Debentures sent up agreeable to the Speciman sent us in the Secretarys Letter of the 22^d^ March 1747 distinguishing each Year, to which Account we beg leave to refer *valediction 3*

Portsmouth An Account of Corn & other Commodities Exported from this Port which are Entituled to a Bounty from Christmas 1744 to Christmas 1749

From Christmas 1744 to Christmas 1745	*Quarters*	*bushels*	Bountys		
Wheat –	7287.	4	1821	17	6
Wheaten Flour –	1771.	0	442	15	0
Barley –	199.	0	24	17	6
Malt –	1314.	$6^1/_2$	164	7	$0^1/_4$
			2453	17	$0^1/_4$
Whereof paid at this Port			Nil –		
Debentures sent up to be paid in London			2453	17	$0^1/_4$

– Other Goods –
– Nil –

From Christmas 1745 to Christmas 1746

			£	s	d
Wheat –	2497.	0	624	5	0
Barley –	341.	3	42	13	5¼
Wheaten flour –	1821.	6	455	8	9
Malt –	2391.	6	298	19	4½
			£1421	6	6¾
Whereof paid at this Port –			Nil –		
Debentures sent up to be paid in London			1421	6	6¾

– Other Goods –

British Manufactur'd Silk only			
94 lb' Avoirdupoize at 3s Per *weight*	14	2	0
Whereof paid at this Port –	14	2	0
Debentures sent up to be paid in London	Nil		

From Christmas 1746 to Christmas 1747

	Quarters	bus*hels*			
Wheat –	4645.	6	1161	8	9
Wheaten flour –	1399.	6	349	18	11
Barley –	68.	0	8	10	0
Malt –	122.	2	15	5	7½
			£1535	3	1½
Whereof paid at this Port –			Nil –		
Debentures sent up to be paid in London			1535	3	1½

Other Goods

British Manufactur'd Silk Stockings, &cetera			
398 lb'.8 oz.4 dwt at 1s.3d' Per	24	18	1¼
Ditto – Silk & Worsted Stuffs 241 lb' at 6d Per	6	0	6
	30	18	7¼
Whereof paid at this Port –	30	18	7¼
Debentures sent up to be paid in London	Nil –		

From Christmas 1747 to Christmas 1748

	Quarters	bus*hels*			
Wheat –	25101.	2	6275	6	3
Wheaten flour –	2887.	4	771	17	6
Malt –	192.	6	24	1	10½
			£7021	5	7½
Whereof paid at this Port –			1399	12	6
Debentures sent up to be paid in London			5621	13	1½

– Other Goods –

British Manufactured Silk and Worsted Stuffs			
467 lb's at 6d'	11	13	6
Irish Linnen 420 yds at 1½d Per Yard	2	12	6
British made Sail Cloth 770 Ells at 2d Per Ell	6	8	4
	£20	14	4
Whereof paid at this Port–	£20	14	4
Debentures sent up to be paid in London	Nil		

From Christmas 1748 to Christmas 1749 –

	Quarters	bus*hels*			
Wheat –	24885.	4	6221	7	6
Wheaten flour –	5414.	4	1353	12	6
Malt –	2590.	6½	323	17	0¼
			£7898	17	0¼
Whereof paid at this Port –			£2730	5	3¾
Debentures sent up to be paid in London			£5168	11	8½

Other Goods

British Manufactur'd Silk 38 lb' at 1s.3d' Per lb	2	7	6
Ditto – Silk & Worsted Stuffs 28 lb' at 6d' Per lb'	.	14	0
	£3	1	6
Whereof paid at this Port –	3	1	6
Debentures sent up to be p*ai*d in London	Nil –		

W C
R T

Custom House Portsm° 31st May 1750

657 CUST 58/1

1 June 1750

From W. C[ooley] and R. T[urvin] (Custom House, Portsmouth). Hand iii.

Inclosed we transmit your Honours an Account of Goods not Enumerated lately Seiz'd by the Officers in this Port to which we beg leave to refer *valediction 4*

658 CUST 58/150, p. 56

2 June 1750

From W. Levinz ('Levine'), R. Chandlor, Sam. Mead and Edw. Hooper (Custom House, London). Hand iii.

We received your Letter of the 18th Ultimo ⌜acquainting us⌝[48] that you have suspended John Forrest Extra Tidesman at your Port, for being Disguised in Liquor on his Duty, and you having in your said Letter represented to us that he is by no means a fit Person to be Employ'd in the Service, We have Dismiss'd the said Forrest and you are to call in his Commission and Cancel it, and transmit it to us with your next Accounts by the Carrier. *Valediction 1*

659 CUST 58/150, p. 56

2 June 1750

From W. Levinz ('Levine'), Sam. Mead, R. Chandlor and Edw. Hooper (Custom House, London). Hand iii.

In Answer to the Account of Seizures transmitted in your Letters of the 26th & 29th Ultimo We direct you to Prosecute the Goods thereinmention'd to Condemnation in the Exchequer at the Kings Charge, And we have no Objection to the Officers Prosecuting the rest of the Goods in like manner, at their own Charge, Corresponding with our Sollicitor and the Register of Seizures *valediction 1*

In margin: Noted the 9th June 1750

660 CUST 58/1

2 June 1750

From W. C[ooley] and R. T[urvin] (Custom House, Portsmouth). Hand iii.

Herewith we transmit your Honours the Abstract for the Month of May last, together with the undermentioned Accounts, to which we beg leave to refer *valediction 4*

Nil List of Bonds
Tea & other Goods Enumerated with petty receipts Endors'd
Absent Officers

PS/ From the Book kept in this Office it appears that the ⌜Weights⌝[49] & Scales Coal & Corn bushels at this Port, were try'd the 4th Ultimo by the Surveyor & Landwaiters & that they found the same to be exact & true & that the Stamps for marking Hides, Skins, Linnen, Seiz'd Goods & Sail Cloth are in good & Sufficient repair & fit for the uses designd

661 CUST 58/1

8 June 1750

From W. C[ooley] and R. T[urvin] (Custom House, Portsmouth). Hand iii.

Inclosed we transmit your Honours an Account of Goods Enumerated and Goods not Enumerated, lately Seizd by the Officers in this Port, to which we beg leave to refer *valediction 4*

[48] Written over an illegible erasure.
[49] MS. 'Weight'.

662 CUST 58/150, p. 57

9 June 1750

From Edw. Hooper, Sam. Mead, W. Westby and W. Levinz ('Levine') (Custom House, London). Hand iii.

In answer to the Account of Seizures transmitted in your Letter of the 1st Instant We have no objection to the Officers Prosecuting the Goods thereinmentioned to Condemnation, in the Exchequer at their own Charge, Corresponding with our Sollicitor & the Register of Seizures *valediction 1*[50]

663 CUST 58/1

11 June 1750

From W. C[ooley] and R. T[urvin] (Custom House, Portsmouth). Hand iii.

In Obedience to your Honours Commands of the 26th April last, we transmitted you Mr Baskervilles Account on Oath setting forth the particular Circumstances attending a Seizure of Wine on board his Majestys Ship, Prince Henry Captain Jasper and the Obstructions he met with on board the said Ship, not having since we transmitted your Honours the said Account, received any Directions thereon, We beg to receive your immediate Orders relating thereto, as we expect the Ship will Sail in a few days, We are further to acquaint your Honours two Officers have been continued on board the Prince Henry to prevent the Wine being Run, which we shall continue until the Ship Sails, or we receive your Directions to the contrary, *valediction 5*

664 CUST 58/1

12 June 1750

From W. C[ooley] and R. T[urvin] (Custom House, Portsmouth). Hand iii.

We have here Inclosed a List of such Stationary Wares as are much wanted for the Service of this Port, with which we beg to be immediately supply'd and the same shall be frugally Manag'd with the greatest frugality *valediction 4*

PS/ The last Supply was Craved the 25th of November 1749.

Portsmouth A List of such Stationary Wares as are much wanted for the Service of his Majestys Customs, humbly Crav'd to be Allowd, – Vizt –

4 Quire Quarter Book Paper In*wards*
2 Quire *Imperial Paper Unruled
3 Rheams fine *Pott Cutt
4 Rheams 2d *Pott Uncutt
6 Quire *Demy Cutt
3 Quire Ditto Uncutt

80	Blue Books –	4	Leaves
50	–	2	–
60	–	6	–
40	–	8	–
30	–	10	–
30	–	12	–
20	–	14	–
12	–	16	–
12	–	24	–
12	–	20	–

1 Dozen *Demy Pocket Books
2 Gallons Black Ink
1 Quart Red Ink
4 *Pounce Boxes
4 Sand Boxes
4 Round Pewter Ink Stands
3 Bags Sand
4 Books 1 Quire *Demy in Marble

3 Quire *Boardings
4 Quire loose reports Inwards
3 Ditto – Outwards
2 Ditto Coal Warrants
1500 Quils
3000 Wafers
1000 large Wafers for *Cocq*ue*ts & cetera
12 Past Board Files with Tags
3 Dozen Tags for Files
1 Report Book Inwards
1 Ditto – Outwards
1 Dozen Lead Pencils
4 Penknives
1 Dozen Tape
2 Journal Books for the use of the Com*mander* & Mate of the Greenhill Yatch
1 Book *Imperial Paper Unruled
2 Quire Paper for Wooll brought & Carried Coastwise agreeable to ye Print*ed* Form
1/2 Pound *Pounce
1 Pound Sealing Wax
2 Quire Baggage Sufferances
2 Ditto Petty Receipts
2 Ditto *Over Entrys
2 Ditto Damage Certificates
1 Abstract Book
2 Quire Blank Abstracts
2 Quarter Books Enumerated Goods
3 Quire loose Accounts of Seizures of Goods Enumerated & Goods not Enumerated

---

50 In the margin is the signature 'June 21st 1750 Pusey Brooke Surv*eyo*r Gen*eral*', presumably on examining the letter book in his inspection of the outport's business (see no. 677 and above, pp. xiii, xxxiv).

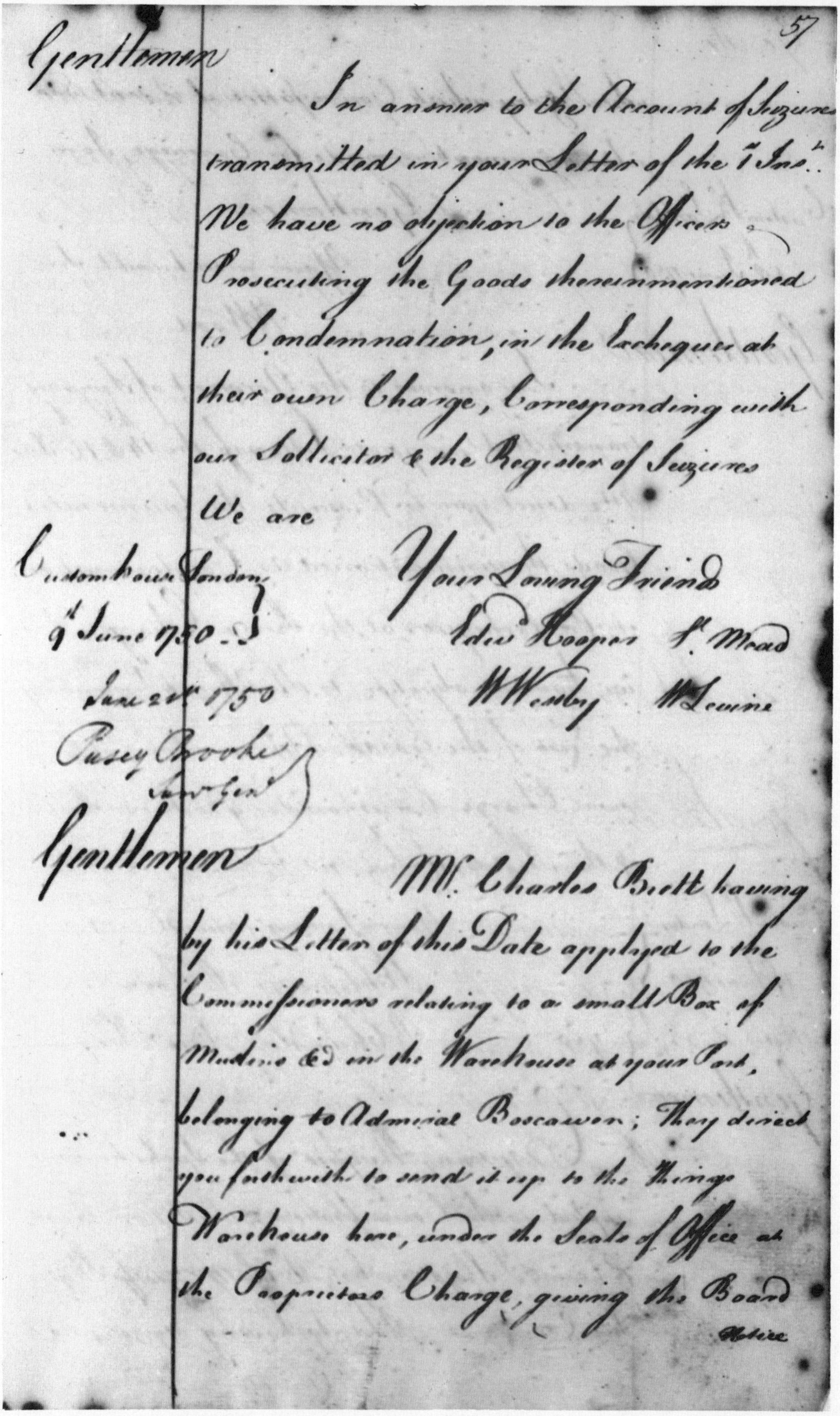

57

Gentlemen

In answer to the Account of Seizures transmitted in your Letter of the 7 Inst. We have no objection to the Officers Prosecuting the Goods therein mentioned to Condemnation, in the Exchequer at their own Charge, Corresponding with our Sollicitor & the Register of Seizures We are

Custom house London
9 June 1750

Your Loving Friends
Edw Hooper S. Mead
W Wellsby W Levinz

June 2 1750
Pusey Brooke
Surv Gen

Gentlemen

Mr. Charles Brett having by his Letter of this Date applyed to the Commissioners relating to a small Box of Muslins &c in the Warehouse at your Port, belonging to Admiral Boscawen; They direct you forthwith to send it up to the Kings Warehouse here, under the Seals of Office at the Proprietors Charge, giving the Board Notice

Fig. 6 LETTERS FROM THE BOARD OF CUSTOMS TO THE PORTSMOUTH CUSTOMS OFFICERS 9 AND 18 JUNE 1750 (nos 662, 667). P.R.O. CUST 58/150, p. 57

665 CUST 58/1

14 June 1750

From W. C[ooley] and R. T[urvin] (Custom House, Portsmouth). Hand iii.

Inclosed we transmit your Honours an Account of Goods Enumerated & Goods not Enumerated lately Seiz'd by the Officers in this Port to which we beg leave to refer *valediction 4*

666 CUST 58/1

16 June 1750

From W. C[ooley] and R. T[urvin] (Custom House, Portsmouth). Hand iii.

Inclosed we transmit your Honours an Account of Goods not Enumerated lately Seiz'd by an Officer in this Port, to which we beg leave to refer *valediction 4*

667 CUST 58/150, pp. 57–8

18 June 1750

From W. Wood (Custom House, London). Hand iii.

Mr Charles Brett having by his Letter of this Date applyed to the Commissioners relating to a small Box of Muslins &cetera in the WareHouse at your Port, belonging to Admiral Boscawen; They direct you forthwith to send it up to the Kings WareHouse here, under the Seals of Office at the Proprietors Charge, giving the Board ⌜Notice⌝[51] when & by what Conveyance it is sent, and what agreement is made for Carriage, *valediction 2*

668 CUST 58/150, p. 58

19 June 1750

From J. Evelynn, W. Levinz ('Levine'), R. Chandlor and Edw. Hooper (Custom House, London). Hand iii.

In answer to the Account of Seizures transmitted in your Letters of the 14th & 16th Instant We direct you to Prosecute the Enumerated Goods thereinmentioned to Condemnation in the Exchequer at the Kings Charge, And we have no objection to the Officers Prosecuting the rest of the Goods in like manner at their own Charge Corresponding with our Sollicitor & the Register of Seizures, *valediction 1*

Noted the 22^d^ June 1750

669 CUST 58/1

20 June 1750

From W. C[ooley] and R. T[urvin] (Custom House, Portsmouth). Hand iii.

Inclosed we send your Honours an Account of the Sale of Tackle, Furniture &cetera belonging to a Sloop Seiz'd by Captain Charles Coombs Commander of the Greenhill Yatch at this Port, Condemn'd in Michaelmas Term last, the Kings Moiety whereof amounting to £2. 12. 11 We have this day remitted to H^y^ Simon Esqr Receiver of the Petty Receipts; And in relation to the Sloop which shou'd have been burnt agreeable to your Honours Order of the 24th January last, We are to acquaint your Honours that after she having been hauld up as far as possible on the shore and well fastend, she notwithstanding by means of a very high Tide and a Storm of Wind at the same time, broke loose and drove out of the Harbour, sunk, and is lost beyond all recovery so far as we can judge; And as the Officer was on her being burnt entituled to the usual Reward on such occasions, We humbly refer it to your Honours whether on her being destroyed by this Accident Captain Coombs may not hope for the usual Allowance seeing her not being burnt agreeable to Law & your Honours Order, was occasioned by no neglect or fault of his, which is humbly submitted *valediction 4*

Portsmouth,

An Account of the Sale and Produce of the Tackle, *Apparrel and furniture of a Sloop Seiz'd by Captn Chas Coombs the 6th October 1749 return'd in an Indenture of Appraisement from this Port, Condemn'd in his Majestys Court of Exchequer in Michaelmas Term last, and Publickly sold here by order of the Honourable Commissioners Dated the 24th January 1749

[51] Written only as catchword at foot of page.

Wm Cooley Collector *Debtor* –				Per Contra *Creditor*			
1 Mast, Boom, Bowsprit Gaff and Topsail Yard	1	5	6	Sollicitors Charge in Condemning the Vessel &cetera	1	6	8
1 Mainsail, Foresail, Square Sail & two Jibbs,	3	16	6	Charges in Unriging and Transporting the said Sloop	0	12	0
3 Anchors, 1 Cable, Blocks *Dead Eyes, Old Iron &cetera	2	2	6	Officers Moyetie –	2	12	11
Total Produce	7	4	6		£4	11	7
				By Kings Moyetie remitted to H^y Simon Esqr of William Cooley on Philip Hyat at sight –	2	12	11
					£7	4	6

670
20 June 1750

CUST 58/1

From W. C[ooley] and R. T[urvin] (Custom House, Portsmouth). Hand iii.

In obedience to your Honours Order signify'd to us by Mr Wood in his Letter of the 18th Instant, We are to acquaint your Honours we have this day sent up to the Kings Warehouse under the Seals of Office directed to your Honours by the Waggon of Geo. Clarke which will be at the Whitehart in the Burrough of Southwark on Friday the 22^d instant, a small Box Containing Muslins belonging to Admiral Boscawen for the Carriage whereof we have agreed that Two Shillings & Nine pence shall be paid *valediction 3*

671
21 June 1750

CUST 58/150, pp. 58–9

From W. Wood (Custom House, London). Hand iii.

Captain Hughes of the Lark having applied to the Commissioners in relation to some China &cetera Seiz'd on board his Majestys Ship under his Command, And he having represented that they are for his own private use, you are to report particularly the Circumstances of this Seizure and whether the Officer has any Objection to their being return'd to the Captain *valediction 2*

672
22 June 1750

CUST 58/1

From W. C[ooley] and R. T[urvin] (Custom House, Portsmouth). Hand iii.

Inclosed we transmit your Honours an Account of Goods Enumerated lately Seiz'd by an Officer in this Port, to which we beg leave to refer *valediction 4*

673
23 June 1750

CUST 58/150, pp. 59–60

From W. Wood (Custom House, London). Hand iii.

Mr Thomas Osborne Bookseller of this City having applied to the Commissioners representing that he is inform'd an Edition of a Book Entitled The Report of Cases in Law of the late Willm Peere Williams Esqr in three Voll^s folio is now printed or printing in Dublin, with intent to be Imported into this Kingdom, contrary to an Act made in the 12th Year of his Present Majesty,[52] desiring that Directions may be given to the Officers of the Customs to stop the said Books; And the said Osborne having given it under his hand that he will be at the Expence of Seizing such Books and Prosecuting the Persons importing them, and to give the Officer his Share of all Penaltys & Forfeitures arising by the said Act and also to Indemnify the Officers for all such Seizures; The Commissioners direct you to give it in strict Charge to the Officers at your Port to stop all such Books as shall be Imported giving the Board an Account of your Proceedings *valediction 2*

[52] Statute 12 Geo. II, c.36.

674 CUST 58/150, p. 60
23 June 1750

From W. Westby, J. Evelynn, W. Levinz ('Levine') and Edw. Hooper (Custom House, London). Hand iii.

Inclosed you will receive a Writt of Delivery for the Enumerated Goods return'd in an Indenture of Appraisement from your Port, and Proclaimed in the Exchequer last Term, which have been Condemn'd Amounting to Forty nine Pounds four Shillings and three Pence, We direct you to sell the said Goods Publickly to the highest bidder, putting them up at such Prizes as the Goodness of the Commoditys deserve, *valediction 1*

In margin: Writt Dated 12th June 1750

⌜£49. 4. 3⌝[53]

675 CUST 58/1
23 June 1750

From W. C[ooley] and R. T[urvin] (Custom House, Portsmouth). Hand iii.

Inclosed we transmit your Honours an Account of such Goods as are now in his Majestys WareHouse at this Port, which have been brought in for Security of the Duties, and have here remained unentered upwards of Six Months, to which we beg leave to refer and desire your Honours Orders for the Sale thereof. *Valediction 4*

676 CUST 58/1
23 June 1750

From W. C[ooley] and R. T[urvin] (Custom House, Portsmouth). Hand iii.

In Obedience to your Honours Order signify'd to us by Mr Wood in his Letter of the 21st Instant, We do humbly report the Circumstances attending the Seizure of some China, India Handkerchiefs, Callicoe &cetera on board his Majestys Ship Lark under the Command of Captain Hughes, which are as follows Vizt That on the 3d Instant was Seiz'd having been run out of his Majestys Ship Lark, Fifty three Pounds Tea, Eighty India Handkerchiefs and Twenty seven Pounds of Sewing Silk, immediately after which Mr Mears one of the Tidesurveyors received an Information that there was remaining on board a considerable quantity of Prohibited Goods which was intended to be clandestinely run on shore therefore agreeable to His Information he went on board the said Ship to make a strict Rummage in doing which he found in the Captains Cabbin & the Gunroom the Goods agreeable to the Inclosed Account, which he brought on shore conceiving the same to be justly forfeited; Mr Mears begs to assure your Honours provided you are pleased to order the Seizure to be return'd Captain Hughes, he shall have no Objection thereto, entirely submiting the same to your Honours Consideration, *valediction 5*

PS/ An Account of the Seizure was transmitted your Honours in our joint Letter of the 8th Instant in the usual form

> Portsmouth An Account of the Goods Seizd by Mr Jno Mears Tidesurveyor at this Port, on board his Majestys Ship Lark Capt Hughes from Jamaica Vizt
>
> One box Containing One Dozen Cups and Saucers, One Dozen Coffee Cups, Two Tea Potts and Stands Two Tea Jars, Two Milk Potts, Two Sugar Basons Covers and Stands, Two Slop Basons, Two plates and Two Boats all of China, Two Pieces Containing Forty India Handkerchiefs, Sixteen Muslin Handkerchiefs, One Piece quantity Eleven Yards and a half *Dimity, Six pieces Containing Twenty five Yards *Chints, One India Counterpain and One Piece Containing six Yards Callicoe

677 CUST 58/150, pp. 61–5
25 June 1750

From Pusey Brooke (Custom House, Portsmouth) to the Collector and Controller. Hand iii.

Having Examined your Books and inform'd my self as to the manner in which the Business of this Port has been carried on since my last Survey, I find it necessary to add to those you have before Received, the following Directions and Instructions *valediction 2*

Collector and Comptroller

That in Order to avoid Disputes which frequently happen amongst the Coal Meters and to prevent any attemps in the Coal Merchants by Management to procure favourite Meters, you are to take care that all such Meters are from this day employed in due Course according to the Dates of their respective Deputations, begining first with the Oldest Meter.

---

53 With line above and below; see App. I, no. 25.

To the end that immediate recourse may be had to such Directions as you have already received, or shall hereafter be sent you by the Commissioners, tis necessary that an Index be made in your Book of Orders.

That for the time to come Duplicates of all Ships registered at this Port, are to be transmitted to the Board immediately after such Registers are taken pursuant to an Act pass'd in the 7th & 8th of Wm 3d[54]

That you are to keep Monthly and Quarterly States of Bonds in Books properly prepar'd for that purpose.

That no Goods of the Growth or Produce of the East Indies are under any pretence whatsoever to be Admitted to an Entry let the Quantity be never so small, without an Order being first obtained from the Board

That you are without loss of time to call upon John Moore Master of the George and Ann to pay the Duties of Twenty Chalders and thirteen bushels of Coals which have been due ever since August 1748 and if the same is not immediately paid you are to lay the ⌜whole⌝[55] Case before the Commissioners for their Directions, and you are to be particularly carefull that nothing of the like kind happens for the future.

That Sixty five barrs of Iron were reported the 6th August 1748 in the Ann & Dorothy from Arundel, with which the said Vessell was Suffered to proceed to Sea without an Entry Inwards being made thereof, owing to which, the Dutys have been lost to the Crown, you are therefore to lay a particular Account of this Affair before the Commissioners for their Directions, and be careful to prevent any thing of the like kind for the future, or the Collector will in all such Cases be surcharged with the Dutys since a Report is deem'd in Law an actual Importation

That you are not to pay Captain Coombs either Wages or Victualling Money for a Boy allowed to the Greenhill Yatch, till he has provided one capable of performing the Duty required

Landsurveyor –

That you are frequently to Visit the Coal Meters when Employed on Duty, and in case you observe that they keep their Accounts on loose pieces of paper, or in any Instance make use of Chalk in tallying, you are immediately to lay the same before the Collector & Comptroller in order to the Suspension of such Meter.

Mr Spry Supervisor –

In Order that Thomas Comden Riding Officer at Titchfield which is upwards of Two Miles from any part of the Sea Coast, may be more properly stationed, he is hereby directed to remove from Titchfield to Maon; and you are to take care that from Michaelmas next he accordingly resides at Maon.

Captn Coombs –

That notwithstanding you have been frequently called upon to provide a Boy capable of performing the Duty required from him on board the Greenhill Yatch under your Command yet you have neglected the same, and applied the Money Allowed by the Crown for that purpose to your own private use, for which shamefull behaviour you are hereby reprimanded.

That contrary to the Commissioners general Orders and my repeated Directions it appears that you very generally lye ashore to the great neglect of your Duty, which affords a bad Example to the Mate & Mariners under your Command; and for this extraordinary Misbehaviour you are once more reprimanded, and if the practice is not discontinued for the time to come, I shall be under the necessity of suspending you in order to your Dismission

Mr Norman Coastwaiter

That you are to give diligent attendance at the Custom House or on the Keys, as the Service may require and carefully to enter into your Coast Books all such Sufferances for Landing or Shipping of Goods as shall be Directed to you, and not transcribe the Deputy Customers Books as is now practised by you, for which you are hereby blamed.

Collector & Comptroller

That these Directions & Instructions are to be Enter'd in your Book of Orders, and Copies of so much thereof given to the other Officers as respectively relates to them.

---

54 Statute 7 & 8 Wil. III, c.22.

55 Written above 'Old', which is struck out.

678 | CUST 58/150, pp. 66–7

26 June 1750

From W. Wood (Custom House, London). Hand iii.

Mr West Secretary to the Lords of the Treasury having transmitted to the Commissioners Extract of a Letter from Mr Porter his Majestys Minister at Constantinople to His Grace the Duke of Bedford dated the 13th April last, giving an Account That the Ship New Phillis Capt Long which arrived there from London & Smyrna a few days ago, departs from thence in three days, and as there has been a Plague Accident among the Franks the said Ship will take in very few Goods there, And their Lordships having directed that all necessary precautions be used in Case of the Arrival of any Ships from Constantinople, or Turkey, with foul Bills of health; The Commissioners direct incase the above Ship or any others shall arrive on your Coast with foul Bills of Health, that you do not Suffer the Captain or any of the Crew ⌜to come on Shore,⌝[56] but acquaint them that they must forthwith repair to the place appointed for the Performance of Quarentine & remain there untill Directions shall be given in relation to the Ship & Cargoe, And you are immediately to acquaint the Board of the Arrival of any Ships from Constantinople or Turkey which shall bring foul Bills of health *valediction 2*

679 CUST 58/150, p. 67

30 June 1750

From W. Westby, Sam. Mead and R. Chandlor (Custom House, London). Hand iii.

In answer to the Account of Seizures transmitted in your Letter of the 22^d Instant; We direct you to prosecute the Rum thereinmention'd to Condemnation before the Justices of the Pease at the Kings Charge, acquainting us when Condemn'd *valediction 1*

Noted the 2^d July 1750

680 CUST 58/150, pp. 67–8

30 June 1750

From W. Westby, Sam. Mead and R. Chandlor (Custom House, London). Hand iii.

Mr Matthew Harrison having by his Memorial of the 27th Instant apply'd to us, praying the delivery of One Quarter Cask Spanish Wine Seized on board the Duke Cumberland ⌜R^d⌝[57] Sparshott Master from London for want of a Coast Dispatch, and ⌜Proof⌝[58] having been made here on Oath, from the Entry that the Duties are paid, you are to deliver the said Wine to the Proprietor upon his giving the Officers concern'd a moderate Satisfaction *valediction 1*

Noted the 2^d July 1750

681 CUST 58/1

30 June 1750

From W. C[ooley] and R. T[urvin] (Custom House, Portsmouth). Hand iii.

Herewith we transmit your Honours the Abstract for the Month of June last together with the undermentioned Accounts to which we beg leave to refer *valediction 4*

Nil List of Bonds
Tea & other Goods Enumerated with petty receipts Endors'd
Absent Officers
State of Bonds for Midsummer quarter last

PS/ From the Book kept in this Office it appears that the Weights and Scales Coal & Corn bushels, at this Port were tryed the 5th Instant by the Surveyor and Landwaiters & that they found the same to be exact and true, and that the stamps for marking Hides, Skins, Linnens, Seiz'd Goods & Sail Cloth are in good & Sufficient Repair and fit for the uses design'd.

W C
R T

---

56 Written over an illegible erasure.
57 Inserted.
58 MS. 'Proop'.

682 CUST 58/1

2 July 1750

From W. C[ooley] and R. T[urvin] (Custom House, Portsmouth). Hand iii.

Inclosed we transmit your Honours an Account of Goods Enumerated and Goods not Enumerated lately Seiz'd by the Officers in this Port to which we beg leave to refer *valediction 4*

683 CUST 58/150, p. 68

3 July 1750

From Beaumont Hotham, Edw. Hooper, W. Levinz ('Levine') and M. Stapylton (Custom House, London). Hand iii.

We received your Letter of the 23^{d} Ultimo transmitting an Account of several Goods which have lain in the WareHouse at your Port upwards of Six Months for Security of the Dutys, And direct you to sell the same Publickly to the highest bidder, and apply the Produce agreeable to Law, *valediction 1*

684 CUST 58/1

4 July 1750

From W. C[ooley] and R. T[urvin] (Custom House, Portsmouth). Hand iii.

In our joint Letter of the 8th Ultimo we transmitted your Honours an Account of Goods Enumerated and Goods not Enumerated lately Seizd by the Officers in this Port, but not having yet received your Honours Directions thereupon, we are apprehensive that the said Letter is miscarried, we therefore send your Honours Inclosed a Duplicate of the said Account, to which we beg leave to refer *valediction 3*

685 CUST 58/150, pp. 68–9

7 July 1750

From Beaumont Hotham, Edw. Hooper, W. Levinz ('Levine') and M. Stapylton (Custom House, London). Hand iii.

In answer to the Account of Seizures transmitted in your Letter of the 8th Ultimo We direct you to Prosecute the Tea thereinmentioned to Condemnation in the Exchequer at the Kings Charge; And we have no Objection to the Officers prosecuting the rest of the Goods in like manner at their own Charge Corresponding with our Sollicitor and the Register of Seizures, *valediction 1*

Noted the 9th July 1750

686 CUST 58/150, p. 69

7 July 1750

From Edw. Hooper, G. Vaughan, Sam. Mead and W. Levinz ('Levine') (Custom House, London). Hand iii.

In answer to the Account of Seizures transmitted in your Letter of the 2^{d} Instant, We direct you to Prosecute the Rum and Brandy thereinmentioned to Condemnation in the Exchequer at the Kings Charge, And we have no Objection to the Officers Prosecuting the Sloop, Boat, and Goods in like manner at their own Charge, Corresponding with our Sollicitor and the Register of Seizures, *valediction 1*

Noted the ⌜9th⌝[59] July 1750

687 CUST 58/150, pp. 70–1

7 July 1750

From W. Wood (Custom House, London). Hand iii.

The Commissioners having received an Anonimous Letter setting forth that great Quantities of Brandy is run ashore at Gosport out of the Men of War, Inclosed you will receive Copy of the said Letter, and you are to enquire very strictly into what is therein complained off reporting to the Board your Proceedings *valediction 2*

June 16th 1750

As I thought it my Duty to acquaint you that great part of the Dutys is lost by Smugling, search the Hulk and the Sunk Ships at Sheerness and you will find large Quantitys of Wine and Brandy run aboard of them from Different Boats passing as Merchants Boats so that whole Cargoes are Lodged by the Boatswains of the Hulks Son in Law and others concern'd there; At Portsmouth there they take Brandy on a Venture and run it all ashore at Gosport Jos. Townsend and Mich^{l} Garden and others as they know practice that this 8 or 9 Years and Masters of Men of War and People that you Credit with Deputations at different Ships and Places, I am

Yours to Command at all Times

Q D C[60]

---

59 Altered from '19th'.

60 Possibly '*Quem Decet Celari*' (i.e. who should be hidden).

688 CUST 58/1

7 July 1750

From W. C[ooley] and R. T[urvin] (Custom House, Portsmouth). Hand iii.

Inclosed we transmit your Honours[61] the undermentioned Accounts the Same being due from this Port for Midsummer Quarter last, to which we beg leave to refer *valediction 4*

Corn & other Goods Exported which are Entituled to a Bounty
Naval Stores from Rushia and Levonia
Ships &cetera from the British Plantations in America

689 CUST 58/1

11 July 1750

From W. C[ooley] and R. T[urvin] (Custom House, Portsmouth). Hand iii.

We are to acquaint your Honours on the 9th Instant, Thomas Gorden late a Tidesman and Boatman at this Port, with the Allowance of £5 Per Annum P*er* Incidents resign'd his Deputation *valediction 5*

690 CUST 58/1

12 July 1750

From W. C[ooley] and R. T[urvin] (Custom House, Portsmouth). Hand iii.

By your Honours Order signify'd to us by Mr Wood in his Letter of the 7th Instant, We are directed to Examine into the Circumstances of an Anonimus Letter, sent your Honours, setting forth that great Quantities of Brandy is run on shore at Gosport out of the Men of War; In Obedience to your Honours said Order, We are to acquaint you we have called all the Officers before us, and carefully examined them, touching what is complain'd off in the said Anonimous Letter, and we humbly beg leave to assure your Honours, we have no reason to believe there is any foundation for what is alledged, imagining if such Practices were carried on at this Port they must inevitably be soon discovered by the Officers, who we have no other reason than to believe execute their several Employments faithfully and honestly. *Valediction 5*

691 CUST 58/150, p. 71

14 July 1750

From Beaumont Hotham, G. Vaughan, Sam. Mead and Wil. Levinz ('Levine') (Custom House, London). Hand iii.

Mr Brooke Surveyor General of Hants and Dorset having in his Letter of the 5th instant, transmitted us an Estimate of the Charge of Building a New Shed for the accommodation of the Surveyor and Landwaiters of your Port, Amounting to Eight Pounds, you may order a Shed to be forthwith Built on the best and Cheapest Terms you can, taking care the Charge does not exceed the Estimate, and when finished transmit us the Tradesmens Bills of particulars for our further Orders, *valediction 1*

692 CUST 58/1

14 July 1750

From W. C[ooley] and R. T[urvin] (Custom House, Portsmouth). Hand iii.

We are to acquaint your Honours that on Tuesday last, the 10th Instant John Mears one of the Tidesurveyors at this Port resign'd his Deputation *valediction 5*

693 CUST 58/1

14 July 1750

From W. C[ooley] and R. T[urvin] (Custom House, Portsmouth). Hand iii.

Inclosed we transmit your Honours an Account of Goods Enumerated lately Seiz'd by the Officers in this Port to which we beg leave to refer *valediction 4*

694 CUST 58/1

18 July 1750

From W. C[ooley] and R. T[urvin] (Custom House, Portsmouth). Hand iii.

In our joint Letter of the 12th Ultimo Inclosed we transmitted your Honours an Account of such Stationary Wares as were much wanted for the ⌜use⌝[62] of this Port, and that the last Supply was Crav'd the 25th November 1749, We therefore beg your Honours will be pleased to give Directions that we be immediately supply'd with Stationary Wares, otherwise we must be obliged to supply our selves here in order to carry on the business of the Port, *valediction 3*

---

[61] 'Honours', repeated, struck out.
[62] MS. 'use use'.

695 CUST 58/1

20 July
1750

From W. C[ooley] and R. T[urvin] (Custom House, Portsmouth). Hand iii.

In your Honours Letter of the 23^{d} Ultimo we received a Writt of Delivery for the Enumerated Goods return'd in an Indenture of Appraisement from this Port and Condemn'd in the Exchequer last Term, Amounting to Forty nine Pounds four Shillings & three Pence, the said Goods were in obedience to your Order put up to Sale at the Appraisement, the Brandy was all Sold, but the Tea appraised at 5s Per Pound no one woud bid on, nor shall we be able to get the Appraised Value for the same; We are to acquaint your Honours four Shillings & Six pence Per Pound have been offer'd us for the said Tea, We therefore humbly beg to know if your Honours are pleased to agree to our selling the said Tea for the Price offer'd or to put it up in our next Sale at four Shillings & Six pence Per Pound *valediction 5*

696 CUST 58/150, p. 72

21 July
1750

From G. Vaughan, Edw. Hooper, W. Levinz ('Levine') and M. Stapylton (Custom House, London). Hand iii.

Mr Brooke your Surveyor General having in his Letter of the 30th Ultimo laid before us an Account of the Services of the Riding Officers belonging to your Port, mentioned on the back hereof, who by our Order of the 18th March 1748 were Continued at the Additional Allowances set against their respective Names to Lady=day 1748, And he being of Opinion that it is for the Interest of the Revenue to continue the said Allowances, We therefore agree to Your paying the same accordingly from Lady=day 1748 to Lady day 1750 for which the Collector may take Credit in his Account of Incidents annexing Copy of this Letter with proper Receipts thereto as Vouchers *valediction 1*

		£	s	d
Thos Comden – Riding Officer	from Lady=day 1748 to Lady day 1750 at £5 Per Annum	10.	0.	0
John Wood – Ditto –	The like time at – Ditto –	10.	0.	0
Jno Newnham Ditto –	The like time at Ditto –	10.	0.	0
Jeremiah Fardell – Ditto –	The like time at Ditto –	10.	0.	0
Wm Goddard – Ditto –	The like time at Ditto –	10.	0.	0
		£50.	0.	0

697 CUST 58/1

21 July
1750

From W. C[ooley] and R. T[urvin] (Custom House, Portsmouth). Hand iii.

Inclosed we transmit your Honours an Account of Goods Enumerated & Goods not Enumerated lately Seiz'd by an Officer in this Port, to which we beg leave to refer *valediction 4*

698 CUST 58/150, p. 73

24 July
1750

From W. Levinz ('Levine'), Sam. Mead, Beaumont Hotham and G. Vaughan (Custom House, London). Hand iii.

Mr Brooke Surveyor General of Hants & Dorset, having in his Letter of the 22^{d} Ultimo represented to us that a settled Tidesman has been almost constantly Employed to ⌜assist⌝[63] the Collector in the WareHouse for above Fifty Years at an Expence of Thirty Pounds Per Annum to the Crown and proposing in order to lessen the Charge, to appoint John Stretch weighing Porter to Assist the Collector in the WareHouse in the room of Jno Ring Tidesman and Boatman Deceased, with an Additional Allowance of Ten Pounds Per Annum, to make up his Sallary Thirty Pounds Per Annum, We have agree'd thereto, and the Collector may pay him after the Rate of Ten Pounds Per Annum by Incidents for the said Service from the date of this Order, and take Credit for it from time to time in his Account of Incidents, referring therein to the date hereof. *Valediction 1*

In margin: ⌜1747 Feb 20⌝[64]

---

63 MS. 'assit'.

64 Added, possibly in a different hand.

699
24 July
1750

CUST 58/150, p. 74

From W. Wood (Custom House, London). Hand iii.

Complaint having been made to the Board by the Master Wardens and Fellowship of the Company of Comb Makers of this City setting forth that diverse Combs ready wrought have of late been brought into this Kingdom contrary to Law to the great prejudice of many hundreds of the said Trade, they have therefore prayed that the Commissioners wou'd be pleased to give Directions to their Officers to put the Laws in Execution and not Suffer any Combs to be Admitted to an Entry, as they are Prohibited to be Imported; And the Commissioners having advised with their Sollicitor who has Reported, "That[65] by the Act of 3 Edward 4 Cap 4 Sec 1 Combs are Prohibited to be Imported into this Kingdom, except such as are made and wrought in Ireland, which are not Prohibited," The Commissioners direct you to give it in strict charge to all the officers at your Port, to prevent the Importation and Entry of Combs, except from Ireland, & incase they meet with any, they are to Seize & prosecute the same agreeable to Law, *valediction 2*

700
26 July
1750

CUST 58/150, p. 75

From W. Wood (Custom House, London). Hand iii.

Benjamin Bevis Master of the Industrious Rebecca lately arrived from Malaga having landed here all her Cargoe except three ⌜Hogsheads⌝[66] of Wine reported for your Port; The Commissioners have ordered her to be cleared and to proceed with the said Wine to your Port accordingly, *valediction 2*

701
27 July
1750

CUST 58/1

From W. C[ooley] and R. T[urvin] (Custom House, Portsmouth). Hand iii.

We crave leave to transmit your Honours Inclosed a Petition of the Officers at this Port, who were Employed in the Service of the Quarentine, signed by such of them as are still living, and remaining in the Port, And least the former shou'd be mislaid have likewise sent you Copy of the Account of Charges attending the said Quarentine, Containing the several Allowances Craved by each Officer respectively Amounting in the whole to £612. 1. 10 – In relation to which we beg leave to assure your Honours that what is sett forth in the said Petition is real fact, and truth, that the service was duely attended and faithfully perform'd, and that the Allowances are no more than have usually been paid on the like Occasions: And beg leave to refer it to your Honours Consideration whether the delaying the Payment of such Allowances may not tend greatly to the Disadvantage of the Service in case of another Quarentine, for as none but our best and ablest Tidesmen are fit for such Service, it must be a great Discouragement to them to be obliged to go upon such Service again, while they find themselves under Difficulties by reason of the Expence of the former, for we are assured many of them are still in Debt by that means, and expect relief only from the Payment of the said Allowances; We therefore humbly hope your Honours will take the Case into Consideration, so as we may have Orders for Payment of the said Bill of Quarentine Charges, *valediction 3*

702
28 July
1750

CUST 58/150, p. 75

From W. Levinz ('Levine'), Edw. Hooper and M. Stapylton (Custom House, London). Hand iii.

Inclosed you will receive a Writt of Delivery for the Enumerated Goods, return'd in an Indenture of Appraisement from your Port, and Proclaim'd in the Exchequer last Term, which have been Condemn'd, Amounting to Fifty seven Pounds Two Shilling and Six pence – We direct you to sell the said Goods Publickly to the highest bidder putting them up at such prices as the Goodness of the Commoditys deserve, *valediction 1*

In margin: Writt Dated 19th July 1750
⌜£57. 2. 6⌝[67]

---

[65] Each line of this quotation is introduced by a double quotation mark.
[66] MS. 'H'd'ds' (for 'H'h'ds').
[67] Underlined; see App. I, no. 26.

703
28 July
1750

CUST 58/150, p. 76

From W. Wood (Custom House, London). Hand iii.

By this Post you will receive from Mr Simon the Sollicitor an *Extent against Messrs Philpot and Hutchinson Merchants of this City who are failed considerably Indebted to the Crown; And the Sea Horse Capt Tollman of which they are Owners, being daily expected from York River in Virginia, with a large Cargoe of Tobacco on account of the said Messrs Philpot & Hutchinson; Incase she puts into your Port, you are immediately to carry Mr Simons Directions into Execution and acquaint the Board and him with your Proceedings *valediction 2*

704
28 July
1750

CUST 58/150, pp. 76–7

From W. Wood (Custom House, London). Hand iii.

You are immediately on Receipt hereof to draw out and transmit to the Board an Account of all Tobacco Bonds standing out at Your Port (not Including those have been or are in Process, or Older than three Years) with the Names of the Principals and the Securities, the Dates of the Bonds and the Amount of the Duties for which they are given, as also all such Sums as have been Discharged by Endorsm*ent* on any of the said Bonds, either by Drawbacks or Payment in Money according to the underwritten Form, *valediction 2*

The above Account made out & transmitted 1st Aug*ust* 1750

Dates of the Bonds	Principals Names –	Securities Names	Amount of the Duties for which the Bonds are given.	How much has been Discharged of the said Bonds	To Distinguish whether in Money or by Debentures

705
31 July
1750

CUST 58/150, p. 77

From Edw. Hooper, G. Vaughan, Sam. Mead and W. Levinz ('Levine') (Custom House, London). Hand iii.

In answer to your Letter of the 23^{d} Instant acquainting us that you cannot dispose of the Tea thereinmentioned at the Appraised Value; We direct you to put up the same again ⌜to⌝[68] Publick Sale at the price proposed by you, or such other price as the Goodness of the Comodity deserves *valediction 1*

706
31 July
1750

CUST 58/150, p. 78

From Edw. Hooper, G. Vaughan, Sam. Mead and W. Levinz ('Levine') (Custom House, London). Hand iii.

Captain Barker of his Majestys Sloop the Wasp, having by his Letter of the 25th Instant, applyed to us, desiring that the Goods Seiz'd by him out of a Cutter, as mentioned in your Letter of the 5th March last may be Prosecuted at the Kings Charge, We agree thereto, as the said Goods are Condemn'd and you are to govern your selves accordingly *valediction 1*

707
1 August
1750

CUST 58/1

From W. C[ooley] and R. T[urvin] (Custom House, Portsmouth). Hand iii.

Inclosed we transmit your Honours an Account of all Tobacco Bonds, standing out at this Port, agreeable to the Form sent us in Mr Wood's Letter of the 28th Ultimo, to which we beg leave to refer, *valediction 3*

708
2 August
1750

CUST 58/150, p. 78

From Edw. Hooper, G. Vaughan, Beaumont Hotham and M. Stapylton (Custom House, London). Hand iii.

In answer to the Accounts of Seizures transmitted in your Letters of the 14th & 21st Ultimo We direct you to Prosecute the Enumerated Goods thereinmentioned to Condemnation before the Justices of the Peace, at the Kings Charge, And we have no Objection to the Officers Prosecuting the China Ware in like manner, at their own Charge acquainting us when Condemn'd, *valediction 1*

Noted the 4th Aug*ust* 1750

---

68 Inserted.

709
2 August
1750

CUST 58/1

From W. C[ooley] and R. T[urvin] (Custom House, Portsmouth). Hand iii.

Inclosed we transmit your Honours an Account of Goods Enumerated, lately Seiz'd by an Officer in this Port, to which we beg leave to refer *valediction 4*

710
4 August
1750

CUST 58/150, p. 79

From W. Wood (Custom House, London). Hand iii.

The Speedwell James Creagh Master from Maryland another Ship belonging to Messrs Philpot and Hutchinson being Expected with a Cargoe of Tobacco on Account of the said Messrs Philpot and Hutchinson, Incase ⌜she⌝[69] puts into your Port, you are immediately to carry Mr Simons Directions into Execution and acquaint the Board and him with your Proceedings pursuant to my Letter of the 28th Ultimo *valediction 2*

711
4 August
1750

CUST 58/150, pp. 79–80

From W. Wood (Custom House, London). Hand iii.

The Commissioners direct you to draw out and transmit them as soon as possible an Account of the Number of Hogsheads and quantity of Pounds of Tobacco Imported into and Exported from your Port, with the Net Amount of the Dutys paid and Drawback thereon from Christmas 1748 to Christmas 1749 and from that time to Midsummer 1750 as also an Account of what has been Sent Coastwise and to what Ports for the same time, *valediction 2*

⌜ The above Account transmitted 7th Aug*ust* 1750⌝[70]

712
4 August
1750

CUST 58/150, p. 81

From Edw. Hooper, M. Stapylton, W. Levinz ('Levine') and G. Vaughan (Custom House, London). London). Hand iii.

Having considered your Preparatory Account of Incidents for the Quarter ended at Lady=day last, Amounting to Eighteen Pounds, Eleven Shillings and five pence half penny, The Collector may pay the same with the privity of the Comptroller, and take Credit for it in his Account of Incidents, annexing this Letter with proper receipts thereto as Vouchers.

By Our Order of the 2^{d} June last, we Dismis'd John Forrest Extra Tidesman at Your Port, for being Disguish'd in Liquor, You may pay him his Allowance by Incidents to the Date of ⌜Our⌝[71] said Order, for which the Collector may take Credit in the manner before directed, *valediction 1*

In margin: £18. 11. 5$^{1}/_{2}$[72]

713
6 August
1750

CUST 58/1

From W. C[ooley] and R. T[urvin] (Custom House, Portsmouth). Hand iii.

Herewith we transmit your Honours the Abstract for the Month of July last, together with the undermentioned Accounts to which we beg leave to refer *valediction 4*

Nil List of Bonds
Tea & other Goods Enumerated with petty receipts Endors'd
Absent Officers

PS/. From the Book kept in this Office it appears that the Weights and Scales, Coal & Corn bushels at this Port, were try'd the 5th Ultimo by the Surveyor & Landwaiters & that they found the same to be exact & true & that the Stamps for marking Hides, Skins, Linnens Seiz'd Goods & Sail Cloth, ⌜are in – ⌝[73] good & Sufficient repair and fit for the uses design'd

WC RT

---

69 MS. 'the'.
70 Added.
71 Written over 'this'.
72 With line above and below.
73 Written over an illegible erasure.

714
7 August
1750

CUST 58/150, p. 80

From W. Wood (Custom House, London). Hand iii.

John Tilham being recommended to the Commissioners to be a Tidesman & Boatman at Your Port, in the room of John Forrest deceas'd, They direct you (in case he is to act as a Boatman) to examine into his Qualification and if you find him Sufficiently Qualified, you are by return of the Post to transmit the Board a Certificate thereof, in the manner required by my Letter of the 21st June 1743 *valediction 2*

715
7 August
1750

CUST 58/1

From W. C[ooley] and R. T[urvin] (Custom House, Portsmouth). Hand iii.

In Obedience to your Honours Directions signify'd to us by Mr Wood in his Letter of the 4th Instant, Inclosed we transmit you an Account of Tobacco Imported into & Exported from this Port &cetera agreeable to the Form required to which we beg leave to refer *valediction 3*

Portsmouth

An Account of all the Tabacco Imported into & Exported from this Port, as also what as been sent Coastwise from Christmas 1748 to Christmas 1749

Imported		Nett	Exported –		Drawback	Quantity	To
N° of hogsheads	Number of Pounds *weight*	Amount of Duties Paid	N° of hogsheads Exported	N° of Pounds *weight*	thereon	sent Coastwise	what Ports
203	174,660	623 6 6¼	197 –	171,298	535 6 1½	8 hogsheads & 2 Small Casks came formerly from London 1 hogshead Containing 976 lb's from Cowes	London
The like Account from Christmas 1749 to Midsum*m*er 1750							
						16 Bags Containing 16 Cwt from Weymouth	London

W C R T

Custom House Portsm° 7th Aug*ust* 1750

716
11 August
1750

CUST 58/150, pp. 81–2

From M. Stapylton, W. Levinz ('Levine'), W. Westby and Edw. Hooper (Custom House, London). Hand iii.

In answer to the Account of Seizures transmitted in your Letter of the 2d Instant, we direct you to Prosecute the Brandy thereinmention'd ⌜to Condemnation,⌝[74] in the Exchequer at the Kings Charge Corresponding with our Sollicitor and the Register of Seizures *valediction 1*

717
11 August
1750

CUST 58/1

From W. C[ooley] and R. T[urvin] (Custom House, Portsmouth). Hand iii.

Inclosed we transmit your Honours an Account of Goods not Enumerated lately taken by Captain Hanbury of his Majesty's Sloop Hazard, and Seiz'd by an Officer in this Port, to which we beg leave to refer *valediction 4*

---

74 Inserted.

718
14 August
1750

CUST 58/150, pp. 82–3

From R. Chandlor, Edw. Hooper, W. Levinz ('Levine') and M. Stapylton (Custom House, London). Hand iii.

It appearing by your last Months Abstract that there is remaining in the Collectors, hands the Sum of £500. 16. 5¾ of the Kings Money; We direct you forthwith to Remit the same together with what you have since received to the Receiver General, Pursuant to the Condition of the Collectors Bond.

In answer to the Account of Seizures transmitted in your Letter of the 11th Instant We have no objection to the Officers Prosecuting the Wine thereinmentioned to Condemnation in the Exchequer at the Officers Charge Corresponding with our Sollicitor & the Register of Seizures. And you are to report to us, whether Capt Hanbury has taken up his Commission &cetera to Seize Goods transmitted you in our Letter of the 6th Feb*ruar*y last he having made a Seizure and carried the same into Weymouth. *Valediction 1*

In margin: Noted the 17th Aug*ust* 1750

719
14 August
1750

CUST 58/1

From [W. Cooley] and [R. Turvin] (Custom House, Portsmouth). Hand iii.

Inclosed we transmit your Honours the Charge & Answer of Richard Chambers and James Redstone Tidesmen & Boatmen at this Port, who were boarded on the Ship Lyon of London Wm Tobin Master lately arrived from Cadiz, laden with Salt & Wine for this Port & Amsterdam, having reason to believe the said Officers have been neglectfull of their Duty We have Suspended them, our reasons for so doing We beg leave to acquaint your Honours are as follows

That about two of the Clock in the Morning on Wednesday the 8th Instant was stopt on Gosport Beach by Captain Hanbury of his Majestys Sloop Hazard, ten Casks of Spanish White Wine, who acquainted us had great reason to believe had been Run out of the Lyon Wm Tobin Master then lying at Spithead, (in which Ship Chambers & Redstone was placed as a Guard,) on receiving such an Information from Capt Hanbury Mr Baskerville ⌜Tidesurv*eyo*r⌝[75] at this Port, went on board the said Ship, taking with him the Report the Master had made at the Custom House (Copy of which is herewith Inclosed) by which it will appear Twenty nine Quarter Casks by him was reported, Twenty two for Amsterdam & Seven for Portsmouth, but on Mr Baskerville's examining into the Cargo, agreeable to the Masters report he only found nine, instead of Twenty nine Quarter Casks on board so that there is great reason to believe Twenty Quarter Casks have been run on Shore, ten of which have only been Seiz'd; On the whole we humbly submit it to your Honours Consideration whether by the Circumstances beforementioned it does not appear that a fraud have been Committed and that it has the appearence of a very great neglect of Duty in the Officers who were Boarded on the Ship, altho we dont know on which of the Officers particularly to fix the Charge, or, on ⌜Whose⌝[76] Watch the Fraud was committed, Yet we think it our Duty to lay the same before your Honours, for your Directions thereon, which when received will be duely observ'd *valediction 4*

720
15 August
1750

CUST 58/1

From W. C[ooley] and R. T[urvin] (Custom House, Portsmouth). Hand iii.

On the request of Richard Chambers & James Redstone Officers at this Port, Inclosed we transmit your Honours their Affidavits relating to their Charge for neglect of Duty, which we Yesterday transmitted your Honours in our joint Letter, Off this We beg leave to assure you that neither Chambers who have been an Officer at this Port upwards of Twenty four Years & Redstone One Year, were to our knowledge ever before charged with neglect of Duty, but on the contrary have faithfully & honestly Discharged the trust committed to their Charge and Inspection in the Service of the Customs, We therefore humbly Submit their present Case to your Honours consideration, *valediction 3*

---

75 Written only as catchword at foot of page.

76 Written over an illegible erasure.

721
16 August
1750

CUST 58/150, pp. 83–4

From R. Chandlor, Edw. Hooper, W. Levinz ('Levine') and M. Stapylton (Custom House, London). Hand iii.

We received your Letter of the 14th Instant enclosing the Charge And ⌜Answer⌝[77] of Rd Chambers and James Redstone Tidesmen and Boatmen at your Port who were boarded on the Ship Lyon Wm Tobin Master lately arrived from Cadiz laden with Salt & Wine; And you are immediately on receipt hereof to go on board the said Ship and take an Account of the Marks and Numbers of the Casks of Wine on board, and transmit the same to us, as also the Marks & Numbers of the Casks of Wine that are Seiz'd which you shou'd have done at the time you sent the Account, it being a material Circumstance to have enabled us ⌜to judge⌝[78] this Affair, *valediction 1*

722
16 August
1750

CUST 58/150, p. 84

From R. Chandlor, Edw. Hooper, W. Levinz ('Levine') and M. Stapylton (Custom House, London). Hand iii.

In pursuance of a Warrant of the Treasury, We have Issued our Deputation for Richard Temple to be a Waiter & Searcher at your Port, in the room of John Mears Preferr'd; and when he has perfected the Inclosed Bond with two Securities whose Sufficiency you are to Certify to Mr McSwiney Examiner of Officers Securities, You may admit him to his said Employ, giving him all due Encouragement for his Majestys Service letting him know he must Qualify himself as the Law directs, reporting to us the day he is admitted, and you are to call in Mears Deputation & Cancel it & transmit it to us with your next Accounts by the Carrier, *valediction 1*

723
20 August
1750

CUST 58/1

From W. C[ooley] and R. T[urvin] (Custom House, Portsmouth). Hand iii.

Inclosed we transmit your Honours a Schedule of Accounts, due from this Port for Midsummer Quarter last, the same being this day forwarded by the Waggon of Geo. Clarke which will be at the Whitehart in the Burrough of Southwark on Wednesday the 22d Instant, for the Carriage whereof we have agreed that Two Shillings & Sixpence shall be paid, *valediction 3*

Portsmouth

A ⌜Schedule⌝[79] of Accounts due from this Port for Midsummer Quarter last, sent by the Waggon of Geo. Clarke, which will be at the Whitehart in the Burrough of Southwark on Wednesday the 22d August 1750

Collectors Quarter Book	Preparatory Account of Incidents and Tradesmens Bills
Comptrollers Ditto	Personal Prosecutions
General Incidents w*ith* the Establishm*ent*	Enumerated Goods Per Act 12th Geo 1[80]
10 Bounty } Debentures & 1 Foreign } 1 *over Entry	Ships Reports Inwards & Outw*ar*ds
Coal Incidents	Journals of the Commander & Mate of the Greenhill Yatch
Imports & Exports	Do of the Chief Boatman at Hayling
Wooll bro*ught* & Carried Coastwise	
Civil List Receipt & Repayment	
Deputation of John Mears, Jno Forrest & Thos Gorden	

The undermentioned Accounts for said Quarter was sent the Honble Commissioners the 7th July 1750

Naval Stores from Rushia & Levonia
Corn Exported with the Amount of the Bounty due thereon and other Bountys.
Ships &cetera which Discharged in this Port from the British Plantations

[77] Altered from 'answer'.
[78] Inserted.
[79] Altered from 'chedule'.
[80] Statute 12 Geo. I, c.28.

724
20 August 1750

CUST 58/1

From W. C[ooley] and R. T[urvin] (Custom House, Portsmouth). Hand iii.

We have your Honours Letter of the 16th Instant in which we are directed immediately to go on board the Ship Lyon Wm Tobin Master, to take an Account of the Marks & Numbers of the Casks of Wine, on board the said Ship; We are to acquaint your Honours the said Ship Sailed on her intended Voyage, the very next day after the Wine was Seiz'd, which supposed to be run out of her, but of this we can assure your Honours that the Nine Pipes which stand Reported with the Twenty two Quarter Casks Wine for Amsterdam were Mark'd with the Letters ⌜To⌝[81] as Mr Baskerville the Tidesurveyor who was on board the said Ship, well remembers as to the two Quarter Casks which were only remaining out of the Twenty two reported for Amsterdam one of them Mr Baskerville likewise remembers was Mark'd in the very same manner as those which have been Seiz'd, they being all Mark'd with the Letter F but with no Numbers, In obedience to your Order of the 14th instant, We are to acquaint your Honours Captain Hanbury of his Majestys Sloop Hazard has taken up his Commission &cetera to Seize Goods, but it has been since we were directed by your Honours to report whether he had or not, *valediction 5*

725
22 August 1750

CUST 58/1

From W. C[ooley] and R. T[urvin] (Custom House, Portsmouth). Hand iii.

Inclosed we transmit your Honours Capt Hanburys Bond duely executed *valediction 4*

726
22 August 1750

CUST 58/1

From W. C[ooley] and R. T[urvin] (Custom House, Portsmouth). Hand iii.

In obedience to your Honours Orders of the 16th instant on the 18th we admitted Mr Richard Temple to his Employment of Waiter & Searcher at this Port in the room of Jno Mears preferr'd *valediction 4*

727
22 August 1750

CUST 58/1

From W. C[ooley] and R. T[urvin] (Custom House, Portsmouth). Hand iii.

Inclosed we transmit your Honours an Account of Goods Enumerated lately Seiz'd by the Officers in this Port, to which we beg leave to refer *valediction 4*

728
23 August 1750

CUST 58/150, p. 85

From Beaumont Hotham, Edw. Hooper, W. Levinz ('Levine') and M. Stapylton (Custom House, London). Hand iii.

We received your Letter of the 20th Instant acquainting us with the Marks & Numbers of the Wine which was run out of the Lyon William Tobin Master from Cadiz, and Seiz'd by Captain Hanbury of his Majestys Sloop Hazard. And it appearing that the said Wine was run out of the Ship, whilst Richard Chambers and James Redstone Tidesmen & Boatmen, were Boarded; We have Dismiss'd them, and you are to call in their Commissions & Cancel them, and transmit them to us with your next Accounts by the Carrier *valediction 1*

729
28 August 1750

CUST 58/150, pp. 85–6

From G. Vaughan, Edw. Hooper, W. Levinz ('Levine') and M. Stapylton (Custom House, London). Hand iii.

Application having been made to us, desiring that Geo. Spry Supervisor of the Riding Officers at your Port, may have Leave to be Absent a Month for recovery of his health, We have agreed thereto, without loss of Pay and you are to take care the service does not Suffer during his Absence, *valediction 1*

---

[81] Written as a monogram.

730
28 August
1750

CUST 58/150, p. 86

From G. Vaughan, Edw. Hooper, W. Levinz ('Levine') and M. Stapylton (Custom House, London). Hand iii.

In answer to the Account of Seizures transmitted in your Letter of the 22^d^ Instant, We direct you to prosecute the Goods thereinmentioned to Condemnation in the Exchequer at the Kings Charge, Corresponding with our Sollicitor and the Register of Seizures, *valediction 1*

In margin: Noted the 30th of August 1750

731
30 August
1750

CUST 58/150, pp. 86–8

From W. Wood (Custom House, London). Hand iii.

Mr Samuel Chandler Attorney at your Port, having laid before the Board his Bill of Charges, in carrying on several Prosecutions, And it appearing that no use was made of the two Examinations taken from one Hixon for which the Articles mentioned in the Inclosed Account are Charged Amounting to £6. 11. 11. he being a Person of bad Character; The Commissioners direct you to Examine into the same, and report to them by whose Orders the Business was done, and whether the several Expences charged therein, really attended the same, *valediction 2*

To The Honble Commissioners of the Customs
to Samuel Chandler

Attending Hixon to take Instructions for his Affidavit against Crips and several other Smuglers in Sussex and Hampshire	0.	6.	8
Drawing the same –	0.	13.	4
Engrossing it –	0.	6.	8
Paper and Stamps –	0.	1.	1
*Jurat in the Exchequer –	0.	1.	0
Paid the said Hixon for his Expences in Pursuance & by Order of Mr Cooley the Collector –	0.	8.	0
Paid for Chariot with Clerk to Fareham to get Hixon's further Affidavit against Crips & the other Smuglers as to times and places &cetera but could not meet with him	0.	13.	6
Expences there –	0.	6.	0
Journey and time –	1.	0.	0
Paid for Chaise with the Collector to Fareham to examine the said Hixon again –	0.	13.	6
Expences on both & Horses &cetera –	0.	10.	6
Journey and time –	1.	0.	0
Drawing his Second Affidavit –	0.	6.	8
Ingrossing the same –	0.	3.	0
Stamps and *Jurat –	0.	2.	0
	£6.	11.	11

732
30 August
1750

CUST 58/150, pp. 88–9

From C. Vaughan, Edw. Hooper, Beaumont Hotham and M. Stapylton (Custom House, London). Hand iii.

Having granted our Commission for George Garthwaite to be Extra Tidesman and Boatman at your Port, in the room of James Redstone Dismist, you are to take care he be under Oath & Security for the faithful Discharge of the said Employ, and Qualifies himself as the Law directs, paying him the like Allowance of Five Pounds Per Annum by Incidents as was paid to his Predecessor, for which the Collector may take Credit from time to time in his Account of Incidents refering therein to the date hereof *valediction 1*

PS/ since writing the above the said Garthwaite has given Security here

733
1 September
1750

CUST 58/1

From W. C[ooley] and R. T[urvin] (Custom House, Portsmouth). Hand iii.

Inclosed we transmit your Honours an Account of Goods not Enumerated, lately Seiz'd by the Officers in this Port, to which we beg leave to refer *valediction 4*

734
3 September
1750

CUST 58/1

From W. C[ooley] and R. T[urvin] (Custom House, Portsmouth). Hand iii.

We are to acquaint your Honours last night arrived and was immediately Conducted to the place for the performance of Quarentine by Captain Coombs of the Greenhill Yatch, the Ship Recovery H^{y} Nell Master from Santa Cruize, Inclosed we transmit your Honours the Questions put to the Master of the Ship and his Answers thereto, to which we beg leave to refer. By to Morrows post we shall be able to transmit your Honours a Manifest of the Ships Cargoe together with the Bills of health, *valediction 5*

Questions to be put to the Masters of Ships on their Arrival from the Island of Sicily, or other Places in the Mediterranean

1	The Name of the Ship or Vessel.	The Recovery
2	The Name of the Com*mander* or other Person having Charge of her –	Henry Nell
3	At what place the Cargoe was taken on board –	Santa Cruize
4	What Place or Places the Ship or Vessel touch'd at in her Voyage	Torbay
⌜5	Whether such places, or any, and w*hi*ch of them were infected w*i*th the Plague	None⌝[82]
⌜6⌝[83]	How long such Ship or Vessel has been on her Passage or Voyage	40 Days
7	How many Persons were on board when the said Ship set Sail –	Seven
8	Whether any, and what Persons during thc Voyage on board, have been, or now are infected with the Plague, & what Number are so	None
9	How many Died in the Voyage & of what Distempt*er*;	None
10	What Ships or Vessels, he, or any of his Ships Company went on board during the Voyage	None
11	What Person from other Ships ⌜came⌝[84] on board his in the Voyage and to what place such Ships belong	None
12	The true Contents of his Loading to the best of his Knowledge;	Wooll, Gum, Almonds, Wax Roots & Oyl

N B/ You are by the first opportunity after you have received Answers to the above Questions, to transmit the Same to the Commissioners.

735
4 September
1750

CUST 58/150, pp. 89–90

From W. Wood (Custom House, London). Hand iii.

Mr John Quallett having by his Memorial of the 29th Ultimo applyed to the Commissioners relating to three Casks of *Arrack, landed out of the Young Eagle and Secured in the WareHouse at your Port, I am directed to send you Copy of the said Memorial, and you are to examine into the Allegations therein Contained, and report a true state of the case with your opinion *valediction 2*

May it please your Honours

At the arrival of the Ship Young Eagle under my Command belonging to the Squadron of his Majestys Ships Commanded by the Honourable Admiral Boscawen from the East Indies, there were lodged in the Custom House of this Port, about 160 Gallons of *Arrack in three Casks from the above said Ship, being the remaining part of the Sea Store belonging to Capt Hislop Lieu^{t} Mollman and self, for the Security of his Majestys Dutys, humbly pray your Honours will please to give Orders for its Delivery, I am

Honourable Sirs Your Honours most Ob*edien*t humble Servant

J. Quallett

Portsmouth 29th Aug*us*t 1750

---

[82] Inserted.
[83] Altered from '5'.
[84] Altered from 'cane'.

736
4 September 1750

CUST 58/150, pp. 90–1

From W. Wood (Custom House, London). Hand iii.

In my Letter of the 30th April last I transmitted you an Act of the last Session for Inforcing the Laws against the Clandestine Importation of Soap, Candles, and Stearch into this Kingdom,[85] and the Commissioners having caused several Clauses in the said Act to be printed, have directed me to send you Twenty five of the ⌜*said*⌝[86] Clauses to be Distributed to the Tidesmen and Preventive Officers at your Port, And they direct you to take care that the said Law be Effectually put in Execution, so far as you and they are respectively concern'd, and you are to cause this Letter to be Enter'd in your Book of Orders, and signify the Receipt thereof to the Board by a Postcript to your said Letter. *Valediction 2*

The above Clauses are sent you by the Portsmouth Waggon Wm Connop who sets out the 6th instant

737
4 September 1750

CUST 58/1

From W. C[ooley] and R. T[urvin] (Custom House, Portsmouth). Hand iii.

Inclosed we transmit your Honours the Dayly Muster of the Mariners on board the Ship ⌜Recovery⌝[87] Hy Nell Master lately arrived from Santa Cruize now under Quarentine at this Port, Inclosed we likewise transmit your Honours the Bills of health and Manifest of the Ships Cargoe, to which we beg leave to refer, *valediction 3*

To whom these may concern

An Account of all Goods taken in on board the ⌜Recovery⌝[88] Hy Nell Master at Santa Cruize in South Barbary, in the Months of June and July 1750

Eight large Casks of *Sweet Oil Containing near four Tons
Twenty two Casks of *Gum Sandrick and Six Chests of *Sweet Oil Containing about 4½ Tons,
Thirty seven *Serons of bitter Almonds Containing about 5 Tons
Sixty seven *Serons ⌜Bees⌝[89] Wax Containing about Seven Tons
Seventeen *Seerons of Roots, for Chymists Containing about 3 Tons
Seventy nine Bags of Wooll Containing about 14 Tons
About fifteen Tons of Ballast, besides Provisions all which we carried from London

This is the true Contents on Oath.

Hy Nell

738
5 September 1750

CUST 58/150, pp. 91–2

From Wil. Wood (Custom House, London). Hand iii.

The Commissioners have directed me to acquaint you that they have thought fit to order Capt Frith of the Richmond Sloop and Capt Mears of the George the Second to repair forthwith to your Port, and in Conjunction to conduct from the Motherbank the Ship Recovery lately arrived there from Santa Cruize in Barbary, to Standgate Creek to perform Quarentine, and you are to take care that no person be Suffered to come on shore from the Recovery or go on board her during the time she shall remain in the Motherbank. *Valediction 2*

---

85 Statute 23 Geo. II, c.21.
86 Inserted.
87 MS. 'Reovery'.
88 MS. 'Reovery'.
89 MS. 'Beex'.

739
5 September
1750

CUST 58/1

From W. C[ooley] and R. T[urvin][90] *(Custom House, Portsmouth). Hand iii.*

In your Honours Letter signified to me by Mr Wood I have received inclosed therein Mr Samuel Chandlors Bill of ⌜law⌝[91] Charges, for carrying on several Prosecutions, but it appearing to your Honours that no use was made of the two Examinations taken from Nicholas Hixon for which the articles mentioned in his Bill are Charged, Amounting to £6. 11. 11 your Honours are therefore pleased to direct me to examine into the same, and report by whose Orders the Business was done and whether the several Expences Charged by Mr Chandlor really attended the same; In answer to which I am to acquaint your Honours the Business was done in pursuance of your Orders to me Dated the 15th & 21st April & 20th May 1749 on my transmitting Hixons several Affidavits as will appear by my Letters bearing date the 3^{d}, 7th, 9th and 24th April 6th & 26th May 1749 in which I gave your Honours from time to time an Account of my Proceedings, as to Mr Chandlors Bill that I have Examined and believe the several Expences charged therein really attended the same, with great regard I am

Your Honours &cetera

WC RT

740
6 September
1750

CUST 58/150, pp. 92–3

From W. Levinz ('Levine'), R. Chandlor, W. Westby and G. Vaughan (Custom House, London). Hand iii.

We received your Letter of the 1st instant transmitting an Account of a Seizure, of One hundred and Sixty four half Kegs of Spruce Beer, made by Wm Baskerville & others, on board a Ship from Dantzick, for being concealed and not reported, and having referr'd the same to our Sollicitor, he has reported that it is Forfeited if the Officers can distincly prove that the Seizure was made, before the second report, and that the Master may be Prosecuted for the Treble Value which we signify to you for your Government. *Valediction 1*

741
6 September
1750

CUST 58/1

From W. C[ooley] and R. T[urvin] (Custom House, Portsmouth). Hand iii.

We have your Honours Order signified to us by Mr Wood in his Letter of the 4th Instant, Inclosing Copy of the Memorial of Mr John Quallett to your Honours relating, to three Casks of *Arrack landed out of the Young Eagle and secured in his Majestys Warehouse at this Port, and by your said Order we are directed to report a true state of the Case, with our opinion; In obedience thereto, we are to acquaint your Honours we have Examined into the Allegations of the said Memorial & do report that there is, as set forth in the Memorial of Mr Quallett three Casks of *Arrack landed out of the Young Eagle, now in the Warehouse at this Port, to which the delivery of We have no objection on Payment of the Dutys, provided your Honours approve thereof, it being our opinion the Allegations sett forth in Mr Qualletts Memorial is just & true, *valediction 5*

742
6 September
1750

CUST 58/1

From W. C[ooley] and R. T[urvin] (Custom House, Portsmouth). Hand iii.

Inclosed we ⌜transmit⌝[92] your Honours an Account of the Musters of the Mariners on Board the Recovery now under Quarentine at this Port, as taken by Capt Coombs of the Greenhill Yatch, to which we beg leave to refer *valediction 3*

---

[90] As the first person singular is used throughout the letter, it is probably from Cooley alone, though signed with Turvin's initials as well.
[91] Inserted.
[92] MS. 'tramit'.

743
6 September
1750

CUST 58/1

From W. C[ooley] and R. T[urvin] (Custom House, Portsmouth). Hand iii.

Herewith we transmit your Honours the Abstract for the Month of Aug*ust* 1750 together with the undermentioned Accounts, to which we beg leave to refer *valediction 4*

Nil List of Bonds
Tea and other ⌜Goods⌝[93] Enumerated w*ith* Petty Receipts Endors'd
Absent Officers

PS/ From the Book kept in this Office it appears that the Weights & Scales, Coal and Corn bushels at this Port, were tryed the [94] Ultimo by the Surveyor & Landwaiters, & that they found the same to be exact & true, and that the Stamps for marking Hides, Skins, Linnens, Seiz'd Goods & Sail Cloth are in good and Sufficient repair & fit for the uses design'd

W C R T

744
8 September
1750

CUST 58/150, p. 93

From W. Levinz ('Levine'), G. Vaughan, M. Stapylton and W. Westby (Custom House, London). Hand iii.

In answer to the Account of Seizures transmitted in your Letter of the 4th instant We direct you to Prosecute the Goods thereinmentioned to Condemnation before the Justices of the Peace at the Kings Charge, acquainting us when Condemn'd, *valediction 1*
In margin: Noted the 11th of Sept*ember* 1750 –

745
8 September
1750

CUST 58/1

From W. C[ooley] and R. T[urvin] (Custom House, Portsmouth). Hand iii.

Inclosed we transmit your Honours an Account of the Dayly Muster of the Persons on board the Recovery Hy Nell Master from Santa Cruize now under Quarentine at the Motherbank, sign'd by Capt Coombs of the Greenhill Yatch to which we beg leave to refer *valediction 4*

PS/ The above Ship still remains at the Motherbank, Captn Mears of the Geo*rge* the 2d is arrived here as mentioned in your Honours Letter of the 5th but Capt Frith of the Richmond Cutter is not yet arrived, as soon as he does we shall take care to send the Vessel round agreeable to your Order.

746
8 September
1750

CUST 58/1

From W. C[ooley] and R. T[urvin] (Custom House, Portsmouth). Hand iii.

Inclosed we transmit your Honours a Certificate whereby it will appear that Capt Coombs of the Greenhill Yatch, in the Service at this Port, hath duely perform'd his Contract agreeable to what was transmitted in our joint Letter bearing date the 13th November 1743 Vizt for the Quarters ended Lady day & Midsummer last, and therefore we pray your Honours Order for paying the said Capt Coombs the Sum of Twenty three Pounds five Shillings, being after the rate of Thirty Shillings Per Ton Per Annum for Thirty one Tons Burthen, *valediction 5*

PS/ We have received your Honours Order signify'd to us by Mr Wood in his Letter of the 4th Instant which we shall take care be duely observ'd

W C R T

Portsmouth

These are to Certify that upon a Carefull Survey made for the half Year ended at Midsummer last, it appeared to us that the Greenhill Yatch and Boats belonging to her Employed in the Service of his Majestys Customs at this Port together with all the Materials have been duely kept and are in good & Sufficient repair; And that Captain Coombs the Commander thereof, Hath well and duely perform'd his Contract & is thereby Entituled to half a Years Allowance amounting to Twenty three Pounds, five Shillings Witness our hands at the Custom House this 8th Sept*ember* 1750

W Cooley Collector — Wm Baskerville Tidesurv*eyo*r
R Turvin Deputy Comptroller — Wm Read Shipw*righ*t

---

93 MS. 'Goods Goods'.
94 Space left blank.

747
10 September
1750

CUST 58/1

From W. C[ooley] and R. T[urvin] (Custom House, Portsmouth). Hand iii.

Inclosed we transmit your Honours an Account of the Daily Muster of the Persons on board the Recovery H^y Nell Master from Santa Cruize now under Quarentine at the Motherbank, as taken by Capt Coombs of the Greenhill Yatch, to which we beg leave to refer *valediction 4*

748
11 September
1750

CUST 58/150, pp. 93–5

From Wil. Wood (Custom House, London). Hand iii.

Mr Thomas Warren having by his Memorial of the 7th instant, applyed to the Commissioners relating to One hundred & Seventy nine half Kegs of Spruce Beer under Seizure at your Port for being concealed and not reported, Inclosed you will receive Copy of the said Memorial, and you are to Examine into the Allegations therein contained, and report a true State of the Case to the Board for their further Orders, *valediction 2*

Honourable Sirs

I am desired to acquaint your Honours that the Ship Adelgunda Euphrosia Joachim Hoephner Master, is arrived at Portsmouth from Dantzick, and that when the said Master Reported his Ships Cargoe, he Reported One hundred Kegs of Spruce Beer and at the same time told the Collector that incase he found there was any more on board belonging to his Men, he wou'd come and make a Post report, which the Collector readily consented to, and on a strict enquiry amongst his Men, he found they had a large Quantity on which he went onshore to the Custom House and reported them, but the Surveyor of the Port going on board the Ship whilst the Master was at the Custom house, and finding One hundred and seventy nine Half Kegs of Spruce Beer, has taken them away and refuses admitting them to an Entry, they not being in the first report, and as the Master had been admitted to make a Second Report in which they were included before the Surveyor had laid hands on them; and as it is humbly presumed such a Quan*tity* cou'd not possibly be concealed, I am desired to crave your Honours Order, they may be admitted to an Entry, I am

Your Honours most Obedient humble Servant
Thomas Warren

7th Sept*ember* 1750

749
11 September
1750

CUST 58/150, p. 96

From M. Stapylton, W. Levinz ('Levine'), J. Evelynn and G. Vaughan (Custom House, London). Hand iii.

We received your Letter of the 6th Instant in return to the Memorial of Mr Jno Quallett relating to three Casks of *Arrack landed out of the Young Eagle, and secured in his Majestys Warehouse at your Port, and it appearing that there was no design of Fraud, You are to deliver the said *Arrack to the Proprietors on their paying the duties for the same, *valediction 1*

750
11 September
1750

CUST 58/1

From W. C[ooley] and R. T[urvin] (Custom House, Portsmouth). Hand iii.

Inclosed we transmit your Honours signd by Capt Coombs of the Greenhill Yatch an Account of the daily Muster of the Persons on board the Recovery H^y Nell Master from Santa Cruize which Ship proceeded this day from the Motherbank for Stangate Creek under the care of the Richmond and George the Second, Cutters pursuant to your Honours Order of the 5th Instant *valediction 5*

751
12 September
1750

CUST 58/150, pp. 96–7

From W. Levinz ('Levine'), M. Stapylton, J. Evelynn and R. Chandler (Custom House, London). Hand iii.

Having granted our Commission for Richard Mann and John Tilham to be Preferable Tidesmen and Boatmen at your Port, in the room of Richard Chambers dismist and John Forrest deceas'd; You are to take care they be under Oath & Security for the faithfull Discharge of the said Employ, paying them the like Allowance by Incidents as was paid to their Predecessors, for which the Collector may take Credit from time to time in his Account of Incidents referring therein to the date hereof, *valediction 1*

752
13 September
1750

CUST 58/150, p. 97

From W. Levinz ('Levine'), M. Stapylton, J. Evelynn and G. Vaughan (Custom House, London). Hand iii.

Having granted our Deputation for John Tilham to be a Coalmeter at your Port, You are to take care he be under Oath and Security for the faithfull Discharge of the said Employ and Qualifies himself as the Law directs, *valediction 1*

753
14 September
1750

CUST 58/1

From W. C[ooley] and R. T[urvin] (Custom House, Portsmouth). Hand iii.

We have your Honours Order signified to us by Mr Wood in his Letter of the 11th Instant, together with the Memorial of Mr Thomas Warren relating to 179 half Kegs Spruce Beer under Seizure at this Port, for being concealed on board the Ship Euphrosia Joackem Hoephner Master from Dantzick, and not reported; In obedience to your Honours Order we have examined into the Allegations of Mr Warrens Memorial, and Inclosed we transmit your Honours a State of the Case, which we have received from Mr Baskerville one of the Tidesurveyors who made the said Seizure, to which we beg leave to refer your Honours. In the first part of Mr Warrens Memorial to your Honours he mentions that when the Master Reported his Ships Cargoe, he Reported One hundred Kegs of Spruce Beer and at the same time told the Collector that in case he found any more on board belonging to his Men he wou'd come and make a Post Report (this is true) and the Collector did tell the Master at the time he swore him to his Report, that if he shoud find any more Spruce Beer on board than what he had first Reported, that it woud be proper to make an addition to his said Report *valediction 5*

Gentlemen

You having been pleased to communicate to me a Letter from Mr Secretary Wood, Inclosing the Memorial of Mr Thos Warren in relation to a large Quantity of Spruce Beer which I seizd out of the Ship Adelgunda Euphrosina Jochim Hoephner Master from Dantzick; In answer to which I beg leave to observe that on the 28th Ultimo I went on board the said Ship in order to make a Rummage having great reason to believe that there was a much larger Quantity on board than what the Master had Reported at the Customhouse, which was only One hundred half Kegs and which was Enter'd and landed, before I went off to make the said Rummage, when I came on board the said Ship was inform'd the Master was on shore, on which I made my Application to the Mate & Mariners, and asked them if there was any more Spruce Beer then on board to which being answered in the Negative, I proceeded to make a strict Rummage in the Execution of which I found Concealed in the Cargoe of Plank & Pipe Staves One hundred & twenty six half Kegs Spruce Beer, all which I Seiz'd & brought on shore to his Majestys Warehouse. Mr Warren in his Memorial to the Commissioners setts forth that the said Spruce Beer was Included in the Masters Second Report before I laid hands on them which is false, for during the time I was Rummaging the said Ship (and[95] had Seiz'd the greatest part of the said Beer) the Master came down on the Jetty head alongside of which his Ship lye and seeing me and the Tidesmen on board and being inform'd by his People that his Ship had been Search'd and the said Spruce Beer found & Seizd went

[95] MS. omits opening bracket.

immediately to the Customhouse and made an Addition to his Report of Two hundred half Kegs, which Addition I am Possitively assured was not made till all or the greatest part of the said Spruce Beer was Seizd – Mr Warren in his Memorial further ⌜presumes⌝[96] to alledge that the same cou'd not possitively be concealed it being so large a Quantity.

In answer to which I (as well as the Tidesmen who Assisted in making the said Seizure) am ready if required to make Affidavit that the same was Secreted and Concealed in Several parts of the Ship and that in the most artfull manner – I further beg leave on this occasion to observe that some time after I had made the said Seizure the Master came to me and treated for a Composition, telling me that if I woud relinquish the same he wou'd make me sufficient satisfaction; I have only further to observe that the Mariners on board the said Ship whose Property the said Spruce Beer was, finding the same was Seiz'd and justly forfeited, ⌜Confess'd to y^e ⌝[97] Tidesmen on board that the same was never intended to have been Reported or Entered; I am humbly of Opinion these reasons will be thought Sufficient for Prosecuting the said Seizure, as it evidently appears the same was intended to have been clandestinely run and that what is alledged by Mr Warren in his Memorial will be deem'd but a Slender pretence to cover a plain intended Fraud, and as such is humbly submitted to the Honourable Board, being with great regard Gentlemen

Your most &cetera

Wm Baskerville Tidesurv*eyo*r

Sept*ember* 14th 1750

To The Collector & Comptroller

754
20 September
1750

CUST 58/150, pp. 97–8

From J. Evelynn, R. Chandlor, W. Westby and M. Stapylton (Custom House, London). Hand iii.

We received your Letter of the 8th Instant Inclosing a Certificate whereby it appears that the Greenhill Yatch and Boats belonging to her in the Service at your Port, under the Command of Captain Coombs, are in good and Sufficient repair. The Collector may pay the Commander thereof the usual Allowance for keeping the said Yatch and Boats in Wear and Tear, for the Quarters ended at Lady day and Midsummer last, and take Credit for the same in his Account of Incidents annexing this Letter with proper receipts thereto as Vouchers, *valediction 1*

In margin: ⌜Original transmitted with the Account of Salarys and Incidents for Christmas Quarter 1750⌝[98]

755
20 September
1750

CUST 58/150, p. 98

From J. Evelynn, R. Chandlor, W. Westby and M. Stapylton (Custom House, London). Hand iii.

The Collector and Comptroller of the Customs at Sunderland, having in their Letter of the 25th Ultimo acquainted us that the Fortune Wm Tewart Master was Cleared there the 2^d April last, with 56 Cha*ldron*s Coals New Castle measure for Yarmouth; and it appearing that the said Ship Sailed from your Port to Arundel, We direct you to report to us what part of the abovementioned Coals were landed at your Port, in the whole and what Duties were paid for the same, *valediction 1*

756
22 September
1750

CUST 58/1

From W. C[ooley] and R. T[urvin] (Custom House, Portsmouth). Hand iii.

Inclosed we transmit your Honours an Account of such Stationary Wares as was received at this Port the 6th Instant all which shall be managed with the greatest frugality *valediction 4*

---

96 MS. 'persumes'.

97 Inserted in space left blank or written over an illegible erasure.

98 Added.

Allow'd Portsmouth

4 Quire Quarter Book Paper Inw_ar_ds	1 Q_uar_t red Ink & Stone bottle
⌜3 Quire Reports Outwards⌝[99]	3 Sand Boxes, 3 Bags Sand
3 Rheams fine *Pott	
⌜1 Report book Inwards⌝[1]	1500 Quills
9 Quire *Demy	12 Pastboard files with Tags
⌜2 Journal books Sloop⌝[2]	
3 Quire *Imperial	1 Doz_en_ lead Pencils
⌜2 Quire Paper for Wooll bro_ugh_t & Carried Coastwise⌝[3]	
4 Rheams 2^{d} *Pott	3 Bodkins
⌜2 Quire *Over Entrys⌝[4]	1 Book *Imperial⌜*V_at_ B_lued_⌝[5]
50 Blue Books – 2 Leaves	½ Pound *Pounce
40 – 8 Leaves	2 Gallons Black Ink & *Rundlet
	4 Round Pewter Stand Dishes
20 – 14 Leaves	4 Books 1 Quire *Demy in Marble
80 – 4 Leaves	3000 Wafers, 3 Doz_en_ Tags for files
60 – 6 Leaves	3 Penknives, 1 Dozen Tape
30 – 10 & 12 Leaves	2 Alphabet books 4 Quire *Demy
12 – 16. 20 & 24 Leaves	1 lb' Sealing Wax
1 Dozen *Demy Pocket Books	4 Quire Reports Inw_ar_ds 2 Quire Coal Warrants
2 Quire Damage Certificates, 1 Abstract book	1 Report Book Outwards
2 Books Quarterly Accounts of Enumerated Goods, 3 D^{o} Loose	1 Permit Book, 2 Quire Baggage Sufferances –

⌜2 Quire *Over Entrys, 2 Quire Petty Receipts, 1 Quire Abstracts⌝[6]

99 Inserted.
1 Inserted.
2 Inserted.
3 Inserted.
4 Inserted.
5 Or, possibly, 'V_ellum Bound_'.
6 Written between the two columns with the book turned sideways.

Appendix I

Portsmouth entries in the register of seizures 1748–1750

These are all the entries indexed under (and headed) Portsmouth in the three annual volumes of the register of seizures covering the period from Christmas 1747 to Christmas 1750: P.R.O. CUST 21/52–54. The contents of the volumes are 'A Transcript of all the Indentures of Appraisement Entered with the Register of Seizures'. A single entry may include goods from more than one seizure but they will all come from a single port.

For the procedure in seizure cases see pp. xxv–xxvi. The date of registration, heading the entry in the register, is here given in the margin. In each entry the register names only one of the officers making the seizures, others being simply 'etc.'; his name is followed often by a number of which the significance is not clear and by a date which is probably that of the earliest seizure included in the entry. The name with a sum of money that follows the total in some entries is presumably that of the purchaser who has paid more than the appraised value of the goods.

Most of the incorrect addition noted below (App. I, nos 2, 4, 14, 31) probably comes from miscopying individual items; thus in no. 31 the amount of the moiety shows that the total is correct as given. In App. I, no. 7, however, the total is almost certainly given incorrectly here, correctly in no. 290: £132.15s. from 590 lb. of tea would be exactly 4s.6d. a pound.

Calendared.

1 CUST 21/52, ff. 70v–71r

23 June 1748 Foster Perry, etc., 19 Nov. 1747.

	£	s.	d.		£	s.	d.
32 lb. chocolate	1	1	4	3½ yds *dowlas		3	6
8 yds *dowlas		6	8	5 gall. Lisbon wine	1	5	0
3 handkerchieves		3	0	6¾ yds *duroy		7	10½
19 gall. red wine	4	15	0	8¼ yds silk	1	13	0
5 bottles oil		7	6	6¼ yds *camlet ('Camblet')		18	9
87¼ yds *hollands linen	8	14	6	52½ yds blue silk	7	17	6
69¼ yds *Britannias linen	2	17	8½	119 yds black silk	14	17	6
41 yds *diaper	3	1	6	76½ yds *diaper	5	14	9
202 yds canvas	8	8	4	108 yds *hollands linen	6	15	0
11 pairs cotton stockings		13	9	12 cotton handkerchieves		6	0
63½ gall. port wine	11	18	1½	6½ yds striped cotton		10	10
28 pairs milled stockings	1	8	0	29¾ yds flowered linen	1	2	3¾
27 pairs worsted stockings	2	7	3	26½ yds checked linen		19	10½
8 cotton handkerchieves		8	0	96 pairs small silk stockings	4	16	0
64 yds Dutch calico	11	4	0	5lb. 13oz. sewing silk	4	13	0
24 yds Dutch calico	2	2	0				
					111	17	6¾

13 Aug. 1748: discharged on recovery in the Court of the Exchequer, 'as appears per Tally dated the 9 Instant'; King's moiety £55. 18s. 9½d. *Initials of* R[ic.] C[handler].

2
23 June 1748

CUST 21/52, ff. 71v–72r
John Ring, etc., no. 1, 27 July 1747.

	£	s.	d.		£	s.	d.
2 gall. brandy		11	0	12 lb. 12 oz. tea	3	3	9
4 lb. 2 oz. raw coffee		6	2¼	8 gall. *geneva	2	0	0
3¾ gall. *geneva		18	9	153 lb. tobacco	3	16	6
14 gall. brandy	4	4	0	15 gall. brandy	3	15	0
9¼ gall. brandy	2	6	3	47½ gall. brandy	11	17	6
13 gall. rum	4	2	3	2 lb. tea		10	0
8 lb. 6 oz. tea	2	1	10½	5 gall. brandy	1	5	0
25 gall. rum	7	10	0	29 gall. brandy	7	5	0
51 lb. tea	12	15	0				
					68	7	0¾ [1]

Condemned and discharged; writ of delivery 14 July 1748. [2]

3
21 October 1748

CUST 21/52, ff. 129v–130r
James Martin, etc., no. 3, 11 July 1748.

	£	s.	d.		£	s.	d.
343 lb. tobacco	8	11	6	76½ gall. brandy	22	19	0
44 gall. rum	13	4	0	28 gall. rum	9	2	0
6 lb. tea	1	7	0	104 lb. tobacco	2	12	0
22¼ gall. brandy	5	19	3	4 gall. *arrack	2	0	0
					65	14	9

Condemned and discharged; writ of delivery 13 Dec. 1748. [3]

4
21 November 1748

CUST 21/52, ff. 125v–126r
Ric. Dick, etc., no. 1, 25 June 1748.

	£	s.	d.		£	s.	d.
1 lb. 10 oz. tea		7	3¾	72 gall. *geneva	16	4	0
4 gall. brandy	1	0	0	7½ gall. brandy	1	17	6
778½ lb. tobacco	19	7	9	3 lb. tea		13	6
61 gall. rum	18	6	0	36 gall. *arrack	18	0	0
					76	6	0¾ [4]

Condemned and discharged; writ of delivery 13 Dec. 1748. [5]

5
21 November 1748

CUST 21/52, ff. 127v–128r
Wil. Baskerville, no. 18, 16 Sept. 1748.

	£	s.	d.
898 gall. brandy	269	8	0

'Claim'd by (*space left blank*)' [6]

---

[1] Correctly £68.8s.0¾d.
[2] See no. 82.
[3] See no. 221.
[4] Correctly £75.16s.0¾d.
[5] See no. 221.
[6] See nos 129, 131, 153, 162, 173, 323, 365, 425.

6 CUST 21/52, f. 129v–130r

21 November 1748 Ric. Chambers, etc., 20 June 1748.

	£	s.	d.
36 lb. chocolate	1	4	0
42 gall. red wine	5	5	0
80 lb. *castile soap	2	13	4
74 lb. wax candles	1	17	0
100 lb. tallow candles	1	13	4
50 gall. Madeira wine	7	3	0
13 gall. port wine	2	12	0
48½ yds flowered and striped satin	6	1	3
Boat, oars	1	10	0
55 gall. port wine	9	15	0
43 gall. Spanish wine	8	12	0
29 flasks Florence wine		9	8
280 lb. sheep's wool	7	0	0
56 lb. worsted	7	9	4
24 gall. wine	1	4	0
Trimming for lady's sash	1	1	0
Gauze handkerchief, embroidered with gold	1	1	0

	£	s.	d.
2 pair women's ruffles and 1 pair men's ruffles, wrought	2	2	0
Black silk *capuchin with lace		5	0
1 dozen pairs women's gloves		4	0
12 remnants (45 yds) of ribbon		12	0
3 snuff-boxes		8	0
40¼ yds black velvet	32	4	0
8 yds silk		16	0
3 yds white *dimity		3	0
2 yds yellow *holland		2	0
1½ yds woollen crepe ('Krap')		1	6
10 lb. Spanish snuff	2	0	0
21½ gall. red wine	3	6	6
	108	14	11
Sam. Hood	5	0	0

Condemned and discharged; writ of delivery 13 Dec. 1748.[7]

7 CUST 21/53, ff. 20v–21r

8 February 1748/9 Cha. Markland, etc., no. 7, 20 July 1748.

	£	s.	d.
590 lb. *bohea tea	132	5	0[8]

Condemned and discharged; writ of delivery 28 Feb. 1748/9.[9]

8 CUST 21/53, ff. 53v–54r

5 May 1749 Jos. Seale, etc., no. 14, 15 Feb. 1748/9.

	£	s.	d.
8½ gall. rum	2	11	0
23 gall. rum	6	18	0
15 gall. rum	4	10	0
286 lb. tobacco	5	19	2
4 gall. *Hungary water	1	12	0

	£	s.	d.
9 gall. rum	2	18	0
1000 lb. tobacco	20	16	8
4 gall. brandy	1	0	0
196 gall. brandy	44	2	0
	90	6	10

Condemned and discharged; writ of delivery 24 May 1749.[10]

7 This note, opposite App. I, no. 3, on f. 130r, probably applies to App. I, no. 6, as well.
8 £132.15s. in no. 290.
9 See nos 87, 92, 186, 208, 290.
10 See no. 349.

9 CUST 21/53, ff. 58v–59r

5 May 1749 Henry Duncan, etc., no. 4, 6 Nov. 1748.

	£	s.	d.		£	s.	d.
58 lb. tobacco	1	4	2	38 gall. rum	11	8	0
38 gall. rum	12	7	0	12 gall. rum	3	12	0
30½ gall. rum	10	2	0	18½ gall. rum	5	19	6
20½ gall. rum	6	19	0	4 gall. brandy	1	0	0
19 gall. rum	6	8	6	4½ gall. *arrack	2	5	0
1 lb. 10 oz. tea		7	8½	4½ gall. rum	1	9	3
40 gall. *geneva	9	0	0	2¼ gall. brandy		12	4½
15 gall. rum	4	17	6	3 gall. rum		19	6
148 lb. tobacco	3	1	8	13 gall. brandy	3	18	0
12 gall. rum	3	12	0	7 gall. rum	2	9	0
					91	12	2

Condemned and discharged; writ of delivery 23 May 1749. [11]

10 CUST 21/53, ff. 58v–59r

6 May 1749 Wil. Tasker, etc., 8 Nov. 1748.

	£	s.	d.		£	s.	d.
26 gall. white wine	6	10	0	1 firkin cod's sounds		5	0
28 gall. Lisbon wine	5	12	0	2 Turkey mats	3	13	6
28 gall. Spanish wine	5	12	0	Small boat, oars	1	10	0
Wherry boat and materials	3	10	0	11 painted straw mats	2	4	0
				28 gall. wine	5	1	6
37 lb. refined sugar		12	4	3 pairs *holland sheets, 64½ yds	4	16	9
50 lb. Irish soap		16	8				
45 gall. spruce beer	1	2	6	15 yds *dimity	1	10	0
					42	16	3
				Sam. Hood	1	0	0

King's moiety £21.18s.1½d., paid into the Exchequer 2 June 1749.

11 CUST 21/53, ff. 74v–75r

10 June 1749 Ric. Chambers, etc., 10 May 1749.

	£	s.	d.
50½ yds velvet	40	8	0
17½ yds white *dimity	3	1	3
40 muslin handkerchieves, bordered	6	10	0
66 yds *dimity	12	6	0
	62	5	3
John Banks	6	0	0

Moiety £34.2s.7½d., paid into the Exchequer 4 Aug. 1749.

12 CUST 21/53, ff. 74v–75r

10 June 1749 Wil. Baskerville, etc., 29 May 1749.

	£	s.	d.		£	s.	d.
6 pieces, 8 quarters wide, of clear muslin	78	0	0	India *dimity counterpane, wrought	5	5	0
1 piece, 6 quarters wide, of *book clear muslin	15	0	0	Boat, oars, rudder	3	10	0
12 muslin aprons, clear	10	16	0	17½ yds muslin, stamped	5	5	0
					117	16	0
				Sam. Hood	5	0	0

Moiety £61.8s., paid into the Exchequer 1 July 1749.

[11] See no. 349.

13
10 June
1749

CUST 21/53, ff. 74v–75r

Wil. Baskerville, etc., 29 May 1749.

	£	s.	d.
13 pieces of *morees, ell wide	39	0	0
1 piece of *morees, yard wide	5	10	0
5 pieces of *morees, 6 quarters wide	26	5	0
Boat, oars, anchor	2	15	0
	73	10	0
Sam. Hoods	1	0	0

Moiety £37.5s., paid into the Exchequer 1 July 1749.

14
22 October
1749

CUST 21/53, ff. 128v–129r

Wil. Baskerville, etc., no. 7, 28 Apr. 1749.

	£	s.	d.		£	s.	d.
8½ gall. rum	2	11	0	32½ lb. tea	9	4	3
28 gall. *arrack	14	0	0	17½ lb. tea	4	7	6
18 gall. rum	5	8	0	176 lb. coffee	18	1	0
16¼ gall. brandy	4	13	5	25½ gall. brandy	20	0	3
25¼ lb. tea	7	4	3				
					72	9	8[12]

Condemned and discharged; writ of delivery 13 Dec. 1749.[13]

15
22 November
1749

CUST 21/53, ff. 129v–130r

Wil. Hyslop, no. 7, 24 Aug. 1749.

	£	s.	d.
170 gall. rum	51	0	0
148 gall. brandy	37	0	0
27 lb. *bohea tea	6	15	0
	94	15	0

Condemned and discharged; writ of delivery 13 Dec. 1749.[14]

16
22 November
1749

CUST 21/53, ff. 129v–130r

Tho. Merritt, etc., 20 June 1744.

	£	s.	d.
Several parcels of prohibited East India goods, 'vizt Silks *Chints Counterpanes *Cherryderry &c"	44	9	4
Sherwood	1	0	0

One-third £15.3s.1½d., paid into the Exchequer 22 Dec. 1749.

---

[12] Correctly £75.9s.8d.

[13] See no. 530.

[14] See no. 530.

17 CUST 21/53, ff. 129v–130r
22 November 1749 Wil. Baskerville, etc., 3 Sept. 1749.

	£	s.	d.		£	s.	d.
80 yds *holland	12	0	0	4 artificial flowers, 2 dog's collars		6	0
12½ yds flowered silk	1	11	3	4 pairs necklaces, 1 stone ring		9	0
7½ yds yellow silk	1	6	3	4 small boxes with fishes for cards		5	0
19 yds blue flowered silk	4	15	0	4 pairs women's slippers, 16 fans	1	3	0
58 yds flowered and checked cotton	3	19	0	4 horn tobacco-boxes, 1 dozen large spoons, 1 dozen teaspoons, soup ladle		7	0
10 yds silver lace	2	10	0	4 boats and materials	25	10	0
3 gauze embroidered handkerchieves	1	17	6		60	2	0
2 worked and 6 gauze caps	1	7	0	John Percival	1	0	0
2 tippets, 2 stomachers		5	0	Sloop, about 14¾ tons, with tackle, etc.	14	14	0
3 pairs ear-rings ('Drops for the Ears)'	1	1	0				
3 dozen stone waistcoat buttons	1	10	0				

Condemned and discharged; writ of delivery 13 Dec. 1749. [15]

18 CUST 21/53, ff. 129v–130r
22 November 1749 Cha. Coombes, no. 1, 6 Oct. 1749.

	£	s.	d.
172 gall. brandy	43	0	0
90 gall. rum	27	0	0
9 lb. tea	2	5	0
	72	5	0

Condemned and discharged; writ of delivery 13 Dec. 1749. [16]

19 CUST 21/53, ff. 130v–131r
22 November 1749 Wil. Baskerville, etc., 4 Aug. 1749.

	£	s.	d.		£	s.	d.
138 yds *dimity	34	10	0	4 muslin aprons and 3 handkerchieves, wrought	10	3	0
125 yds calico	21	1	6	Parcel of China ware	11	1	3
22 yds *diaper	1	7	6	2 small bottles oil of cinnamon	1	10	0
92 yds *morees	20	14	0		112	7	3
25 yds muslin	12	0	0	Holden	5	0	0

Condemned and discharged; writ of delivery 13 Dec. 1749. [17]

20 CUST 21/53, ff. 130v–131r
22 November 1749 Wil. Baskerville, etc., no. 8, 26 Aug. 1749.

	£	s.	d.		£	s.	d.
103 gall. brandy	25	15	0	41 gall. brandy	10	5	0
90 gall. brandy	22	10	0	4 gall. *geneva	1	0	0
7½ lb. green tea	2	5	0	51 gall. brandy	12	15	0
19 gall. rum	5	14	0	10 gall. rum	3	0	0
					83	4	0

Condemned and discharged; writ of delivery 13 Dec. 1749. [18]

[15] This note, opposite App. I, no. 18, on f. 130r, probably applies to App. I, no. 17, as well. See nos 452, 459, 462, 474, 536, 546, 669.
[16] See no. 530.
[17] This note, opposite App. I, no. 20, on f. 131r, probably applies to App. I, no. 19, as well.
[18] See no. 530.

21 CUST 21/53, ff. 130v–131r

22 November 1749 Tho. Chadwick, etc., 20 Apr. 1749.

	£	s.	d.		£	s.	d.
Parcel of China ware	4	4	9	134 lb. soap	4	9	4
13 yds muslin	4	11	0	40 yds muslin	8	15	0
Parcel of China ware	3	9	0	5⅝ yds velvet	5	16	0
7 yds muslin	4	18	0	7 dozen 8 bottles French red wine	9	4	0
Parcel of China ware	1	9	6	786 lb. *castile soap	26	4	0
1 cwt 1 qr 14 lb. rice	1	5	8	Parcel of eastern ware		18	6
36 gall. wine, 5 gall. vinegar	7	11	6		82	16	3
				John Percival	1	0	0

Condemned and discharged; writ of delivery 13 Dec. 1749.[19]

22 CUST 21/54, ff. 19v–20r

6 February 1749/50 Ric. Chambers, etc., no. 4, 12 Nov. 1749.

	£	s.	d.		£	s.	d.
3 gall. brandy		17	6	10 gall. brandy, 25 gall. rum	10	0	0
23 lb. tea	5	15	0	154 gall. brandy, 25 gall. rum	46	0	0
4 gall. brandy, 3 gall. rum	2	0	0	8 gall. brandy	2	0	0
5 gall. brandy, 11 gall. rum	4	11	0		71	3	6

Condemned and discharged; writ of delivery 27 Feb. 1749/50.[20]

23 CUST 21/54, ff. 21v–22r

6 February 1749/50 Wil. Baskerville, etc., no. 7, 15 Nov. 1749.

	£	s.	d.
70 gall. brandy, 20 gall. rum	23	10	0
150 gall. brandy	37	10	0
60 lb. *bohea tea	15	0	0
7 gall. rum	2	2	0
	78	2	0

Condemned and discharged; writ of delivery 27 Feb. 1749/50.[21]

24 CUST 21/54, ff. 66v–67r

23 May 1750 Wil. Baskerville, etc., 20 Jan 1748/9.

	£	s.	d.		£	s.	d.
50 lb. whalebone	10	0	0	14 dozen 11 bottles French red wine	22	7	6
21 iron locks, tin coffee pot	1	8	9	9 dozen 11 bottles French white wine	14	17	6
8 lb. shoemaker's thread		1	4	5 dozen French red	7	10	0
17 lb. soap		8	6	5 dozen French white	7	10	0
3 small bottles anchovies		2	0	Parcel of China ware	7	3	6
4¼ yds cotton		7	9½	22 lb. chocolate		11	0
					72	7	10½
				Sam. Hood	1	0	0

Moiety £36.13s.11½d., paid into the Exchequer 16 June 1750.[22]

[19] This note, opposite App. I, no. 20, on f. 131r, probably applies to App. I, no. 21, as well.
[20] See no. 587.
[21] See no. 587.
[22] See nos 325, 609.

25
23 May 1750

CUST 21/54, ff. 66v–67r
John Barker, no. 3, 24 Feb. 1749/50.

	£	s.	d.
147 gall. brandy	36	15	0
3½ gall. rum		19	3
46 lb. *bohea tea	11	10	0
	49	4	3

Condemned and discharged; writ of delivery 12 June 1750.[23]

26
30 June 1750

CUST 21/54, ff. 92v–93r
John Cross, etc., no. 4, 14 Mar. 1749/50.

	£	s.	d.		£	s.	d.
4 lb. green tea	1	2	0	5 gall. brandy	1	5	0
1 lb. *bohea		5	0	3 lb. tea		15	0
70 gall. brandy	17	10	0	21 gall. brandy	5	5	0
16 gall. *arrack	8	0	0	21½ lb. tea	6	5	6
12 gall. brandy	3	0	0	25 gall. brandy	6	5	0
18 gall. brandy	4	10	0	12 lb. tea	3	0	0
					57	2	6

Condemned and discharged; writ of delivery 19 July 1750.[24]

27
22 November 1750

CUST 21/54, ff. 156v–157r
John Stretch, no. 3, 8 Nov. [1750].

	£	s.	d.		£	s.	d.
510 gall. brandy	127	10	0	40 lb. green tea	11	0	0
180 gall. rum	49	10	0	5033 lb. tobacco	125	16	6
540 lb. *bohea tea	121	10	0				
					435	6	6

Condemned and discharged; writ of delivery 13 Dec. 1750.

28
22 November 1750

CUST 21/54, ff. 157v–158r
John Barker, etc., no. 5, 18 Aug. 1750.

	£	s.	d.		£	s.	d.
30 gall. rum	8	5	0	7 gall. brandy	1	15	0
10 gall. brandy	2	10	0	246 gall. spruce beer	32	16	0
17 lb. *bohea tea	4	5	0	35 gall. rum	9	12	6
30 lb. *bohea tea	7	10	0				
					66	13	6

Condemned and discharged; writ of delivery 14 Dec. 1750.

29
22 November 1750

CUST 21/54, ff. 159v–160r
Rob. Knipper, etc., no. 9, 3 June 1750.

	£	s.	d.		£	s.	d.
35½ lb. green tea	10	13	0	14½ gall. rum	3	17	0
18 lb. *bohea	4	19	0	4 lb. *bohea tea	1	0	0
20 gall. rum	5	10	0	1 lb. green		5	6
137 gall. brandy	34	5	0	10 gall. brandy	2	15	0
					63	4	6

Condemned and discharged; writ of delivery 13 Dec. 1750.

[23] See nos 581, 592, 674, 695, 706.
[24] See no. 702.

30 CUST 21/54, ff. 159v–160r
22 November 1750 David Shirley, etc., 16 June 1750.

	£	s.	d.		£	s.	d.
16 yds cut velvet	10	8	0	271 gall. Spanish white wine	54	4	0
10 lb. soap		5	0	8 lb. *castile soap		4	0
Parcel of China ware	1	9	0		66	10	0
				Punch-Bowl, small sloop, about 6 tons, with tackle, *apparel, furniture	8	10	0

Condemned and discharged; writ of delivery 13 Dec. 1750. [25]

31 CUST 21/54, ff. 159v–160r
22 November 1750 Wil. Baskerville, etc., 22 May 1750.

	£	s.	d.		£	s.	d.
14 yds muslin	2	6	0	Parcel of China ware	2	11	0
14 yds muslin		17	6	27 lb. sewing silk	37	16	0
18 yds muslin	2	14	0	Parcel of China ware	3	3	0
Parcel of China ware	3	16	9	16 muslin handkerchieves	2	0	0
Parcel of China ware	6	15	3	11½ yds *dimity	2	11	9
2 muslin neckcloths		2	0	6 yds calico		15	0
					65	7	3 [26]
				John Sorriff	12	0	0

Moiety £38.13s.7½d., paid into the Exchequer 14 Dec. 1750. [27]

32 CUST 21/54, ff. 160v–161r
22 November 1750 Tho. Hanbury, etc., no. 8, 1 Sept. 1750.

	£	s.	d.		£	s.	d.
15 gall. rum	4	2	6	110 gall. brandy, decayed	5	10	0
50 gall. brandy	12	10	0	60 gall. rum, decayed	3	0	0
140 lb. *bohea tea	35	0	0	5 gall. brandy	1	7	6
523 lb. tobacco	13	1	6	2½ gall. rum		15	0
					75	6	6

Condemned and discharged; writ of delivery 13 Dec. 1750.

[25] This note, opposite App. I, no. 29, on f. 160r, probably applies to App. I, no. 30, as well.
[26] Correctly £65.8s.3d.
[27] See no. 676.

Appendix II

List of Portsmouth Customs letter books 1726–1762

These are all the surviving letter books down to the end of 1760; they come from the records of the Portsmouth Custom House (above, p. xxxi). The volume number recorded in the P.R.O. list at the end of each entry must originally have been on each volume, but is now missing from some; thus, of the three volumes used for the present edition it survives only on CUST 58/150 (above, p.xxxiii).

Out-letters, from Portsmouth to the Board of Customs

P.R.O. CUST	58/1	16 Sept. 1748 – 22 Sept. 1750: vol. 1A
	2	9 May 1760 – 16 Dec. 1761: vol. 1B

In-letters, from the Board of Customs to Portsmouth

P.R.O. CUST	58/142	22 Sept. 1726 – 24 Mar. 1730/1: vol. 2
	143	3 Apr. 1731 – 23 July 1737: vol. 3
	144	23 July 1737 – 24 July 1740: vol. 4
	145	25 July 1740 – 29 Apr. 1742: vol. 5
	146	30 Apr. 1742 – 25 Nov. 1743: vol. 6
	147	26 Nov. 1743 – 20 Sept. 1745: vol. 7
	148	26 Sept. 1745 – 15 Jan. 1747/8: vol. 8
	149	19 Jan. 1747/8 – 6 Feb. 1749/50: vol. 9
	150	8 Feb. 1749/50 – 11 Mar. 1752: vol. 10
	151	14 Mar. 1752 – 29 Nov. 1753: vol. 11
	152	29 Nov. 1753 – 29 Dec. 1756: vol. 12
	153	4 Jan. 1757 – 7 Sept. 1758: vol. 13
	154	9 Sept. 1758 – 10 Oct. 1759: vol. 14
	155	12 Oct. 1759 – 25 Nov. 1760: vol. 15
	156	26 Nov. 1760 – 18 Feb. 1762: vol. 16

Appendix III

List of Board of Customs central personnel 1748–1750

This information is taken from P.R.O. CUST 18/236–247 (quarterly establishment lists, Lady Day 1748 to Christmas 1750). The names are of all those listed as 'employ'd in the Business in General and not confin'd to any Port', except those with responsibilities for particular areas that did not include Portsmouth. However, some central officials of the service were omitted from the lists because they were paid no salary from the Customs establishment; the Receiver-General is a notable example.

Commissioners
- By successive commissions of 27 July 1747, 30 Dec. 1748, 14 Apr. 1750
  - Sir John Evelyn, Bart.
  - Brian Fairfax (died 9 Jan. 1748/9)
  - Wardell Geo. Westby
  - Sir Rob. Baylis (died 21 Nov. 1748)
  - Ric. Chandler
  - Beaumont Hotham
  - Sam. Mead
  - Gwyn Vaughan
  - Wil. Levinz
  - Edw. Hooper (added in commission of 30 Dec. 1748)
  - Sir Miles Stapylton, Bart. (added in commission of 14 Apr. 1750)

Secretary
- Wil. Wood
- Plantation and western clerk
  - John Fremantle (*also* Freemantle)

Solicitor for the port of London and the western ports of England and Wales
- Geo. Medcalfe

Solicitor for bonds and criminal prosecutions
- Henry Simon

Paymaster of Incidents
- Wil. Leach

Controller-General
- Rob. Parsons

Controller of the issues and payments of the Receiver-General
- Aug. Schutz

Register-General of all trading ships belonging to Great Britain
- Tho. Boothby Schrymsher (to 22 Feb. 1747/8)
- John Eckersall (from 23 Feb. 1747/8)

Inspector-General of Imports and Exports
- Henry Pelham
- Assistant
  - John Oxenford

Inspector of the Outport Collectors' Accounts
- John Roberts

Examiners of the Outport Books
John Creswicke
Edw. Williams
Ben. Martin (*also* Martyn)
Henry Saxby

Surveyor-General of Hampshire and Dorset
Pusey Brooke

Examiner of the sufficiency of officers' securities and to solicit the payment of debts outstanding in the plantation receipt
Owen McSwiny (*also* McSwiney)

Appendix IV

Tables of the Customs establishment at Portsmouth 1671–1750

The information is taken from:

P.R.O. CUST 39/10 (list of established officers, Michaelmas 1671 with apparently later additions)
P.R.O. CUST 58/349 (accounts of expenses at Portsmouth, 1689–1702: account for Midsummer 1702)
P.R.O. T 42/2 (list of established and other Customs officers, Michaelmas 1717)
P.R.O. CUST 18/236–247 (quarterly establishment lists, Lady Day 1748 to Christmas 1750; there was no formal change in this period).

All salaries are given for the full year to show the cost of the allowed establishment. In practice the amount spent was often less as a result of vacancies (see Appendix V); thus in 1748–50 the quarterly total of £288.7s.4d. was fully spent in only five of the twelve quarters.

The records of the establishment are an inadequate guide to the number of Customs employees at Portsmouth. They exclude those paid solely by a patent officer (such as the Deputy Customer: see no. 97) or by fees (such as the coal meters: see nos 358, 364, 373) and the growing number paid solely from the incidents account (see Appendix VI). Conversely, the Surveyor-General's report in 1750 (no. 677) shows that although payments were being made for a ship's boy on the yacht none was actually employed. Nor are these records a guide to the income of those listed. As the notes show, payments from the establishment had to cover such expenses as clerks' salaries or the upkeep of horses, but for most officers were supplemented from other sources: fees, seizures and allowances from the incidents account (see Appendix VI).

1	Collector	£40
1671	Surveyor	35
	Waiter and Searcher	30
	Waiter and Searcher at Gosport	25
	Four tidesmen and boatmen, £10 each	40
	Total	£170

2	Collector and Customer	£60
1702	plus, for a clerk	20
	Surveyor, to keep a horse and visit the coast eastward to Chichester	60
	Two landwaiters, £40 each	80
	[Deputy] to act for the Controller and Searcher, to have their fees, and from the Queen	13
	Commander of the sailing-boat	30
	Two tidesmen and boatmen, £30 each	60
	Tidesman	30
	Two boatmen, £25 each	50
	Waiter and Searcher at Fareham, to inspect and take account of the coast vessels	20
	Waiter and Searcher at Gosport	25
	Waiter and Searcher at Emsworth	20
	plus, for the wool business	65
	Riding Surveyor at Titchfield	50
	Total	£583

3	Collector, for himself and clerk	£60
1717	Surveyor	60
	Deputy Controller and Searcher, besides the whole fees	13
	Two landwaiters, £40 each	80
	Commander of the sailing-boat	30
	Coastwaiter and tidesman	30
	Tidesman	30
	Tidesman and boatman	30
	Two boatmen, £25 each	50
	Waiter and Searcher at Fareham	45
	Waiter and Searcher at Gosport	35
	Waiter and Searcher at Emsworth, and for the wool business, for himself, servant and two horses	90
	Waiter and Searcher at Cosham	45
	Riding Surveyor at Titchfield	50
	Total	£648

4	Collector, for himself and clerks	£60
1748–50	Deputy Controller, to have £20 from the Controller or the whole fees, and from the King	25
	Surveyor, to keep a horse and visit the coast eastward to Chichester	60
	Two landwaiters, £40 each	80
	Additional landwaiter	40
	Coastwaiter	40
	Tidesurveyor	50
	Two tidesmen, £30 each	60
	Tidesman and boatman	30
	Two boatmen, £25 each	50
	Supervisor of the Riding Officers in this port and the Isle of Wight	100
	Waiter and Searcher at Fareham, £25 to take account of the coast vessels, £20 to keep a horse	45
	Waiter and Searcher at Gosport	35
	Waiter and Searcher and Riding Officer at Emsworth	60
	Waiter and Searcher at Cosham, to keep a horse	45
	Riding Officer at Titchfield	45
	Greenhill yacht: commander	50
	mate	25
	eight mariners, £15 each	120
	boy	8
	victualling eleven men, 7½d. per day each	£125.9s.4d.
	Total	£1153.9s.4d.

Appendix V

Table of Customs establishment office-holders at Portsmouth 1671–1750

The information is taken from:

P.R.O. CUST 39/10 (list of established officers, Michaelmas 1671 with apparently later additions)
P.R.O. PRO 30/32/15–29 (quarterly establishment lists, Midsummer 1673 to Christmas 1689)
P.R.O. CUST 39/11–13 (quarterly establishment lists, Lady Day 1674, Lady Day 1679, Lady Day 1691)
P.R.O. CUST 18/1A–247 (quarterly establishment lists, Midsummer 1675 to Christmas 1750)
P.R.O. CUST 58/349 (Portsmouth, accounts of expenses, Michaelmas 1689 to Christmas 1702)

as well as (for 1748–50) from the letters printed in this volume. The order in which the posts were listed changed slightly from time to time; the order here and the titles in the margin are based on the lists of 1750 or the last appearance of posts abolished earlier. Most of the lists normally enter the date of an officer's admission to a post and the date of the warrant or order appointing him, and both are given here; the year of the warrant is omitted if it is the same as the year of admission, and 'warrant' without a date following means that the list enters the date only of the warrant without noting whether this was the date of admission also. If a post is known to have been relinquished through death or superannuation this is noted here. The loss of some lists means that exact dates cannot always be given, but some further details may be supplied from the *Calendar of Treasury Papers*, 1557–1728 (6v., 1868–89), *Calendar of Treasury Books*, 1660–1718 (32v., 1904–69) and *Calendar of Treasury Books and Papers*, 1729–45 (5v., 1897–1903) as well as from the earlier Portsmouth letter books (see Appendix II).

Not only did the titles of posts change from time to time, sometimes confusingly, but at any time there might be inconsistency in what a post was called, while some established officers also held posts paid from the incidents account or from fees. Thus, for instance, when the death of Thomas Trehearne, Waiter and Searcher at Cosham, was reported to the Board of Customs he was called Tidesurveyor (see no. 505). Officers paid from the establishment were in any case far from being the only Customs employees at Portsmouth (see the note at the beginning of Appendix IV).

1	Collector		
Collector	John Pocock	from 29 Sept. 1671	to 24 June × 29 Sept. 1676
	Collector and Surveyor		
	John Pocock	from 25 June × 30 Sept. 1676	to 24 June 1679
	Fra. Weaver	25 June 1679	24 June 1680
	Collector		
	Fra. Weaver	from 25 June 1680	to 29 Sept. 1686
	Customer and Collector *or* Collector and Customer		
	Fra. Weaver	from 30 Sept. 1686	to 29 Sept. 1689
	John Weaver	26 Dec. 1689 × 30 Sept. 1690	25 June × 24 Sept. 1705 (died)
	Sam. Binks (*also* Bincks)	24 Sept. 1705 (warrant)	25 Dec. 1715
	John Arnold	2 Mar. 1715/6 (warrant)	24 June 1725
	Pusey Brooke	26 Mar. × 25 June 1726	24 June 1735
	Collector		
	Pusey Brooke	from 25 June 1735	to 6 May 1746
	Wil. Cooley	7 May 1746 (warrant 17 Apr.)	still in post 25 Dec. 1750

2 Deputy Controller

To act for the Controller and Searcher		
Peter de Cardonnel (*also* de Cardonel)	from 26 Dec. 1686 × 26 Mar. 1688	to 25 Mar. 1691 × 25 Mar. 1692
Dan. de Cardonnel (*also* de Cardonnell, de Carnonell)	26 Mar. 1691 × 26 Mar. 1692	29 Sept. 1711
Deputy Controller and Searcher		
Dan. de Cardonnel (*also* de Cardonell, de Cardonnell)	from 30 Sept. 1711	to 29 Sept. 1724
Deputy Controller		
Wil. Smith	from 30 Sept. 1724 (warrant 18 Sept.)	to 25 Mar. 1726
Lancelot Hicks	28 Dec. 1730 (warrant)	13 June 1731
Rob. Turvin	14 June 1731 (warrant 22 Apr.)	still in post 25 Dec. 1750

3 Surveyor

Surveyor		
Nic. Badcock	from 29 Sept. 1671	to c. 17 June 1672
And. Percivall	17 June 1672 (order)	25 Mar. 1674
Dan. Shewell	26 Mar. 1674	25 Mar. 1676
John Salisbury	12 Nov. 1681 (order 12 Nov.)	25 Dec. 1683 × 25 Dec. 1684
Tho. Ogle	26 Dec. 1683 × 26 Dec. 1684	30 Sept. × 25 Dec. 1685
Tho. Davies	30 Sept. × 25 Dec. 1685	31 July 1689
Laur. Cole	1 Aug. 1689 (warrant 27 July)	25 Mar. 1693 × 25 Mar. 1695
John Mellish	26 Mar. 1693 × 26 Mar. 1695	23 Jan. 1697/8 (died)
Gilb. Poulson	1 Feb. 1697/8 (warrant)	25 Mar. 1711
Rob. Eden	26 Jan. 1711/2 (warrant)	28 Aug. 1719
Cha. Morgan	29 Aug. 1719 (warrant 6 Aug.)	8 Mar. 1747/8 (died)
Cha. Markland	16 Apr. 1748 (warrant 29 Mar.)	still in post 25 Dec. 1750

4 Landwaiters

Waiter and Searcher		
Rawleigh Hull	from 29 Sept. 1671	to 24 Nov. 1679 (died)
Tho. Dicken	26 Dec. 1679	25 Dec. 1683 × 25 Dec. 1684
Waiter		
Jos. Battelley (*also* Battailey, Battailhey, Battelhey, Battialhey)	from 26 Dec. 1683 × 26 Dec. 1684	to 24 June 1698
Landwaiters		
John Mellish	from 1 Feb. 1697/8 (warrant)	to 24 June 1709
Jos. Battelley (*also* Batailhe, Battailhe)	25 June 1698	29 Sept. × 25 Dec. 1706 (died)
Tho. Legh (*also* Leagh, Leigh)	19 Nov. 1706 (warrant 19 Nov.)	26 Mar. × 2 May 1723
John Sherer	25 June 1709 (warrant)	15 Feb. 1730/1 (died)
Rob. Reynolds	3 May 1723 (warrant 24 Apr.)	2 Sept. 1725 (died)
Eli Stanyford	26 Dec. 1726 (warrant 16 Dec.)	28 Apr. 1733 (died)
John Williams Flower	26 Dec. 1730 (warrant 29 Sept.)	26 Dec. 1733 × 25 Mar. 1734
Tho. Whitehorne	26 Dec. 1733 (warrant 8 May)	still in post 25 Dec. 1750
Stan. Pugh	2 Feb. 1733/4 (warrant 24 Jan.)	to 25 Dec. 1737
Edw. Skeat	7 July 1738 (warrant 29 Dec. 1737)	still in post 25 Dec. 1750

5 Additional landwaiter

Additional landwaiter		
Tho. Wiggett (*also* Wigget)	from 1 Jan. 1723/4	to 29 Sept. 1747
Tho. Merritt (*also* Merrit)	25 Apr. 1748 (warrant 15 Oct. 1747)	still in post 25 Dec. 1750

6 Coastwaiter

Coastwaiter		
Stan. Pugh	from 31 May 1725 (warrant 26 Mar.)	to 1 Feb. 1733/4
Ric. Smalley	4 Feb. 1733/4 (warrant 24 Jan.)	26 Mar. × 24 June 1735 (died)
John Barnston	8 Aug. 1735 (warrant 31 July)	21 Jan. 1738/9
Wil. Henn	3 Apr. 1739 (warrant)	9 June 1740 (died)
Tho. Norman	10 July 1740 (warrant 18 June)	still in post 25 Dec. 1750

7 Tidesurveyor

Tidesurveyor		
Edw. Berkley	from 4 Aug. 1731 (warrant 29 June)	to 22 Feb. 1735/6
Wil. Baskerville	8 Mar. 1735/6 (warrant 3 Mar.)	still in post 25 Dec. 1750

8 Tidesmen

Chief Boatman		
John Ewins (*also* Evans, Ewens)	from 26 Dec. 1683 × 26 Dec. 1684	to 26 Mar. × 26 May 1692 (died)
John [1] Skinner	26 May 1692 (warrant)	29 Sept. 1698
Tidesmen and boatmen		
Sam. Plumb	from 30 Sept. 1698 (warrant 27 Sept.)	to 24 June 1703
Tho. Robinson	30 Sept. 1698 (warrant 27 Sept.)	24 June 1703
Tidesmen		
Sam. Plumb (*also* Plume)	from 25 June 1703	to 25 Dec. 1724
Tho. Robinson	25 June 1703	12 Dec. 1719 (died)
John Bayles	1 Mar. 1719/20 (warrant 12 Feb.)	26 Dec. 1734 × 25 Mar. 1735 (died)
Wil. May	4 Jan. 1726/7 (warrant 16 Dec. 1726)	21 Dec. 1749 (died)
John [2] Ring	5 Mar. 1734/5 (warrant)	18 Mar. 1749/50 (died)
Tho. Garret	24 Feb. 1749/50 (warrant 13 Feb.)	still in post 25 Dec. 1750
James Mitchell	not yet in post 25 Dec. 1750 (warrant 3 Oct.)	

9 Tidesman and boatman

Boatman		
Wil. Cliff	from 26 Dec. 1684 (warrant 2 Oct.)	to 25 Dec. 1689 × 29 Sept. 1690
Walt. Edwards	26 Dec. 1689 × 30 Sept. 1690	24 June 1704
Tidesman and boatman		
James Adams	from 31 July 1704 (warrant)	to 25 Mar. 1725
John Wills	11 Oct. 1725 (warrant 10 Aug.)	25 Dec. 1741
John Williams	15 Jan. 1741/2 (warrant 7 Jan.)	still in post 25 Dec. 1750

---

1 Jos. in CUST 18/39–44 (Lady Day 1697 to Michaelmas 1698), probably by mistake: he is John in the lists for the same quarters in CUST 58/349.

2 Rob. in CUST 18/184 (Lady Day 1735), probably by mistake.

10 Boatmen

Boatmen and tidesmen *or* tidesmen and boatmen *or* tidesmen

John Bull	from c.29 Sept. 1671	to 29 Sept. 1671 × 25 Mar. 1673
Edw. Burgh (*also* Brough)	c.29 Sept. 1671	26 Mar. × 24 June 1674
Pascoe Silk (*also* Silke)	c.29 Sept. 1671	c.25 May 1676
Wil. Golding (*also* Goulding)	c.29 Sept. 1671	30 Sept. × 25 Dec. 1683
Gabriel Clousley (*also* Clousely, Clously, Clowsly, Cowseley)	29 Sept. 1671 × 26 Mar. 1673	26 Dec. 1675 × 25 Mar. 1676 (died)
Henry Smith	25 June 1674 × 26 Mar. 1675	24 June 1682
John Baxter	c.25 May 1676	24 June × 29 Sept. 1676
Nat. Andrews	1 Aug. 1682 (order)	30 Sept. × 25 Dec. 1683
Rob. Knight	30 Sept. × 25 Dec. 1683	25 Dec. 1689
John Francklyn	26 Dec. 1683 × 26 Dec. 1684	30 May 1685
Tho. Edmonds	31 May 1685	25 June × 29 Sept. 1689 (died)
Henry Chapman	25 June × 30 Sept. 1689	25 Dec. 1689 × 29 Sept. 1690

Boatmen

John Somers (*also* Sommers, Summers)	from 26 Dec. 1689 × 30 Sept. 1690	to 24 June 1704
Henry Chapman	26 Dec. 1689 × 30 Sept. 1690	25 Apr. 1692
Tho. Spott	26 Apr. 1692 (warrant 25 Apr.)	24 June × 29 Sept. 1696
John Parraguanath	25 June × 30 Sept. 1696	25 Mar. 1697
Wil. Drake	21 May 1697 (warrant)	14 Jan. 1701/2 (died)
Tobias Drake	28 Mar. 1702 (deputation 5 Feb. 1701/2)	24 June 1704
Tho. Trehearne (*also* Traherne, Trehern, Treherne)	31 July 1704 (warrant)	3 Oct. 1723
Tho. Sykes (*also* Sikes)	8 Sept. 1704 (warrant)	30 Sept. × 14 Dec. 1721
Edw. Skeat (*also* Skeats, Skeet, Street)	15 Dec. 1721 (warrant 6 Dec.)	6 July 1738
Tho. Smith	8 Oct. 1723 (warrant 2 Oct.)	30 Sept. × 25 Dec. 1725
Tho. Billson (*also* Bilson)	19 Feb. 1727/8 (warrant 13 Feb.)	22 May 1750 (superannuated)
Wil. Rout	8 July 1738 (warrant 29 Dec. 1737)	25 June × 29 Sept. 1744
Wil. Robinson	26 Mar. 1745 (warrant 11 Dec. 1744)	24 June 1746
Rob. Knipper	10 Dec. 1747 (warrant 15 Oct.)	still in post 25 Dec. 1750

11 Commander of the sailing-boat

Commander of the sailing-boat

Tho. Burford (*also* Burfield)	from 30 Sept. 1698 (warrant 27 Sept.)	to 29 Sept. 1727
vacant	30 Sept. 1727	24 June 1737
post abolished	25 June 1737	

12 Supervisor of the Riding Officers

Supervisor of the Riding Officers in this port and the Isle of Wight

Geo. Spry	from 25 Mar. 1741 (warrant 20 Jan. 1740/1)	still in post 25 Dec. 1750

13 Waiter and Searcher at Fareham

Waiter and Searcher at Fareham

John Merrick	from 26 Dec. 1689 × 30 Sept. 1690	to 25 Mar. 1709
Ben. Merrick	18 Apr. 1709 (warrant)	30 Sept. × 25 Dec. 1709 (died)
Sam. Blanchard	26 Dec. 1709	25 Dec. 1716 × 25 Mar. 1717
Tho. Newnham	26 Dec. 1716 × 26 Mar. 1717	25 Mar. × 13 Apr. 1724
Tho. Newnham jun.	14 Apr. 1724 (warrant 8 Apr.)	29 Sept. 1727
Tho. Newnham sen.	24 Oct. 1727 (warrant 21 Sept.)	25 Mar. 1729
John Newnham (*also* Newham)	26 Mar. 1729 (warrant 6 Feb. 1728/9)	still in post 25 Dec. 1750

14 Waiter and Searcher at Gosport

Waiter and Searcher at Gosport

John Bromley	from 29 Sept. 1671 × 26 Mar. 1673	to 24 June × 25 Dec. 1673
Tho. Dicken (*also* Dickens, Dickin)	25 June × 26 Dec. 1673	25 Dec. 1679
Nat. Lee	26 Dec. 1679	24 June 1680
Wil. Smith	25 June 1680	30 Sept. × 2 Dec. 1682
Wil. Pickford	2 Dec. 1682 (order)	25 Mar. 1685
John Francklyn	30 May 1685 (warrant 30 May)	25 Dec. 1686 × 25 Mar. 1688
Jos.[3] Sandford (*also* Sanford)	26 Dec. 1686 × 26 Mar. 1688	25 June × 3 July 1712
John Hicks	3 July 1712 (warrant 3 July)	27 Nov. 1713
Cha. Young	7 Jan. 1713/4 (warrant)	4 Aug. 1721
Tho. Dumbrell	5 Aug. 1721 (warrant 9 July)	29 July 1723 (died)
Tho. Wilkes (*also* Wilks)	8 Aug. 1723 (warrant 5 Aug.)	25 Dec. 1725
Edm. Smith (*also* Smyth)	14 Mar. 1725/6 (warrant)	25 Mar. 1745
John Noel	17 Apr. 1745 (warrant 9 Apr.)	still in post 25 Dec. 1750

15 Waiter and Searcher and Riding Officer at Emsworth

Waiter and Searcher at Langstone and Emsworth

Wil. Butcher	from 30 Sept. 1671 × 26 Mar. 1673	to 24 June 1674 × 25 Mar. 1675
John Hedger	25 June × 30 Sept. 1675	25 Mar. 1679

Waiter and Searcher at Emsworth

John Hedger	from 26 Mar. 1679	to 25 Dec. 1690
Nat. Spencer	26 Mar. 1691 × 26 Mar. 1692	25 Dec. 1715
Tho. Till	13 Jan. 1715/6 (warrant 3 Jan.)	25 Mar. 1719

Waiter and Searcher and Riding Officer at Emsworth

Tho. Till	from 26 Mar. 1719	to 18 Nov. 1720
John Till	19 Nov. 1720 (warrant 14 Nov.)	26 Mar. × 18 Apr. 1735
Ric. Libbard	19 Apr. 1735 (warrant 3 Apr.)	still in post 25 Dec. 1750

16 Waiter and Searcher at Cosham

Waiter and Searcher at Cosham

John[4] Gardiner (*also* Gardner)	from 5 June 1710 (warrant)	to 25 June × 29 Sept. 1723 (died)
Tho. Trehearne (*also* Traherne)	4 Oct. 1723 (warrant 30 Sept.)	8 Nov. 1749 (died)
John Mears	21 Feb. 1749/50 (warrant 13 Feb.)	9 July 1750
Ric. Temple	18 Aug. 1750 (warrant 25 July)	still in post 25 Dec. 1750

---

[3] John in CUST 18/39 (Lady Day 1697), probably by mistake.
[4] James in CUST 18/115 (Midsummer 1717), probably by mistake.

17 Riding Officer at Titchfield	Riding Surveyor at Titchfield		
	Jos. Clapp (*also* Clap)	from 1 Mar. 1696/7 (warrant)	to c.24 June 1723
	Jos. Clapp jun.	20 July 1723 (warrant 1 July)	25 Dec. 1725
	Riding Officer at Titchfield		
	Tho. Comden (*also* Combden)	from 26 Mar. × 25 June 1726	still in post 25 Dec. 1750
18 Greenhill yacht[5]	Commander		
	Cha. Coombes	from 10 Nov. 1727 (warrant 3 Nov.)	still in post 25 Dec. 1750
	Mate		
	James Goodman	from 3 Nov. 1727	to 30 Sept. × 25 Dec. 1729
	unnamed	30 Sept. × 25 Dec. 1729	25 Dec. 1750
	Eight mariners		
	unnamed	from 3 Nov. 1727	to 25 Dec. 1750
	Boy		
	unnamed	from 3 Nov. 1727	to 25 Dec. 1750

[5] The yacht Greenhill moved to Portsmouth from Newport, where John Button (died 19 Sept. 1727) had been commander, James Goodman mate (CUST 18/155, f.24: Michaelmas 1727); previously she had been stationed at Cowes (e.g. CUST 18/115: Midsummer 1717). She was thus not the same as the earlier sailing-boat at Portsmouth (App. V, no. 11).

Appendix VI

Tables of Customs salaries paid on the incidents account at Portsmouth 1702–1744

The information is taken from:

P.R.O. CUST 58/349 (accounts of expenses at Portsmouth, 1689–1702: account for Midsummer 1702)
B.L. Harley MS. 7432 (list of established and other Customs officers, 1711)
P.R.O. T 42/2 (list of established and other Customs officers, Michaelmas 1717)
P.R.O. T 42/3 (list of non-establishment Customs salaries, 1720)
B.L. Additional MS. 8831 (list of established and other Customs officers, Christmas 1744)

All payments are given for the full year. Those called 'additional' are to establishment office-holders (see Appendix V).

Payments from the incidents account each year in salaries from Christmas 1732 to Christmas 1748 are listed in no. 377, and in allowances to Riding Officers from Lady Day 1744 to Lady Day 1750 in nos 295 and 696. These show that the 1744 list below is incomplete. No. 200 throws some further light on salary payments from the incidents account in the 1740's.

1 **1702**	Tidesmen:	John Summers, additional	£5
		Tobias Drake, additional	5
	John Merrick, Jos. Sandford, Nat. Spencer, additional £5 each		15
	Tho. Sykes (succeeding Tho. Shortridge)		30
	Boy to Tho. Burford:	Peter Summers,	15
	Tho. Burford, additional		5
	Collector:	J[ohn] W[eaver], additional for a clerk	10
	Total		£85

2 **1711**	Tidesmen:	Tho. Trehearne	£10
		Tho. Sikes	10
	Boatmen:	Peter Summers	30
		John Robinson	35
	Commander of the boat:	Tho. Burford	10
	Coastwaiter:	Sam. Plumbe	20
	Boatmen:	Wil. Smith	35
		Tho. Feild	35
	Tidesurveyor:	Jos. Bagshaw	60
	Tidesmen:	Sam. Plumbe jun.	30
		James Adams	5
		Jos. Sandford	5
		Tho. Robinson	5
	Total		£290

3 **1717**	Commander of the sailing-boat:	Tho. Burford, additional	£10
	Tidesurveyor:	Jos. Bagshaw	60
	Coastwaiter and tidesman:	Sam. Plume sen., additional	20
	Tidesman:	John Robinson, additional	5
	Tidesman and boatman:	James Adams, additional	5
	Boatmen:	Tho. Trehearne, additional	10
		Tho. Sykes, additional	10
	Tidesman and boatman:	John Robinson	30
	Boatmen:	Peter Somers	30
		Wil. Smith	30
		Tho. Feild	30
	Tidesman and boatman:	Sam. Plume jun.	30
	Total		£270

4 1720	Boatmen:	Tho. Sikes, additional	£5
		Tho. Traherne, additional	5
	Tidesmen and boatmen:	John Robinson,	30
		Peter Summers	25
	Commander of the sailing-boat:	Tho. Burford, additional	5
	Coastwaiter:	Sam. Plume. additional	15
	Boatmen:	Wil. Smith	30
		Tho. Field	30
	Tidesurveyor:	Jos. Bagshaw	60
	Tidesman and boatman:	Sam. Plume jun.	30
	Tho. Burford, Peter Summers, further £5 each		10
	Total		£245
5 1744	Coastwaiter:	Tho. Norman, additional	£5
	Boatmen:	Tho. Bilson, additional	5
		Wil. Robinson, additional	5
	Deputy Searcher for assisting the landwaiters:	Jos. Townsend	20
	Riding Officer:	Wil. Goddard	45
	Tidesmen and boatmen:	Peter Summers	30
		Tho. Squibb	30
		Ric. Chambers	30
		John Gilbert	30
		James Fryer	30
		Tho. Dellymore	30
		David Shirley	30
		Tho. Presland	30
		Henry Duncan	30
		Tho. Merritt	30
		James Martin	30
		Ric. Corker	30
		John Blissett	30
		John Ferry	30
		Wil. Hyne	30
	Extra tidesmen and boatmen ('Besides the usual day pay when Employ'd'):	Wil. Baskerville jun.	5
		Tho. Jones	5
		John Savage	5
		John Dixon	5
		Ric. Fitchett	5
		John Battershall	5
		Henry Duncan	5
		Wil. Brown	5
		Ben. Summers	5
		Jeffrey Wright	5
		Gilb. Stoakes	5
		Wil. Vernon	5
		James Dicks	5
		Wil. Battershall	5
		Anth. Haswell	5
		Foster Perry	5
		John Martin	5
		Jos. Robinson jun.	5
		John Fivefoot	5
		Rob. Newnam	5
	Waiter and Searcher at Gosport:	Edm. Smyth, additional	5
	Weighing porter at Gosport:	Tho. Cartwright	20
	Waiter and Searcher at Cosham:	Tho. Traherne, additional	5
	Riding Officer at Cosham:	Geo. Everden	45
	Riding Officer at Stokes Bay:	John Wood	45

Greenhill yacht:	mate, additional	10
	eight mariners, £3 each, additional	24
	victualling eleven men, ½d. per day each, additional	£ 8. 7s.3½d.
	for keeping the sloop in wear and tear	£ 46.10s.
Total		£838.17s.3½d.

Appendix VII

Table of Statutes referred to in the Introduction and text

For individual references see the Index, under Acts of Parliament. The titles of Acts down to 1714 are those given in *The Statutes of the Realm* (9v. and index, 1810–28; those of later Acts are from *The Statutes at large*. The years are those of the parliamentary sessions.

PUBLIC ACTS

1463	3 Edw. IV, c.4	[Prohibition of import of specified manufactured goods.]
1487	3 Henry VII, c.8	An Act against merchants carrying of goods from one port to another without a certificate from the Customer where the goods were first entered.
1661–2	14 Cha. II, c.11	An Act for preventing frauds and regulating abuses in His Majesty's Customs.
1689	1 Wil. & Mary, st.1, c.12	An Act for the encouraging the exportation of corn.
1695–6	7 & 8 Wil. III, c.22	An Act for preventing frauds and regulating abuses in the plantation trade.
1698–9	10 Wil. III, c.3	An Act to prohibit the exportation of any corn, malt, meal, flour, bread, biscuit or starch for one year from the tenth day of February one thousand, six hundred, ninety-eight.
1698–9	10 Wil. III, c.16	An Act to prevent the exportation of wool out of the kingdoms of Ireland and England into foreign parts and for the encouragement of the woollen manufactures in the kingdom of England.
1699–1700	11 Wil. III, c.20	An Act for taking away the duties upon the woollen manufactures, corn, grain, bread, biscuit and meal exported.
1708–9	8 Anne, c.2	An Act to prohibit the exportation of corn, malt, meal, flour, bread, biscuit and starch, and low wines, spirits, worts and wash drawn from malted corn.
1718–19	5 Geo. I, c.11	An Act against clandestine running of uncustomed goods and for the more effectual preventing of frauds relating to the Customs.
1718–19	5 Geo. I, c.27	An Act to prevent the inconveniences arising from seducing artificers in the manufactures of Great Britain into foreign parts.
1719–20	6 Geo. I, c.21	An Act for preventing frauds and abuses in the public revenues of Excise, Customs, Stamp Duties, Post Office and House-Money.

1720–1	7 Geo. I, st. 1, c. 3	An Act for repealing an Act made in the 9th year of the reign of Her late Majesty Queen Anne, entitled, An Act to oblige ships coming from places infected more effectually to perform their quarantine; and for the better preventing the plague being brought from foreign parts into Great Britain or Ireland or the isles of Guernsey, Jersey, Alderney, Sark or Man; and to hinder the spreading of infection.
1720–1	7 Geo. I, st. 1, c. 7	An Act to preserve and encourage the woollen and silk manufactures of this kingdom, and for more effectual employing the poor, by prohibiting the use and wear of all printed, painted, stained or dyed calicoes in apparel, household stuff, furniture or otherwise, after the twenty-fifth day of December one thousand, seven hundred and twenty-two (except as therein is excepted).
1721–2	8 Geo. I, c. 15	An Act for encouragement of the silk manufactures of this kingdom; and for taking off several duties on merchandises exported; . . . .
1721–2	8 Geo. I, c. 18	An Act to prevent the clandestine running of goods and the danger of infection thereby; and to prevent ships breaking their quarantine; and to subject copper ore of the production of the British plantations to such regulations as other enumerated commodities of the like production are subject.
1722–3	9 Geo. I, c. 21	An Act for enabling His Majesty to put the Customs of Great Britain under the management of one or more Commissions; and for better securing and ascertaining the duties on tobacco; and to prevent frauds in exporting tobacco and other goods and merchandises or carrying the same coastwise.
1726	12 Geo. I, c. 28	An Act for the improvement of His Majesty's revenues of Customs, Excise and inland duties.
1732	5 Geo. II, c. 22	An Act to prevent the exportation of hats out of any of His Majesty's colonies or plantations in America; and to restrain the number of apprentices taken by the hat makers in the said colonies or plantations; and for the better encouraging the making hats in Great Britain.
1739	12 Geo. II, c. 36	An Act for prohibiting the importation of books reprinted abroad, and first composed or written and printed in Great Britain; and for repealing so much of an Act made in the 8th year of the reign of Her late Majesty Queen Anne as empowers the limiting the prices of books.
1740–1	14 Geo. II, c. 3	An Act to prohibit, for a time therein limited, the exportation of corn, grain (rice excepted), meal, malt, flour, bread, biscuit, starch, beef, pork and bacon.
1741–2	15 Geo. II, c. 19	An Act for granting to His Majesty an additional duty on foreign cambrics imported into Great Britain; and for allowing thereout a bounty upon certain species of British and Irish linens exported.
1744–5	18 Geo. II, c. 36	An Act for prohibiting the wearing and importation of cambrics and French lawns.

1746–7	20 Geo. II, c.47	An Act to continue several laws for prohibiting the importation of books reprinted abroad, and first composed or written and printed in Great Britain; . . . and relating to rice, to frauds in the Customs, to the clandestine running of goods and to copper ore of the British plantations; . . . .
1747–8	21 Geo. II, c.1	An Act for continuing the duties upon malt, mum, cider and perry in that part of Great Britain called England, and for granting to His Majesty certain duties upon malt, mum, cider and perry in that part of Great Britain called Scotland, for the service of the year one thousand, seven hundred and forty-eight.
1747–8	21 Geo. II, c.2	An Act for granting to His Majesty a subsidy of poundage upon all goods and merchandises to be imported into this kingdom; and for raising a certain sum of money by annuities and a lottery, to be charged on the said subsidy; and for repealing so much of an Act made in the 20th year of His present Majesty's reign as enacts that prize goods and merchandise may be exported without paying any duty of Custom or Excise for the same.
1747–8	21 Geo. II, c.4	An Act to prohibit assurance on ships belonging to France and on merchandises or effects laden thereon, during the present war with France.
1747–8	21 Geo. II, c.7	An Act for granting an aid to His Majesty by a Land Tax to be raised in Great Britain, for the service of the year one thousand, seven hundred and forty-eight.
1747–8	21 Geo. II, c.14	An Act for permitting tea to be exported to Ireland and His Majesty's plantations in America, without paying the inland duties charged thereupon by an Act of the 18th year of His present Majesty's reign; and for enlarging the time for some of the payments to be made on the subscription of six millions, three hundred thousand pounds, by virtue of an Act of this session of Parliament.
1747–8	21 Geo. II, c.26	An Act for explaining, amending and enforcing an Act made in the 18th year of the reign of His present Majesty, entitled An Act for prohibiting the wearing and importation of cambrics and French lawns.
1747–8	21 Geo. II, c.30	An Act for encouraging the making of indigo in the British plantations in America.
1748–9	22 Geo. II, c.1	An Act for continuing and granting to His Majesty certain duties upon malt, mum, cider and perry, for the service of the year one thousand, seven hundred and forty-nine.
1748–9	22 Geo. II, c.2	An Act for granting an aid to His Majesty by a Land Tax to be raised in Great Britain, for the service of the year one thousand, seven hundred and forty-nine.
1748–9	22 Geo. II, c.36	An Act for the more effectual preventing the importation and wear of foreign embroidery and brocade, and of gold and silver thread, lace or other work made of gold or silver wire manufactured in foreign parts.
1748–9	22 Geo. II, c.37	An Act for the better securing His Majesty's duties arising upon coal, culm and cinders exported beyond sea.

1748–9	22 Geo. II, c.40	An Act for enlarging and maintaining the harbour of Ramsgate and for cleansing, amending and preserving the haven of Sandwich.
1748–9	22 Geo. II, c.42	An Act for granting to His Majesty the sum of one million out of the Sinking Fund, for the service of the year one thousand, seven hundred and forty-nine; . . . and for continuing the bounties on the exportation of British and Irish linens; . . . .
1749–50	23 Geo. II, c.2	An Act for granting an aid to His Majesty by a Land Tax to be raised in Great Britain, for the service of the year one thousand, seven hundred and fifty.
1749–50	23 Geo. II, c.3	An Act for continuing and granting to His Majesty certain duties upon malt, mum, cider and perry, for the service of the year one thousand, seven hundred and fifty.
1749–50	23 Geo. II, c.13	An Act for the effectual punishing of persons convicted of seducing artificers in the manufactures of Great Britain and Ireland out of the dominions of the Crown of Great Britain; and to prevent the exportation of utensils made use of in the woollen and silk manufactures from Great Britain or Ireland into foreign parts; and for the more easy and speedy determination of appeals, allowed in certain cases, by an Act made in the last session of Parliament, relating to persons employed in the several manufactures therein mentioned.
1749–50	23 Geo. II, c.20	An Act for encouraging the growth and culture of raw silk in His Majesty's colonies or plantations in America.
1749–50	23 Geo. II, c.21	An Act for granting to His Majesty the sum of nine hundred thousand pounds out of the Sinking Fund, for the service of the year one thousand, seven hundred and fifty; . . . and for enforcing the laws against the clandestine importation of soap, candles and starch into this kingdom.
1749–50	23 Geo. II, c.24	An Act for the encouragement of the British white-herring fishery.
1749–50	23 Geo. II, c.26	An Act to continue several laws for the better regulating of pilots for the conducting of ships and vessels from Dover, Deal and Isle of Thanet up the rivers of Thames and Medway; and for permitting rum or spirits of the British sugar plantations to be landed before the duties of Excise are paid thereon; . . . .
1749–50	23 Geo. II, c.29	An Act to encourage the importation of pig and bar iron from His Majesty's colonies in America; and to prevent the erection of any mill or other engine for slitting or rolling of iron, or any plating forge to work with a tilt hammer, or any furnace for making steel in any of the said colonies.
1749–50	23 Geo. II, c.32	An Act for granting to His Majesty certain duties upon such species of sailcloth as are therein mentioned, which shall be imported from Ireland into Great Britain during the time therein limited.
1749–50	23 Geo. II, c.34	An Act for permitting raw silk of the growth or produce of Persia, purchased in Russia, to be imported into this kingdom from any port or place belonging to the empire of Russia.

1753	26 Geo. II, c.6	An Act to oblige ships more effectually to perform their quarantine; and for the better preventing the plague being brought from foreign parts into Great Britain or Ireland or the isles of Guernsey, Jersey, Alderney, Sark or Man.
1756–7	30 Geo. II, c.1	An Act to prohibit, for a time to be limited, the exportation of corn, malt, meal, flour, bread, biscuit and starch.
1766–7	7 Geo. III, c.3	An Act to prohibit, for a limited time, the exportation of corn, grain, meal, malt, flour, bread, biscuit and starch, and also the extraction of low wines and spirits from wheat and wheat flour.
1846	9 & 10 Victoria, c.22	An Act to amend the laws relating to the importation of corn.

Glossary

ALLOWANCE WINE: *possibly* damaged or unmarketable wine which, imported on a merchant ship in casks, might be taken by the Customs for sale for brandy or vinegar, the purchase price, within fixed limits, being returned as an allowance to the importer (Saxby, pp. 375, 621), nos 220, 223, 226

ANCHOR: cask containing 8⅓ gall. (*O.E.D.*, anker 2), nos 153, 365, 425, 520, 552, 581

APPAREL, APPARELL, APPARREL, APPARRELL: outfit or rigging of a ship, defined more precisely in no. 9 as sails and colours only (*O.E.D.*, apparel sb 4), nos 9, 83, 157, 169, 342, 536, 669, App. I 30

ARRACK: spirits of eastern origin (*O.E.D.*, arrack), nos 113, 120, 123, 135, 245, 340, 352, 375, 387, 418, 423, 432, 433, 437, 615, 620, 625, 638, 735, 741, 749, App. I 3, 4, 9, 14, 26

BANDANNO: handkerchief or other piece of silk cloth, with spots left white by knotting when dyed (*O.E.D.*, bandanna; Wilhelmsen, p. 131), no. 77

BEJUTAPAUT: type of Indian cotton cloth (Wilhelmsen, p. 128, where *bejutapant* is perhaps incorrect: cf. Postlethwayt, i, p. 928), nos 56, 77

BOARDING, BOARDING BILL: certificate, with receipt for payment, of boarding ships or other work by tidesmen and boatmen paid by incident (Crouch, pp. 130–1), nos 191, 267, 351, 400, 514, 591, 664

BOHEA: type of black tea (*O.E.D.*, bohea), 462, 464, App. I 7, 15, 23, 25–29, 32

BOOK CLEAR MUSLIN: type of muslin folded like a book when sold in the piece (*O.E.D.*, book sb 18), App. I 12

BRAWLE, BRAWLEY: type of Indian cloth, striped blue and white (*O.E.D.*, brawl sb^4; Wilhelmsen, p. 127), nos 42, 56, 77

BRITANNIAS LINEN: type of linen (*O.E.D.*, Britannia 2, 3), App. I 1

BUMM: bomb, no. 130

BUSHEL IRON : small scrap iron sold by the bushel (*O.E.D.*, bushel sb^1 3b), no. 130

BYRAMPAUT, BYRAMPUT: type of Indian cloth, nos 42, 56

CAMBRICK: type of white linen cloth (*O.E.D.*, cambric 1), nos 61, 182, 534, 562

CAMLET: cloth of various types and materials, originally in imitation of a type of eastern cloth (*O.E.D.*, camlet sb), App. I 1

CAPUCHIN: woman's cloak and hood (*O.E.D.*, capuchin 2), App. I 6

CARRIDARRY, CHERRYDERRY: type of Indian cotton cloth (Wilhelmsen, p. 128), nos 42, 56, 77, App. I 16

CASTILE SOAP, CASTLE SOAP: type of hard soap made with olive oil and soda (*O.E.D.*, castile soap), no. 296, App. I 6, 21, 30

CELLO, CHELLO: type of Indian cloth (*O.E.D.*, chello), nos 42, 56, 77

CHARTER PARTY: written agreement between ship-owner and merchant for hire of vessel, safe delivery of cargo (*O.E.D.*, charter-party 2), no. 4

CHINTS: painted or dyed Indian cotton cloth (*O.E.D.*, chintz 1), nos 42, 77, 437, 441, 451, 676, App. I 16

CHOPPS OF THE CHANNEL: the entrance into the English Channel from the Atlantic (*O.E.D.*, chop sb^2 4b), no. 611

COCKET, COCQUET: sealed certificate of Customs officer that goods have been entered and duty paid (Crouch, pp. 72–4; *O.E.D.*, cocket sb^1 2; Postlethwayt, i, pp. 175–6), nos 42, 44, 56, 68, 77, 411, 468, 476, 514, 515, 630, 640, 664

COHORNE SHELL, COHORN SHELL: grenade fired from a small mortar (*O.E.D.*, coehorn b), nos 110, 130

COINAGE DUTY: extra duty on the import of wine, vinegar, cider, beer and spirits, to defray the costs of the Royal Mint (Saxby, pp. 46–7), nos 65, 368, 377

COPEE: type of Indian cotton cloth (Wilhelmsen, p. 128), no. 42

CUTTANEE: type of Indian silk or silk and cotton cloth (Wilhelmsen, p. 129), nos 42, 56, 77

DAGGER: two-masted ship of a type used for fishing (*O.E.D.*, dogger^1 1), no. 652

DEAD EYE: pierced wooden block used to extend the shrouds or stays (*O.E.D.*, dead-eye, dead man's eye), no. 669

DEMY: writing-paper 15½ × 20 in. (*O.E.D.*, demy 3), nos 191, 267, 351, 400, 514, 591, 664, 756

DIAPER: type of linen or cotton cloth woven with a diamond-shaped pattern (*O.E.D.*, diaper sb 1), App. I 1, 19

DIMITY: type of cotton cloth woven with a raised pattern (*O.E.D.*, dimity), no. 676, App. I 6, 10–12, 19, 31

DOWLAS: type of linen cloth (*O.E.D.*, dowlas 1a), App. I 1

DUROY: type of woollen cloth (*O.E.D.*, duroy), App. I 1

EXTENT: writ to recover debts due to the Crown (*O.E.D.*, extent sb 2a), no. 703

FIRE MONEY: *possibly* payment to defray fuel costs (*O.E.D.*, fire sb B 5) *or* composition for fines for having fire on board ship in harbour (Beawes, pp. 147, 190), no. 89

GENEVA: gin (*O.E.D.*, geneva[1]), nos 439, 467, App. I 2, 4, 9, 20

GUINEA STUFFS: types of Indian cotton cloth exported to west Africa (*O.E.D.*, Guinea 1; Wilhelmsen, p. 102), no. 56

GUM SANDRICK: resin, from varied trees, used in making pounce (q.v.) and varnish (*O.E.D.*, gum sb[2] 3a, sandarac 2), no. 737

HALF SAY: *possibly* light quality of say, a type of woollen cloth (*O.E.D.*, say sb[1] 1; cf. Beck, say, where double say is mentioned), no. 79

HOLLAND, HOLLANDS LINEN: type of linen cloth (*O.E.D.*, Holland 2), App. I 1, 6, 10, 17

HUNGARY WATER: distilled infusion of rosemary flowers in wine (*O.E.D.*, Hungary), App. I 8

IMPERIAL: writing-paper 22 × 30 in. (*O.E.D.*, imperial A 8b), nos 191, 267, 351, 400, 514, 591, 664, 756

JURAT: memorandum as to when, where and before whom an affidavit was sworn (*O.E.D.*, jurat[2]), no. 731

KENDALL COTTONS: type of woollen cloth (Wilhelmsen, p. 42), no. 79

LAWN: type of linen cloth (*O.E.D.*, lawn sb[1]1), nos 61, 182, 562

LONG ELLS: type of woollen cloth, the same as perpets, q.v. (Beck, perpets; *O.E.D.*, long a[1] A 18), no. 79

MAIN WHALE: the lower of the wales, extra-thick planking at various heights along the side of a ship (*O.E.D.*, main a 11, wale sb[1] 4b), no. 589

MANCHESTER STRIPES: type of striped cotton cloth (*O.E.D.*, Manchester 1, 3), no. 79

MARSEILLES QUILTED: type of cotton cloth, quilted (*O.E.D.*, Marseilles 1; Wilhelmsen, p. 170), nos 500, 510

MATT: bag of matting, used to hold dry goods (*O.E.D.*, mat sb[1] 1d), nos 161, 164, 172, 271

MEAD FLOUR: made (i.e. artificial) flower (cf. corresponding entry in App. I 17), no. 462

MENDES HOLLAND: unidentified type of holland, q.v., no. 462

METAGE: fee paid for officially measuring goods (Crouch, p. 35; *O.E.D.*, metage 2), nos 68, 377

METING: measuring (*O.E.D.*, meting vbl.sb[1]), no. 68

MONMOUTH CAP: flat, round cap (*O.E.D.*, Monmouth 1), no. 79

MOREES: *possibly* the same as moreen, a type of woollen or woollen and cotton cloth (*O.E.D.*, moreen), App. I 13, 19

MUSTER: type of grey woollen cloth (Beck, musterdevilliers; *O.E.D.*, muster sb[2], musterdevillers), nos 56, 77

NECCANEE, NICCANEE, NICEANEE: type of Indian cloth (*O.E.D.*, niccanee), nos 42, 56, 77

NEGANEPACEL: *possibly* miscopied form of neganepaut, q.v., no. 42

NEGANEPAUT: type of Indian cloth (*O.E.D.*, negannepant, perhaps correctly *negannepaut*: cf. bejutapaut, above, and Postlethwayt, i, p. 928), no. 56

OVER ENTRY: certificate of repayment of duty mistakenly overpaid (Crouch, pp. 182–3, 191; *O.E.D.*, over-entry; Postlethwayt, i, p. 174), nos 180, 228, 350, 351, 400, 447, 590, 649, 664, 723, 756

OWLER: smuggler of wool or sheep out of England (*O.E.D.*, owler), no. 397

PASPORT: licence to import or export goods without paying the usual duty (*O.E.D.*, passport sb[1] 4), no. 128

PERPET: perpetuana, a type of hard-wearing woollen cloth (Beck, perpets, perpetuana; *O.E.D.*, perpet, perpetuana), no. 79

PHOTA: type of Indian cloth (*O.E.D.*, phota), no. 42

PISTOLE: any of several kinds of gold coin (*O.E.D.*, pistole), no. 87

PISTOL LAWN: unidentified type of lawn, q.v., no. 182

PLAIN: plain cloth, a type of flannel (*O.E.D.*, plain sb[1] 9), no. 79

PORTAGE, PORTAGE BILL: statement, with receipt, of payment of portage, an allowance to a ship's master for reporting its cargo correctly to the Customs (Crouch, pp. 198–9; Postlethwayt, i, pp. 174–5), nos 14, 180, 228, 294, 350, 447

POTT: writing-paper 15½ × 12½ in. (*O.E.D.*, pot sb[1] 10), nos 191, 267, 351, 400, 514, 591, 664, 756

POUNCE: fine powder used to prevent ink from spreading when writing over an erasure or on unsized paper (*O.E.D.*, pounce sb[2] 1), nos 191, 267, 351, 400, 514, 591, 664, 756

PREFERABLE: first to be called on after establishment employees (*O.E.D.*, preferable A 1), no. 200

ROMALL, ROMAU: type of patterned silk or cotton cloth (*O.E.D.*, romal 1), nos 42, 56, 77

ROYAL: writing-paper 24 × 19 in. (*O.E.D.*, royal A 11), no. 591

RUNDLET, RUNDLETT: container of varied size (*O.E.D.*, runlet[1], nos 400, 591, 756

SANGE'S: type of wine or spirit, *possibly* from Spanish *sanguesa*, raspberry, *or sanguaza*, red juice of fruits or vegetables, no. 387

SEERON, SERON: bale or package made up in an animal's hide (*O.E.D.*, seron), no. 737

SETTLED MAN, SETTLEMAN, SETTLE TIDESMAN: employee established in his particular post (*O.E.D.*, settled 8b), nos 68, 200, 364

SITTERON: citron, no. 101

SNOW: type of small three-masted ship (*O.E.D.*, snow sb²), nos 260, 269, 277, 283, 301, 310

SOWER: sour, no. 223

STRETCHER: piece of wood used as a footrest in a rowing-boat (*O.E.D.*, stretcher 7), no. 552

STRIKE: wooden corn-measure of varied capacity (*O.E.D.*, strike sb 4), no. 258

SUPERSEDEAS: writ ordering the stay of legal proceedings or suspending an officer's powers (*O.E.D.*, supersedeas 1), nos 618, 625

SWEET OIL: olive oil or other mild-tasting oil (*O.E.D.*, sweet a and adv C 1), no. 737

SWEET WATER: scent (*O.E.D.*, sweet water 2), nos 338, 344

TAFFATY, TAFFITY: type of glossy silk or other cloth (*O.E.D.*, taffeta A), nos 42, 77

TAMARIND, TAMARINDS: pulp from the pods of the tamarind tree (*O.E.D.*, tamarind 1), nos 432, 633

TRANSCIRE: warrant issued by Customs officers, permitting the passage of goods (Crouch, p. 17; *O.E.D.*, transire sb), nos 258, 468

ULAGE, ULLAGE: amount remaining in a cask or package that has leaked or been partly used (*O.E.D.*, ullage sb 2a), nos 258, 365, 390

VAT BLUED: blue-tinted paper, nos 267, 591, 756

Index

1 References to the Introduction are by pages, in roman numerals; all other references are to entry numbers.
2 No attempt is made to differentiate between persons bearing the same name, except where a person is identified by a description in italics; this description need not apply to the person at the time of the record.
3 Outside the vicinity of Portsmouth, place-names are normally entered under the parishes existing at the time of the record. Cross-references to these are given from the name of the county (for England and Wales) or country.
4 The following subject headings are used in the Index, as well as others to which cross-references are given: administration, local; administration, national; aliens; antiquities; Army; articles of utility; arts; buildings and grounds; Church, clergy and religion; documents and diplomatic; drainage; fauna; flora; food and drink; games and entertainments; industry and production; languages; law and justice; medicine; natural phenomena; Navy; newspapers; trade and commerce; transport and communications; war and rebellion.
5 In the entries of ships' names (under ships and shipping) no attempt is made to differentiate between ships bearing the same name or to bring together references to the same ship under different names.

Portsmouth Record Series

PUBLICATIONS

The Portsmouth Record Series began publication in 1971. Primarily it is intended to make the written sources for Portsmouth's history widely available. But beyond this it is hoped that the Series may help to set a new pattern for the publication of local records in Great Britain. For well over a hundred years record societies and other bodies have been publishing documents that are the sources of local history. But since 1945 the establishment of local record offices has made the majority of manuscripts easily available to research, while cheap photographic methods enable the searcher to use records from scattered repositories without recourse to printed texts. It is with this in mind that the Portsmouth Record Series has been planned. It is proposed to print complete texts only of three types of record: first, a very few documents that are of basic importance to the history of the City; second, any records of Portsmouth that are sufficiently unusual to give their publication more than purely local interest; and third, records of types found elsewhere but hitherto unpublished. For the rest the Series will consist of calendars, catalogues, indexes and bibliographies.

The volumes already published in the Series are:

1 *Borough Sessions papers 1653–1688*: a Calendar compiled by Arthur J. Willis and edited by Margaret J. Hoad with an Introduction by Margaret J. Hoad and Robert P. Grime (1971).
2 *Portsmouth and Sheet Turnpike Commissioners' Minute Book 1711–1754* edited by William Albert and P.D.A. Harvey (1973).
3 *Book of Original Entries 1731–1751* edited by N.W. Surry and J.H. Thomas (1976).
4 *Maps of Portsmouth before 1800*: a Catalogue compiled by D. Hodson (1978).
5 *Records of university adult education 1886–1939*: a Calendar compiled by Edwin Welch (1985).
6 *Portsmouth Dockyard papers 1774–1783: the American War*: a Calendar compiled by R.J.B. Knight (1987).
7 *Records of the Portsmouth Division of Marines 1764–1800* edited by J.A. Lowe (1990).

LIST OF SUBSCRIBERS TO THE SERIES

September 1993

INDIVIDUALS

Andrews, Miss P.M., 45 Hillmead Gardens, Bedhampton, Havant
Arthur, Ms S.D., 5 Grand Parade, Old Portsmouth
Attrill, Councillor J.R., 5 Masefield Avenue, Paulsgrove
Balch, J.T., 7 Sawyers Crescent, Copmanthorpe, North Yorkshire
Batchelor, W.J., 224 Freshwater Drive, Hamworthy, Poole, Dorset
Benfield, C.T., 39 King George Road, Portchester
Cleal, Ms P., 42 Fifth Street, Fratton
Easton, R.E., 6 Colinton Avenue, Portchester
Emery-Wallis, Councillor F.A.J., Froddington, Craneswater Park, Southsea
Groves, W.E.S., 66 Penny Street, Portsmouth
Hughes, Mr and Mrs M.F., 5 Cyprus Road, Hatch Warren, Basingstoke
Karn, M.J., Somerley House, Bell Lane, Birdham, Chichester, West Sussex
Linington, J.G., 5 Pembroke Road, Portsmouth
MacDougall, P., 2 James Street, Rochester, Kent
Norman-Rogers, P., 6 Blackmoor Walk, Havant
Payne, S.P., 33 Hartford House, Blount Road, Pembroke Park Portsmouth
Pinhorn, M.A., Norman's Place, Newbridge, Isle of Wight
Poate, J.V., WWF International UK Ltd, Claire House, Bridge Street, Leatherhead, Surrey
Pomeroy, S.J., 49 Preston Road, North End
Quail, Mr and Mrs A.J., 2 Sussex Terrace, Southsea
Riddell, Mrs C., 48 Common Lane, Tickhill, South Yorkshire
Smart, J.G., 57 Devonshire Avenue, Southsea
Surry, N.W., 38 Cross Street, Sudbury, Suffolk
Taplin , Honorary Alderman E.H., 10 St Ronan's Road, Southsea
Tweed, R.B., 48 St Matthew's Road, Cosham
Webb, J.G., 11 Blount Road, Pembroke Park, Portsmouth
Welch Dr E., 7487 Forest Turn, Lantzville, British Columbia, Canada
Willis-Fear, M.J.W., 42 Kendall Road, Crumpsall, Manchester
Wooden, F.E., 32 Miller Drive, Fareham

INSTITUTIONS (Great Britain and Ireland)

Aberystwyth, National Library of Wales (copyright library)
Birmingham, Reference Library
Bognor Regis, West Sussex Institute of Higher Education
Cambridge, University Library (copyright library)
Chester, City Record Office
Dublin, Trinity College Library (copyright library)
Durham, University Library
Edinburgh, National Library of Scotland (copyright library)
Exeter, University Library
Glasgow, Strathclyde University Library
Gosport, Museum
Leicester, University Library
Liverpool, University Library
London, British Library (copyright library)
Institute of Historical Research
London Library
National Maritime Museum
Public Record Office
Royal Historical Society
Society of Antiquaries of London
University Library
Norwich, East Anglia University Library
Oxford, Bodleian Library (copyright library)
Portsmouth, City Museum and Art Gallery
City Records Office
Grammar School
High School
University Library
Southampton, University Library
Winchester, Hampshire County Library
Hampshire Record Office
King Alfred's College

INSTITUTIONS (overseas)

United States of America
Ann Arbor (Mich.), Michigan University Library
Cambridge (Mass.), Harvard College Library
Chicago (Ill.), Newberry Library
Los Angeles (Calif.), California University Research Library
Princeton (N.J.), University Library
San Marino (Calif.), Huntington Library

An EXPLANATION of the References in the following horizontal Columns.

☞ These Columns shew the several Branches of Duties, to which each Species of Goods or Merchandize is liable.

O.S. signifies the Old Subsidy, N.S. the New Subsidy, ⅓ S. the one third Subsidy, ⅔ S. the two thirds Subsidy, I. 1690, Impost Duty 1690, I. 1692⅔, Impost Duty 1692⅔, S. 1747, Subsidy of 1747, Coin. Coinage Duty, N. D. on App. New Duty on Apples imported, D. Discount allowed for prompt Payment.

The RATES of MERCHANDIZE INWARD[S] … MENT, for the Payment of the Subsidy, &c. of … on each Species of Goods so rated, according to th[e] … upon all Goods and Merchandizes to be imported … DUTIES ad valorem; and the Total Amount o[f] … in Time.

I N W A R[DS]

GOODS and MERCHANDIZE w[…]

B.

This col. answers to that before the rates. ☞

Duties	No.	Goods and Merchandize
O.S. N.S. ⅓ S. ⅔ S. S. 1747	1	Babies, or puppets for children, the groce, containing 12 dozen
Ditto	2	Babies heads of earth, the dozen — — —
I. 1692⅔	3	All other toys for children, not any where particularly rated in the firs[t] … value upon oath, or of their rate in the second column of Rates … But, if painted, prohibited to be imported.
O.S. N.S. ⅓ S. ⅔ S. I. 1692⅔ 1 s. D. 6¼ S. 1747	4	Babies jointed, the dozen (Toys) — — —
		Backs for chimnies, Vide in Iron.
O.S. N.S. ⅓ S. ⅔ S. S. 1747	5	Bacon, of Ireland, the flitch — — —
I. 1692⅔ 4 d. per lb. gross D. 6¼	6	Bacon, of Ireland, and besides for every pound weight
O.S. N.S. ⅓ S. ⅔ S. I. 1692⅔ D. 6¼ Seco. 25 per cent. on Fren. goods S. 1747	7	Bacon, of Westphalia, or Hamburgh, viz. if …
O.S. N.S. ⅓ S. ⅔ S. I. 1692⅔ 4 d. per lb. gross. D. 6¼ S. 1747	8	Bacon, or the like, the hundred weight containing 112 lb. viz. if …
O.S. N.S. ⅓ S. ⅔ S. S. 1747	9	Bags, with locks, the dozen — —
I. 1690 5 s. per 112 lb. D. 6¼	10	Bags, with locks, and besides for every hundred weight, con[taining] …
O.S. N.S. ⅓ S. ⅔ S. S. 1747	11	Bags, with steel rings, without locks, the dozen — —
I. 1690 5 s. 6 d. per 112 lb. D. 6¼	12	Bags, with steel rings, without locks, and besides for every hundred weight, cont[aining] …
I. 1692⅔ for every 20 s. of the rate or value on oath, 1 s. D. 6¼	13	Bags, and besides, if the leather be the most valuable part of the bags, For every 20 s. of their respecti[ve] …
New duty on hides for every 20 s. value on oath, 3 s. and additional duty on hides ditto, without discount	14	Bags, and besides, if the leather be the most valuable part of the bags, For every 20 s. of their real val[ue] …
O.S. N.S. ⅓ S. ⅔ S. I. 1692⅔ for every 20 s. of the rate or value on oath, 1 s. gross. D. 6¼ S. 1747	15	Bags, called runnet-bags, the dozen — —
O.S. N.S. ⅓ S. ⅔ S. S. 1747	16	Balances, vocat. gold balances, the groce, containing 12 dozen pair
O.S. N.S. ⅓ S. ⅔ S. S. 1747	17	Balances, vocat. ounce balances, the groce, containing 12 dozen pair
O.S. N.S. ⅓ S. ⅔ S. S. 1747	18	Balances, vocat. the sort, containing 4 dozen — —
I. 1690 5 s. per 112 lb. D. 6¼	19	Balances, and besides for such of the said balances as are made of iron, for every hundre[d] …
I. 1692⅔ for 20 s. of the rate 1 s. D. 6¼	20	Balances, and besides for such of the said balances as are made of brass, for every 20 s. …
O.S. N.S. ⅓ S. ⅔ S. S. 1747	21	Balks, great, the hundred containing 120, of Africa, Asia, or Ireland
O.S. N.S. ⅓ S. ⅔ S. I. 1690 for every 20 s. of the rate or value 2 s. D. 6¼ S. 1747	22	Balks, great, the hundred containing 120, of the British Plantations in America, … of all other places —
O.S. N.S. ⅓ S. ⅔ S. S. 1747	23	Balks, of Africa, Asia, or Ireland —
O.S. N.S. ⅓ S. ⅔ S. I. 1690 for every 20 s. of the rate or value 2 s. D. 6¼ S. 1747	24	Balks, of the British Plantations in America, … of all other places, in British ships —
Ditto with ¼ gross O.S.	25	Balks, of all other places, in ships not belonging t[o] …
O.S. N.S. ⅓ S. ⅔ S. S. 1747	26	Balks, middle, the hundred containing 120, of Africa, Asia, or Ireland
O.S. N.S. ⅓ S. ⅔ S. I. 1690 for every 20 s. of the rate or value 2 s. D. 6¼ S. 1747	27	Balks, middle, of the British Plantations in America, … of all other places, in British ships —
Ditto with ¼ gross O.S.	28	Balks, middle, of all other places, in ships not belonging t[o] …
O.S. N.S. ⅓ S. ⅔ S. S. 1747	29	Balks, small, the hundred, of Africa, Asia, or Ireland —
O.S. N.S. ⅓ S. ⅔ S. I. 1690 for every 20 s. of the rate or value 2 s. D. 6¼ S. 17[47]		Balks, small, the hundred, of the British Plantations in America, …

Note. All timber in balks, of eight inches square or upwards, are to pay according to the measure of timber for every load, containing 50 feet square.